REVOLUTIONIZING
FRENCH COOKING

Other books by Roy Andries de Groot

Feasts for All Seasons
The Auberge of the Flowering Hearth
Esquire's Handbook for Hosts

Metric Equivalents for Standard U.S. Measures

1 tsp	5 milliliters 5 grams
2 tsp	10 milliliters 10 grams
1 Tbs	15 milliliters 15 grams
⅓ cup	1 deciliter less 1⅓ Tbs (0.079 liter)
1 cup	¼ liter (o.236 liter)
2 cups	½ liter less 1½ Tbs (0.473 liter)
4 cups	1 liter less 1 deciliter (0.946 liter)

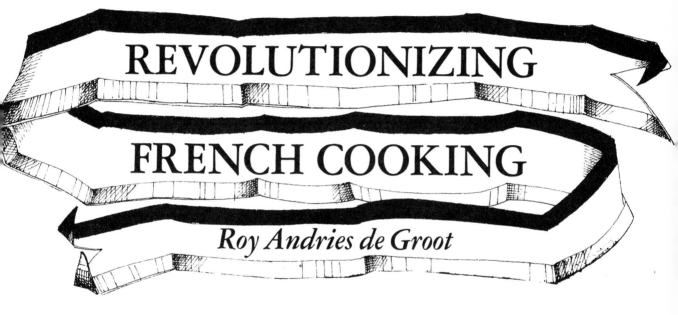

REVOLUTIONIZING

FRENCH COOKING

Roy Andries de Groot

Illustrations by Bill Goldsmith

McGRAW-HILL BOOK COMPANY

New York/St. Louis/San Francisco/Düsseldorf/Mexico/Toronto

Book design by Judith Michael

Copyright © 1975, 1976 by Roy Andries de Groot.
All rights reserved.
Some of the material in this book appeared
in Esquire magazine in slightly different form.
Printed in the United States of America.
No part of this publication may be reproduced,
stored in a retrieval system, or transmitted,
in any form or by any means, electronic, mechanical,
photocopying, recording, or otherwise,
without the prior written permission of the publisher.

1 2 3 4 5 6 7 8 9 DODO 7 9 8 7 6

Library of Congress Cataloging in Publication Data

De Groot, Roy Andries
  Revolutionizing French cooking.

  Includes indexes.
  1. Cookery, French. I. Title.
TX719.D373   641.5′944   76-10947
ISBN 0-07-016240-9

To Don Erickson

loyal friend, constructive editor
whose imagination launched this book

incisive gastronomic critic, superb amateur cook
who prepared (and rejected)
the <u>Selle de Veau à la Prince Orloff.</u>

Acknowledgments

This book, which interprets a revolutionary new gastronomic technique, which translates the superb skills of some of the greatest chefs of the world into workable terms for the American amateur cook, and which adapts supreme French professional recipes into precise procedures for the home, could not have been written without the dedicated help of friends, associates and expert technicians in the culinary and literary arts. To all of them I offer my warmest thanks:

To Bill Goldsmith, a brilliant artist of extraordinary sensitivity, for his interpretation, in his jacket and chapter illustrations, of the delicacy, lightness and transparency of this new French Low-High Cuisine. To my wife, Katherine, and to Anna McArtor, who traveled with me back and forth across France, tasting the dishes, watching the chefs at work, collecting the recipes and assembling the notes. To Juanin Clay and Pat Lennox who did much of the research and who helped with the testing and retesting of the recipes. To my other researchers, tasters, readers and typists, including Margaret Fung, Edna Gengerke, Adele Hoenig, Johanna Wright and Lucille de Zalduondo for their devotion to the ideal of accuracy in every detail.

To the editorial and production staff of the publisher, including my editor, John Jacob Simon, always a charming and positive literary critic, as well as an outstanding amateur cook whose continuing advice helped to shape and sharpen the recipes. To his efficient and understanding literary assistant, Jennifer Gerard, as well as to Cicely Nichols, for meticulous control and admirable literary navigation.

To the great French chefs who made this book possible, by inviting me to their restaurants, by preparing their magnificent dishes for my tasting, by demonstrating their techniques in their kitchens, by recording their thoughts into my microphones, by writing out for me their original recipes, and by giving me permission to use their names, their words, and their recipes, translated and adapted to American ingredients, kitchen equipment and cooking procedures. (For amateur cooks who collect the recipes of great chefs, it is good news that both Paul Bocuse's new book, *La Cuisine du Marché*, and Michel Guérard's *La Cuisine Minceur* will soon be available in an English translation and that other books are being planned or written by Alain Chapel, Jean and Pierre Troisgros, and Roger Vergé.)

Finally, a loving tribute to my dog, Otoña, who traveled across France with me, who lay patiently and quietly in her corner by my desk during almost two years of writing and was always willing, at any moment, to rush to the kitchen and taste absolutely anything.

Roy Andries de Groot
New York City
July 16, 1976

Contents

CHAPTER THREE / THE BASIC TECHNIQUES OF THE LOW-HIGH KITCHEN — 59

CHAPTER FOUR / HORS D'OEUVRES AND CANAPÉS

CHAPTER SEVEN / FISH AND SHELLFISH   169

CHAPTER EIGHT / POULTRY AND GAME   **219**

CHAPTER NINE / BEEF 273

CHAPTER TEN / LAMB 293

CHAPTER ELEVEN / VEAL 307

CHAPTER TWELVE / A FEW MULTI-PURPOSE SIMPLE SAUCES 331

CHAPTER THIRTEEN / SOME FAR-FROM-THE-ORDINARY SALADS AND VEGETABLES 349

Chapter One
The New Low-High Cuisine

in which we examine a French revolution and
find out who started it, and when, and why.

I was having breakfast with Chef Jean Troisgros on my last day at the great three-star restaurant that he runs with his brother, Pierre, in the textile town of Roanne in central France. We were eating *les petits oeufs de poules naines à la coque,* boiled baby pullets' eggs straight from the nest. We dug out the inside of each egg – hardly more than a single mouthful – with *mouillettes,* narrow fingers of toast very lightly spread with hazelnut-flavored farm butter. In the middle of the table was a big bowl of Montmorency cherries just picked from the tree, a basket of croissants hot from the oven, and a jar of Jean's own whole-strawberry jam.

Le Restaurant des Frères Troisgros is, in my opinion, the best restaurant in France – perhaps, the best in the world. I had just completed eight working days with Jean and Pierre tasting and testing in their dining rooms and kitchen many of their marvelous culinary inventions. They had presented me with copies of some of their recipes and had recorded on my tapes their detailed advice. Now, Jean was discussing their basic gastronomic philosophy.

I said that I considered him and Pierre to be the leading exponents of the so-called "new-new cuisine" of France – the new approach to great French eating that is widely known as the "new Low-High cuisine." I knew what it was in terms of eating at the table, but I wanted Jean to give me a definitive statement of its basic principles.

We were joined at this point by one of the top gastronomic writers of France, Christian Millau, who was on a restaurant tour and had stayed overnight at the Hotel Troisgros. Christian and his partner, Henri Gault, publish the most prestigious of French food and wine magazines, *Le Nouveau Guide de Gault-Millau*. Breaking open his first egg, Christian was more than ready to join the discussion of the new developments in the gastronomy of France.

"In ancient China," Christian began, "when a Chinese host invited a friend to a feast, he said: 'Come. We will eat fat.' And in the great, historical family portraits in the Louvre or the Rijksmuseum, the men and women of nobility and wealth are always shown as being much fatter than the ordinary working people. Even in more modern times, the idea of the jolly and successful fat man was part of the unchanging tradition of society. Think of Mr. Pickwick in Charles Dickens. But that whole concept has been buried by our current generation. It would have been a twentieth-century tragedy if our great chefs had failed to recognize the new trend. Let us be thankful they have decided to be involved."

"I think we all understand," Jean added, "that the new international interest in health and weight control is not just a passing fad, but a permanent new direction in gastronomy. So we *cuisiniers* are adding our grain of salt to the new movement. We are helping to make a pleasure out of a necessity."

"It is much more than that," Christian said. "Such great cooks as Jean and Pierre, Michel Guérard, Jacques Manière, Roger Vergé and many others are, in fact, inventing a superb new cuisine, almost without butter, cream, other fats, starches, or sugar. It is *la nouvelle révolution française*."

What emerged from the discussion was that this new-new Low-High cuisine is not a slimming diet. It has nothing to do with the mineral oil and sugar substitute recipes of what the French call *La Cuisine Diététique*. This new-new cuisine still gives first priority to the high pleasure of great eating – but it is great eating that is at the same time digestible, healthy, light, natural and simplified by the exclusion of most of the carbohydrates and sugars, of flour-thickened sauces and starchy stuffings. The idea is that you should continue to eat in the style of high cuisine but with low likelihood of gaining weight and low prospects of damage to health. The eternal roller-coaster ride – the ups and downs of undisciplined stuffing followed by agonizing self-denial – is eliminated once and for all. It is indeed the new French revolution.

"Well, a gastronomic revolution is hardly something new in French history," said Jean. "In the last three hundred years, there have been more cuisine revolutions than political. The progression of French eating – in every way as temperamental and volatile as our French character – has never gone forward in a logical straight line. It has twisted and turned. It has been through violent upheavals. It has had amazing upsurges and disastrous collapses."

Before the early 1500s, there was no such thing as a French cuisine. Eating was still at what you might call the near-cave-man stage. The women who slaved over the hot fires never sat at table with the men. The long trestles of rough boards had neither place settings nor knives, forks, or spoons. The men sat in their hunting clothes on long benches. When the huge joint of still partly raw, spit-roasted meat was placed in the center of the table, they drew their daggers from their belts and slashed off huge chunks, holding them in their hands. Having no napkins, they simply waved their bloody, greasy, sticky fingers in the air to dry them. At table, France was in no way ahead of England, Germany, or Spain and was far behind the civilized nobility of Florence, Rome, or Venice.

The first gastronomic revolution was brought to France by Catherine de' Medici, daughter of Lorenzo of Florence, when she became engaged to the Duke of Orléans (later, King Henri II). On a visit to her fiancé, she was horrified by the food and the manners at table. So, in 1533, when she left Florence to become Queen of France, she brought with her sixteen crack Florentine cooks and a whole wagon train of herbs, spices and vegetables, including a green leaf that grew wild on the Florentine hills but had never before been tasted in France – *spinaci*. (This is why, on a French menu, any dish with spinach is still called *à la Florentine*.) Male-chauvinistic Frenchmen dislike admitting that the basic foundation of *La Grande Cuisine* (as well as the prototypes of handmade, silver cutlery) were imported into France by an Italian woman.

The next revolution in French cuisine began in 1682, when Louis XIV completed the palace of Versailles and, as part of its immense show-off, launched the wildest era of conspicuous consumption of food. When the king dined, an almost endless parade of huge and highly decorated dishes passed before him, each borne on the shoulders of four men. He would take one bite from each, then wave it back to the kitchen for later reheating and serving to members of the court and their guests. The royal waste of food was one of the seeds of the French Revolution – it has passed into tradition with the famous argument at the gates of Versailles over the relative merits of bread and cake. Meanwhile, all the noblemen in their own châteaux in every part of France were imitating the king and hiring the most brilliant cooks they could find. Cooking became (and still is) one of the most honored of French professions.

The era of super luxury came to a crashing end in 1789 when the Bastille was stormed and noble heads were soon being neatly sliced off by the guillotine. The thousands of chefs all over France – fearing that they would be classified as bootlickers of the rich and also sent to the guillotine – went underground. For almost fifteen years, *La Grande Cuisine* disappeared. Great eating was automatically associated with the oppressors of the people and was not even mentioned in whispers.

By about 1800, the chefs, having exhausted their savings, had to do something. The famous Parisian *cuisinier* Beauvilliers is generally credited with the brilliant idea that changed the life of France. He decided to demonstrate his devotion to Democracy by opening a restaurant at which he would offer for the delectation of the *bourgeoisie* the greatest dishes he had created for his former noble employers. Beauvilliers slyly called it his "Restaurant of the Republic - Palace of Equality," and it was instantaneously such a raging success that other chefs in hiding opened their own luxurious restaurants in virtually every city of France.

The greatest name to emerge from this tremendous resurgence of French gastronomy was Antonin Carême, who raised *La Grande Cuisine Française* to its highest peak of all. He cooked for the kings of France and England, as well as for the Tsar of Russia.

Under the world-wide influence of Carême, which lasted

one hundred years, until the appearance of Escoffier, grand dining became more and more an ostentatious and snobbish status symbol, more and more committed to excessive waste. Ice was not yet being used as a preservative and Carême had only four simple ways of preventing mountains of food from going bad: salting, smoking, sun-drying, or marinating in vinegar. To hide the off-taste in most fish and meat, sauce was piled on top of sauce, filling was stuffed inside filling. A banquet might last for eight hours and offer a hundred separate dishes.

The next revolutionary change came just before 1900 when Escoffier almost single-handedly brought *La Grande Cuisine* into the twentieth century. He had primitive ice boxes that enabled him to change many of the techniques and codify the basic rules of French grand cooking. But he was still planning his menus for bored tsars, emperors, and kings to whom sumptuous waste was a way of life. He was still gilding the lily. It was still very much *La Grande Cuisine*. Then, after Escoffier died, a thousand chefs continued to try to imitate him, while the world and its sybaritic mood gradually changed as food abundance gradually became food shortage. It was again time for a change – another turning point in French gastronomic history.

THE COURSE OF HISTORY IN A SINGLE DISH

The roots of the new-new Low-High cuisine are clearly seen in the evolution of one of the most famous dishes of *La Grande Cuisine*. Its name is known to every serious gastronome: *Selle de Veau à la Prince Orloff*. In the middle 1800s, the Russian Prince Orloff was Minister in Paris for Tsar Nicholas I and was a regular customer at the then-famous Parisian Restaurant Tortoni, where the *chef de cuisine* was the great Urbain Dubois. When Orloff returned to St. Petersburg, he persuaded Dubois to go back with him as his personal chef, and Dubois stayed in St. Petersburg for twenty years. There was plenty of good veal in Russia, but Orloff disliked the taste of it. So he kept urging Dubois to mask the flavor of the meat with all kinds of aromatic stuffings and sauces. Finally, perhaps in desperation, Dubois created the famous dish in which an entire saddle of veal is slit across the bones in dozens of places – each slit is filled with a complicated mixture of a *duxelles* or minced mixture of chopped wild mushrooms and shallots, a *soubise* or garnish of onions and aromatic rice and layers of sliced foie gras and black truffles; everything, finally, is covered by a Mornay sauce loaded with grated Gruyère cheese. When all this was reheated and browned, the flavor of the veal disappeared. Prince Orloff felt that a great new dish had been created and gave his name to it as a crown jewel of *La Grande Cuisine Française*.

Just about a hundred years later, Julia Child included a simplified version of the recipe (leaving out the super-expensive foie gras and truffles) in the first volume of her *Mastering the Art of French Cooking*. A friend of mine, a young man who is a highly skilled amateur cook, tried Julia's recipe for a party. Afterwards, he wrote me about it. He admires Julia and follows every fine shading of her instructions. After he had browned and braised the solid piece of veal, he thought it smelled and tasted marvelous. He almost wondered why the rest of the recipe was necessary. He minced the mushrooms and sautéed them with shallots for the *duxelles*. He sliced the onions and sautéed them for the *soubise*. He kept thinking hungrily of that beautifully browned veal waiting in the pot. Julia's instructions worked perfectly. The mushroom *duxelles*, by itself, tasted fine. The onion-rice *soubise*, by itself, was elegant. He whipped up the white Mornay sauce with butter, flour, milk, heavy cream and grated Gruyère. The veal was sliced open and stuffed in layers. Then it was covered with the sauce, more grated Gruyère and oodles of melted butter and browned and bubbled in a hot oven. Not a single square inch of the original veal was visible.

After dinner, with the help of some good Cognac to open them up, the cook persuaded his guests to talk frankly about the veal main course. They thought that the solid veal at the center was lovely, but its character was too much masked by the stuffings and sauce – unnecessarily gussied up. The dish seemed too complicated – overluxurious – absurdly pretentious.

Was this a purely American reaction? Would a French gourmet have agreed? Recently, James de Coquet, the much-admired food and wine columnist of the Paris newspaper, *Le Figaro*, wrote: "In this dish, the attractive veal is put into the minority by the sauce, the *duxelles* of mushrooms, the *soubise* of onions, the slices of black truffles and all the other unnecessary impedimenta. It finishes up as a dish that is ruined!" De Coquet went on to report that when Chef Urbain Dubois ended his service in Russia and returned to Paris in 1870, he wrote a cook book for the average French housewife in which he said: "The ambition of every good cook must be to make something very good with the fewest possible ingredients." Thus, in the view of James de Coquet, Dubois himself wrote the epitaph for his own Veal Orloff! Perhaps – a hundred years too soon – he was sounding the first clarion call for the new-new Low-High cuisine?

At breakfast in Roanne, I turned to Jean Troisgros who, as all young cooks must, had begun his training with the classical techniques. "Would you," I asked, "be willing today to prepare a Saddle of Veal Prince Orloff?"

Jean fairly snorted: "No! Never! That's an antique, a museum-piece, good for a professional cooking competition. It was one of the dishes I prepared when I won my 'Best Chef of France' award, quite a few years ago. It was an interesting exercise for a young chef. But not for his customers. First, you have to cook the veal. Then you have to spoil it by letting it cool down. Then you have to cut it open in a dozen places to make sure it dries out. Then you have to dominate it with foie gras and truffles *and* an onion *soubise and* mushrooms *and* a cheese Mornay *and* what else? Then you must reassemble it. Then you must reheat it. Then you must be crazy!

"It would be far better to serve the veal as a plain roast," Jean continued, "perfectly hot and savory from the oven. If you want a *soubise* of simmered onions with it, serve them, freshly prepared, in a separate dish. The mushrooms, also freshly sautéed, in another separate dish. And if you absolutely insist on foie gras with it, then have it as the first course of the meal. I would agree with that menu. With all the ingredients of a Veal Orloff served separately and in the proper order, you can make a very digestible and pleasant menu, but if you bang them all together inside the meat, I predict you'll be sick!"

Jean's attitude towards Veal Orloff is the best possible illustration of the most basic principle of the new-new Low-High cuisine — the continual drive, with every recipe, towards simplification. Jean dislikes Veal Orloff because it is an endless repetition, because it offers no opportunity to the cook to be inventive, because it is overcomplicated, overrich and indigestible.

WHO INVENTED THE LOW-HIGH CUISINE?

Very few great new ideas are the flash of a single mind. Most evolve from the constructive interplay of the thoughts of many specialists. The new-new cuisine is no exception. Almost thirty years ago, after the end of World War II, I talked to the two greatest chefs since Escoffier about the future of French gastronomy. The magnificent Alexandre Dumaine was still at his Restaurant de la Côte d'Or in the village of Saulieu. The giant, Fernand Point, was at his Restaurant de la Pyramide in the town of Vienne just south of Lyon. Although both were brilliant masters of *La Grande Cuisine,* both were convinced that it must be modernized and simplified. They wanted to cut down on the enormous catalog of classic sauces. They wanted, gradually, to eliminate the overaromatic and overrich garnishes and stuffings. They believed that good ingredients should be tasted for themselves.

Chef Paul Bocuse was trained by Papa Point and absorbed these ideas. Soon after 1965, when Paul won three stars for his superb restaurant at Collonges-au-Mont-d'Or, I visited him and recorded our discussion. He told me about his *Nouvelle Cuisine.* Dozens of classic dishes had been adapted by Paul and his disciples (called by their *ancien régime* critics of that time "the gastronomic Mafia"), but as I tasted these dishes, I sensed an ambivalent attitude in their preparation. These young chefs seemed to me to be unsure whether their clients would be willing to switch from the completely rich to the completely light. So they compromised with half-light, half-rich dishes. While loudly proclaiming that they were

going forward, they were still looking backward. My dis-
illusionment was fairly complete when Bocuse and his col-
leagues formed a trade association and named it La Grande
Cuisine Française! Ten years later, Paul's recipes, including
those in this book, had moved much closer to a convinced
lightness and simplicity.

The second major attempt to modernize *La Grande Cuisine*
came from the brilliant, young Chef Michel Guérard when he
was still running his Paris bistro, Le Pot au Feu. He decided
to go the whole way and convert some classic dishes into
dietetic slimming recipes, complete with mineral oil, sugar
substitutes and low-fat yoghurt. I bow to no one in my admiration of Michel's imagination and skill, but, frankly, I find
no pleasure in mineral oil. Other Young Turk chefs of Paris
have picked up some of Michel's ideas and are now promoting
La Cuisine Diététique. Michel calls his version *La Cuisine
Minceur*. He has given me several recipes for this book, but
none contain any mineral oil or sugar substitute. This is not
a diet book.

Then, on a visit to Chefs Jean and Pierre Troisgros, I was
served their ''Duck with Fresh Figs'' (page 246), their ''Sirloin
Steak with Lemon and Capers'' (page 286), and their ''*Yakisuki
à la Française*'' (page 274), and I knew that the perfect balance
between *La Nouvelle Cuisine* and *La Cuisine Diététique* had been
precisely achieved. It was the new-new cuisine – the Low-
High cuisine – the new revolutionary gastronomy of natural-
ism and simplicity. How had it been done? I asked Jean
Troisgros, ''Did you invent it?''

''No. Not at all,'' Jean replied. ''As you know, I followed
Paul Bocuse as the assistant chef to the great Fernand Point.
He first laid down the principles of a truly light, simple cuisine. We often discussed the fact that we did better work (and
were happier) when we cooked as we pleased, rather than
when we were blindly and slavishly following the inexorable
and inflexible rules of *La Grande Cuisine*. We wanted to cook
specially for each of our clients – as if they were guests in our
own house. We began preparing each dish slightly differently
each time. In one evening, I might try twenty variations of
sea bass. That was the start of the great urge to experiment.''

"Was that when you began cutting out the butter and cream?" I asked.

"Not altogether. We still use butter and cream, but in new ways that eliminate the old indigestibility and super richness," Jean said. "What was wrong, in the old days, was the endless cooking and reducing of the butter and cream. They used to put in gallons of cream and pounds of butter and flour, then boil it down – concentrating and reconcentrating the fats and the starches. That was why the old cuisine was so unhealthy. Today, we use butter and cream without endless boiling, with complete protection of the essential lightness. Come, let me show you."

We had talked so long over breakfast that it was almost lunch time and Jean took me to the kitchen where Pierre and his brigade were preparing for the midday rush. "Look," said Jean, "there is not a single sauce simmering in advance on the stove. The butter is still in the refrigerator. So is the cream. When the first customers arrive, we start from scratch. That is a basic principle of the new-new cuisine. No stale flavors – no washed-out feeling – of anything that has been boiling on the stove for hours and hours."

"How do you give body to your new-style sauces?" I asked.

"The word *roux* has been eliminated from our dictionary," Jean continued. "That eternal and inevitable butter-flour mixture used for thickening everything in sight, which never provided any flavor of its own, has been thrown out of the kitchen window. Now, we thicken our sauces by reduction – a simple process which not only provides a better body to the sauce, but also concentrates and sharpens the flavor – an essence, a magnification of the basic character of the dish. Finally, at the very last moment before serving, we melt in a small quantity of butter or cream, with no cooking at all, to complete the sauce with a sense of light and simple softness."

"How do you lighten and simplify your desserts?" I asked.

"Instead of throwing in masses of processed sugar," Jean said, "we now draw out the natural sweetness of very ripe fruits – we reduce and concentrate the natural grape sugars in sweet wines. This brings a natural quality to our desserts – a much better, healthier and more satisfying way to end a meal."

"Not all of those ideas," I countered, "are absolutely new."

"Certainly not," Jean said, "some of what we do comes straight from Grandmother. Her cooking somehow went out of fashion. The snobbish gourmets of Paris looked down their noses at it, because they thought it was too simple. So they turned back to the super-fancy-pants, show-off cuisine of the kings of France at the Palace of Versailles, as interpreted by Escoffier. For nearly a hundred years, Escoffier has eclipsed Grandmother. Now, our new-new cuisine is a return to Grandmother, but with this difference – it is now being modernized and perfected by professional chefs, using to the maximum their imaginations and skills. Our new-new cuisine is, speaking in culinary terms, the concentration to an essence of French bourgeois country cooking, which, after all, has always been ultimately the best. The difference, now, is that we cook things less and that we avoid excess. What I hate most is the cuisine where there is too much of everything – too many embellishments in the dish – too many garnishes on the plate – and totally too much of everything everywhere for the diner to eat without after-dinner discomfort. Excess serves no purpose. In our new-new recipes there is no excess of anything."

REVOLUTIONARY, YET PRACTICAL ADVICE FROM PARIS

From Roanne, I returned to Paris and recorded a series of talks with one of the most brilliant *cuisiniers* of the city, Chef Jacques Manière, at his famous and great bistro, Le Pactole, on the Boulevard St-Germain. He, too, has accepted the Low-High concepts, but interprets the new movement in his own special way. I asked whether he thought that the new-new cuisine was as good as the old.

"It is perfectly possible to have a *grande cuisine* with marvelous flavors and savors," Jacques replied, "yet dramatically low in butter, cream and all other fats. I have been experimenting more and more in my own kitchen with low-fat and low-sugar dishes – yet trying to avoid any compromise in the pleasures and satisfactions of great eating. I must say that I am enchanted with my own food!"

I asked him what kinds of foods he used for his Low-High dishes.

"Clearly," Jacques continued, "one must turn towards those creatures of which the flesh is less fatty, less rich. These include capon and chicken; nonoily fish such as sea bass, sole, and turbot; fatless cuts of lamb and veal; steamed liver; lobster and crayfish; mushrooms; mussels; shrimp; veal brains and sweetbreads . . . – all these are thoroughly low in fat and not exactly sad to eat!"

I ask how he planned his menus around these dishes.

"Once you have chosen the main dish, you plan the first course and the dessert for the most perfect possible balance. You can add many different kinds of vegetables, undercooked, of course, without butter, and, to end the meal, nothing more than ripe fresh fruits. You can add body to your sauces with low-fat white or pot cheese. If I occasionally use a small amount of oil, it is to add flavor and therefore I use very small quantities of such strong oils as first-pressing green olive, or cold-pressed walnut. If, occasionally, I dare to enrich a dish with a minimum addition of, say, basil butter, I allow myself this luxury because I have saved so much in other directions."

Which cooking methods did he prefer?

"Many of my dishes are steamed, or cooked wrapped in aluminum foil or parchment paper – a method which requires no pre-buttering of the cooking vessel and which holds in maximum flavor. To balance the absence of fatty richness, I make everything strongly aromatic with such characterful herbs and spices as basil, whole green peppercorns, shallots, tarragon and thyme, among others. I use no added sugar whatsoever in my desserts. I rely entirely on the natural sweetness of the fruits. If you take very fresh fruits and simply mash them lightly with a fork, then freeze them, you can produce superbly refreshing sherbets. I drink one glass of wine with every meal – to help sustain the pleasures of the table. Instead of coffee with cream and sugar, I drink smoky lapsang souchong – China tea so full of·character that nothing need be added. Great menus can be planned by the intelligent balance of the simplest of preparations."

TASTING AND TESTING THE NEW-NEW LOW-HIGH RECIPES

There is an intense practicality about the recipes in this book. Each is the invention of a working chef with all the mechanical problems calculated down to the last detail. For every recipe, I visited the restaurant and tasted the dish as prepared by the chef. Then I went into the kitchen and helped in preparing it a second time. Finally, I recorded the answers to my questions about the ingredients, the sequence of the work, the timing, the utensils and so on, all generally confirmed by a copy of the original recipe, often written out by hand by the chef.

Then, in my small kitchen in New York, we prepared the recipes with standard products from the local markets. I deliberately did not use a professional, multiburner, restaurant-type cooking stove, but the standard home equipment as it is sold to millions of American amateur cooks. Although some of these recipes involve a fair amount of work, they are perfectly adapted to the new kitchen machines (page 80) which are now being used as much by French chefs in their professional kitchens as by American amateurs. (The chefs, after all, in these days of the cost squeeze, are as much concerned with labor-saving as we are.) Each recipe in this book begins with a clear estimate of the time and work involved. If some special ingredient is needed for a particular recipe, there is a warning in the introduction. Finally, at the end of each main dish recipe, there is a suggestion about the best wine to accompany the dish – the wine actually served to me by the chef at my first tasting, with an American alternative.

Most of these recipes are the inventions of the great, three-star chefs. But by no means all. Of several hundred recipes, this is my selection of those which in their making and eating were the most interesting and pleasureful. Some are from two-star or one-star restaurants, others from young *cuisiniers* who as yet have no stars but have such a brilliant potential that they will unquestionably be the three-stars of the future. (The chefs are discussed in the next chapter.) Almost all the recipes are from France, but a few are from other countries – usually with a strong French influence – and a very few are included to prove the point that the new-new cuisine can sometimes be as ancient as the hills of China, India, or Japan. (The great three-star Chef Roger Vergé once offered me a marvelous side dish of perfectly fresh, crisply undercooked vegetables. When I congratulated him on their preparation and presentation, he said: "I am not quite sure whether it is the new-new cuisine of France, or the old-old cuisine of China!")

No printed recipe, of course, can tell you everything. You must make some of the decisions. You must taste to achieve a fine balance of the freshly ground aromatic herbs and spices which are all-important in this new cuisine. Since the sauces are thickened by being boiled down, instead of by the incorporation of butter and flour, you must be the precise master of your cooking heat. Finally, your ingredients must have a glowing freshness. Stale meats and tired vegetables simply will not do in this new cuisine, where the flavors come not from the rich sauces but from the natural juices of the raw materials. These extraordinary recipes offer no instant key to three-star cooking at home. They are worth an extra effort to meet their challenge.

IF YOU MUST MENTION CALORIES!

Let us again be quite clear in saying that, although these recipes are exceptionally low in fats and sugars, they are not designed to be a reducing regimen. They put eating pleasure first and aim only secondarily at eliminating the blown-up, tight-belted feeling at the end of the meal. They avoid the eternal cycle of gaining weight for fun and having to reduce for health.

I feel that these elegant dishes should not be demeaned by the boring technicality of calculating calories. I will not allow my party atmosphere to be poisoned by low mathematical haggling and, therefore, the dirty word "calorie" will not appear anywhere else in this book. If you actually enjoy the mathematics of nutrition, you can, naturally, compare many of these recipes to their classic counterparts and work out the savings as a result of the elimination of the traditional amounts of butter, cream, flour, cooking oil and sugar. I find no pleasure or satisfaction in that kind of figuring. These recipes are, first of all, for the pleasures of the table – the double pleasures of eating lightly and superbly at the same time.

*   *   *   *

After Henri Gault and Christian Millau had dined on one of the extraordinary new-new, Low-High dinners of Jacques Manière in Paris, they wrote of his cuisine (and, by inference, of all the great chefs who practice the Low-High techniques) that it is "the really great, the simple, the pure, the intelligent and generous new gastronomy of our time." With this new cuisine – with these new recipes – one of the important questions of our era is answered. Great cooking and great eating are not being eliminated from the modern world. We can adapt and continue this wonderful thing, this great conceptual pleasure principle of French cooking, this supremely attractive art of absorbing essential nourishment by a ritual of delight and sensual satisfaction. Great dining remains alive and well.

Chapter Two
The Chefs

in which the great contemporary chefs discourse
upon the subject of the new Low-High cuisine,
and we find them united in a fierce struggle against
the tide of mediocrity by their dedication to
gastronomic perfection.

The recipes in this book were given to me in all parts of France (and a few in other countries) over many months of travel. Finally, as I translated, tested and adapted them, I became strongly aware of their extraordinary variety – not only of the primary ingredients and cooking methods, but of every detail of the techniques of preparation. Each recipe has a personality of its own which reflects the character of the professional chef who invented it. Each chef cooks in a unique way – a way based on life experience and on particular interests and skills, all molded by individual temperament.

Yet this variety is something quite new in French gastronomy. If this book had been written even twenty or thirty years ago, a discussion of the contemporary chefs would have made dull reading. Apart from one or two giants in each generation who succeeded in breaking out of the standard mold, there would have been a deadly sameness about the other *cuisiniers* – about their training, their careers, the way they organized their kitchens and about their techniques at the cooking fires. A chef was not regarded as an independent artisan with a creative mind of his own. He was a workman – a working brother of the bricklayer, the carpenter, the plumber, the assembly technician in a factory. Professional cooking was defined as a technical trade with a training program involving a body of fixed rules to be memorized. There was only one cuisine to be learned and practiced – *La Grande Cuisine* – with no permissible variations. Each new chef, as he completed his apprenticeship, was dedicated to the endless repetition of a range of classical dishes. Each recipe was so much enshrined in tradition that no chef dared to change a single word.

The great Swiss chef Albert Stockli told me that when he was a young apprentice in Paris, he once dared to suggest an obvious improvement in the preparation of a classic *Soupe de Poisson* to the almighty, haughty *chef de cuisine* who ruled the kitchen. "My boy," said the old man, drawing himself up and bristling from every pore, "there are five thousand recipes in our French *Grande Cuisine* and only after you have learned every word of them by heart will you be accepted and listened to as a cook."

Today, that point of view no longer rules the kitchens of France. The chefs worthy of the name cook as they please. The men and women on whom I report in this chapter are creative artisan craftsmen. In their field, they are in the same class as cabinet makers, brilliantly designing and constructing new pieces of furniture; or botanists, producing new varieties of flowers for our pleasure. To know and understand the recipes of these chefs, you must listen, as I did, to their voices . . .

CHARLES BARRIER AT HIS THREE-STAR CHEZ BARRIER IN TOURS ON THE LOIRE

Even among the seventeen top three-star restaurants of France, some are clearly more starry than others. If I could have my dictatorial way, I would give three and a half stars to some and, to a very few, a dazzling four stars. Among the few on my list would unquestionably be Chef Charles Barrier who runs the greatest restaurant in the City of Tours and is the pride of the entire Loire Valley.

Barrier is one of the great examples of the poor boy who not only made good in his home town, but has become one of the national leaders in the modern movement of French gastronomy. He was born, almost sixty years ago, in a cave in one of the hills looking down on the river just outside the city. "It was poverty in the pure state," Barrier once confided. "After my father was killed in World War I, there was never enough bread for my mother and her eight children. When we were desperately hungry, we would walk over to the back kitchen door of the nearby château, where the family was still in residence. The cook would invite us in and give us food. He had a big belly and looked as though he got all he wanted. So when I was asked, one day, what I wanted to do with my life, I didn't hesitate for a moment."

At twelve, Barrier was apprenticed in the kitchen of a local restaurant. At fourteen, he moved to an ancient, low-beamed *auberge* just across the river. Its customers were mostly coachmen and carters, so it served meals to both man and horse. Barrier saved his money and, by the time he was seventeen, was able to go to Paris and work his way around the great kitchens there, learning fast and beginning to think deeply, as he put it, about "the art and meaning of cooking." During World War II Barrier joined the army and concentrated on driving the Germans out of France.

After victory, Barrier returned to Tours and found that the *auberge* had been blown up by the retreating German army. He bought the ruins and set about rebuilding it as the small restaurant of his dreams. He has never moved and, in thirty years, has never ceased to improve it towards an ideal of perfect country simplicity. In 1968, he was awarded the highest accolade of three stars.

When I first met Charles Barrier, almost ten years ago, he was already in revolt against *La Grande Cuisine* of Paris. When I asked him what was the essence of his brilliant cooking, he replied: "Above all, it is honesty and simplicity." He went on: "The grand cuisine that catered to the wealthy snobs of Paris was never particularly honest or simple and never, in my opinion, represented the authentic cooking of France. That was always the simple yet perfect cooking of the farms and small towns of our Provinces. There may be new fads, fancies and fashions every month in snob circles in Paris, but the authentic country cooking continues unchanging and eternal and it is to this honesty and simplicity that we are now returning. Perhaps new-new cuisine is not correctly named. Perhaps it ought to be called the old-old cuisine."

Many of Barrier's freshest fruits and vegetables are from his own farm – a quite large piece of land almost next door to the cave where he was born. "My motive when I bought it was not entirely agricultural," said Barrier, "It was also a protest (and my revenge) against the abject poverty of my childhood."

My adaptation of Charles Barrier's recipe for his "Fricassee of Chicken with Jumbo Shrimp *à la Tourangelle*" is on page 236.

CHEF GEORGES BLANC AT HIS TWO-STAR AUBERGE CHEZ LA MÈRE BLANC IN VONNAS IN THE REGION OF BRESSE

If you turn off the *autoroute* about ten miles south of the Burgundian wine town of Macon, you find yourself on narrow, winding country roads that lead you to the tiny village of Vonnas, which has one of the most excellent small country *auberges* of France. It has been run by the Blanc family for four generations. For the first three, the name of the *auberge* was strictly accurate – Mother cooked and Father managed the inn. Now, with thirty-two-year-old Georges and his lovely Jacqueline, the roles are reversed. He is the brilliantly inventive young cook. She is the *maîtresse de la maison*, with an irresistibly charming sense of hospitality and a flair for organizing impeccable service.

Georges in the kitchen is a Young Turk who balances a devotion to the rich cooking of his native Bresse with a mastery of the most advanced principles of the Low-High cuisine. Side by side on his menu, he offers Bresse chicken poached in what must be a quart of heavy cream, or the same chicken lightly sautéed with vinegar and served with its natural, unthickened juices in a deep soup plate.

Georges was born in the *auberge* where his mother was the famous cook – famous, above all, for her chicken in cream and her frogs' legs sautéed in butter. At sixteen he enrolled in the Swiss professional restaurant school in Lausanne. After graduation he "made the tour" of the great kitchens of Paris and the resort hotels and then came home to Vonnas to be the assistant chef to his mother for almost ten years of her meticulous regional training. In 1968, his mother retired and he took over. Georges already has two stars – in my opinion he deserves three.

The adaptations of Georges Blanc's recipes are his "Chicken Half-Melted in a Provençal *Potage Pistou*" on page 144 and his "Squabs Filled with a *Ragoût* of the Forest" on page 258.

CHEF PAUL BOCUSE AT HIS THREE-STAR CHEZ BOCUSE IN COLLONGES-AU-MONT-D'OR NEAR LYON

Paul has quite recently been called "the most famous French chef in the world." In fact, you might say that he is now less of a chef and more of an international ambassador for French gastronomy. He is also a TV star performer and a commercial wine merchant. One of Paul's closest friends, also a three-star chef, told me: "Paul can still cook better than any of us when he wants to. At the moment, he is too busy."

To say that Paul comes from a long line of *cuisiniers* and *restaurateurs* is an enormous understatement. The Bocuse family has been serving food in the village of Collonges-au-Mont-d'Or since 1765. Originally they were millers. Farmers came to the Bocuse mill with their sacks of wheat and then hung around waiting for them to be ground into flour. Madame Bocuse began serving them a light, inexpensive lunch. She was an excellent cook, and in a few years she was making more money on her lunches than Monsieur Bocuse was getting for his milling. So the mill was closed down and the Bocuses turned full time to the restaurant business. The original, large restaurant is still standing in the center of town, still serving *la friture* and *la grillade* – fried chicken, grilled ham and steaks – with no pretensions to *La Grande Cuisine*. It makes a nice profit on business banquets and wedding receptions. It looks for no fancy listings in gastronomic guide books.

It was Paul's mother who first had the idea of an enlargement of the business towards *La Grande Cuisine* and the tourist trade. She bought an old warehouse below the village down by the main highway which runs along the left bank of the River Saône between Burgundy and Lyon. She began converting it into a second restaurant, a luxury establishment. She also succeeded in planting in Paul's mind the seeds of an ambition to join the immortals of French gastronomy.

As a boy, Paul began working in some of the best restaurants of Lyon. He showed such immediate potential that he was accepted as an apprentice by the supreme French chef of the time, Fernand Point, at his Restaurant de la Pyramide in the town of Vienne, just south of Lyon. There, and in later, brief working periods in Paris, Paul completed his gastronomic education in about half the normal time. By 1954, he was ready to come home to Mama and take over her luxury warehouse. From that date, his internal fires of ambition, imagination and skill shot him upwards with the flare of a meteor. In 1954, the Bocuse name was not even listed in the gastronomic guides. In 1956, he was in the guides, still unstarred. In 1960, one star. In 1961, he won the national award as "Best Chef of France." In 1962, two stars. In 1965, three stars. The entire sequence was the fastest rise to acceptance by the top establishment of any chef in French gastronomic history.

My translations and adaptations of a few of the recipes given me by Paul during my various visits with him are his "Pâté of Saône Eels," on page 116, "Pumpkin Soup in a Pumpkin," on page 162, his famous "Truffle Soup of the Élysée Palace," on page 165, the "Navarin of Lobster" on page 200, his very personal "Turkey down the Hole," on page 268, his ideas for my "Sauce Gribette," on page 338, and his modernization of the ancient "Sauce Saupiquet" on page 344.

CHEF RENÉ BRUNET AT HIS TWO-STAR AUBERGE ET RESTAURANT DES ESCALES DE RENÉ BRUNET AT VARCES IN THE SOUTHEASTERN ALPS

Brunet has often been called "the chef of chefs." He has never received a great deal of publicity, but he is enormously admired by his peers among the two-star and three-star chefs of France. He has been described to me as "the pure perfectionist who has never cut a single corner."

Brunet calls his restaurant "Escales" – Ports of Call – because in the Navy he went around the world several times. He returned close to his birthplace among the High Alps to a built-up commercial suburb of Grenoble. Dining on the terrace in the flowered and tree-shaded garden that surrounds his *auberge*, René talked in his enthusiastic, excited voice, the words tumbling out, his eyes shining, his hands waving. "If I can claim any success as a cook," he told me, "I owe it all to one man, who was never in his life in a kitchen. He was a great gourmet. He was more than a father to me. After I had trained as a young cook and war came in 1940, I joined the Navy and was given the job of being private cook to this great Admiral. Wherever we were, on whatever ship he was commanding, he demanded from me a beautiful and varied dinner table. Wherever we touched port – in all the exotic places of the earth – he gave me shore leave to shop in the food markets, to study the local cuisine, to bring back new ideas for his table. He was demanding. He gave me daily constructive criticism. When he died, my heart was broken."

When Brunet came out of the Navy he had the spirit, but neither money nor practical plans. He walked around Grenoble looking for work. In the suburb of Varces, he stopped for a drink at a small bistro where the main entertainment on the ground floor was a bowling alley and upstairs a tiny dance hall. It was going broke and it was for sale. Brunet managed to borrow $500 for a down payment and started work. He has worked eighteen hours a day ever since. Over the years, he bought bits of adjoining land to make a private garden around his restaurant. At the end of six years, he had his first star. Eight years later, two stars. He now easily deserves three.

René was almost bouncing up and down in his chair as he said: "In these modern days there is a lot of talk about cooking green beans so slightly that they crackle in your mouth. That's supposed to be the latest thing. Well, my God, I was making my green beans crackle twenty years ago! What is important is not 'the latest thing' nor big international publicity, but the movement towards more healthy cooking. Believe me, I need steady clients. I can't afford to have them die on me. And I believe that loss of health, in terms of food, comes from three basically dangerous elements, which I have been eliminating more and more from my cooking. The first two are the fattening elements, butter and cream. The third is the cholesterol element in eggs."

I asked him how he had worked them out of his cooking without compromising his quality.

"At six o'clock every morning," René continued, "I am alone at my stoves. I prepare three basic stocks fresh every morning. Each is an absolute essence of bones, meat, chicken, fish, vegetables, aromatic herbs, with all the nutritive elements, but not a bit of fat. I refine them and refine them until they are a pure essence of flavor – the gelatinous, thickening base of everything I prepare for the rest of the day.

"So butter and cream play no part in your cooking?" I asked.

"That is always the temptation – the easy way," René said. "You take your steak, your veal, your chicken, anything you have – you fry it in half-an-inch of butter – you add red wine, white wine, Cognac, whiskey and, at the last moment, you slather it all with pints of the heaviest cream. The client says, 'Oh, this is magnificent!' But for how long will he keep coming back to enjoy it? How long will I keep him as a healthy and hungry client? When will he crack between my fingers?"

After tasting Chef René Brunet's "*Coulis* of Crayfish," his "Oysters *à la* Brunet," his "Duck Livers with White Grapes," one can hardly escape the feeling that the new-new cuisine is not quite so new-new as all that! It was probably discovered by René Brunet at least thirty years ago.

There are adaptations of his "*Rouelle* Steak of Veal" on page 313, and his "Lime Sherbet with Chasse Spleen" on page 376.

CHEF ALAIN CHAPEL AT HIS THREE-STAR CHEZ LA MÈRE CHARLES IN MIONNAY IN THE REGION OF AIN NORTHEAST OF LYON

Of all the regions of France this is the land known for its supreme gastronomic luxury. Ain for its cattle and dairy farms. Bresse for its chickens. The forests of Les Dombes for wild game. "The cooking of Lyon has become world-famous," Alain Chapel told me, "but it is really the cooking from here, from this immense and rich region about forty miles northeast of the city. It is a simple, bourgeois cooking, but the products from which it is constructed are about as near to perfection as a bountiful Nature can make them."

Of this superb region, Alain Chapel, by his brilliant, off-beat, often iconoclastic imagination and supreme culinary skills, has made himself in an extraordinarily short time the gastronomic king. Chez La Mère Charles was a country bistro of the simplest kind, owned and run by a lady cook called Mother Charles. Shortly before World War II, Alain's father and mother bought her bistro but kept her on for a time as cook. Struggling to upgrade everything, they gradually built a reputation with the Lyonnais as a fine place to stop during weekends in the country and, in 1958, earned one star. Meanwhile, their small son, Alain, had fallen in love with the kitchen and, his revolutionary spirit already developing, had decided that he was damn well going to show them all how much better everything could be done. He went off to be an apprentice of the great Chef Jean Vignard in Lyon and showed such brilliant potential that he was accepted as an assistant to the supreme master of the time, Fernand Point, at his Restaurant de la Pyramide in Vienne. Alain subsequently made the rounds of the great kitchens of Paris. In 1967, La Mère Charles having retired, Alain's father invited him to come home and be the *chef de cuisine*. The rest is gastronomic history – an extraordinary display of culinary fireworks.

Alain changed and improved everything – the menus, the service, the landscaping of the lovely garden, the comfort and luxury of the *auberge*. Within two years he had two stars. In 1972, he won the national competition for "Best Chef of France." In 1973, at thirty-five, he was awarded three stars. The famous French gastronomic critics Henri Gault and Christian Millau rated Chapel as having one of the four supreme restaurants of France (with Paul Bocuse, Paul Haeberlin of Alsace, and the Troisgros brothers) with nineteen points out of a possible twenty – higher than any of the *grand luxe* restaurants of Paris.

After dinner, Alain and I sat in his garden by the fountain in the cool of a lovely July evening discussing the new French gastronomic revolution. "More than anyone else," Alain said, "it was the immortal Fernand Point who instilled in all of us the spirit of the searching artist. He was the detonator who triggered the explosions of our creative imaginations."

"Then do you feel that Point invented the new-new cuisine?" I asked.

"Yes, insofar as there is, really, a new cuisine," said Alain. "I would prefer to call it a return to a 'cuisine of love' – so much love of one's work that one refuses to repeat it endlessly and thoughtlessly, but wants to continually change it and create with it something nearer to perfection. To achieve this we are turning back to the eternal verities of our mothers and grandmothers. If I could not go on creating – if I were forced to repeat myself every night – you wouldn't find me here. I would have gone fishing."

My adaptations of two of Chef Alain Chapel's recipes are his "Canapés *Fritures* of Tiny Whole Fish" on page 94 and "Baby Chicken Sautéed with Garlic" on page 222.

CHEF CLAUDE DARROZE AT HIS RESTAURANT DARROZE AT LANGON IN THE GRAVES DISTRICT OF BORDEAUX

There is a feeling of security for the future of French gastronomy when you meet Claude Darroze. Still relatively unknown at the age of thirty-three, he is a brilliantly inventive, supremely skilled and obviously fast-rising new culinary star. Darroze opened his ôwn restaurant – his first – only about a year ago and as yet has no stars. He is already presenting a menu worthy, in my opinion, of several stars and firmly within the basic principles of the Low-High cuisine.

There is no mystery about the sudden success of Claude Darroze. He is the son of Jean Darroze, who for about fifty years has been the leading *cuisinier* of the southwestern Landes region. You might say that Claude was born with a boxwood spoon in his mouth. After stirring sauces for his father, he was apprenticed at sixteen to the great Chef Pierre Laporte in Biarritz; then to the Hôtel de Paris in Monte Carlo, where he won the prize as the best cook of the region; to Paris and the supreme elegance of the Hôtel Plaza Athenée; to Switzerland and the Palace in St. Moritz; and back home to his father's *auberge* in the Landes. But, Claude told me, "the clash of the generations" occurred and he decided that he wanted to be boss of his own kitchen in his own restaurant.

At that point, Claude had a lucky break. The great French culinary superstar Raymond Oliver, who demonstrates his cooking to millions of viewers on TV, needed someone to run a small, country hotel in the wine town of Langon among the vineyards of Bordeaux, almost next door to Château d'Yquem. The local châteaux owners and their cellar masters needed a fine restaurant where they could entertain their customers. Oliver turned over the hotel and restaurant to Claude Darroze, who was joined by his elder brother, Francis, as director of the dining room. I lunched with them for the first time after they had been open for only a month or two and at once, as I sniffed and tasted the first dish they set before me, I knew that I was in the presence of a *maître cuisinier*.

An adaptation of Chef Claude Darroze's "Quail with Semillon Grapes" is on page 251.

CHEF GEORGES DUMAS AT THE THREE-STAR LASSERRE IN PARIS

"Our clients eat less nowadays and demand that their food be lighter," Chef Dumas told me – speaking from his extraordinary vantage point as second in command of the kitchen at Lasserre. There is perhaps no restaurant in the world more completely devoted to the ancient and historic principles of Escoffier than the three-star Lasserre. In its beauty, its devoted clientele, its elegance and its entirely classical menu, it often seems to me – although I am sure I am wrong – that nothing, not a single detail of the rich and showy food preparation and service has changed at Lasserre in a hundred years. And yet, apparently, its kitchen staff is well aware of the new Low-High cuisine.

Georges Dumas began his culinary training at sixteen in Lyon, the heartland of French gastronomy. Inevitably, as does any young, ambitious cook, he came to Paris and worked at the Café de la Paix, moved around for a while, did some summer seasons at resort hotels and then, in 1947, joined René Lasserre with whom he has remained, with minor interruptions, for almost thirty years. In 1972, competing with more than two hundred chefs from all over Europe, Georges Dumas won the *Coupe Culinaire Pierre Taittinger* for the best new dish invented during the year.

There are translations and adaptations of two of Georges Dumas's recipes here: *"Noisettes* of Lamb with Champagne" on page 299 and "Rack of Lamb *Jardinière*" on page 300.

CHEF HENRI EUDES AT HIS CAFÉ DE LA GARE IN HASTINGS-ON-HUDSON

Chef Eudes is that rare person, the man who deliberately reformed and reshaped his life and made a success of it in a new direction. For sixteen years, he was known to most New York gastronomes as a top *maître d'hôtel.* Few people knew that he was also a professionally trained, high-cuisine cook. Suddenly, he left Manhattan behind and opened his own miniature Franco-American bistro, Le Café de la Gare, near the old railroad station in the small town of Hastings-on-Hudson, about twenty miles north of New York City. His cuisine is classic French but brilliantly simple in the most modern style.

Henri was born in the center of Paris and, while still quite a small boy, he came under two powerful gastronomic influences. One was his mother, "the greatest cook I have ever known." The other, an uncle, worked for a placement bureau for professional chefs and was required by his job to dine every night at one or another of the great restaurants of Paris. He often took young Henri along with him and the boy developed an appreciative and critical taste for *La Grande Cuisine.* By the time he was sixteen, Henri was safely enrolled in the Hotel and Restaurant School of Paris. From there, he pursued his training – with the invaluable help of his uncle's placement bureau – in such famous establishments as the Grand Hotel in Deauville, the Hermitage in Monte Carlo, the Savoy in London and the Mid-Ocean Club in Bermuda. From the latter it was only a short step to New York.

Many of Henri's recipes come from his mother and grandmother who now live in a tiny village in the ancient agricultural district of the Mayenne, west of Paris, roughly between Normandy and Brittany. This is country food prepared with an extraordinary lightness and simplicity. A near-perfect example is my translation and adaptation of Henri Eudes' recipe for "Bay Scallops *à la Mayennaise*" on page 203.

CHEF FRANCIS GARCIA AT THE ONE-STAR LA RÉSERVE IN PESSAC OUTSIDE BORDEAUX

This handsome, small hotel and excellent restaurant surrounded by its private park is the "local bistro" of the great wine makers and grand château owners of the supreme Bordeaux wine districts of the Medoc and the Graves. This is where they bring their V.I.P. customers and journalist friends to talk about and show off their wines. So the first absolute demand on La Réserve is that it must maintain an enormous wine cellar, covering virtually every vintage of every important vineyard in Bordeaux. There would be quite a stink if, say, Baron Phillippe de Rothschild brought someone to dinner and found that his 1961 Mouton-Rothschild was not on the list! Second, the food at La Réserve must be designed to go with (and to show off) the great red and white Bordeaux wines.

These inflexible and high-pressure requirements have broken many a good chef at La Réserve. Now the highly skilled, very young Chef Francis Garcia seems to be meeting his multiple problems with dash and sparkle. He was born in Bordeaux, twenty-seven years ago, but left it quite young and did his apprenticeship training in the truffle country of the Dordogne and Perigord in southwestern France. "It was a small restaurant," Francis told me, "but the old chef was a tough taskmaster and he banged into me the basic disciplines. Yet, perhaps, I was still too young to take myself very seriously. In various succeeding jobs, I still considered myself as primarily a worker for profit – looking for the easy job which paid the most money for the least work. Then, suddenly, I realized I was getting nowhere. I had a crisis within myself. With a friend, I fitted out a small sailboat and, for two years, sailed around the world. I thought things through. I decided to devote the rest of my life to the serious pursuit of perfection in the art of *la cuisine*." When Francis returned to Bordeaux, he got his first new job in the kitchen of one of the top restaurants of the city, Dubern, where, at the age of twenty-four, he was promoted to *chef de cuisine*. A couple of years later, when problems developed at La Réserve, Garcia was offered the challenging job of executive chef.

"I am trying, above all, to modernize the spirit of our cooking here," he told me. "We now follow the Bocuse, Guérard and Troisgros principles with our gastronomic creations in the new, light style, without complicated sauces or stuffings, with everything designed to stress the natural flavors of our superb Gironde ingredients prepared with our great Bordeaux wines. . . ."

An adaptation of Chef Francis Garcia's "Salad of Raw Sea Bass and Trout with Red Caviar" is on page 107.

CHEF MICHEL GUÉRARD AT HIS TWO-STAR LE POT AU FEU, IN EUGÉNIE-LES-BAINS IN THE SOUTHWESTERN REGION OF THE LANDES

Michel Guérard, at forty-three, seems to be the most debated and discussed personality of the gastronomic world. You can hardly open a magazine without finding his picture and a feature about him. There is hardly a food page that is not printing garbled versions of his recipes. Depending on your point of view, he is either a new Messiah or a publicity-hungry iconoclast. If the subject of Guérard comes up at a gathering of gastronomes in London, New York, or Paris you may hear him referred to variously as a member of the gastronomic Mafia, a gentle and logical food philosopher, the gastronomic *enfant terrible* of our time, a businessman of food interested mainly in the profits, or the greatest cook of the twentieth century. One three-star chef told me: "Guérard is the most formidable innovator since Escoffier." Another, equally prestigious, said to me: "Michel can have three stars any time he wants them."

Today, deliberately rejecting the adulation of Paris, he "hides away" in the distant Spa Hotel that he shares with his wife, Christine, in the foothills of the Pyrenees Mountains while the gastronomic world beats a path to his kitchen door — mainly, perhaps, to watch him juggle the various high toques he wears at provocative angles.

The first hat Guérard wears (and this, perhaps, is his primary role) is that of one of the most brilliant technicians of French high cuisine, capable of reproducing any of the greatest dishes of French history in a bravura style. His second hat is that of the high priest of the new religion, *La Cuisine Minceur*, using dramatic, low-calorie, diet recipes (some of them containing such currently frowned-on ingredients as mineral oil and sugar substitutes) that have his fans gasping with admiration and his critics snickering behind their hands. In his third hat he is the administrator of the kitchen personnel of a growing chain of nightclub restaurants – a job which keeps him on the move between Paris, New York, Rio de Janeiro, Monte Carlo, and Bahia, with very little connection to the art of cooking. His fourth hat – and, in my view, by far the most important – is that of an interpreter of an airy, delicate, lacy, cuisine – the cuisine that has been an important influence in the development of the Low-High techniques. To understand Guérard's many roles fully, it is necessary to differentiate between the Guérard romantic myth and the hard realities of his career.

Almost no one had heard of Michel before 1958 when, at twenty-five, he was an intensely ambitious, deeply determined, hard working *sous-chef* in the kitchen of the famous Hôtel Crillon in Paris. Suddenly, he sprang into public view as the youngest winner in the history of the quadrennial national competition for the title of "Best Chef of France." It brought an instant blaze of publicity in the magazines and newspapers – but, as he put it to me: "You can't exploit that kind of success unless you have your own restaurant." So he disappeared again and there was silence from Michel Guérard for almost ten more years. Then came the explosion.

Guérard decided to open his own restaurant, but because he had very little capital all he could manage was to convert a tiny somewhat broken-down former bar and grill into a shoestring bistro called Le Pot au Feu in the grim and grimy industrial suburb of Asnières, a good three-dollar taxi ride from the center of Paris. "For the first two years, the place was half empty," Michel told me. "Then, one day, I was down in the Beaujolais buying wine and accidentally ran into Paul Bocuse and Jean Troisgros. We knew each other. We had met before, very briefly. We talked about the philosophy of cooking and a bond of sympathy seemed to be forged between us. The next time they were in Paris, they came to eat at Le Pot au Feu.

They admitted, later, that that first experience was both a surprise and a shock! But they understood what I was trying to do and they were enthusiastic about the basic ideas. They talked to the food writers, especially to Gault and Millau, and the next thing I knew, there was a major feature about me in the newspapers. That was all it needed."

"Why?" I asked. "What was the essence of your instant success? What were you doing that so quickly attracted so many people?"

Michel replied: "The secret was, finally, fairly simple. It was my rebellion against the monotony of repetitious classical cuisine. I was expressing a philosophy I had gradually developed since my childhood. I was born in a small village not far from Paris. My father was a grocer, but he died when I was so young that I never really knew him. My mother then married a butcher. So, you see, I was never very far from food. My grandmother, who, incidentally, had her portrait painted by Claude Monet, was a fine, professional cook who often catered some quite large dinners."

During World War II times were very bad. One day, Michel's parents told him that they had pretty well run out of money and could no longer afford to keep him at home and continue his education, so he had better go out and find a job.

"I wasn't much troubled about leaving home," Michel continued. "I had known what I wanted to do ever since I baked my first cake in my mother's kitchen. At fifteen I apprenticed myself to a baker-caterer on the outskirts of Paris. This man, Monsieur Alix, a fine artisan, became my true father. He was extremely severe, but it was a formidable training, with disciplined experience of everything: baking, pastry, the complete preparation of catered dinners . . . . we even had our own small vineyard and made our own house white wine. We made all our own jams and jellies. We put up fruits – and even snails – in sealed glass jars. Pâtés. Terrines. Everything. For me, it was the kind of complete and detailed apprenticeship training that, I am sad to say, has now virtually disappeared. Monsieur Alix had an amazing sense of renewal, of change toward improvement. He was never content to repeat the same thing over and over again. Every week, for example, he tried to invent an entirely new cake. It was damned diffi-cult. Many a week, it was a failure and we just threw it out. But, you see, the idea of constant renewal was already taking hold inside me. Endless repetition became, for me, a poi-sonous form of monotony."

His abhorrence of repetition was the ruling factor when Michel opened Le Pot au Feu. He refused to repeat any of the classic *Grande Cuisine* dishes. He adapted and changed every-thing – constructing a menu so brilliant, so dramatically dif-ferent, so shockingly untraditional, yet so supremely success-ful in terms of sensuous pleasure, that within a few months he had all of gastronomic Paris and then all of the gastronomic world battling for his twenty-eight seats. He was "dis-covered" by the opinion-molding gastronomic writers of Paris. The crowds at his front door became steadily larger. You gen-erally had to wait ten days for a reservation for lunch or dinner. When you got there, you were virtually shoe-horned in. The room had the ambience of a small barn. The service was frenzied. But the food was divine. Each dish was so light that it seemed almost transparent. When the Young Prince walked, slightly languidly, into the dining room from his kit-chen, the excited conversation of all the diners was hushed. A new star had been born.

Almost before anyone expected it, Le Pot au Feu had two stars and an official of the *Guide Michelin* said confidentially that Michel Guérard's would almost certainly be the first small bistro ever to receive three stars. It did not happen.

Guérard had come in with the flash of a rocket. At the crest of his trajectory, like a rocket, he was suddenly extinguished. The roadway in front of his bistro was scheduled to be wid-ened into a new superhighway approach to Paris. Guérard's little building was condemned to be razed. The bulldozers came. Le Pot au Feu was gone. Michel was so hurt and mad that I very much doubt whether he even looked for another place. For four years he had been working dog-hard. He was overweight. His kidneys were giving him trouble. He was sick in body and at heart. He had just met Christine who was young and slim and who owned a Spa Hotel in the far-away Landes where the special feature was a hot-springs treatment for obesity. He married Christine and left Paris for Eugénie-les-Bains. Paris mourned. The third star was left dangling in limbo.

When I visited Christine and Michel in the Landes I found him still questioning everything, still fighting the boredom of repetition, even of the recipes of his own invention. He said: "My cuisine here in Eugénie-les-Bains, where I have reopened my Pot au Feu – and, in fact, wherever my recipes may be prepared – has a double objective: to help gourmets to eat well while losing weight and, perhaps even more important, to eat superbly while neither gaining nor losing."

The translations and adaptations of the recipes which Michel Guérard has given me are "A Curative Consommé" on page 150, "Frogs' Legs Soup" on page 155, "Mushroom Soup Without Butter" on page 157, "*Pot au Feu* of Mixed Fish" on page 182, "Lobster Baked with Its Coral" on page 194, "Chicken-in-the-Pot" on page 232, "Turkey-in-a-Bag" on page 265, "*Blanquette* of Veal in a Steamer" on page 316, "French *Osso Buco* with Oranges" on page 319, his ideas for my "*Sauce Gribette*" on page 338, his "Mayonnaise Without Oil" on page 341, "Virgin Tomato Sauce" on page 345, "Black Truffle Salad" on page 351, "Terrine of Carrots" on page 358, "*Gâteau* of Mushroom, Spinach and Tomato" on page 361, "*Granita* of Unsweetened Bitter Chocolate" on page 368, and "Hot Soufflé of Butterless, Sugarless Pears" on page 378.

CHEF PAUL HAEBERLIN AT HIS THREE-STAR AUBERGE DE L'ILL IN THE VILLAGE OF ILLHAEUSERN IN ALSACE

This *auberge* – one of the four supreme restaurants of France – is run by the two brothers, Paul in the kitchen and Jean-Pierre directing the dining room. When I first visited them, more than ten years ago, Jean-Pierre told me: "The most significant thing about us, Monsieur, is that we were both born in a room above this restaurant, here on the banks of the River Ill. We are not imported. We and our food are products of the region. Our grandfather started a small bistro here which became famous in the region for a single special dish, prepared wonderfully by our grandmother – her *matelotte*, or cream stew of the fat eels which were caught in the river right at our kitchen door. In those early days, before there were very many automobiles, customers took the train to the nearby town of Mulhouse and my father drove a one-horse carriage to collect them at the station and bring them to the restaurant. The old horse was so slow that we called him 'Le Rapide.' Incidentally the dish is still on our menu. We now call it *La Matelotte d'Anguille à la Manière de Grandmaman.* That is our secret, Monsieur, regionalism and continuity."

The restaurant was blown up during the fierce fighting of World War II. Jean-Pierre and Paul rebuilt it as one of the most beautiful restaurants of France, set in a manicured garden sloping down to the willow-lined, slow-moving, swan-populated river. Paul had prepared himself for more than ten years for this new beginning. At fifteen, he was apprenticed to the great chef of a local Alsatian restaurant. "The old man," Paul told me, "had been, in his younger days, chef to the Russian Tsar Nicolas II in St. Petersburg and to the Greek King Constantine I in Athens. He trained me in the most classic discipline of *La Grande Cuisine.* In retirement, he had bought a small Alsatian restaurant and he longed, more than anything, to train his son to succeed him. But the boy wanted nothing to do with cooking and went off to Paris. So all the love of the old man became focused on me, but with extreme perfectionism and severity. I absorbed it all, but I never forgot my Alsatian roots and my mother's devotion to the peasant dishes of our region."

When he took over in his bright new kitchen in 1950, Paul had not the slightest intention of allowing the Auberge de l'Ill to become merely an Alsatian outpost of *La Grande Cuisine.* He had a master plan. Building on the conceptual base of his grandmother's *matelotte* of eels, he analyzed, one by one, the simple, traditional farmhouse dishes of Alsace and, with his classic techniques, gave them elegance, lightness, and refinement. Gradually, he produced a menu which became a glorified and magnified interpretation of the great cuisine of Alsace. Paris became aware of Paul Haeberlin. Three years after he took over he was awarded his first star. Four years later two stars. Another eight years, in 1965, three stars. The French gastronomic critics, Henri Gault and Christian Millau, who also list numerical ratings for the great restaurants, give the Haeberlin brothers nineteen points out of a possible twenty – a supreme score allowed to no restaurant in Paris and shared by only three others, Paul Bocuse, Alain Chapel and the Troisgros brothers (pages 26, 29 and 50).

Adaptations of two of Chef Paul Haeberlin's feather-light recipes are his "Turbot Swimming in Its Aromatic Bouillon" on page 214 and "Almost Sugarless Champagne Sherbet Bubbling in Champagne" on page 372.

CHEF MIMI LENSALADE AT HER BEACH BISTRO, AU RESCAPÉ AT ST-GIRONS-PLAGE

The French region of Les Landes, the vast area of marsh lands and pine forests southwards from Bordeaux to Biarritz and the Spanish border, is a wild and lonely land, but no one goes hungry or thirsty. There are fat geese, foie gras, ortolans and Armagnac. It is *par excellence* the home of hunters and fishermen. Along the wide, sweeping, lonely beaches, the Atlantic rollers pound the sand like thunder and the fishing is magnificent. When you bring in a big sea bass on the beach of St-Girons-Plage, you carry it at once, if you are wise, to the extraordinary beach restaurant, Au Rescapé, which looks like a typical Cape Cod shore dinner shed. It is owned and run by Mimi Lensalade, one of the finest regional cooks of the southwest of France. She might be defined as one of France's best kept gastronomic secrets!

She was born only about eight miles away in the village of Linxe, where her parents owned a small *auberge*. Many of the winter hunters who came there by horse and mule and stayed a few days were also summer fishermen at the beach where, they said, there was absolutely no place to eat. So eventually Papa bought a plot on the beach and began building, mostly by himself, the bistro that he called Au Rescapé, meaning in the local Landais dialect, "At the Restful Café." He was a fine, traditional Landais cook and, as a child, Mimi learned the techniques by helping him. But, by the age of twenty, she wanted no part of the restaurant business and went off to the University in Paris, to be, as she told me, "as far from the Landes as I could get." After graduation, she went to Morocco and ran a successful business there for ten years. But the news came that her father was incurably ill and, being a dutiful only child, she came home. While her father, growing gradually weaker, sat in an armchair on the terrace, Mimi organized the kitchen, perhaps as it had never been organized before. The local fame and prestige of the restaurant grew steadily. Two years ago, Papa died. Mama is now almost eighty-five. When I asked Mimi what she saw in her future, she said: "I will stay and look after *Maman*. Then perhaps I will give up here and go off to Tahiti!" I somehow doubt that she will.

Some of Mimi's cooking is pure Landais, which means that it is rich with duck and goose fat. But she is too sensitive not to be aware of the new movement towards the lighter cooking and a fine example is her recipe for "Grilled Sea Bass with Contrasting Green and Red Sauces," adapted on page 336.

CHEF JACQUES MANIÈRE AT HIS LE PACTOLE IN PARIS

The only accurate way to define Chef Manière is as the mystery giant of Paris. Among the true connoisseurs of the city, there is simply no dispute about his being among its three or four top *cuisiniers*. The gastronomic critic Jean Didier rates Manière in his prestigious *Guide Kléber* as *Grande Cuisine* and writes: "His cooking is an astonishing exaltation . . . a daily discovery of the art of living in evolution." The top French critics, Henri Gault and Christian Millau, in their *Nouveau Guide Gastronomique,* give him their top rating with eighteen points out of a possible twenty (the same as most of the exalted, three-star, world-famous restaurants of Paris) and write: "A fabulous cuisine . . . audacious, fantastic, with incomparable excitement of flavors, inventive to the point of genius, with his Raw Salmon and Chives, his Fish Steamed in Parsley, his Chicken *à la Vapeur*, his Sugarless Crushed-Fresh-Fruit Sherbets . . . all so simple and marvelous . . . the exact image of the new-new cuisine of France. Manière is, at his best moments, the greatest *cuisinier* in the world . . . even at his worst, he is still very, very good." Yet the lordly and powerful *Guide Michelin* does not even list Jacques Manière's restaurant, the small, bistro-style Le Pactole. There are no stars; for *Michelin,* it does not exist. One can only guess that the temperamental Manière and the conservative *Michelin* have had some kind of a fight, which neither now wants to discuss. I respect their privacy.

But I cannot remain silent about the entirely superb qualities of Jacques Manière's Low-High cuisine at Le Pactole. (Incidentally, the Pactole was the river in which King Midas bathed, leaving the waters loaded with gold – hardly a good simile in terms of Jacques's restaurant. He has exactly fifteen tables. His only riches are in his cuisine.) Jacques is, today, one of the most active and persuasive leaders in the new-new gastronomy of France. Whenever he is challenged to "take out the fat" he comes up with an invention in which you feel not only that nothing is lost in pleasure at the table, but that superb qualities are gained by his brilliant lightening and simplification. And yet Jacques is not a lifetime professional chef. He came to the business quite late in life.

During World War II, as a relatively young man, he joined the Free French army that was fighting the Germans in North Africa and was highly praised for his courage, daring and martial skill. As soon as the war was won and the Germans were ousted from France, his commanders sent him to the Military Academy at St-Cyr, the West Point of France, to be trained as an army officer. He might have made a lifetime career of it (and what a loss to gastronomy that would have been!). But the war had soured him on the military life. "Naturally, they threw me out," he told me, "with my temperament of personal independence."

So he went back to his parents' home in the southwestern region of the Perigeux and used his savings to open a small factory for the canning of black truffles. The production was small, but extremely high quality. "Perhaps because of the smallness of the operation," he said, "I didn't make any kind of big money. My mother had had a restaurant and I became interested in the idea of cooking. I practiced in our kitchen at home and soon was putting together some marvelous dinners for our friends. I loved my kitchen so much that I became entirely convinced that I should plunge into the world of professional cooking. The dining table was, for me, the perfect link between the material riches of the earth and the longing for perfection of the human spirit. So I came to Paris to try my luck. I got a job at the three-star Lapérouse and then at that wonderful small restaurant, Chez Max, where Max, that formidable man, taught me the basics."

Jacques scraped up just enough money to open his first Le Pactole in the unfashionable Paris suburb of Pantin. It could seat only twenty people, but almost at once he gathered around him a regular, admiring clique. "I was not trying to be different," Jacques told me, "but my guiding principle was that I wanted each of my guests to finish dinner and then stand up and say, 'I feel just about ready to start all over again.' That was, to me, the ultimate compliment."

"How can the amateur cook achieve that result at home?," I asked.

"I give you a secret," Jacques said, "You can do it most easily with truffles. They add flavor and texture without richness. They also help every man and woman to be a great lover. If you eat a pound of truffles a day, you will always be a magnificent lover. But, you see, truffles are so expensive, so there are very few great lovers in the world."

In 1967, the building was sold for demolition and Jacques moved to the Boulevard St-Germain on the Left Bank. He loves being so near the church of St-Germain-des-Prés. "Now, every day," he told me, "I can ask God, 'What have you done for me lately?' "

My adaptations of some of Chef Jacques Manière's recipes are "Stuffed Aromatic Mushrooms" on page 96, his ideas for "Raw Salmon with Caviar," on page 105, "Boiled Shrimp with Mayonnaise Almost Without Oil" on page 109, "Fish Steamed on a Bed of Parsley" on page 175, "Calf's Liver Steamed *à la Soubise*" on page 322, "Low-Fat Lemon-Yoghurt Sauce" on page 340, "Aromatic Cold Sauce Entirely Without Oil," on page 343, and his ideas for the "Salad with Whipped White Cheese" on page 350.

CHEF MARC MENEAU AT HIS TWO-STAR AUBERGE DE L'ESPÉRANCE IN ST-PÈRE-VÉZELAY

One can hardly avoid sensing an important future for Chef Meneau, a local boy who is making it so well in his home town that his prestige is expanding far beyond his region. He was born in a house almost next door to his present *auberge* in the tiny village of St-Père, on the short road between Avallon and Vézelay. His parents owned a small local restaurant with no pretensions. Marc helped in the kitchen and decided to be a *cuisinier*. After graduating from the Hotel and Restaurant School, he was apprenticed to one of the major chefs of the northeastern region in the town of Charleville. Marc came home to marry the daughter of a local *restaurateur* and in 1968 he and his wife, Françoise, took over the Meneau family restaurant. They wanted, naturally, to expand and improve it, and in 1974 when a handsome old house just outside the village came into the market at a price they could just afford, they bought it and have converted it into a charming *auberge*. Meanwhile, in 1970, Marc, at the age of twenty, won his first star. In 1974 came the second. I asked him: "How soon do you think you will be ready for the third star?"

"Never I hope," he replied, "It is not the kind of life that Françoise and I want – with its crowds of critical and demanding customers, with all its publicity and inescapable show-off. I want to continue standing quietly in front of my cooking stoves, experimenting, creating new and lovely things to eat. Françoise and I want to stay, shall we say, with a comfortable two stars."

Adaptations of a few of Chef Marc Meneau's recipes are his "Tiny Garden Vegetables with Coriander *à la Grecque*" on page 110, his ideas for a "Salad with White Cheese Dressing," on page 350, "Mousse of Celery Root" on page 359, "Spinach Creamed with Peaches Instead of Cream" on page 363, and his memorable "Sherbet of Champagne-Rum Punch with Smoky Lapsang Souchong Tea" on page 374.

CHEF DANIEL MÉTÉRY AT THE RESTAURANT CLOVIS OF THE HOTEL WINDSOR IN PARIS

In the textile town of Roanne in central France there must be many boys who regard the glory of Le Restaurant des Frères Troisgros and say to themselves, "That's where I would like to be." Daniel Météry is one who made it. He was born in Roanne where his grandmother was a well-known local cook. At sixteen Daniel, with a strong recommendation from his high school professor, persuaded the Troisgros to take him on as a three-year apprentice. In the third year, he won the national competition as "Best Apprentice Cook of France."

From this initial success Daniel moved on to an impressive sequence of jobs. There were two years as an assistant to Paul Bocuse. Then, naval service during which he was chief cook in a submarine. ("Not much room to turn around, but I managed to keep the men satisfied, happy, and active.") Then he stormed the gastronomic gates of Paris. He joined the kitchen of Maxim's and rose rapidly to be *chef saucier*. When Michel Guérard (page 35) opened his now-fabled restaurant, Le Pot au Feu, Météry agreed to head the kitchen team as *chef de cuisine*, under Guérard's executive direction. It was – as we all now know – a sensational, creative, and experimental success in which Météry played an important role. When the restaurant was suddenly closed and its great kitchen team broke up, Météry, still only twenty-eight, took over the direction as executive chef of the new Restaurant Clovis in the rebuilt and redecorated Hôtel Windsor. There Daniel is presenting a menu composed mainly of great dishes of his own adaptation or invention, continuing a career that I predict will eventually achieve the peaks of recognition.

My adaptations of Chef Daniel Météry's recipes are his "Lobster Swimming in Its Bouillon" on page 196, "Bay Scallops in Their Natural Juices" on page 203, "Chicken with Lime Juice" on page 230, "Parisian Veal Sweetbreads" on page 323, and his magnificent *Mirliton* of Normandy" on page 381.

CHEF LOUIS OUTHIER AT HIS THREE-STAR L'OASIS AT LA NAPOULE ON THE MEDITERRANEAN COAST

Probably the secret of Chef Outhier's extraordinary popularity and prestige all along the Côte d'Azur is that he seems to have become a true Man of the Midi. Other great chefs have been attracted to the lovely life of Provence but have not been entirely absorbed. Outhier, you feel, must have been born there. For more than twenty years he has been running his luxurious beach restaurant in the small resort village of La Napoule, about five miles west of Cannes. The house was originally a private villa which Outhier bought and converted to a *pension de famille*, a vacation boarding house open only in the summer at which the guests paid a weekly rate that included a fixed-menu dinner with everyone sitting family style around a single dining table. Within a few months, the food prepared by Outhier was the talk of the region from Nice to Marseilles. Outhier tried to restrict his dinners to his residents. He failed. Every night, each guest begged to be allowed to bring in "a couple of old friends" who "just happened" to be visiting La Napoule for the evening. The local trick was to find out who was staying with Outhier and get yourself invited for dinner. Guests sunning themselves on the beach were approached by total strangers offering to pay for an invitation to dinner.

So, in 1954, Outhier doubled the size of the dining room, built a fountained and tree-shaded courtyard between the house and the sea for open-air tables and invited in the public. "Very soon," Louis told me, "the restaurant diners had chased away the residents and we closed the *pension de famille*."

It was a bravura performance by Outhier – made all the more remarkable by the fact that one of the most famous restaurants of the time was almost next door to him in La Napoule. Such was the prestige of the great La Mère Terrat that every evening the parked Rolls Royces of the millionaires from Cannes and Nice jammed the little plaza down to the beach. "She was extraordinary," Louis said, "a fortress of *La Grande Cuisine*. I was warned that she was impregnable." Yet, today, the restaurant of La Mère Terrat no longer exists and Outhier has three stars.

Sitting with Louis in the shade of a tree by the fountain in his courtyard I probed for the secret of such an overwhelming gastronomic success. "There is no secret," he said, "it was a matter of fantastic good luck with my teachers, very hard work, slow but steady progress and a passion for cooking. My grandparents worked a lovely old mill near Besançon, in the rich farm region of the Franche Comté and their food was fabulous. I can still remember every detail of those meals. My parents moved to Alsace and, there, the moment I was old enough, I apprenticed myself to a marvelous cook, Denis Michelon, at his restaurant The Golden Barrel in the city of Belfort. He was a great man and I believe I would have stayed with him for the rest of my life if he had not one day suddenly dropped dead. Looking around for another job, I was fantastically lucky to be taken on by the great Chef Fernand Point at his La Pyramide, almost exactly at the moment when he was hiring two other young beginners, Paul Bocuse and Jean Troisgros. A couple of years later, I came here to the South by accident. The chef of the Hôtel Carlton in Cannes needed an assistant so he called Monsieur Point and I was chosen. It was for three weeks. I fell in love with the Midi and here I am."

Adaptations of Chef Louis Outhier's recipes are "Chicken with Madeira and Baked Apples" on page 228 and his "Cold Breast of Duck Bathed in Red Wine" on page 241.

CHEF LUCIEN SARRASSAT AT HIS CHEZ SARRASSAT IN THE VILLAGE OF ST-GERAND-LE-PUY NEAR VICHY

Sarrassat has been called "the most illustrious unknown Chef of France." His cooking, to my taste, is worthy of three stars. He has none. He is not even listed in the *Guide Michelin*. He does not want to be. Every year, around August, when the standard questionnaire arrives asking for new information on his restaurant, he tears it up and throws it into the fire. He told me: "I am a tiny restaurant, *Monsieur*. I have only six tables. We are only nine miles from Vichy and all the *grands gourmets* know me. They call me and I propose a menu. I have no printed menu. I propose dishes each evening, according to what has come in during the day, according to the cuts of Charolais beef hanging in my larder, according to the pike or salmon that my fishermen friends have caught today in the Allier River, or according to the game birds brought in by my hunting friends. I am a one-man operation, *Monsieur*. What would I do with tourists?''

Most of Sarrassat's regular customers call him ''the madman perfectionist.'' When he makes his hors d'oeuvre Lyonnais sausage, he refuses to grind the meats but cuts, chops and works them by hand. When he prepares his famous Crayfish in Champagne, I have seen him throw in a whole bottle of Dom Perignon. For his *mille-feuilles à la crème* he puts on a fantastic, bravura performance, with six forks spread fanwise in each hand, eclipsing any rock-'n'-roll drummer. The result is heavenly, consistently the best *mille-feuilles* I have ever tasted. And any evening, if things are not going right in the kitchen – even if only three of his six tables are filled – the ''FULL UP'' sign will go up on the front door and the key will be turned in the lock. Or the sign on the locked door may read ''CLOSED TODAY – GONE HUNTING.'' This usually means that something has gone wrong with the old weight-operated *rotisse*-spit at the open fireplace and Sarrassat is busily tinkering with it. Tomorrow ''the madman perfectionist'' will want to spit-roast a whole lamb.

Lucien Sarrassat was born on his grandfather's farm in 1914. Both his father and mother were pastry cooks and his father had worked under Escoffier in the kitchen of the Ritz in London. Lucien was apprenticed at the age of twelve to the great Chef Rabette at the famous Majestic Hotel in Vichy where he remained for thirteen years. He had an urge to travel and worked, in turn, at Prunier's in Paris, at the Casino in Algiers and at the great, now closed, Shepherd's Hotel in Cairo. But he never stayed long. He always wanted to return quickly to his beloved Bourbonnais country. So, at the age of twenty-eight, he bought a small stable in St-Gerand-le-Puy and converted it himself into his *auberge* and restaurant, where he has remained ever since.

Why does he stay in this remote and undeveloped land – he who has the hand and the skill of a great *cuisinier*? Because he is only six miles from the village where he was born, St-Germain-des-Fosses. Because he is in Charolais beef country and can see from his windows those magnificent beef cattle, seeming miraculously to be made all of steak. Because he can make the Bourbonnais *tourtes.* Because he can get the large round country loaves; the vegetables picked this morning; the farm-bred chickens, ducks, and geese; the crayfish, salmon and trout from the nearby rivers. Because it is a paradise of fresh, natural, pure produce. Because, when one has the character of Sarrassat, one does not wish to accommodate oneself to the pressures of the world, to the dishonesty and bad faith of large cities.

Chef Lucien Sarrassat's recipe for "Pike Baked on a Bed of Aromatic Vegetables" is on page 178.

CHEFS JEAN AND PIERRE TROISGROS AT THEIR THREE-STAR RESTAURANT DES FRÈRES TROISGROS IN ROANNE

Of these extraordinary men in this extraordinary restaurant I wrote in 1972 that they were the best *cuisiniers* in France — possibly in the world. After spending a good deal of time with them in the course of writing this book, I can find no reason to change my original opinion. Apart from the impeccable food and service, apart from the extraordinary warmth of the welcome offered to every patron by every man, woman and child of the large Troisgros family, there is in their kitchen an unceasing drive to experiment, to improve, to work out new ideas, to continually move forward. One result of this restless urge is the group of superb Troisgros new-new cuisine recipes in this book.

Jean and Pierre's father, Jean-Baptiste, once told me, "Our results may appear simple, but our methods are quite complicated." The restaurant is the dream vision of this single Burgundian family over four generations and almost ninety years. The grandfather ran a café restaurant in Beaune, the wine capital of Burgundy. Jean-Baptiste began working out his perfectionist ideas there and then later at his own restaurants — first in Burgundy and then in the textile city of Roanne on the upper Loire. Papa did not hope to be a great cook, but he had high ambitions for his two sons, Jean and Pierre. He told me before his death in 1974, "When they were baptized, I dropped a little salt and olive oil into the holy water so they would also be anointed as good chefs."

As they grew up in and around the restaurant, bottling the good Burgundies in their cellar and doing all the odd jobs of the kitchen and dining room, Papa always insisted that if they wanted to be true masters of the art of cuisine, they would have to do ten years of classical training in Paris. Just as the city was being liberated from the German occupation, Jean arrived and got his first job, at the age of eighteen, grilling hamburgers at the American Red Cross. Pierre soon followed and, almost as if they were inseparable twins, they always managed to work together after that. They were at the famous Hôtel Crillon, at Maxim's, and finally at the foremost *grande cuisine* restaurant of Paris, Lucas-Carton, where the kitchen was ruled with a rod of iron by a magnificent chef-disciplinarian, Père Richard. He became the major force in their gastronomic education. After their ten years of training, they could have stayed on in Paris and become star high-cuisine chefs. But they wanted none of it – neither the pressures of the city nor the boredom of the endless repetition and waste of *La Grande Cuisine*. They moved to Lyon and completed their training in the kitchen of the supremely great Chef Fernand Point at his La Pyramide in Vienne, where they began developing the experimental ideas which have resulted in the new-new cuisine.

In 1955 Papa Jean-Baptiste sent his sons a telegram: "I AM TIRED. COME HOME. I GIVE YOU MY RESTAURANT." Then began the long slow work of changing the Troisgros bistro into a great experimental restaurant. In 1957, they won their first star. Eight years later, in 1965, the second star. In 1968 the highest rating, three stars. For the twenty years that Jean and Pierre have continued to work together in Roanne, there has never been a single day, seven days a week, when at least one of them was not in charge of the restaurant. The parade of dramatic, experimental dishes that they continually present on their menus and to their regular customers and friends is an overwhelming *tour de force*.

My translations and adaptations of some of the recipes of Chefs Jean and Pierre Troisgros are "Steak *Tartare* Skating on Ice" on page 92, "Canapé *Tourte à la Bourbonnaise*" on page 97, "Melon and Ham Sailboats" on page 99, "Salad of Spinach Leaves and Duck Livers" on page 100, *"Rillettes* of Rabbit" on page 121, "Burgundian Soup of Mixed Fish" on page 140, "Mussel Soup" on page 159, "Lobster Flamed with Calvados" on page 189, their ideas for the *"Navarin* of Lobster" on page 200, "Sea Bass Crusted with Tarragon" on page 207, their ideas for the "Squab Sautéed with Garlic" on page 222, *"Fricandeau* of Chicken in Vinegar" on page 239, "Roast Duck with Figs" on page 246, "Duck Livers with White Turnips" on page 249, "Turkey Poached in Wine" on page 263, "Balinese *Yakisuki à la Française*" on page 274, "Sirloin Steak with Lemon and Capers" on page 286, the Troisgros family recipe for a "Pluperfect Pot Roast of Veal" on page 310, *"Sauce Antibeoise* for Fish" on page 335, their ideas for the "Salad with Whipped White Cheese" on page 350 and the "Salad of Green Beans with Raw Mushrooms" on page 353.

CHEF ROGER VERGÉ AT HIS THREE-STAR HOSTELLERIE DU MOULIN DE MOUGINS NEAR CANNES IN PROVENCE

Vergé, a man with a large, bushy walrus moustache, who looks a bit like a Victorian British army officer, became, in 1974, at the age of forty-six, the latest and seventeenth member of the "grand club" of French three-star chefs. He was born in the French central mountains of the Auvergne, on the border of the region of the Bourbonnais, the native land of the French Bourbon kings (from which also derives the name of that certain well-known whiskey) – both regions famous for their gastronomies. "So, you see, perhaps the love of food was in my blood," Roger told me. "And, to make matters even better, in my native village of Commentry, not far from Vichy, my father was an Auvergnat while my mother was a Bourbonnaise. Papa was the blacksmith of the village and instilled in me, almost as soon as I could talk and think, the advantages of the life of a skilled artisan working for oneself, never an employee of anyone.

"But the big interest in my life at that time was my aunt,

who was entirely devoted to a single hobby, the art of high cuisine. She worked at some ordinary job five days a week, but on weekends spent her entire free time in a huge, professionally equipped kitchen she had set up for herself, experimenting with the most complicated and difficult recipes. Then, faced with the problem of using up these monster dishes she produced for fun, she opened out a huge dining table for about twenty people in her enormous kitchen and invited family and friends to formidable lunches which lasted for the rest of the day and into the night. I was enormously impressed. You could taste something new there every few minutes. My aunt never made a penny out of it. It was all for the pure joy of gastronomic creation. I began to feel the joy myself. I was six at the time and still much too small to reach up to my aunt's stove, so she put a small, low table alongside and lifted the pots down for me to smell them and stir them."

At twelve, Roger dreamed of being an aviation engineer. "It was the idea of travel – of seeing the world." Then, when he was about fifteen, his father suddenly died and there were family financial problems. He had to find a way of earning a living quite quickly. There was no more possibility of thinking about the years of study that might be involved in aviation engineering. He remembered the joys of his aunt's kitchen and apprenticed himself to the chef of a small bistro in the village. The old man was retired from being a chef at the great La Tour d'Argent in Paris. Roger worked hard for three years. Then the old chef told him he must go to Paris and gave him a letter of introduction to La Tour d'Argent. They hired Roger at once.

"But, instantly, I hated the big city," Roger said. "Within two days, I had walked out of La Tour d'Argent and was back in my village. My mother was furious. The old chef at the bistro slapped me across the face, took my arm with a grip like a vise, marched me back to the railroad station, put me on the next train to Paris and yelled, as the train was pulling out, 'Don't you ever come back.' The chef at La Tour d'Argent understood and took me back. I stayed for almost a year and then went on to the famous Plaza Athenée, where I worked under the fabled Chef Lucien Diat."

Then, young Vergé, now about twenty-three, turned back to

his dream of traveling. With letters of introduction from the world-famous Chef Diat in his pocket, Roger could get a job virtually anywhere. First, he helped to open the new Hotel El Mansour at Casablanca in Morocco. Next, he moved to Algeria. Then, to Nairobi in Kenya. This led to a job as executive chef to a company that was opening a string of hotels and restaurants across Central Africa – the dream job of his young life, taking him to such remote and dramatic places as Entebbe, Bulawayo, Dar es Salaam, and Zanzibar, among others, and giving him an extraordinary gastronomic experience through training and working with young African, Indian and Portuguese cooks. "I discovered at that time," Roger told me, "the multiple cuisines of India and the Far East. Even today, twenty years later, those influences are still in my cuisine. They taught me how to use and control the hot spices. I still make Indian curries, not only for some of my customers, but also because I adore them myself.

"I loved my time in Africa," Roger continued, "I loved the warm climate, the brilliance of the air and sky, the strong character of the foods. When, eventually, I returned to Paris, I had the deepest feeling of despair. Most of all, I was desperate about the unchanged repetition of *La Grande Cuisine*. Then, I discovered the Midi and, particularly, Provence. It was the life and the food here that, finally, reconciled me to a return to working in France. For the next few years, always in the Midi, I was *chef de cuisine* and manager of various hotels and restaurants. But, I often thought of my father and his sense of freedom in being an artisan, in business for himself. I was a success. I was earning good money. But I was still an employee of others."

Then one day Roger found an old mill with its wheel still intact in the village of Mougins about five miles inland from Cannes. It had already been converted into a small bistro, but it was badly managed; the food was poor, the house dilapidated, the business failing. Vergé bought it and began working harder than ever before. He improved and enlarged the house. He landscaped the gardens. He built a series of terraces at various levels for dining out in the scented night air. Above all, he slaved in the kitchen. He had learned, in the

previous ten years, the basic principles of the cooking of
Provence. He loved it and was determined to stay with it
in his restaurant. "In Provence, the local ingredients make
the greatness of the cuisine, but all must be prepared in the
local way that best brings out their flavors. You cannot live
in Provence and depart from Provence in your kitchen."

So he began working with all his imagination and skill to
perfect, so to speak, his personal vision of an improved, lightened, sharpened, simplified, but nonetheless authentic,
Vergé-style cuisine of Provence. He has succeeded. He has
succeeded, also, in creating one of the most beautiful restaurants in France.

His work was recognized by one star in 1970. Two years
later came the second star and in 1974, the third. It was,
clearly, a meteoric rise to the top. "I started here with the de-
termination to get three stars. But, *mon Dieu*, it has come
almost too fast. We are overwhelmed. We are out of breath."

Now that he has the customers – they come to a three-star
restaurant from all over the world – his battle is to maintain the
quality of the products for his kitchen. At crack of dawn one
morning I went with him to the farmers' market of Cannes.
It was like trying to keep up with a darting lizard. He was
here, there, everywhere, picking rock fish one by one out of a
barrel, choosing tiny tomatoes so small they were still like
bunches of grapes on the stem, prodding the vegetables, tasting the fruits, squeezing the cheeses. There is something
marvelous and memorable about the products of the strong
sunlight of Provence. Equally memorable is the determina-
tion of Roger Vergé to find absolutely the best of everything.

"You know, this kind of restaurant is not very profitable,"
he told me. "For serving about one hundred dinners a night,
I have to have a staff of more than fifty. I need not tell you
about operating costs. The margin of profitable success is
quite narrow and getting narrower all the time. But, living
and working and experimenting here, in this beauty and this
climate and with this air and these singing birds, is so near to
a joyous perfection of satisfaction that I never, if I can help it,
want to do anything different.

"And as to our new-new cuisine, this Low-High cuisine on

which you have asked so many questions, I feel that *la cuisine* is a profession very close to an art. To do it well you must first of all respect the highest standards set by the great masters of the past. You cannot disregard the supreme achievements of French gastronomic history. But, in the end, one must find in one's own kitchen an expression of oneself. In the same way that a musician, a painter, a sculptor dramatizes the self in the work. If I can achieve that here in Provence, I cannot be anything else but happy. We are surrounded by an ambience of gaiety, a softness and sweetness of life . . . and marvelous, marvelous food. I want to express in my cooking the delicacy, the lightness, the subtlety of the air, the colors, the perfume of Provence."

My translations and adaptations of Chef Roger Vergé's recipes are: his "Fish-Garlic Soup of Provence" on page 135, "Lobster in Sauternes" on page 191, "Sea Bass in Lettuce Leaf Packages" on page 209, "Smelt with Oranges and Lemons" on page 212, "*Gibelotte* Country Aspic of Rabbit" on page 255, "Lamb *à la Moussaka*" on page 294, "Sauce in the Style of a Béarnaise but Without Butter" on page 333, his ideas for a "*Sauce Gribette* for Meat and Fish" on page 338, his ideas for "White Cheese with Herbs" on page 350, "*Salade Mesclün*" on page 355, and his "*Salade Mikado*" on page 356.

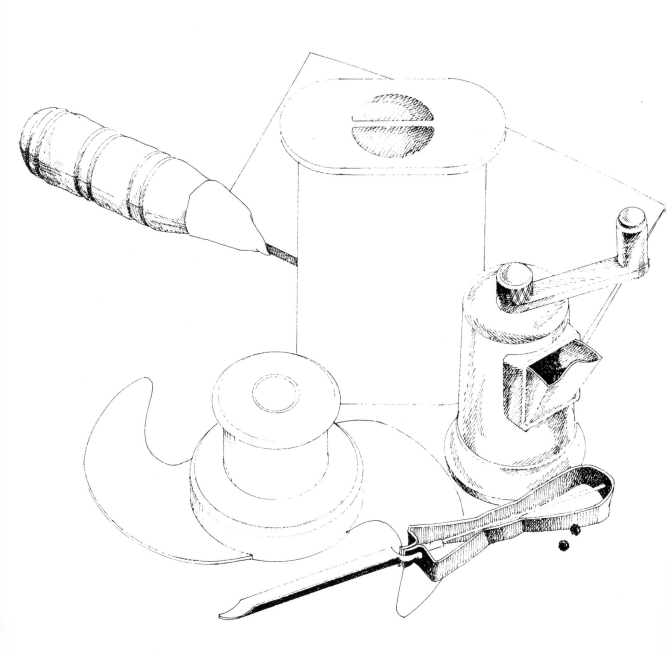

Chapter Three
The Basic Techniques of the
Low-High Kitchen

in which, by means of some provocative
suggestions, the author prompts us to
undertake a short self-analysis to uncover
our subconscious habits at the chopping
block and the hot stove.   A short account
of American wines and of what's in a label.

During my kitchen talks with the great chefs about the Low-High cuisine, there was one universal point they all stressed again and again – the essential requirement of flexibility on the part of the amateur cook in interpreting the new recipes. Many of us have become lazy about our food planning and shopping. We see the word "asparagus," for example, in the ingredients list of a recipe so we write "asparagus" in our shopping list without giving it a second thought. We almost never ask the primary question: is it in season? We seldom check the recipe to see how important a part is played by the asparagus. Would canned or frozen be good enough? If not, would it be better to substitute for the asparagus some other vegetable currently in fresh supply?

It might not have mattered so much in an old-style recipe whether or not the asparagus was freshly picked; it would probably have been heavily sauced with lemon butter and garnished, perhaps, with grated Parmesan cheese and mashed hard-boiled egg yolks. That kind of gastronomic coverup has been eliminated from the Low-High cuisine. Now at every season of the year it is essential to use the fruits and vegetables that are fresh and ripe in the market. That is the key to the success of these Low-High recipes. Chef Pierre Troisgros told me: "Our recipes are not legal regulations. They are suggestions. The first rule of our new-new cuisine is that we should all cook, not by rules, but as we please. If the recipe contains green beans and you don't happen to like green beans, replace them with some other green vegetable. Make your shopping list your own – not ours. Above all, follow the dictates of the seasons. If our recipe calls for sea bass, but cod is at its peak, then by all means prepare the recipe with cod. At all times, in the new-new cuisine, flexibility is the password."

Clichés in the kitchen

When the modern French chefs began seriously analyzing the ancient recipes of *La Grande Cuisine*, they found a large number of traditional operations that were really unnecessary and could be eliminated. We have the same problem with our old-style recipes in our old-style cook books. The same traditional steps are repeated so often in so many different recipes that, to me, they have become kitchen clichés. For example:

1. A majority of main-dish recipes include onions, usually chopped or minced. Almost without exception, before being incorporated into the dish, they are sautéed in butter. Why? The original theory, I suppose, was that (a) the sautéeing would evaporate from the onion some of its more pungent flavor oils, (b) the texture of the onion would be softened and somehow made nicer to eat and (c) the butter soaked into the onion would enrich the dish on the now questionable theory that enrichment of everything was a worthy end in itself. As to the last objective, the Low-High point of view is that deliberate enrichment for its own sake is no longer in tune with modern demands. As to (a) and (b), there are now better non-clichéed ways of preparing onions without the use of butter and these are discussed in this chapter on page 83 and in the recipes.

2. There is the same problem with mushrooms. Almost invariably in old-style recipes we are instructed to sauté them in butter. It is true, of course, that a fresh mushroom is a kind of sponge and that it contains a certain amount of water which does somewhat dilute its flavor. By heating the mushrooms, we expel the water, creating a slight vacuum inside the mushroom which demands to suck up something to replace the water. Why must that something be butter? Why not wine? Or a fatless aromatic bouillon? Ways of eliminating kitchen clichés with mushrooms are discussed in the recipes.

3. The hoariest of all kitchen clichés are the traditional methods of thickening sauces. You have some lovely natural juice from the cooking – perhaps the juice of just-steamed clams, or the defatted natural gravy from a roast of beef – and you want to give it some body and texture without diluting or modifying its natural flavor. The old clichéd way, endlessly repeated in thousands of recipes, was to work in a butter and flour *roux*. Chef Michel Guérard told me: "That word *roux* should be expelled from the gastronomic dictionary." Or, we were instructed to thicken the sauce by whipping in cholesterol-loaded egg yolks. Butter, flour, or eggs added no character of their own to the sauce beyond a glutinous thickness and they certainly diminished the natural flavors. The great modern French Chefs – the Troisgros brothers, Michel Guérard, Roger Vergé, Paul Bocuse – decided that there must be a better way of thickening sauces. They have come up with half a dozen better ways that have greatly advanced the major revolution that is the Low-High cuisine. Basic principles are discussed in this chapter, starting on page 77, and in the main body of the recipes.

The remainder of this chapter, then, is an alphabetical list of some of the principal kitchen problems – with my suggestions as to how the old work clichés can be eliminated by the application of the Low-High principles of lightness and simplicity. Note that I say "my suggestions." This chapter represents my point of view. The recipes do not. They are the reflections of the varying philosophies of the different chefs. In my translations and adaptations I have tried to be true to the personal methods of each chef. (For example, the Troisgros brothers prefer white pepper and it is used in all their recipes. Michel Guérard prefers black pepper and it appears in all his recipes.) Deliberately, I have not superimposed my own uniformity on the healthy variety of these recipes. The onions and mushrooms are not always sautéed in the same way. The sauces are thickened in all kinds of ways. But you do not have to follow blindly. Remember what Pierre Troisgros said about absolute flexibility. Experiment. Try one way after another. Find out which way you prefer. Finally, you will be in the best possible position to cook exactly as you please.

AROMATIC HERBS AND SPICES

No department of the kitchen better illustrates the essential truth of what has just been said above. The freshest possible herbs and spices are all-important in the Low-High cuisine. Without the heavy sauces and the dominant garnishes, the aromatic ingredients make or unmake the character of the dish. We have all been brainwashed with fixed rules for aromatic affinities. We have been brought up to believe that tarragon is the perfect herb with fish – that only rosemary goes with lamb – only sage with onions – only basil with tomatoes. All clichés. Never be hidebound by the list of aromatics in a recipe. You can produce a hundred variations of the same dish by experimental juggling with the herbs and spices.

The most important of the new Low-High cuisine rules is to always use as the first choice the scissor-snipped fresh leaves of the herb plant. This is far more important than sticking to a particular herb named in the recipe. If the list calls for tarragon and none is available, but fresh basil is, then by all means switch to basil. Within reason, you should start your Low-High experiments with the assumption that any fresh herb leaf can be used to replace any other and that you should use dried herbs only as a last resort. Therefore, in the ingredient lists of all the recipes in this book, fresh herbs are always named and measured without the complication of inserting conversions to dried herbs (see below). (The one exception is oregano, which is almost impossible to find fresh.)

As to spices, it is equally essential in the Low-High cuisine that they be freshly ground a few moments before using, to avoid the rapid evaporation of the flavor oils. To eliminate this serious problem, I never buy ready-ground spices. I store in a dark closet apothecary jars with airtight, ground-glass stoppers filled with whole dried berries, whole cloves, cinnamon sticks, mace chips, whole nutmegs, etc., that do not dry out in storage and that can be ground to the finest powder in two or three seconds with one of the new, miniature, electric spice mills (see, in this chapter, under "Machines, Kitchen" on page 80).

Sometimes, of course, you will be forced to use dried herbs.

How much to use? This is a most difficult question. There are so many variables. Your dried herb, when you buy it, may be good quality or bad, reasonably fresh or already stale. Your own storage arrangements may or may not be good. If you keep your jars in a strong light, or in a hot place in the kitchen or, worst of all, if they are not tightly closed, your herbs may be quite weak by the time you come to use them. Sniff them every time you open the jar. If there is any smell of old hay, throw them out.

Taking all these possibilities into account and allowing for the fact that the Low-High recipes of this book demand a definite aromatic character, I would experiment with a basic conversion of ½ to 1 teaspoon of dried herb for each table-spoon of chopped fresh leaf. Then, taste and decide whether your personal preference requires a larger or smaller conver-sion factor. Remember, also, that some varieties of herbs and spices are much more concentrated than others in the dried form. Dried mint, nutmeg, oregano and sage, for example, should be added to a dish very cautiously since they can easily become overdominant. Experiment, develop your judgment. Cook as you please.

How to store fresh green coriander

Two of the most unusual recipes of this book require the fresh green leaves of that extraordinary herb, coriander ("Indian Turkey with Green Coriander" on page 102 and "Hunanese Hot and Sour Fish Soup" on page 143). By the time you have found the coriander (see "Index of Sources" on page 392) and have had experience with it in the recipes, you will either hate it and want to rush the rest of the bunch as quickly as possible to the incinerator, or you will adore it, as I do, so that you will want to store the remainder of the bunch for future use.

Stand the bunch of coriander in a refrigerator jar, as if you were arranging a bunch of flowers in a vase. Fill the jar with enough cold water so that the stems are well covered. Now slide a fair-sized plastic bag down over the leaves and around the outside of the jar, holding the bag in place with a rubber band. Thus the leaves will be surrounded by moist air which is what they need for survival. Stand the jar in the refrigerator. When you need coriander leaves, snip them off with scissors, each time carefully resealing the bag.

ASPICS AND GELATINS

Chef Louis Outhier's brilliant three-star recipe on page 241 for slices of duck breast covered with a red wine aspic points the way towards many Low-High uses of entirely fatless aspics to decorate and flavor many different cold foods. How much more digestible, lighter and less fattening, for example, to serve cold poached salmon with a colorful coating of savory aspic than with a rich egg-and-oil mayonnaise. Aspics are extremely flexible as to colors and flavors. They can be made golden, red, or yellow with wine; green with spinach juice; amber with Madeira or Sherry. They can be made with tomato juice or almost any clear bouillon or stock: beef, chicken, duck, or veal. Subtle variations can be added with small doses of fortified wines and spirits, including Armagnac, Cognac, or Vermouth. Begin, if you want to start experimenting, by preparing a batch of the "Basic Low-High Beef-Chicken Bouillon" on page 68. It can then be converted into:

BASIC LOW-HIGH QUICK MULTI-PURPOSE ASPIC

(about 2¼ cups)

Bouillon, clear, Beef-Chicken or
  other flavor (1¼ cups)
Tomato juice (½ cup)
Vermouth, dry (¼ cup)
Gelatin, unflavored, granulated
  (2 envelopes or 2 Tbs)
Salt, coarse crystal, to taste

Black pepper, freshly ground,
  to taste
Eggshell, crushed in the
  fingers (1)
Egg white, lightly beaten (1)
Armagnac brandy (1½ Tbs)

Preparation in about 25 minutes

This ultrasimple procedure disregards all those rules about separately melting the gelatin and then clarifying the aspic as a secondary operation.

Here it is all done together. Put all the ingredients, except the Armagnac, into a 1-quart saucepan and gradually heat it up, stirring continuously until the gelatin is completely melted, with no lumps, while the liquid comes just to the boil. Turn down the heat to gentlest simmering, cover, then continue simmering for 10 minutes. Turn off the heat and let it cool for ten minutes. Now strain it through a flannel cloth that has been wetted with cold water and lightly wrung out. Into the crystal clear liquid stir the 1½ tablespoons of Armagnac. The aspic should then either be chilled in the refrigerator or kept warm according to how you are going to work with it (see below).

This aspic serves almost all purposes, but if you prefer a specially flavored aspic only for fish, prepare a batch of the "Basic Low-High Fish Bouillon" on page 70 and convert it into:

BASIC LOW-HIGH QUICK ASPIC FOR FISH

(about 1 pint)

Fish bouillon, clear, either Basic
  Low-High recipe, or clam juice,
  or fish cooking liquor with wine
  (1¾ cups)
Dry Vermouth (¼ cup)
Carrot, scraped and diced (1 small)
Yellow onion, peeled and chopped
  (1 small)
Green Pascal celery, destringed
  and chopped (1 small inner
  stalk, with leaves)
Gelatin, unflavored, granulated
  (2 envelopes or 2 Tbs)

Parsley (2 sprigs, with stalks)
Thyme, fresh leaf in season,
  chopped (2 tsp)
Lemon juice, freshly squeezed
  (2 Tbs)
Eggshell, crushed in the fingers (1)
Egg white, lightly beaten (1)
Salt, coarse crystal, to taste
White pepper, freshly ground,
  to taste
Calvados, French apple brandy
  (1 Tbs)

Preparation in about 30 minutes

Proceed exactly as in the previous recipe. Put all the ingredients except the Calvados into a 1-quart saucepan and bring it slowly up to boiling, stirring continuously. Let it gently simmer, covered, for 10 minutes. Then let it cool and rest for 10 minutes. Strain it, exactly as in the previ-

ous recipe, through damp flannel. Stir into it the 1 tablespoon of Calvados and the aspic is ready for you to work with.

How to work with aspic

The most important trick is not to let the aspic become too stiff too quickly. There is an easy way to avoid this. Set out two large mixing bowls. Fill one with ice cubes, the other with hot water. Stand the saucepan with the hot liquid aspic among the ice cubes. In a surprisingly short time the aspic will begin to set. It is important to learn to recognize the various stages. First it becomes thick and syrupy, like honey. This is the moment to spoon it on for glazing. Next it becomes gelatinous, like raw egg white. This is the moment to pour it into a mold. Finally it becomes too stiff to handle. Lift the saucepan out of the ice cubes and half submerge it in the hot water, stirring. Within a few seconds the aspic will be liquid again. Put it back in the ice cubes and wait for it to get syrupy again. Repeat this double play as often as necessary. Of course, all work with aspic must be done several hours in advance so that it can be fully set in the refrigerator before serving. When glazing do not worry about syrupy aspic dripping and running down on the serving platter. It all scrapes off easily when the aspic is fully set.

Making decorative aspic cubes

Pour the liquid aspic into a square cake pan until it is about ¼ to ⅜ inch deep. Set in the refrigerator until the aspic is very firm. Then cut the layer in the pan into squares of any desired size and lift them out with a spatula. These squares catch the light and are extremely decorative.

BOUILLON, BROTH, COURT-BOUILLON, FUMET, STOCK

Since aromatic boiling or simmering (instead of frying in fat) is one of the cornerstones of the Low-High cuisine, it is essential to know how to prepare the fatless and flavorful bouillons which are the foundations of various kitchen operations. They can be broths for boiling meats – court-bouillons for fish – or stocks to be incorporated into light and simple sauces. The old French name court-bouillon meant, literally, a short bouillon, quickly made specifically for poaching fish. Thus it was differentiated from the "stocks" which simmered for days on the back of the stove and were always, so to speak, "in stock." Now, since the Low-High principles require that every meat or chicken bouillon be freshly prepared, they should perhaps be called "Low-High court-bouillons." But tradition in gastronomy dies hard.

Here is my principal beef-chicken bouillon, which I introduced to Chefs Jean and Pierre Troisgros for their "*Yakisuki à la Française*" (page 274). It is, in fact, a broad modification of one of the most marvelous clear soups of the world, the *Soto Ayam* of the island of Bali. It is delicately and subtly spiced and the beef and chicken that are its main ingredients are not overcooked, so they can be used up in other dishes after the bouillon has been strained off. This bouillon can be used in any recipe in this book where the ingredients list beef bouillon or chicken bouillon, or, as a compromise, veal stock. It will add its aromatic character to any dish in which it is used. Quite apart from its being fatless and light, it is the best homemade bouillon I know.

BASIC LOW-HIGH MULTI-PURPOSE BEEF AND CHICKEN BOUILLON

(about 2 quarts – can be frozen in ice-cube trays for later use)

Soup bones, nicely meaty,
  including knuckle (3 lbs)
Soup beef, lean (1 lb)
Macadamia nuts, shelled whole (8)
Shallots, peeled whole (6 cloves)
Garlic, peeled whole (3 cloves)
Onion, peeled and quartered
  (1 medium)
Lemon for juice and grated rind (1)
Coriander seeds, whole (1 Tbs)

Turmeric, ground (2 tsp)
Ginger root, fresh, skinned
  (2 pieces, each about thumbnail
  size)
Salt, coarse crystal, to taste
Black pepper, Indian or Chinese
  Szechuan, freshly ground, to
  taste
Chicken, boiling fowl (about
  3½ lbs)

Carrots, scraped and chunked
  (3 medium)
Celery, green Pascal, destringed
  and chunked (1 stalk)
Leek whites, washed and chunked
  (2 medium)

Yellow onions, peeled and
  chunked (2 medium)
Bay leaf (1)
Parsley, fresh (4 sprigs)
White wine, dry (1 cup)

Active preparation about 20 minutes, plus unsupervised simmering about 3 hours

Put the bones into a soup kettle of roughly 8 quarts capacity, just cover them with freshly drawn cold water and bring rapidly to the boil. As soon as bubbling begins, pour away this first water, cool and wash the bones immediately under cold running water. (This standard technique of professional chefs washes away the bitter-tasting glutinous elements and eliminates the later need for skimming.) Put the bones back into the kettle, add the pound of soup beef, again cover with freshly drawn cold water, but this time to about 6 inches above the top of the bones. Bring rapidly to the boil, then continue bubbling gently, uncovered.

Meanwhile, prepare the aromatic flavoring paste. I put into the container of my Cuisinart chopper-churner (see page 80): the 8 macadamia nuts, the 6 shallot cloves, the 3 garlic cloves, the quartered onion, 1 teaspoon grated lemon rind, the tablespoon of coriander seeds finely ground just before going in, the 2 teaspoons of turmeric, the 2 pieces of ginger root, 1 teaspoon of salt and about 6 grinds of black pepper. I chop and churn these until they are mixed into a smooth, but still slightly grainy paste – usually in about 15 seconds. Rub the chicken inside and out, first with the cut side of half the lemon, then with the flavoring paste, using it all up and piling the last of it inside the chicken. Gently lower the chicken into the boiling bouillon, making sure that it is submerged and adding, if necessary, more boiling water. Keep the bouillon simmering, uncovered, until the chicken is quite soft – usually in about 1½ hours.

When the chicken is done, remove it, let it cool and store, tightly wrapped, in the refrigerator for some other use. Now add to the bouillon: the chunked carrots, celery, leeks and onions, the bay leaf, the 4 sprigs of parsley, and the cup of wine. Keep the kettle bubbling, uncovered, to continue concentrating the flavors for about one more hour. Then discard the bones and let the soup kettle cool, covered. Finally, strain off the aromatic bouillon and store it. Pick out the pieces of lean beef and save them for some later use. Discard all the remaining solids.

In the above recipe and in the one which follows for a fish court-bouillon our objective, of course, is to get enough strength of character into the liquid so that its savory quality will suffuse the flesh of whatever is boiled in it. You cannot get that effect with a bland bouillon – it has to be penetrating and strong. Those qualities seem to come naturally in the balanced spices of the traditional soups of the Far East. In this next recipe, the base of the bouillon is the classic Japanese *dashi*, clear fish soup, which I have adapted to the techniques of the Low-High cuisine.

The modern chefs do not approve of the boiling down of nondescript fish bones of doubtful origin which, they feel, often give a stale and worn-out flavor to a court-bouillon. In the old *Grande Cuisine*, after one of these bone bouillons had been simmering at the back of the coal-fired stove for a couple of days, it took on a slightly smoky flavor and that is the origin of the name *fumet de poisson* meaning, literally, a smoky fish bouillon. To avoid all these dangers, the Low-High method is to start with fresh fish (including some eel for gelatinous body in the bouillon), each fish put in with its bones, flesh, and head intact – all quickly braised with aromatic vegetables in a winey liquid for a minimum time. The resulting court-bouillon has the freshness of just-caught fish and such a smooth texture that it needs no enrichment with butter, cream, or egg yolks.

When choosing the fish for the following court-bouillon remember that soft-fleshed fish (for example, flounder or whiting) tend to break up and purée in the bouillon, while the firm-fleshed fish (cod, halibut, eel, etc.) are more useful because they release a gelatinous body into the broth. Always choose some of these, with their heads and bones, for the following basic recipe. This court-bouillon can be used wherever a fish bouillon appears in the ingredients list in any fish recipe in this book.

BASIC LOW-HIGH COURT-BOUILLON FOR FISH

(about 2 quarts – can be frozen in ice-cube trays for later use)

Kelp seaweed, Japanese kombu (6 oz bag)

Bonito tuna, dry shavings, Japanese katsuobushi (8 oz box)

Kelp, granulated (1 Tbs)

Mixed fish, with heads and bones, see above, washed (about 2½ lbs)

White wine, dry (2 cups)

Carrot, scraped and sliced
(1 medium)

Leek white, washed and chunked
(1 medium)

Yellow onion, peeled and chunked
(1 medium)

Garlic, peeled and sliced (2 cloves)

Black peppercorns, whole (6)

Bay leaf, whole (1)

Parsley, fresh (3 sprigs)

Tarragon, fresh in season (1 sprig)

Thyme, fresh in season (1 sprig)

Salt, coarse crystal, to taste

Active work about 15 minutes plus about 2 hours of unsupervised simmering

The best aromatic fish bouillon begins with a classic, Japanese-style dashi, *a clear bouillon of seaweed and shaved dried tuna — both ingredients available at Japanese markets. Unwind the long leaf of the* kombu *kelp, usually about 4 inches wide and 5 feet long. With sharp kitchen scissors cut off about 2 feet, wash it under running cold water for not more than a couple of seconds, then cut it into 2 inch squares and hold. Open up the package of* katsuobushi *fish shavings, measure 6 cups, fairly loosely packed, then hold. Put 3 quarts of freshly drawn cold water into an 8-quart lidded soup kettle, add the kelp squares and at once set over high heat to bring rapidly to the boil. Make sure that the seaweed squares are thoroughly immersed and are separated around the kettle. Stir in 1 tablespoon of the granulated kelp. As the liquid comes to the boil, watch the kettle carefully and, at the first sign of bubbling, throw in, all at once, the dried tuna shavings and stir them around vigorously. Remove the kettle from the heat the instant the liquid is thoroughly boiling and strain at once through a fine sieve into a large bowl, pressing all the juice out of the seaweed and fish and discarding them. Speed is essential — if the kelp and fish stay in the water too long, they give off a slight bitterness. Put back the now clear bouillon into the kettle and reheat to gentle simmering for its conversion into a Low-High court bouillon.*

Add to the bouillon: the 2½ pounds of mixed fish, the 2 cups of wine, the carrot, the leek, the onion, the sliced garlic, the 6 peppercorns, the bay leaf, the 3 sprigs of parsley, 1 sprig each of fresh tarragon and thyme and, after tasting (since the kelp and tuna will already have provided some salt), additional salt as needed. Let all this gently simmer, covered, for about 1 hour, then let it cool, strain off the court bouillon and store it in the refrigerator or freezer. Discard all the solids remaining in the kettle.

FINAL NOTE: *If you are lazy or pressed for time, you can substitute canned beef bouillon or bottled clam juice for these Low-High stocks.*

BRAISING INSTEAD OF FRYING

One night in the High Alps while the winter winds were howling around her Auberge of the Flowering Hearth, Mademoiselle Ray Girard demonstrated to me the meaning of the ancient French cooking phrase *la braise*, from which is derived our modern word "braising." The huge central hearth of the Auberge was roaring with the flames from a pile of large logs – the spaces between them filled with glowing embers. Mademoiselle Ray brought from the kitchen a flattish, wide, black iron pot almost entirely filled by a rack of veal standing on a bed of aromatic vegetables, with slices of ham and not more than half a cup of wine. Using a big poker, an iron shovel and tongs, she worked the pot almost into the center of the fire, so that it rested on a layer of red embers entirely surrounded by flames. Then she shoveled more embers on top of the concave lid and left the pot, as she said, *pour cuisiner dans la braise*, to cook in the braise. She referred to the base of aromatic vegetables under the meat as *la fond de la braise*, the base of the braise. The phrases were all based on the ancient name of the glowing embers of a wood fire, *les braises.*

Mademoiselle Ray went on to explain what was happening to the meat inside the braising pot. The heat, entering evenly from all sides, would drive the collagen juices of the meat towards its center where they would be hydrolyzed into protein elements and steam. This would set up internal pressure and begin to break down the toughness of the fibers of the meat. Then, as the pressures were released, the juices would work their way outwards again and finally, expelled from the meat, would combine with the juices of the vegetables to form the superb natural sauce. There was no added fat in the pot and even the fats dripping from the meat would be skimmed off.

As Chef Jean Troisgros has told me many times: "The new-new cuisine is teaching all of us to return to the ancient methods of cooking." Once you understand how braising works, you can convert many standard recipes (which call for frying or grilling the meat with lashings of fat) to the braising method where the meat always comes out moist and soft, with aromatic flavoring from the variable array of vegetables added to the braising pot. The perfect example of the braising technique is the Troisgros family recipe for a "Rump of Veal" on page 310.

BUTTER VERSUS OIL

The great Escoffier, at the turn of the century, was once reported to have exclaimed: *"La Grande Cuisine* demands butter, butter and more butter." Ever since, butter has been a kind of status symbol of high cooking—a sacred cow with a superiority so lordly that it was never questioned. Whenever I open one of the standard cook books of the past twenty years, I find instructions to use butter "generously" and to add it "lavishly" at almost every stage of almost every dish. The Low-High cuisine has taught me that this is a cliché which should be sharply challenged. First, I question the amount of butter suggested in most standard recipes. Almost invariably, when cubes of meat are to be sautéed in advance, the standard instructions are to "first melt into the sauté pan 4 to 6 tablespoons of butter." I at once cut this down to 2 tablespoons. Nothing goes wrong. Now, experimentally, I am cutting down even more. In several of the following recipes, therefore, I include the instruction to "lubricate the bottom of the sauté pan with a minimum of butter." I find that quick sautéeing can be done with the pan just lightly greased and that the proper sealing crust is formed with much less butter soaking into the meat. Meat does not burn if it is kept moving, even over quite high heat. As a general rule, in almost every standard recipe, I now cut the suggested amount of butter in half.

My second challenge of the butter cliché is on the score of the lengthy cooking of butter in a dish. Almost all of the great chefs of the Low-High cuisine are now agreed that it was the lengthy cooking, the slow concentration and reduction of butter and cream that was the main cause of the unhealthy richness of the old high cuisine. When butterfat is baked or simmered for long hours, it tends not only to soften the natural crispness of the texture of the ingredients, but the butterfat itself breaks down into its fatty acids and becomes both unhealthy and unpleasant to the taste. Chef Pierre Troisgros (page 50) argues that, if butter is used at all, it should never be cooked with the dish, but a very small quantity should be melted in at the last moment before serving, when it can provide a sense of luxurious velvet with a minimum of added fattiness. This is the technique that is used in almost all the recipes of this book.

Third, I challenge the universal statement that "there is no substitute for the taste of butter." That could be true on a mountain farm in, say, the High Alps in the summer, when the cows feed on the mountain flowers and lush grasses; when the butter is freshly made every morning from heavy cream that has been allowed to ferment overnight so that the un-pasteurized butter has a marvelous nuttiness and is suffused with the perfume of the flowers. But the average supermarket butter that we use every day is a compromise product, mass produced from unfermented cream; pasteurized to eliminate all the living yeasts; bland, dull, neutral and uniform across the country. We all know the problems with melting butter, when the calcium deposit begins to burn, to brown, then to blacken and become bitter. Standard cookbooks tell us how to make butter easier to handle by clarifying it and converting it into Indian-style *ghee*. Why bother? Why not learn from Chef Roger Vergé and the great *cuisiniers* of Provence who cook with the supreme-quality natural oils now being produced in more and more interesting varieties?

I find I can get much more character into my dishes with considerably less fat, by using small amounts of the finest-quality, first-pressing green virgin olive oil from Provence – not to be confused in any way with standard olive oils on the shelves of the average supermarket. The Provençal olive oil has such a fruitiness, such a flowery bouquet, such a natural quality of the Mediterranean earth that 1 teaspoon of this gorgeous stuff adds more character to the dish than 2 table-spoons of nondescript butter. Other oils, used for various purposes in my kitchen, include a wonderfully light oil pressed from grape pits, a virgin olive oil from Sicily, an oil extracted from sunflower seeds and cold-pressed walnut oil. (See "Index of Sources" on page 392.) Sometimes they replace the butter. Sometimes they are mixed with the butter to liven its dull personality. The objective is always to use less fat and to extract a larger mileage from it in terms of the character and taste of the finished dish.

CHEESES, LOW-FAT

Chef Michel Guérard (page 35) is generally credited with the invention of the brilliant trick (now adopted by many chefs and included in numerous recipes in this book) of adding body and a smooth velvety quality to natural sauces by blending in a creamy whip of low-fat white cheese instead of the traditional butter, flour, or egg yolks. Guérard's national publicity has started a boom in France for a Gervais-type, partially fermented, cheese-yoghurt called Taillefine ("narrow waistline") sold nationally in French drug stores in small 6-ounce packages and claiming to contain 0% fat and 82% water. What has gone out of it with the fat, it seems to me, is any positive flavor or texture – so much so that I for one feel a slight sense of relief that it is not yet being imported into the United States. This is one area where we are quite far ahead of France. I have found in many parts of the United States excellent low-fat cottage, cream-type, farmer, pot, or Italian-style ricotta cheeses. I wish the makers of these excellent products would take one cue from the French and print on their labels – instead of such vague phrases as "Slimmers' Special," or "Weight Losers' Delight" – the precise percentage of butterfat in the cheese. In these Low-High days there ought to be a law requiring all cheeses to be rated by their butterfat content. (As a rough rule of thumb, the average "American cheese" or any standard firm cheese for eating with crackers runs somewhere between 30% and 50% butterfat, whereas soft dessert cheeses such as Brie, Camembert, or Triple Crème can be anywhere from 60% to 80% pure butterfat.) Against these terrifying figures I have found 1%-fat cottage and farmer cheeses, an outstanding New York State 5%-fat pot cheese, a nationally distributed brand of "imitation cream cheese" at from 12% to 14% fat and a number of ricottas at between 12% and 16% fat.

(See "Index of Sources" on page 392.) Finally, if you need a firm cheese for grating, with a memorably nutty flavor, there is the nationally distributed, imported Norwegian Jahrlsberg, an imitation Swiss Gruyère-type with a fine texture (used in the "Carrot Terrine" on page 358). But you should not depend only on national packaged brands in supermarkets. You should also explore your small neighborhood cheese shops where you can often find locally made fresh, white curd cheeses. They can add a touch of freshness and immediacy to many of the recipes in this book.

CREAM, CRÈME FRAÎCHE, LOW-FAT CRÈME DE FROMAGE, SOUR CREAM, LOW-FAT YOGHURT

On the rare occasions when a Low-High recipe calls for cream, it is used in exactly the same way as butter – never added in the early stages as part of the cooking process of the dish, but a minimum amount floated in at the last moment before serving to add velvet without overrichness. Actually, in France, the classic way of thickening sauces is not with sweet cream (called *fleurette*), but with that irresistible dairy product almost unknown until recently in the United States, the luxuriously smooth and thick, nutty and refreshingly acid *crème fraîche*, which is a completely natural product. Since French sweet cream has its lactic yeasts returned to it after pasteurization, it will, if left alone, thicken by natural fermentation into *crème fraîche*, roughly the French equivalent of our sour cream. But not quite. American sweet cream is left sterile of yeasts after pasteurization and does not thicken naturally. So our sour cream has to be manufactured by means of chemical additives and the final result is something much more sour, much less nutty than *crème fraîche*. However, since *crème fraîche* has an average butterfat content of around 35% and American sour cream has about 18%, neither is exactly suitable to perform the thickening functions required by the Low-High cuisine.

My practical kitchen research problem, then, during the writing of this book, was to experiment with all the American low-fat cheeses (see "Cheeses," above) to convert them by any possible means into the kind of thickening cheese cream that Chef Michel Guérard is using with his sauces in France. I believe I have succeeded and, since my new thickening cream is my own invention, I have given it a name of my choosing, *Crème de Fromage Maigre*. Since it will be used in many recipes throughout this book to give body and smoothness to the natural sauces, I am giving the recipe here so that you can begin to practice preparing it in advance and storing a regular supply in the refrigerator where it keeps excellently in a covered jar, ready to be spooned out for any of its various uses. It is made in about five minutes of work and about two hours of solitary fermentation with the help of two now fairly standard kitchen machines: the Cuisinart chopper-churner (see page 80) and a small yoghurt maker. It can, of course, be made without them, using a blender and substitute heat source, but not so efficiently or fast.

BASIC LOW-HIGH CRÈME DE FROMAGE MAIGRE FOR LOW-FAT THICKENING OF SAUCES

(about 2½ cups to be stored in the refrigerator up to 2 weeks as a regular supply)

Pot cheese, low-fat (1½ cups) Ricotta, Italian style, low-fat
Yoghurt, plain, low-fat (½ cup) (¼ cup)

Preparation in about 5 minutes, plus
2 hours of unsupervised fermentation

I put all these ingredients into the bowl of my Cuisinart chopper-churner and run the motor until they are all perfectly blended and just smooth – in no more than 7 or 8 seconds. Transfer the mixture to a round-bottomed beating bowl and, using a large balloon wire whisk, beat furiously, with high whipping strokes to get as much air in as possible, until the mixture is fluffy and light and has expanded to about 2½ cups – usually in 3 to 4 minutes, according to the strength of your arm. Then spoon it lightly into 2 or 3 small covered jars and stand them on the hot plate of a yoghurt maker, so that they will stay at a steady 75°F. to encourage fermentation for about 2 hours. The mixture will thicken, taking on a subtle nuttiness and a refreshingly acid tang. When it tastes right, arrest any further fermentation by transferring the covered jars to the refrigerator.

FINAL NOTE: *This is the basic thickening cream, without aromatic seasoning, so that it cannot upset the balance of any sauce to which it is added. But it can also be seasoned and adjusted for other uses. Work in chopped herbs with salt and pepper for a low-fat replacement of sour cream on, say, a baked potato or as a garnish over vegetables. Thin it with vinegar and it can become a salad dressing. Whip in a very small amount of confectioners' sugar and it can be spooned over fresh raspberries or strawberries almost as if it were* crème fraîche. *You will discover dozens of ways of using it.*

DEMI-GLACE AND GLACE-DE-VIANDE

In a few of the recipes in this book, the chef calls for a spoonful or two of one or the other of the professional flavoring essences that are always available in a restaurant kitchen. *Demi-glace,* half-glaze, is the basic brown sauce made by boiling down unseasoned beef bouillon to concentrate its glutinous thickening elements. It can be added in very small quantities to any sauce to intensify its flavor and body. *Glace-de-viande,* meat glaze, is a kind of beef paste made by reducing and concentrating the defatted pan juices from a beef roast. This also is used in minuscule quantities as a flavor magnifier.

The easy way out for *demi-glace* is to buy one of the reasonably good canned versions now being nationally distributed as brown beef gravy (see "Index of Sources" on page 392). *Glace-de-viande* can be replaced, when you are feeling lazy, by one of those small bottles of concentrated beef extract sold by drugstores for making nourishing protein bouillons for sick people. But be warned that these extracts are so extremely concentrated that you must use only about ¼-teaspoon for each tablespoon of *glace-de-viande* in the recipe.

A far better solution to the problem – if you have the ambition and can spare the small extra amount of time involved – is to make your own Low-High *demi-glace,* with no use of butter or flour and the deliberate avoidance of long simmering. I have worked out my own, reasonably streamlined way for a small home quantity, which produces such a superb result that this little operation is a richly rewarding exercise in low-fat cooking.

BASIC LOW-HIGH BEEF STOCK AND DEMI-GLACE

(about 2 cups – to be kept up to 3 weeks in the refrigerator as a running supply)

Veal for boiling, boneless and
  fatless, preferably shin (1 lb)
Beef chuck, fatless, coarsely diced
  (1 lb)
Carrots, scraped and chunked
  (4 medium)

Tomatoes, cut in half (4 medium)
Yellow onions, washed, not peeled
  (4 medium)
Parsley, leaf and stalks (3 sprigs)
NO SALT OR PEPPER

Preparation in about 20 minutes, plus about 1½ hours of unsupervised simmering

Put all of the ingredients into a 3-quart top-of-the-stove lidded casserole and just cover them with about 1 quart of freshly drawn cold water. Heat it up to gentle simmering and continue, with the surface "just smiling," for an hour and a half. Let it cool slightly and then strain it into a covered storage bowl and hold it in the refrigerator overnight.

In the morning remove every speck of fat. Reheat the stock just to simmering and strain it carefully through a wetted and squeezed-out flannel. You now have a clear and excellently flavored beef stock which is to be reduced to a demi-glace.

Pour it into a 10-inch sauté pan and heat it up to boiling, not rolling, but a merry bubbling to evaporate off the water so as to reduce the liquid and concentrate the flavor. Little bits of scum may form on the surface. Carefully remove them with a wetted stainless steel spoon. When the liquid begins to coat this spoon, indicating that it is becoming syrupy and has been reduced to about 2 cups, the job is done – usually in about 10 to 15 minutes of bubbling. The flavor has now been concentrated three times and you can understand why no seasonings were added at the beginning. If it had been normally salted and peppered at the start, they would now be so concentrated as to make the demi-glace *inedible and unusable. Pour this syrupy* demi-glace *into a covered refrigerator jar with a fairly wide mouth, so that you can spoon out the thick syrup as needed. Although it will not be as dark brown as the professional stuff, it has an excellent body and, to me, a clearness and freshness of flavor that simply does not exist in the classic brown sauces which have been simmered for three days and thickened with butter and flour.*

FATS IN LOW-HIGH COOKING (see "Butter versus Oil")

FISH FOR THE LOW-HIGH CUISINE

Since the great chefs stress that you should be flexible with their fish recipes, always substituting what is the best of the season, you should learn to differentiate in the market between the oily and the nonoily, lean fish.

The principal fat fish to stay away from in the market are: butterfish, herring, mackerel, pompano, sable, shad, tuna, freshwater trout, and whitefish. The principal lean fish, especially good for Low-High cooking, are: from salt water – sea bass, striped bass, bluefish, cod, flounder, grouper, haddock, hake, halibut, mullet, porgy, rockfish, sea trout, smelt, turbot, or whiting; from fresh water – carp, perch, pickerel and pike. All shellfish are lean. (My cook book *Feasts for All Seasons* contains detailed, season-by-season lists of the oily and lean fish – Winter on page 50, Spring on page 215, Summer on page 363, and Fall on page 509.)

GLACE-DE-VIANDE (see "Demi-Glace")

HERBS (see "Aromatic Herbs")

MACHINES FOR THE LOW-HIGH KITCHEN

The recipes in this book can certainly be prepared with the standard American appliances of a reasonably well-planned kitchen, but some special machines are particularly useful in terms of efficiency and speed for the Low-High cuisine. Once butter, cream and flour are eliminated, for example, the body texture of many of the natural sauces is partly controlled by the fine puréeing of fresh vegetables. For super efficiency at this job, there is one machine now so much admired by American amateur and professional cooks that it is generally called "the phenomenal French Cuisinart." In France, where it is made, it has already brought about the major gastronomic revolution of the past twenty years, and in the United States (where I am told that it is now in use in tens of thousands of kitchens) it seems to be well on its way towards repeating its French success. Its scythe-shaped blades are set at a peculiar angle so that, as they cut at very high speed, they also churn and mix the food. In France it is known as *Le Robot Coupe,* the Robot Cutter. When it started coming to the United States, the importers, apparently thinking that the French name would not be understood here, rebaptized the machine with the ridiculous title of "Food Processor." In these days when "naturalness" is stressed, when "processed" has become virtually a dirty word, I felt some resistance to installing a food processor in my kitchen. I had subconscious visions of everything being automatically dehydrated, pasteurized and sterilized! This label thoroughly maligns a brilliant machine which should be named for its precise function as a chopper-churner. Also, I think it is inaccurate to refer to it as a "super blender" because it is ten miles ahead of any electric blender in current use. So I propose to refer to it in this book as the "Cuisinart chopper-churner."

When I first discovered the chopper-churner in France before it had crossed the Atlantic, I recorded a discussion on its use, specifically in relation to the Low-High cuisine, with the famous French food critics, Henri Gault and Christian Millau.

"Our French *Robot Coupe,*" Gault said, "a brilliant new invention, is a precious tool for the easy preparation of the new low-fat, low-starch, low-sugar, yet high-pleasure cuisine. With it, you can emulsify and thicken the sauces by the fine puréeing of vegetables alone, with no use whatsoever of butter or flour."

"I also find it marvelous," Millau added, "for the preparation of low-fat soups. I put in all kinds of nonstarchy vegetables, lightly cooked to hold their natural flavors, then, in two or three seconds, purée them to a smooth, creamy, delicious soup, also with no butter or starch. In other words, cream soups no longer require any cream."

The Cuisinart chopper-churner is so uniquely efficient that

I have used it for a number of the recipes in this book. It can be replaced by a standard electric blender, but then you will have to allow more time for the operation and you will have to keep pushing the food down inside the jug to ensure proper circulation. Or you *could* do the puréeing with a hand food mill, or by rubbing the foods through a fine sieve. As to the Cuisinart chopper-churner's beating function, this can be replaced by an electric rotary beater or by hand beating with a wire whisk.

Freshly grinding the spices

In the light and relatively simple recipes of the Low-High cuisine, the development of flavor depends more than ever on the freshest of freshly ground herbs and spices. The whole spices I prefer to keep on hand – pepper, coriander, allspice, cloves, cinnamon, juniper, nutmeg, etc. – should be ground at the very last moment before use. This can be done with heavy hand pounding in a mortar or by hand grating, but now the Salton people have brought out a miniature electric spice grinder called a "Quick Mill." It is hardly larger than a standard drinking glass and holds a tablespoon or two of any spice. By the timed push of a button, in a couple of seconds or so, it grinds the spice to any desired degree of fineness. When you open the lid after the grinding, the fresh bouquet that pervades the kitchen is such a pleasure that it seems to lighten the work.

Sugarless sherbets for desserts

Some of the best dessert recipes in this book are those for champagne or fresh-fruit sherbets, sweetened mainly by the natural sugar of the fruits and the wine. They can be made, of course, in any kind of ice-cream machine you already own.

If, however, you become a Low-High sherbet aficionado and want to make it faster with a power drive there is now something new and quite exceptional in the way of electric machines to go inside your freezer. This is the Salton blower type that no longer depends on being frozen onto the floor of the freezer (something that is now impossible with frost-free freezers), but that sucks in ice-cold air and blows it around the sherbet container while the motor drives the dashers which churn the sherbet to a smooth velvet. Almost any kind of soft fruit can be crushed with sweet wine into a sugarless sherbet.

OILS FOR LOW-HIGH COOKING (see "Butter Versus Oil")
ONIONS AND SHALLOTS

I have already said, at the beginning of this chapter, that I regard the eternal sautéeing of chopped onions and shallots in butter as an unnecessary cliché. There are various other low-fat ways of preparing onions and shallots for their entry into a dish. Have you ever tried baking whole, unpeeled onions? If not, you will be amazed at how beautifully they turn out. They get rid of all their sharp pungency, develop a softness, a subtle sweetness, a joyous juiciness, yet with the best of the basic onion character enhanced and magnified. It is no trouble, but it must be done slowly, so you have to plan ahead. You can't rush in from work and have your onions ready in fifteen minutes. I have, however, experimented successfully with freezing the baked onions, still in their skins, and tightly wrapped in plastic. Then, when you need a small quantity of onion in a dish, you can peel and grate the frozen onion, instantly, in its hard state.

How to bake onions? You leave them in their skins, rubbing the skin with a tiny bit of oil to avoid burning. You get rid of this oil when you get rid of the skin. Then put them in an open pan and bake them, as if they were potatoes in their jackets, according to the following rough timing. (You will soon get to know the timing idiosyncrasies of your own oven.) They can be baked at virtually any temperature at which the oven may be set for some other dish. For a medium-sized yellow globe onion, allow about 2 hours at 300°F., 1¾ hours at 350°F., 1½ hours at 400°F. Small white boiling onions average about 40 to 50 minutes in a 350°F. oven. As soon as the onion has cooled enough to handle, cut off the root end and squeeze out the moist inside, discarding the skin. Then you can at once chop them into the dish. (Incidentally, they are also fine served hot as a garnishing vegetable or cold in a salad.)

As to shallots, Chef Michel Guérard (page 35) has shown me a new way of precooking them without butter. He puts his chopped shallots into a small saucepan and just barely covers them with dry white wine. He brings it to the boil and bubbles it down until part of the wine is absorbed into the shallots and the rest is reduced to a mere wetness on the bottom of the pan – usually in 2 to 3 minutes. By this time, the shallots have lost their harsh pungency, are nicely softened and happily drunk with wine in preparation for giving their all to the dish. (See my adaptation of Guérard's "Lobster Baked with Its Coral" on page 194.)

SHRIMP BOILED BY THE LOW-HIGH METHOD

Several of the recipes in this book include garnishing with preboiled shrimp. It seems a great pity to buy shrimp ready-cooked and shelled – or even to buy fresh shrimp and boil them in plain water. Such gastronomic laziness produces only a pale shadow of what a fine, fresh, flavorful shrimp can be. My shrimp rules are few and simple. I buy only fresh shrimp in their shells. I cook them by the method which follows, then leave them to marinate in their aromatic liquor and shell them only a few moments before eating them. They are then a revelation of fine flavor and juiciness. (The recipes involving shrimp are Chef Michel Guérard's "Frogs' Legs Soup" on page 155 and Chef Charles Barrier's "Chicken with Shrimp" on page 236.)

BASIC LOW-HIGH METHOD FOR AROMATIC BOILED FRESH SHRIMP

(about 4 portions)

Vinegar, tarragon white wine
  (1 to 2 cups)
White wine, dry (1 to 2 cups)
Garlic, peeled and slivered (1 or
  2 cloves, to your taste)

Bay leaves, whole (2)
Green Pascal celery, with leaves,
  destringed and chopped (2 or
  3 stalks, according to size)
Salt, coarse crystal, to taste

Black pepper, freshly ground, to
  taste
Red cayenne pepper, to taste

Shrimp, jumbo, fresh, in shell
(1½ lbs)

**Active work about 10 minutes, plus about 35 minutes
of unsupervised simmering, then overnight marination**

*First prepare the aromatic boiling liquor – bearing in mind that it must
be quite strong in taste if it is to inject its flavors into the flesh of the
shrimp. In a 2½-quart saucepan put: 1 cup each of the vinegar, the wine
and freshly drawn cold water, the slivered garlic, the 2 bay leaves, the
chopped celery with its leaves, at least 1 tablespoon or more of salt, 6 or
more grinds of the pepper-mill and enough red cayenne pepper to make
the liquid slightly peppery to the tongue. Bring to the boil and simmer,
covered, for roughly 30 minutes to bring out and mingle the flavors. Stir
once or twice during this period.*

*Meanwhile, wash the shrimp under running cold water and pull off
their legs, but do not shell them. When the boiling liquor is ready, drop
in the shrimp all at once, adding, if necessary, more vinegar and wine in
equal parts just to cover them. Return to the boil as quickly as possible,
then at once reduce to simmering and start the timer. Let the shrimp
simmer, covered, for exactly 5 minutes – not a moment longer. Turn off
the heat and let the shrimp cool in the marinade to room temperature.
Then turn the entire contents of the saucepan into a covered storage jar
and refrigerate for at least 24 hours. This is when the shrimp absorbs the
flavors and the process cannot be speeded up.*

Just before serving or adding to a prepared dish

*Take out as many shrimp as you need, shell and devein them. They
can then be quickly reheated – taking care not to overcook them. They
are delightful as an hors d'oeuvre, ice-cold, or in Chef Michel Guérard's
"Black Truffle Salad with Garden Vegetables on page 351.*

FINAL NOTE: *If you store the shrimp longer than 24 hours, there are
two further steps you should take to prevent them from becoming too
strong in flavor. First, remove all of them from the marinade and strain
off all the vegetables, throwing them away. Return the shrimp to the
now clear marinade to keep them nicely moist. Beyond three days, how-*

ever, you should finally discard the marinade altogether and keep the remaining shrimp in a tightly lidded refrigerator container. They will then keep fresh and edible up to about 1 week.

SPICES (see "Aromatic Herbs and Spices")
WINE

At the end of each recipe in Chapters 4 through 11, there is a suggestion of an ideal wine to be served with the dish. Generally, it is the wine that was offered to me by the chef when I originally tasted his preparation of the recipe. The light and simple foods of the Low-High cuisine demand to be teamed with refreshingly light and reasonably uncomplicated wines. For this basic reason, on our side of the Atlantic, the Low-High cuisine makes an excellent marriage with our fruity and light American wines – especially those made from the noble European grape varieties that thrive in the climate and soil of California. Many other states produce charming, simple "country wines" from our native grapes. But in the last twenty years, California has expanded in production and quality into one of the important wine regions of the world. Therefore I also suggest, next to each French wine, an alternative American label equally appropriate to the dish.

It is now fairly easy to find excellent California wines by learning to read the labels. One can judge by tasting experience which company or vineyard names represent the wines that strike the best balance between the quality one prefers and the price one is willing to pay. Next, one should look for the names of the noble grapes, for it is the grapes that largely control the family character and personality of the wine. Among the reds, some of the finest are the powerful and rich Cabernet Sauvignon, the lighter Gamay and Pinot Noir, the dominant and strong Petite Sirah, the solid and spicy Zinfandel and the peasanty Barbera. Among the whites there are the luscious and rich Pinot Chardonnay, the aromatic Johannisberg and White Riesling, the lighter and softer Sauvignon or Fumé Blanc, the delicate and refreshing Pinot Blanc and French Colombard and the gentle and soft Chenin Blanc. And among the rosés there is the refreshing and tangy Grenache. Unfortunately, at present, very few California labels specify the percentage of the named grape variety contained in the wine. Under United States law, a wine may be labeled Pinot Chardonnay even if it contains as little as 51% of that grape. But, obviously, the wine will have a truer Pinot Chardonnay bouquet and flavor if it is 100%. The percentage of the named grape should be legally required on every varietal wine label.

The next thing to look for are the vintage-dated wines, which almost invariably have more varietal character. Finally, one should look for a geographic location on the label. The land under wine grape cultivation in California has expanded almost 300% in the last few years so that it now embraces ranges of climate as wide as in all of France. The northern coastal valleys around San Francisco are comparable to the cool, temperate regions of Bordeaux, Burgundy and Alsace. But in the southern valleys as far south as Bakersfield where the land is half-desert and the vineyards have to be artificially irrigated, the climate is comparable to the Midi and Mediterranean regions of France. In California as in France, grapes grown in a relatively hot climate make wines of less character and personality. So the districts to look for on California labels are those of the northern coastal counties and wine districts: Napa, Sonoma, the Alexander Valley, Mendocino, Livermore, Monterey and Santa Clara.

There are, however, magnificent exceptions to this general rule – small vineyards in unlikely climatic places that produce wines of almost miraculous quality because of some quirk of the contour of the land that seems to draw and direct the cooling breezes from the Pacific. These spectacular results are now being deliberately cultivated by means of a scientific system of weather measurement known as microclimatic control. In earlier days – with California's traditional habit of thinking big – the vintners planted their vineyards in units of thousands of acres. Now they have learned that the noble vines are exceedingly sensitive to minuscule environmental factors such as the precise angle of the land to the sun, the moist morning and evening mists that blow in from the sea, the way the rainwater runs into and off the earth, the deflection of the circulating air by rocks and trees and dozens of variations in the mineral and stone content of the soil. When all of these factors are about dead right for a particular grape variety, such a potentially great vineyard is seldom larger than five to ten acres. By careful cultivation on that scale, the truly great California wines are being produced. This is why it is important to recognize the districts and regions on California labels, just as one does for French wines, and it is always safer to know the specific geographic region where the wine was made. Many California labels already specify this, and these are the wines that are safest to choose. I have kept all these factors in mind for my suggestions of alternative California wines to accompany the recipes of this book. If, in time, you taste every one of my suggestions, you will have covered a wide range of the very best of American wines.

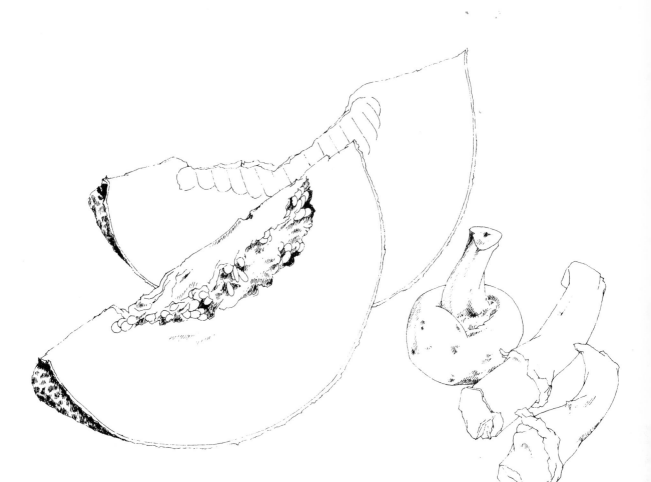

Chapter Four
Hors d'Oeuvres and Canapés

in which a Melon sets sail, Mushrooms are crisply
stuffed, Turkey makes peace with Coriander,
and Beef ventures raw out unto thin ice.

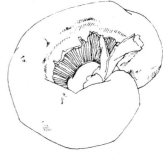

SLICED BIFSTEAK TARTARE SKATING ON THIN ICE

(for 4)

This is one of the cleverest table presentations of Chefs Jean and Pierre Troisgros (page 50) at their three-star restaurant. It is an easy dinner party trick to reproduce at home. The slivers of beef, accented by the Troisgros sauce, are served to each guest on a glistening sheet of ice. This is not just a visual stunt. The enjoyment of the beef is enhanced by the slight stab of cold it gives your tongue as it goes into your mouth. The cold seems to magnify the protean quality of the meat.

Egg yolk, hard-boiled (1)
Olive oil, pure green virgin
   (2 Tbs)
Vinegar, red wine (about 2 tsp)
Lemon juice, fresh
   (about 1½ tsp)
Mustard, preferably Dijon
   (about 1 tsp)
White pepper, coarsely cracked
Salt, coarse crystal

Beef sirloin, best procurable,
   entirely defatted, piece
   about 1 inch thick (1 lb)
Capers (about 2 oz, roughly
   3 or 4 Tbs)
Parsley, chopped leaf (about ¼
   cup)
Tarragon, fresh in season,
   chopped leaf (about ¼ cup)

On the morning of the day – freezing the ice platters – active work about 5 minutes, plus about 2 hours unsupervised freezing

Choose four good-sized dinner plates, each with a depression at least ⅜ inch deep, or four wide soup plates, or four soup bowls at least 8 inches across. Each sheet of ice should be at least ⅜ inch thick or it is likely to break, but there is no problem if it is considerably thicker than that. Fill your plates with cold water almost level with the edge and carefully place them absolutely horizontally in your freezer, leaving them until the water is frozen solid into sheets of ice. According to the efficiency of your freezer, this can take anywhere from 1 to 4 hours.

About 30 minutes before serving

The preparation should now proceed quickly and continuously. Take a plate out of the freezer and hold it upside down, gripping the ice firmly with your fingers, under running warm water, until the sheet of ice detaches itself from the plate – usually in 5 to 10 seconds. Have a handsome napkin ready, prettily folded into a round or square, just large enough to cover the plate under the ice. Lay the detached circle of ice carefully on the napkin, quickly dry the plate, put the napkin and ice back onto the plate and put them immediately back in the freezer to wait. The purpose of the napkins is to absorb drips of water from the melting ice while your guests are eating the beef. Repeat this operation with the three other plates.

Now prepare the sauce. Thoroughly mash the hard-boiled egg yolk in a small mixing bowl, then work into it the 2 tablespoons of olive oil, 2 teaspoons of vinegar, 1½ teaspoons of lemon juice, 1 teaspoon of mustard, plus salt and pepper to taste. Beat it lightly with a small wire whisk until it becomes foamy and velvety. Taste again and adjust any or all of the ingredients if you wish. The sauce should not be so thin that most of it runs onto the ice, nor so thick that it stands up in little piles on the beef. Bring this sauce to the table in a chilled sauceboat resting in crushed ice.

Now slice the beef, using a long sharp knife, into paper-thin one-inch squares, with deliberate and slow strokes. You should finish with about 10 squares per serving.

Last-minute assembly and serving

Lay the beef squares on the ice of each platter in a pretty design of circles, wedges, or modernistic symbolic patterns. Dot each square with one or two capers, sprinkle lightly with parsley and tarragon, then rush the plates to table. At table, dab on small quantities of the sauce. It does not matter if some of the sauce, or some of the parsley or tarragon, gets onto the ice, but too much will spoil the skating-rink effect. With this, the Troisgros brothers served me a fine fruity white Sancerre from the Loire. At my own dining table in New York, I might replace it with an American wine – perhaps a California Napa Valley Fumé Blanc.

CANAPÉS FRITURES OF TINY WHOLE FISH

(for 4)

In his lovely, three-star country restaurant, Chez La Mère Charles, in the rich Ain region northeast of Lyon, Chef Alain Chapel (page 29) serves dinners of exquisite luxury and brilliant preparation. Before you sit down at table, it is almost as if he deliberately tries to shock you by the rough simplicity of his canapés. Alain says: "You must nibble on some little *mise en bouche* [put-in-mouth] to make sure that your apéritif wine does not hurt you too much!" In the garden, before going in to dinner, there arrived a platter of the smallest sand dabs you have ever seen, *les petites solettes des sables de la Vendée* (mini-soles from the beaches of the Vendée near the mouth of the Loire) each about 2 inches long and an inch wide. They were dry fried, so you picked them up with your fingers. As I bit into the first one, I found I was cracking through a head, a prickly backbone and a slightly gritty inside. Alain appeared and asked, in a noticeably offhand tone and with a distinctly wicked grin, how I liked them. I said that they were, obviously, a three-star, super-luxury-fancy-dining-room *pique-nique!* They were certainly not to be forgotten.

Yet, looking back on them, the very naturalness, nuttiness and simplicity of the straight-from-the-sea baby fish was a dramatic contrast to an elegant dinner. I do not guarantee that the recipe below is Alain Chapel's. I did not bother to ask him how he prepares his baby soles. I am addicted to my own way – with the lightest frying batter the world has ever known. It completely seals the fish, holding in the flavor juices and preventing the slightest absorption of any oil. In my kitchen in New York, I use either 3-inch smelt or 1½-inch whitebait (both of which have soft bones) or finger-long sticks cut from boneless fillets of sole or turbot.

Flour, sifted (1 cup)	Sea smelts, cleaned, whole,
Egg (1)	about 3-inch, or other small
Olive oil, pure green virgin	fish, see above (1½ doz)
(3 Tbs)	Oil for deep frying
Salt, coarse crystal	Lemon juice, freshly squeezed
Milk (½ cup)	

About 2½ hours before serving – about 15 minutes active work, plus about 2 hours of unsupervised ripening

Put the cup of flour into a mixing bowl. Separate the egg, putting the yolk into a smaller mixing bowl. Hold the white. Lightly beat into the yolk the 3 tablespoons of olive oil and ¼ teaspoon of the salt. Smoothly work this into the flour. Just warm the ½ cup of milk and add, dash by dash, to the flour paste, using only enough of the milk to make a smooth, very thick cream. The thickness is important, as it controls the thickness of the "glove" that will prevent the absorption of the oil. Let it stand, uncovered, for 2 hours, stirring occasionally.

While the batter is standing, wash, dry, and lightly salt and pepper your fish. Leave them to come to room temperature.

About 25 minutes before serving

Start heating up the oil in the deep-fryer to 375°F. Turn on the oven to keep-warm temperature (150°F.) and place in it a serving platter for the fish. This is the moment to beat the egg white stiff and lightly fold it into the batter. The oil should be hot now. Dip each fish into the batter, turning around so that it is evenly coated, then lower it at once into the hot oil. To prevent the fish from sticking to the sides of the pan or each other, use long kitchen pincers in gloved hand to hold each fish just below the surface of the oil for about 3 seconds. Don't be tempted to crowd the fish. Make as many batches as is necessary. Fry to a deep golden brown, usually in 4 to 5 minutes. As each batch of fish is done, drain on absorbent paper, place it on a serving platter, sprinkle it with salt and return it to the oven to keep warm until ready to serve. At the last moment, lightly sprinkle with lemon juice. With his baby sand dabs, Alain Chapel served me a fine, dry, light white from the village of Condrieu on the Rhône, an American equivalent of which might be a California Pinot Blanc from Sonoma.

CANAPÉ MUSHROOMS WITH LOW-FAT AROMATIC STUFFING

(*for 4*)

When I dined recently in Paris at Le Pactole, the brilliant bistro of Chef Jacques Manière (page 42), who is surely one of the best *cuisiniers* of the city, we agreed that stuffed mushroom caps were just about the ideal canapé. But I complained bitterly that the average stuffing was always loaded to overflowing with butter and cream. I challenged Jacques to produce something that still kept the pleasure of the mushroom, but enhanced it with a stuffing that was light, aromatic and perhaps crackly as a contrast to the texture of the mushroom. The great chef accepted my challenge and, within a few days, invited me to taste and try this recipe.

Mushrooms, whole, medium size, good color and shape, wiped clean (12)
Garlic, peeled (1 clove, whole)
Parsley leaves (small bunch)
Tarragon, fresh in season, chopped (1 Tbs)
Kala Marsala, Indian curry powder, from Indian or Middle Eastern stores (1 Tbs)
Crisp rye wafers (4 or 5)
Egg, lightly beaten (1)
White wine, dry (about 1 Tbs)
Butter (1 Tbs)
Salt, coarse crystal
Black pepper, freshly ground

About 25 minutes before serving – active preparation about 10 minutes, plus about 15 minutes unsupervised baking

Preheat your oven to 400°F. I put into the bowl of my Cuisinart chopper-churner (or you can use an electric blender – see page 82): the mushroom stalks detached from the caps, the garlic clove, a small handful of parsley leaves, the tablespoon each of tarragon and Kala Marsala, the 4 crisp rye wafers, broken into pieces, the egg, 1 tablespoon of the wine, plus salt and pepper, to taste. Run the machine until everything is chopped and thoroughly mixed, usually in about 3 seconds. Do not let it become a pasty purée. If not stiff enough, churn in more crisp rye wafers to make it workable. If it needs thinning, add a teaspoon or two more wine. Fill the mushroom caps with the stuffing, keeping it loose and piling it up slightly. Set the mushroom caps on a lightly buttered baking sheet and put them in the center of the oven until the stuffing is crisp and puffy – usually in about 15 minutes. Chef Manière served with these a very dry Brut Champagne, which was, of course, French, but on our side of the Atlantic might be from California or New York State.

CANAPÉ TOURTE À LA BOURBONNAISE

(4 individual portions)

The three-star brothers Jean and Pierre Troisgros (page 50) serve this attractively simple appetizer in a flaky pastry crust which, in the Low-High tradition, we have eliminated. The name *Bourbonnaise* comes from one of the oldest, most beautiful, and least known of French provinces, the still largely undeveloped country around the spa city of Vichy, the region that gave its name to the long line of French Bourbon kings (and incidentally, also to Bourbon County, Kentucky). The traditional dishes of the Bourbonnais are earthy derivatives of bourgeois and peasant cuisines. This baked potato *tourte* is a shining example. Potatoes are relatively harmless when divorced from their usual marriage with butter and cream, here cut down to the irreducible minimum. This *tourte* can be baked in a 9- or 10-inch quiche pan, but we prefer it in individual soufflé dishes; say 3 inches across and about 1½ inches deep.

Potatoes, medium starchy for
  baking (about ¾ lb, usually
  3 or 4)
Salt, coarse crystal
White pepper, freshly ground
Chervil, fresh in season,
  chopped (2 Tbs)
Chives, chopped (2 Tbs)
Parsley, chopped (2 Tbs)

Tarragon, fresh in season,
  chopped (2 Tbs)
Shallots, minced (2)
Olive oil (1 Tbs)
Butter, melted (1 Tbs)
Veal or ham, lean, slivered
  (about ½ lb to fill about
  1 cup)
Cream, light (⅓ cup)

About 1½ hours before serving – or can be made earlier in the day – about 15 minutes active preparation, plus about 1¼ hours of baking and resting

Pre-heat the oven to 350°F. Peel the potatoes, slice them about ⅛ inch thick and put them in a large mixing bowl. Add salt and pepper to your taste. Now add the chopped chervil, chives, parsley and tarragon, the minced shallots, olive oil, the tablespoon of melted butter, plus the slivered veal or ham. Using a wooden spatula, mix all this carefully, taking care not to break up the potato slices. Spoon the potato mixture in equal parts into the four dishes. Cover each with aluminum foil and set them in the center of the oven to bake for 30 minutes. Warm the cream.

Remove the dishes from the oven, take off the foil and moisten the potatoes with the warmed cream. Replace the foil covering and continue baking for another 15 minutes. Taste to make sure that the potatoes are nice and soft and that all the cream has been absorbed. If not, turn up the oven to 400°F. and continue baking uncovered for another 5 minutes or so, until all the cream has been absorbed. Let the *tourte* rest, covered, in a warm place, so that the flavors combine and ripen, for about another 30 minutes before serving. Each diner digs into his own individual dish.

The Troisgros brothers served this to me in the bar before going into dinner accompanied by a dry, Spanish *fino* Sherry.

LITTLE SAILBOATS OF MELON AND JAMBON CRU

(for 4)

This is not so much a recipe as another of the dramatic serving ideas of Chefs Jean and Pierre Troisgros (page 50). I thought I knew every possible way of bringing the ubiquitous melon and ham together until the Troisgros offered me this charming variation. They, of course, use the *jambon cru,* the sun-dried, raw ham of their Burgundian region. It has a strong enough texture to be stretched out to form sails for the little "boats." On our side of the Atlantic, the best ham to use is the Italian *prosciutto di Parma,* either imported or top-quality domestic. For the rigging of the boats, you will need about half a dozen 3-inch wooden skewers and about a dozen smaller 1½-inch toothpicks, pointed at each end.

Melon, ripe, type according to season (1 medium)

Prosciutto ham, see above, thinly sliced (8 slices, each about 3 x 3 inches)

Lemon peel, for the flags (4 strips)

Lime peel, for more flags (4 strips)

Preparation time about 15 minutes, depending on the dexterity of your fingers

Make the hulls of the 4 boats by cutting the melon into wedges, each 3 to 4 inches long and about 1 to 1½ inches wide. Clean off the seeds and cut off the outer rind, so that the entire wedge is edible. Stick a 3-inch mast into the center and a 1½-inch bowsprit at each end. Now, carefully judging the spaces aboard each boat, cut the slices of ham into two triangular sails to fit fore and aft of the mast. Attach the bottom corners of the two sails to the mast by sticking the top point through them and then carefully pulling them down to deck level. When the bottom corners are about halfway down, thread the top corners and continue pulling bottom corners to the deck. Next, stretch the sails out fore and aft and thread their far corners through the points of the bowsprits. The sails should now be stretched reasonably tight. Cut two little flags of lemon and lime colors and thread them at the top of the mast. Anchor your sailboats in a refrigerated harbor until they are ready to set out for their voyage to the dining table. When the Troisgros brothers placed this charming little conceit before me, they accompanied it with fine, dry, white Sancerre from the Loire. I might replace it by a California Napa Fumé Blanc.

A STARTING SALAD OF RAW YOUNG SPINACH LEAVES WITH DUCK LIVERS

(for 4)

This newest invention by the great Chefs Jean and Pierre Troisgros (page 50), is one of France's concessions to the United States. On a visit to Los Angeles, Jean learned of our California way of starting a meal with a crisp salad. He could hardly believe his eyes and taste buds when he found that one of the regular ingredients was raw young spinach leaves. Spinach served *raw* is simply inconceivable in France. He took the idea back home with him and experimented – with, as always, the argumentative collaboration of brother Pierre. Together, they came up with the idea of adding the luscious texture of thin slices of fresh duck liver to crisp bits of bacon. To keep the salad as light as possible, there is a minimum of oil in the dressing and the livers are boiled instead of sautéed. On days when I can find no duck livers in the market, I make do with chicken livers. They are not quite, but almost as good.

Spinach leaves (10 oz bag or
  1 lb loose)
Egg (1)
Olive oil, pure green virgin
  (1 Tbs)
Lemon juice, freshly squeezed
  (about 2 tsp)
Salt, coarse crystal

White pepper, freshly ground
Mustard, finest Dijon
  (about ¼ tsp)
Chicken bouillon (2 cups)
Duck livers (½ lb)
Butter (2 tsp)
Canadian bacon (6 oz)

About 30 minutes before serving

The young spinach leaves, as soon as they are brought home from the market, should be thoroughly washed under running cold water. Then pick out the youngest and tenderest leaves, pull off the tough stalks and tear by hand the chosen leaves into bite-sized pieces, say, roughly into ½-inch squares. Put these prepared leaves into the crisper of the refrigerator until the last moment.

Hard boil the egg, then peel off the solid white from the solid yolk. Dice the white as decoration for the salad and hold it. Mash the yolk into a small mixing bowl as the base for a modified French *vinaigrette* dressing. Now into the mashed yolk work the 1 tablespoon of olive oil and as many teaspoons of lemon juice as will give only a slightly acid tang to the dressing. It must be just runny enough to toss with the salad. Add salt, freshly ground white pepper and ¼ teaspoon or so of Dijon mustard, all to your taste. (Note that the Troisgros feel that vinegar is too "aggressive" to go well with spinach.) Hold this dressing aside while you prepare the liver.

Put the 2 cups of chicken bouillon into a saucepan and heat it up to simmering. Pick over your half-pound of duck livers, cutting away all bits of tough skin and greenish patches. Pull the livers apart into separate pieces and drop them into the simmering bouillon. Then leave them simmering until they are stiff enough to slice easily with a sharp knife – usually about 5 to 7 minutes. Using a slotted spoon, transfer the livers to a wooden cutting board and slice them fairly thinly. Hold them aside, at room temperature. Set a medium-sized sauté pan over moderate frying heat and melt the 2 teaspoons of butter. While it is heating up, cut the Canadian bacon into thin slivers and sauté them quickly until they are thoroughly crisp.

Just before serving – quickly assembling the salad

This is best served in individual chilled bowls. Put the crisp, torn spinach leaves into a large bowl and lightly toss them with the dressing, making sure that all leaves are nicely coated. Divide the leaves into the separate bowls. Put some of the liver slices and bacon crisps in between the leaves to provide a dramatic texture contrast, but make sure that some pieces of meat rest on top. Sprinkle each serving with the dice of egg white. Serve at once, refreshingly cold. The Troisgros accompany this salad with apéritif-style glasses of a fruity white Sancerre from the Loire, just turned pink and slightly softened with a few drops of crème de cassis, the Burgundian black currant syrup. Or the cassis might be dropped into glasses of California Livermore Sauvignon Blanc.

AN INDIAN STARTING SALAD OF TURKEY BREAST WITH FRESH LEAVES OF CORIANDER

(for 4)

My discovery of this memorable, entirely fat-free hors d'oeuvre was a revelation to me of the universality of the Low-High techniques. The French chefs may currently be the leaders in experimentations with new ideas, but they freely admit that the new cuisine is not a new invention. Both Jean Troisgros and Roger Vergé, among others, have told me that some of their best low-fat ideas have come directly from the cuisines of China, India and Japan, where simple Low-High techniques were practiced at least a thousand years before French cooking was even born. This modern version of an ancient Indian recipe is one example.

For its strikingly unusual quality, it depends on an extraordinary fresh herb, used in many Latin American and Asian countries, but only now becoming known in the United States. This is the fresh leaf of the coriander plant, which has an entirely different character from the seed we all know. It is still a bit hard to find, but well worth the searching out. You may get it in Chinese groceries as "Chinese parsley," in Italian shops as *cilantro*, or in Spanish as *culantro* (see "Index of Sources," page 392). The moment you smell a bunch of it, you will either love it or hate it. I am an aficionado. To me, it has the character of a beautifully clean country stable full of cows and horses, or the slightly sweet mustiness of an old, damp cellar. In any case, it is certainly not a gentle and weak herb.

But its affinity for certain meats and poultry is extraordinary and, with them, it cooks down into something quite memorable. This turkey salad is a fine way to get to know fresh coriander.

Chicken bouillon (about 1 pint)

Turkey breast (about 1 lb)

Mint leaves, fresh in season (½ cup)

Coriander leaves, fresh in season (½ cup)

Serrano chilis, green, hot, canned, chunked, from Mexico, in Spanish stores (2, each about 1½ inches long)

Yellow onions (2 medium)

Tomatoes, skinned and deseeded (2 medium)

Ginger root, fresh (slice about ⅛ inch thick)

Coriander seeds, whole (½ tsp)

Garlic (1 or 2 cloves, to taste)

Lemon juice, freshly squeezed (about 3 Tbs)

Yoghurt, low-fat (3 Tbs)

Grenadine syrup, to add rich color (up to 3 tsp)

Red cayenne pepper

Salt, coarse crystal

Black pepper, freshly ground

Cucumber, skinned and de-seeded (1 small)

Orange, sweet, preferably Temple (1 whole)

Banana, ripe (1 whole)

Lettuce leaves, crisp and bright green, to make a bed for each serving

About 1 hour before serving – active work about 30 minutes, plus 30 minutes unsupervised refrigeration

Put the pint of chicken bouillon into a 1-quart saucepan, heat it up just to boiling, slide in the turkey breast and keep it simmering, covered, until it is just cooked – usually in about 20 minutes. The breast must be covered by the simmering liquid. If not, add a bit more bouillon or water. Test the flesh for perfect doneness by tasting a sliver cut from the center. Then, turn off the heat and let the turkey cool in the bouillon to absorb flavor.

Meanwhile, prepare the aromatic coriander sauce. I use my Cuisinart chopper-churner. You can also use an electric blender or chop by hand, sacrificing efficiency and speed. (See page 82.) I put into the mixing bowl of the machine in this order: ½-cup each (not too tightly packed down) of whole fresh leaves of mint and coriander, the 2 chilis, chunked, 1 of the onions, peeled and chunked, 1 of the tomatoes, chunked, 1 slice about ⅛-inch thick of the fresh ginger root, quartered, the ½ teaspoon coriander seeds, the 1 or 2 cloves of garlic, peeled and quartered, 3 tablespoons of the lemon juice, the 3 tablespoons of yoghurt, 2 teaspoons of the grenadine syrup, a pinch of the cayenne pepper with salt and black pepper to taste. Run the machine until all these are thoroughly mixed and puréed, but not pasty, usually in 10 to 15 seconds. Taste the sauce and adjust it by adding more ingredients as you please. Especially, adjust the lemony flavor to your taste. You can deepen the color by adding a bit more grenadine. Transfer the sauce to a covered bowl and refrigerate at once.

Now remove the turkey breast from its bouillon, drain and place it on a wooden chopping board. With a sharp knife, bone it, removing the skin and any last bits of visible fat. Slice the turkey meat into ⅛-inch thick slivers, each no larger than ½-inch square. Put the meat into a decorative ceramic, glass, or wood serving bowl in which the salad will be brought to table. Add to this bowl the remaining tomato, diced; half the remaining onion, peeled and minced; ½-cup of the cucumber, diced; the orange, peeled, divided into sections, and de-pitted; plus half the banana, thinly sliced. Pour over all this the coriander sauce from the refrigerator and, with wooden salad fork and spoon, toss lightly and thoroughly, but gently enough so that the pieces do not break up or bed down. Cover the bowl and refrigerate for at least half an hour before serving, so that the flavors will mingle and ripen.

Serving at table

Serve the salad on a bed of lettuce leaves on chilled plates. If, by this time, you are beginning to appreciate the bouquet and taste of fresh coriander leaves, add 2 or 3 whole leaves as garnish on each serving. Indians do not usually serve "fire-water" with this, but I like to accompany it with the strong *vin jaune* of France, the Château Chalon of the Jura mountains, or a California apéritif wine of the Santa Clara Valley made from the extraordinary Montonico grape.

ESCALOPES OF RAW SALMON PIQUED WITH TINY TOUCHES OF BLACK BELUGA CAVIAR

(for 4)

The salmon in this now famous hors d'oeuvre is not really raw – not as raw, in fact, as smoked salmon. The basic goal in cooking fish is to solidify the glutinous protein elements of the flesh until they become just firm and opaque. Exactly the same result is achieved without heat by marinating the fish in an acid solution, either lemon or lime juice, or vinegar. The transformation of the fish takes place in a few minutes. It becomes opaque, but retains the irresistible, luxuriously soft, velvety texture of smoked salmon. This is not a new trick. It has been used for centuries by the Peruvians in their *seviche* and by Scandinavians with their *gravadlax*.

I have been served this dish by the Troisgros brothers and by Marc Meneau (page 45) at his Auberge de l'Espérance, but I still think the best of all versions was set before me by the brilliant Chef Jacques Manière (see page 42) at his Le Pactole in Paris. He created the peak of perfection with the sea-saltiness and icy tang of little dabs of black Beluga caviar! This is probably the least expensive way of serving caviar to your guests; a small amount produces a dramatic effect.

The first essential is to do battle with your fishmonger. Force him, if necessary at the point of your sharpest chef's knife, to cut from the midsection of his freshest, fattest salmon neat, round slices no more than ⅛ inch thick and about three to four inches in diameter. He must cut behind the belly opening of the fish, or you will get U-shaped pieces with useless side flaps. When you get the slices home, remove every last speck of skin and bone. Then you are ready for a superb start to your dinner – perfectly easy and quick to prepare.

Salmon, raw, sliced ⅛ inch
thick, see above (4–6 slices
according to size)
Lime juice, freshly squeezed
(about 6 to 8 limes)
Mushrooms, small white
(1 doz)
Shallots, minced finely (1 tsp)
Coriander seed, coarsely
cracked (1 tsp)
Black peppercorns, Indian
Tellicherry or Chinese
Szechuan (about 1 doz)

Green peppercorns,
Madagascar (about 2 doz)
Scallion tops, green, finely
chopped (2 tsp)
Watercress leaves, chopped
(1 Tbs)
Tarragon leaves, fresh in
season, chopped (2 Tbs)
Caviar, black Beluga (2 oz)
Walnut or olive oil, pure green
virgin; optional (4 tsp)
Lemon (1)

About 40 minutes before serving – active preparation about 10 minutes, plus about 30 minutes unsupervised marination

Carefully spread out the salmon slices on a flat serving platter and thoroughly sprinkle and splash them with the freshly squeezed lime juice. Cover with foil and refrigerate for about 30 minutes. About every 10 minutes carefully lift each slice and turn it over so that each is thoroughly moistened on both sides. After the first 10 minutes they will already be partially "cooked" and easier to handle.

Meanwhile, get to work on the mushrooms. Remove the stems. Clean the caps by thoroughly wiping them with a damp cloth. Do not wash them, since they will absorb water. With a very sharp, small knife slice the heads crosswise paper thin and hold them, covered. Cool your serving plates by setting them briefly in your freezer.

Just before serving – assembling the parts

Pour off all surplus lime juice that has not been absorbed by the salmon. Lightly sprinkle minced shallots over each slice of fish, then decorate with mushroom slices. Also sprinkle on the cracked coriander seed, coarsely cracked Indian or Chinese pepper, and a few green peppercorns, all more or less according to your taste. Over the top sprinkle the bright green scallion, watercress, and tarragon. The salmon should not be completely covered by garnishes, since the pink fish is very handsome to see peeking through. Now sparingly drop the caviar over each fillet so as not to overpower the fish. Served exactly like this it's heavenly, but if you want absolute perfection and can afford the extra richness, finally sprinkle on a few drops of virgin walnut oil (or the very best green olive oil). Put wedges of lemon on the table, to be squeezed on just before eating. Accompanying large pieces of dry-grilled country bread magnify the texture and flavor of the salmon. I find this to be a dramatic beginning to a party menu, a much finer and more luscious taste and texture than smoked salmon. If your guests are gastronomically nervous, wait until after they have eaten (and begun praising) before telling them that the salmon was "raw." With this regal hors d'oeuvre, Chef Manière thought a very dry French Champagne was only fitting – naturally. On the American side, a champagne from California or New York State would do nicely.

A STARTING SALAD OF RAW SEA BASS AND TROUT WITH RED CAVIAR

(for 4)

This is an invention of the relatively young, extremely promising Chef Francis Garcia (page 34) at the one-star La Réserve in the wine region of Graves just outside Bordeaux. Cold "cooking" of fish by acid marination in lemon or lime juice is discussed in the previous recipe. The white wine of Graves, of course, participates in this salad and so do the wild *cèpe* mushrooms of the Bordelais region. But I have found it all excellently reproducible with our United States products in my New York kitchen. Before trying this recipe, read the buying instructions for the fish in the previous recipe.

Sea bass, center cut, thin round slices (2)

Brook trout, brown, rainbow, or speckled according to season, boneless, skinned fillets (2)

Lime juice, freshly squeezed (1 cup)

Green beans, cooked until just done but still crisp, then chunked (½ cup)

Mushrooms, fresh white (about 6–8)

Red caviar (3 oz jar)

White wine, dry, preferably Graves (1 Tbs)

Olive oil, pure green virgin (2 Tbs)

Vinegar, white wine (1 Tbs)

Shallots, finely minced (¾ tsp)

Black pepper, freshly ground

Preparation time about 45 minutes, including about 30 minutes unsupervised marination of the fish

Set the sea bass slices and the trout fillets on a platter, then thoroughly splash each piece of fish with the lime juice, cover the platter with foil and set in the refrigerator to marinate for 10 minutes. Then turn each slice and fillet over in the lime juice, cover and put back in refrigerator for another 10 minutes. Repeat the turnover and rewetting and replace in the refrigerator for the final 10 minutes. The fish will be "cooked" and opaque. Drain off the surplus lime juice that has not been absorbed, place fish pieces on wooden cutting board and cut into ½-inch squares. Refrigerate again until ready to use.

While the fish is marinating, begin assembling the salad in a handsome ceramic or glass serving bowl. Put in the ½ cup cold, cooked green beans. Remove the stems from the mushrooms, wipe the caps clean and slice them, crosswise, into very thin slivers, enough to fill ½ cup, and add to bowl. In a small mixing bowl, lightly work together the 3 ounces of caviar, the tablespoon of white wine, the 2 tablespoons of olive oil and the tablespoon of vinegar. When this blend is adjusted exactly to your taste, sprinkle it evenly over the vegetables in the salad bowl. Also sprinkle in the ¾ teaspoon of minced shallots. Now add, evenly across the top, the marinated squares of sea bass and trout from the refrigerator. With a wooden fork and spoon gently toss the entire salad until everything is thoroughly mixed and well coated with dressing. During this tossing, you should grind on pepper to your taste. Usually salt is unnecessary, since the red caviar supplies enough saltiness of its own. Serve the salad in small hors d'oeuvre portions. With this salad Chef Garcia served me a noble, dry white Graves, a Domaine de Chevalier. Among American wines, a replacement might be a California Napa Valley Pinot Chardonnay.

COLD BOILED SHRIMP WITH LOW-HIGH MAYONNAISE ALMOST WITHOUT OIL

(for 4)

Another easy, practical invention by the brilliant Chef Jacques Manière (page 42), at his Le Pactole in Paris.

Pot cheese, low-fat (½ cup)
Egg yolk (1)
Mustard, preferably Dijon
  (½ tsp)
Red cayenne pepper, to taste
Worcestershire sauce (about
  1 tsp)
Lemon juice, freshly squeezed
  (about 2 tsp)
Olive oil, pure green virgin
  (about 1 tsp)

Shrimp, reasonably large,
  preferably boiled and soaked
  in their shells in aromatic
  bouillon, then freshly
  shelled just before serving,
  see page 84 (about 2 doz,
  according to size)
Lettuce, finely shredded (as a
  bed for the shrimp)

Preparation of the sauce in about 7 minutes

Assuming that the shrimp have been boiled, shelled and deveined in advance and are ready, nicely cold, to serve, I put the rest of the above ingredients, in order, into the bowl of my Cuisinart chopper-churner (or, not quite so efficiently, in an electric blender – see page 82): the ½ cup pot cheese, the egg yolk, the ½ teaspoon mustard, a sprinkling of red cayenne pepper, the teaspoon of Worcestershire sauce, the 2 teaspoons of lemon juice and the 1 teaspoon of olive oil. Turn on the machine and run it until the sauce is thoroughly blended and quite smooth – usually in about 5 seconds. Do not overchurn, or it may become pasty. Now pour the sauce into a mixing bowl and taste it. Add, as you please, a few drops more lemon juice and/or a few more grains of red cayenne pepper. Beat furiously for a few seconds with a balloon wire whisk to get air into it and lighten it to the fluffy consistency of mayonnaise. If it is not thick enough, beat in an extra tablespoon of pot cheese. Serve the shrimp neatly laid out on a bed of bright green lettuce. Then dribble the sauce over the shrimp. With this Chef Manière served me a drily refreshing Sauvignon Blanc from Bordeaux. A Sauvignon Blanc from the Livermore Valley of California could substitute.

AN ASSEMBLAGE OF TINY GARDEN VEGETABLES WITH CORIANDER À LA GRECQUE

(for 4)

The phrase *à la Grecque* in classic French cooking is based on an important historical event. In the fifteenth century, the Ottoman sultans of Turkey began oppressing the Greeks who lived in what was then called Constantinople and is now Istanbul. Many thousands of Greek families fled from Turkey and spread out across Western Europe, including France, carrying with them their recipes, which were partly Greek, partly Middle Eastern. The best of these recipes, absorbed into the French cuisine, are always identified as *à la Grecque*. One trick was to poach fresh vegetables with aromatic herbs in a mixture of oil and vinegar, giving the vegetables a refreshingly sharp tang, a salad effect at the start of a meal. Although oil is used in the hot marinade, very little of it is absorbed into the vegetables. The brilliant young Chef Marc Meneau (page 45), has modernized the old recipe at his two-star Auberge de l'Espérance.

When I prepare this recipe in New York, I often find it difficult to get the very small artichokes and onions. Then the only alternative is to buy them precooked in cans. These, of course, require much less simmering in the marinade. The shorter times are given in the recipe below. If you can find small raw artichokes and onions, simply increase their cooking by about 20 minutes.

Olive oil, pure green virgin
(½ to 1 cup)
Vinegar, tarragon white wine
(¼ to ½ cup)
Salt, coarse crystal, to taste
Black peppercorns, whole
(1 doz)
Bay leaves, whole (2)
Fennel seed, whole (1 tsp)
Thyme, fresh in season,
crumbled (1 tsp)
Parsley (1 small bunch)
Carrots, scraped (4 small)
Tomatoes, cherry (4)
Green beans, small, young
(½ lb)

Mushrooms, nice white
(4 small)
Onions, small, white, size of
cherry (4 from smallest-sized
can)
Artichoke hearts, precooked
(4 small, from smallest-sized
can)
Artichoke bottoms, precooked
(4 small, also from can)
Coriander seed, coarsely
cracked (4 tsp)
Watercress (1 bunch)

The day or several days before serving – active preparation about 40 minutes

In a 2-quart saucepan, preferably enameled iron or tinned copper to avoid interaction with the acid, mix: 1 cup freshly drawn cold water, ½ cup olive oil, and ¼ cup vinegar. Bring slowly to simmering while adding 1 teaspoon salt, the 12 peppercorns, the 2 whole bay leaves, the teaspoon of fennel seed, the teaspoon of fresh thyme, and 3 or 4 whole sprigs of parsley with stems. Simmer, covered, about 10 minutes to bring out flavors.

Prepare the vegetables while the marinade is simmering. Wipe the mushrooms clean, then cut their stems off level with the caps; cut the carrots into 1-inch chunks. After the marinade has simmered for 10 minutes, cook the vegetables for the precise time that each requires. Drop in the carrots first. Two minutes later drop in the beans, then the mushroom caps 8 minutes after the beans. Make sure there is enough liquid to cover the vegetables. If not, add more water, oil and vinegar, in the same proportions as above. Let these vegetables cook for about 25 minutes. When the carrots are soft to the center (fish one out to taste), add the tomatoes and the precooked onions, artichoke hearts and bottoms, which should be simmered just long enough to be warmed through, for 4–5 minutes. Let the vegetables cool in the marinade, then bottle them, still in the marinade, in a widemouth screwtop jar and refrigerate overnight. (You can, of course, prepare these vegetables in larger quantities. They keep for several days refrigerated in their marinade.)

On the day – serving at table

Chef Marc Meneau served me, on a chilled plate, one of each of the vegetables nicely sprinkled with coarsely cracked coriander seeds and garnished with watercress. His accompanying wine was a noble, *premier cru,* white Chablis from Burgundy. The American equivalent would be a noble, dry Pinot Chardonnay from the Alexander Valley of Sonoma County in California.

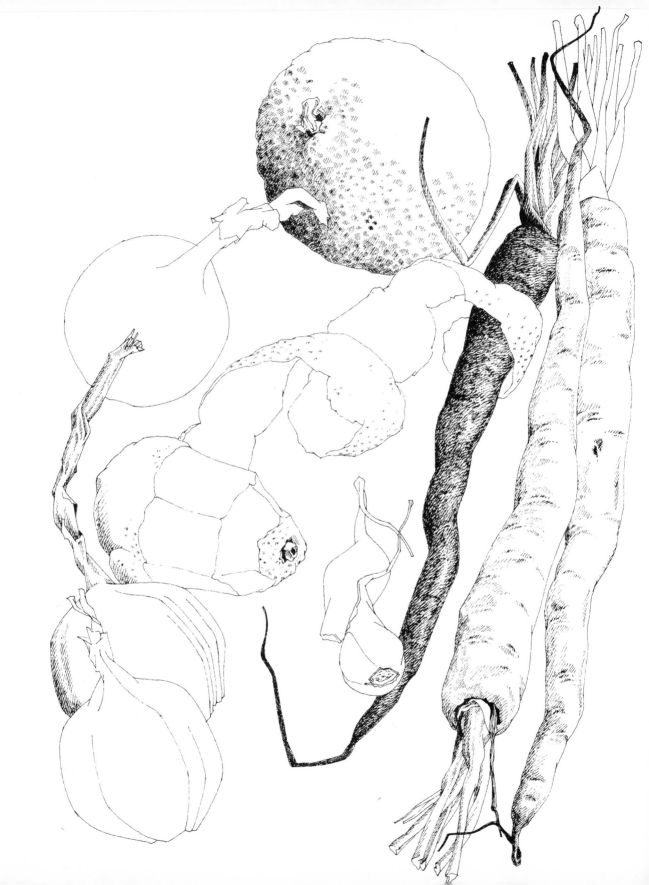

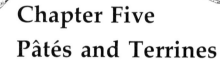

Chapter Five
Pâtés and Terrines

in which we discover that strange bedfellows make
pâtés. Kippers are potted and Eels pâtéed. The
author boldly takes the nearest American approach
to Wild Rabbit rillettes.

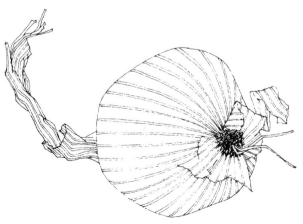

THE ANCIENT BURGUNDIAN PÂTÉ OF SAÔNE EELS

(for 4)

When I visited his three-star restaurant a few miles north of Lyon, the great Chef Paul Bocuse (page 26) gave me this old recipe in honor of his boyhood in his native village of Collonges-au-Mont-d'Or on the banks of the Saône River in the days when it was still unpolluted and filled with large crayfish and fat eels. Sometimes the Bocuse *restaurateur* family would eat their eels hot. Then the dish was called a *matelotte*. At the other times they would prefer them cold in a kind of natural aspic and this was called a pâté.

You can eat eel, which is naturally quite oily, in good Low-High conscience when you cook it in the Bocuse way. Fresh eel boiled in aromatic broth loses a good part of its oil and cools to a firm, light, eminently sliceable and savory starting terrine.

Calf's foot, sawed in half lengthwise (1)

Garlic, finely minced (1 clove)

Yellow onion, peeled and chopped (1 medium)

Tomato, peeled and seeded (2 medium)

Carrots, scraped and sliced (4 medium)

Beef bouillon, clear (about 2 quarts)

Salt, coarse crystal, to taste

Black pepper, freshly ground, to taste

Oranges, nicely sweet (2)

Lemons, fresh whole (2)

Eel, fresh, unsmoked, skinned, boned and cut into 6-inch fillets (4 lbs, before boning and skinning)

Preparation in about 2¼ hours – active work about 20 minutes, plus just under 2 hours of unsupervised simmering

Choose a 4-quart lidded casserole for heating on top of the stove. Into it put: the two halves of the calf's foot, first washed under running cold water; the minced garlic, the chopped onion, one peeled and seeded tomato, and the sliced carrots. Pour in enough beef bouillon to cover the solids. Add salt and pepper to your taste. Bring the contents up to gentle simmering – the surface just smiling, or *riant*, as Paul would say – and keep it all gently simmering, covered, for about 2 hours.

Carefully peel the 2 oranges and 2 lemons, taking off all the white skin down to the citrus flesh. Cut the flesh, across, into thin slices and remove all pits. Choose a rectangular loaf or terrine mold large enough to hold easily all the eel fillets. There should be enough extra room for at least a ¼-inch covering of aspic. Then line the bottom and four sides of the mold with alternating slices of orange and lemon.

When the bell rings for the 2 hours, slip all the fillets of eel into the boiling bouillon, if necessary adding a bit more liquid so that the fish is just covered. Restart your timer at the moment when the bouillon returns to the boil, simmer the eel for no more than 5 minutes, covered, then turn off the heat and remove the lid. First fish out the two halves of the calf's foot. Pull off the gelatinous meat with your fingers and cut it into small pieces. Now start loading your terrine mold. Without disturbing the oranges and lemons, put in a bottom layer of eel fillets. Sprinkle over this about a third of the bits of calf's meat. Then, a second layer of eel fillets and a second layer of calf's meat. Continue layering until all the eel and all the calf's meat is in the mold, making sure that the top layer is all eel.

As soon as all the eel is out of the big casserole, set the remaining liquid over highest heat and let it boil down hard until it is reduced by about half and its flavor and gelatinous texture have been concentrated. While this is in progress, set the mold of eel in the refrigerator to cool. When the bouillon in the big casserole is beginning to be nicely gelatinous, turn off the heat, quickly skim off the fat, strain the liquid through a fine sieve and ladle as much of it into the eel mold as is needed to cover the top layer of the eel with at least ¼ inch of liquid. Cover it with foil and refrigerate overnight. The left-over bouillon will cool into jelly and will be useful for future cooking projects.

Serving at table

Unmold the eel pâté onto a handsome serving platter. It will look lovely with its rounds of oranges and lemons. Garnish the platter with some green parsley and watercress and some red slices of tomato. The pâté should be stiff enough to slice gently with a long sharp knife, using deliberate and slow strokes. Accompany it with thick slices of toasted, un-buttered French bread. Paul said that his parents would serve with this a very light young Beaujolais. At home I might serve instead a fine California Gomay from Monterey.

THE ANCIENT SCOTTISH POTTED PÂTÉ OF MORAY SMOKED HADDOCK

(for 4)

When I recently visited the Scottish Highland whisky country around Dufftown, I dined with special pleasure on some of the excellent Scottish regional dishes, which proved to me that the basic idea of Low-High simplified cooking is almost as ancient as the Highland hills.

Years ago, at just about the same time that the Bocuse family was making its pâtés of eels (see previous recipe), the High-land cooks were making their "pastes" (the Scottish word for pâté) from the marvelously fresh North Sea fish landed each day at dawn at the tiny port of Whitehills at the mouth of the Moray. I went there at crack of dawn to watch the fish being landed. In the wet morning mist the trawlers came in, twist-ing through the harbor bar. They tied up at the jetty and dumped their fish in wooden boxes onto the docks where the auctioneers, calling the bids with their sing-song in the rain, sold out to the buyers within a few seconds. The best and fattest haddocks and herrings were carried at once to the smokehouse at the back of the dock. It was the freshest fish I have ever experienced.

This is my adaptation of an authentic old Scottish recipe. Converting these fish into smoky pastes stored in tightly sealed small crocks was, of course, the basic way of preserving fish long before there were refrigerators. It is still a wonderfully tasty way of starting a meal. Admittedly, there is some butter in these pâtés, but not a quarter of the fat that is in the average *pâté de porc* – nor a quarter of the richness of the butter pastry, the fat bacon, the cheese or eggs in the average *quiche Lorraine*. Also, if there is one thing we have universally across the United States, it is an excellent quality of smoked fish. With the new Cuisinart chopper-churner machine (see page 80), the puréeing of the fish and the mixing in of the aromatic ingredients is a matter of a few seconds.

Smoked haddock or cod fillets
    (1 lb)
Sweet butter (¼ lb)
Pepper, Chinese Szechuan
    (5 or 6 grinds)

Lemon (1)
Paprika, sweet Hungarian
    (½ tsp)

Preparation time about 15 minutes

Set a kettle with about 3 pints of water over highest heat to boil. If the smoked fish fillets are long, cut them in half or quarter them. Place them in a sauté pan, with minimum room to spare. When the water in the kettle is at boiling point, quickly pour over just enough to cover the fish. Put on the lid. Do not put any heat under the pan. Leave the fish to soak for exactly 10 minutes, then drain them. Skin and bone them as necessary. If you are going to do the job by hand, you will have to flake the fish and pound it in a mortar. I chunk it and put it into the bowl of my Cuisinart chopper-churner, adding the ¼-pound butter, sliced, the 5 or 6 grinds of Szechuan pepper, and the juice of half the lemon. I run the machine until everything is just puréed and blended, but not mushy or pasty – usually about 3 seconds. Turn the pâté out into a bowl and taste it. Add, if necessary, tiny extra doses of pepper and lemon juice, until you have the pâté exactly to your taste. Remember that it is to be eaten in small quantities with dry toast, so it should be quite strongly aromatic. Press it fairly tightly into small, lidded, ceramic pâté pots. For decorative coloring as you serve it, sprinkle the top with a little of the paprika. Cool it overnight in the refrigerator. Serve with dry, grilled toast and a fine, gently soft white Graves from Bordeaux, or a Sauvignon Blanc from the Napa Valley.

A HIGHLAND POTTED PÂTÉ OF ABERDEEN SMOKED KIPPERS

(for 4)

For a general discussion of Scottish fish pâtés, see the haddock recipe on page 118. This excellent smoky "paste" of North Sea kippers was served to me in the Highlands, but I have since made it many times with fine Canadian or United States kippers in my New York kitchen.

Smoked kippers, best possible quality (2 pairs, large, or 4 pairs, small) **Sweet butter (¼ lb)**	**Black pepper, freshly ground, to taste** **Lemon (1)**

Preparation time about 10 minutes

Lay the kippers on a cutting board and take them apart. Although a fork and sharp small knife are useful tools, the most effective work is done with clean fingers. Remove the backbone from the split fish, making sure to scrape from the bone any adhering smoky brown bits of flesh. You can put these into a mortar for hand-pounding, but I drop them into the bowl of my Cuisinart chopper-churner (or you can use an electric blender – see page 82). Carefully scrape all the flesh from the back skin of each fillet, removing every little bone. When the edible flesh has been properly harvested and put in with the other morsels of fish, add the ¼ pound butter, sliced, a few grinds of black pepper and the juice of half the lemon. I run my Cuisinart machine until everything is puréed and mixed, but not yet mushy or pasty – usually about 3 seconds. Turn everything out into a mixing bowl and, if needed, add more pepper and lemon juice until you have the pâté exactly to your taste. Remember that it will be eaten in small quantities with dry toast, so it should be quite strongly aromatic. Pack it tightly into small, lidded, ceramic pots and refrigerate overnight. Have with it a fruity, rich, German Riesling white wine from Nierstein on the Rhine. Or serve a fruity white Riesling (sometimes labeled Johannisberg Riesling) from the Napa Valley in California.

THE NEAREST AMERICAN APPROACH TO THE GREAT RILLETTES OF WILD RABBIT BY CHEFS JEAN AND PIERRE TROISGROS

(for 4 to 8, according to size of rabbit)
Rillettes de Tours is one of the great regional hors d'oeuvre specialties of France. It is a marvelously chewy, tasty and unctuous pâté of fat pork invented centuries ago by the thrifty wives of pig farmers along the Loire Valley and around the capital city of Tours to make good use of the unsaleable and unwanted fat back and belly parts of the pig carcass. What we convert into bacon, they make into *rillettes*. It is wonderfully savory eating at the start of a meal, but it is terribly fat – almost a kind of pork butter.

The brilliant Troisgros brothers (page 50) at their three-star restaurant in Roanne, always rethinking every classic dish and trying to find ways of making everything lighter and simpler, came up with the idea of preparing *rillettes* with rabbit, which has virtually no fat. Obviously, if you are going to achieve something of the ambience of true *rillettes*, you must use some pork flavoring in which to cook the rabbit. But once pork is no longer the main ingredient, the amount used is strictly controllable and most of it can be discarded after the cooking. As to the rabbits, very few wild ones are available in our markets. The best I can find for this dish are the so-called "Belgian" breed imported from Canada. If they are not available, our own domestic farm rabbits are a good second choice. It may very well be that a loaf of coarse-textured and crusty bread with a crock of *rillettes* is just about the finest snack in the world.

Rabbits, preferably wild, fresh, skinned and cut up (2, each about 1½ to 2 lbs)
Pork belly or neck, fresh (2 lbs)
Pork fat, fresh, white (½ lb)
Garlic (6 cloves)
Thyme, fresh in season (3 sprigs)

White pepper, freshly ground, to taste
Salt, coarse crystal (1 Tbs per lb of boned rabbit meat)
White wine, lightly sweet (1 cup)

First operation – cooking the rabbit – active preparation about 45 minutes, plus about 4 unsupervised hours in the oven

Begin by boning each piece of rabbit. Cut the meat, across the muscle grain, into chunks about ¼-inch thick. Weigh this boneless meat and hold it. Cut the 2 pounds of pork into thin strips, each about as long as a match, but considerably thicker. Cut the ½-pound of pork fat into large dice.

You will need a tightly lidded casserole (preferably of tinned copper or enameled iron) which can be used both for frying on top of the stove and for baking in the oven. Set the casserole over gentle frying heat and melt the diced pork fat. As soon as the bottom is coated, add the strips of pork belly, stir them around, then add the garlic, whole and unpeeled, the thyme, a few grinds of black pepper, plus 1 tablespoon of salt for each pound of the rabbit meat. Stir everything around and let it all gently melt. Preheat the oven to 300°F. When there is plenty of liquid in the casserole, add the rabbit and also stir it around thoroughly to coat each piece with the juices. Now pour in the cup of white wine, stir around again and set the casserole, covered, in the center of the oven, to stew gently for about 4 hours.

Second operation – making the rillettes in about 1 hour

When the oven stewing is done, remove the sprigs of thyme. Either remove and discard the cloves of garlic or pinch them and mash their pulp into the meat mixture. Have ready the ceramic or stone crocks in which the *rillettes* will be set, stored and, eventually, served. Technique is all important in achieving the texture of true *rillettes de Tours*. *Effilocher* is the French word for the authentic method of tearing the meat into its separate fibers. Using two 4-pronged forks, one in each hand, with the curve of the prongs facing in opposite directions, you literally pull and tear the meat until every solid bit from the casserole has been deliberately disintegrated.

To achieve this effect most efficiently, set a fine mesh wire sieve in a bowl and empty into it (perhaps batch by batch) the contents of the casserole, both the solid meats and the limpid juices. The juice will run through the sieve into the bowl. Now squeeze out more juice from the meat left in the sieve by pressing it with the back of a large kitchen spoon. Then proceed to the tearing apart with the two forks. When the job is done, taste the meat and, if necessary, add more salt and pepper. Remember that *rillettes* are dull if not quite strongly seasoned.

Pile the shredded meat lightly into the small pots and add, tablespoon by tablespoon, just enough of the juice from the bowl under the sieve to solidify the *rillettes* while cooling. Cover with foil, put on the lids and refrigerate at once. *Rillettes* should be eaten quite soft, so bring them back to room temperature before serving them with big chunks of toasted bread. When I have had them with the brothers Troisgros, the wine was a fine, soft, white Vouvray, from the Loire. At home I might drink a California Chenin Blanc.

GREEK PÂTÉ OF TARAMA CARP ROE

(for 4)

This is a Low-High modification of a national Greek specialty. *Tarama* is a form of preserved and salted carp roe which, classically prepared, is whipped up with oodles of olive oil into a kind of mayonnaise. In this version, the oil is cut down to a minimum and the pâté is thickened with a small quantity of dry-mashed potato. *Tarama* can usually be found in Greek groceries. In the more old-fashioned shops, it comes in large wooden barrels and is scooped out as if it were pink ice cream. I usually prepare this pâté in large quantities. In the modern Cuisinart chopping-churning machine, it takes only a few seconds to mix and, when tightly lidded, keeps well in the refrigerator. It is an excellent standby for snacks.

Tarama carp roe, see above (¼ lb)

Garlic, peeled (2 cloves)

Potato, boiled in jacket without salt, then skinned (1 medium)

Olive oil, preferably Greek, pure green virgin (up to 3 Tbs)

Lemon (1)

Red cayenne pepper, to taste

Preparation in about 10 minutes

I break up the *tarama* into chunks and put them into the bowl of my Cuisinart chopper-churner, or you can use an electric blender (see page 82). Add the 2 cloves of garlic, chunked, the boiled potato, chunked, 2 tablespoons of the olive oil, the juice of half the lemon and a pinch of cayenne pepper. I run the machine until everything is thoroughly puréed and blended, but is not yet mushy or pasty – usually about 4 seconds. You should now have a fairly stiff paste. Spoon it out into a mixing bowl and work on it until you have exactly the spreadable pâté consistency and the salty tang that best pleases your taste buds. Remember that this will be eaten in small quantities with dry toast, so it should be quite strongly flavored. Using a wooden spatula with light strokes, work in as needed more lemon juice, pepper and olive oil. (Hold down the oil as much as reasonably possible.) Pack the pâté fairly tightly into small, lidded, ceramic pots and refrigerate sealed, if necessary with aluminum foil, overnight. Serve with dry-grilled chunks of Greek bread and a fine Greek Roditis rosé or a fine California rosé – a Cabernet, Gamay, Grenache, or Zinfandel from Monterey, Napa, Santa Clara, or Sonoma.

TERRINE OF VEAL

(a supply to keep on hand)

I have become so bored and antagonized by the average restaurant *terrine maison* – overenriched, underseasoned, overfatted with massive doses of pork lard, then injected with butter and cream – that the discovery of a low-fat terrine prepared with high imagination was a memorable event. I have translated and adapted this recipe from Brussels for our American kitchens. A fine standby terrine. You will not soon get tired of it.

Pork, fresh, entirely lean, boned leg or loin, ground (1 lb)

Veal, entirely lean, as above, also ground (1 lb)

Chicken livers, very fresh (1 lb)

Boiled ham, dark-smoked, country style, entirely lean, diced (½ lb)

Dry vermouth (about 1 cup)

Juniper berries, whole (1 doz)

Mace chips, freshly ground (½ tsp)

Bay leaf, crumbled (1)

Butter (about 2 Tbs)

Cognac (½ cup)

Beef bouillon (about 1 cup)

Garlic, peeled and chunked (2 cloves)

Shallots, peeled and chunked (6 cloves)

Salt, coarse crystal, to taste

Black pepper, freshly ground, to taste

Nutmeg, freshly ground (1 grind)

Thyme, fresh in season, chopped (2 tsp)

Cinnamon, freshly ground (¼ tsp)

Eggs, grade A, lightly beaten (4 large)

Tomato juice (½ cup)

Milk (½ cup)

Bacon, very lean, sliced (1 lb)

Preparation in about 45 minutes, plus about 5 hours of entirely unsupervised baking and resting

Set out all the meat ingredients to come to room temperature. Put the diced ham into a bowl and pour over it enough of the vermouth to just cover it, stirring around to encourage absorption. Cover and leave it at room temperature. Grind the 12 juniper berries, the ½ teaspoon of mace chips and the whole bay leaf in a spice grinder, or pound them with a pestle in a mortar. Hold them, covered.

Set a medium-sized sauté pan over moderate frying heat and melt in it the 2 tablespoons of butter. Then quickly sauté the pound of chicken livers until lightly browned but still rare and soft inside. Turn up the heat under the pan, pour in the ½ cup of Cognac and flame. When the fire dies down, I remove the chicken livers with a slotted spoon and put them into the bowl of my Cuisinart chopper-churner and, without switching on the machine, leave them there for a few moments. (Or you can use a blender – see page 82.) Now, deglaze the hot sauté pan by adding to the Cognac ½ cup of the beef bouillon, bringing it up to a rolling boil for a few minutes to concentrate and sharpen the flavors.

Now turn back to the chicken livers waiting to be puréed. Add to them, in turn: the previously ground juniper, mace, the crumbled bay leaf, the 2 garlic cloves, peeled and chunked, the 6 shallots, peeled and chunked, 1 teaspoon of salt, a generous grind of pepper, a less-generous grind of nutmeg, the 2 teaspoons of thyme, the ¼-teaspoon of cinnamon, and the 4 eggs, whites and yolks previously beaten lightly together. I then turn on the Cuisinart machine and let it run until all these ingredients are puréed and thoroughly blended, but not so long that they become mushy and pasty – usually 10 to 15 seconds. As soon as the liquid in the sauté pan is reduced by about half, turn off the heat and let it cool.

Now start the assembly of everything in your largest mixing bowl. Put in the chicken livers, then the diced ham with its vermouth, then the ground pork and veal. Now start the thorough mixing. (A wooden spoon will do but no tool is half as effective at eliminating every last lump as the 10 sensitive fingers of your well-washed hands.) As you lift and scoop and turn, begin working in the still-warm bouillon-Cognac blend from the sauté pan. It is all more fun than making mud pies. In fact, the consistency you should aim at is a not-too-sloshy mud. If it is stubbornly stiff, add, ¼-cup by ¼-cup, the tomato juice, a little of the milk plus a little more dry vermouth and beef bouillon. Heaven forbid that you allow it to become too thin. The answer to that problem would be to rush out to your butcher for more solid meat, or, as a last compromise, to add a handful or two of breadcrumbs. Always remember to keep the mixture light by lifting it as you mix, rather than pushing it down and squeezing it together.

You have now assembled about 5 pounds of liquid and solid ingredients. This means that you will need a lidded terrine pan (or more than one) with a total inner capacity of about 6 quarts. I prefer using several pans of different shapes and sizes for easier storage in the refrigerator and longer keeping. Line the bottoms and four sides of each pan with slices of the bacon. Fill each pan with the terrine mixture, packing it tightly into the corners, pressing it down with your fingers and filling each pan to within about half an inch of the top edge. Cover the top of the terrine with bacon. Preheat your oven to 300°F. Prepare a *bain-marie* by filling a large, shallow pan with about 1 inch of boiling water. Set it in the center of your oven. Stand the terrine pans, tightly lidded, in the water and leave them to steam-bake gently for 3 hours.

When the time is up, turn off the oven, but leave the *bain-marie* to cool slowly in the oven. Uncover each terrine and arrange some way for the meat to be weighted down and compressed, so that it slowly settles into a solid, tightly textured mass. I achieve this effect by having pieces of wood cut to size to fit loosely inside each terrine. I cover each piece of wood with foil, lay it on the meat and place a fairly heavy weight on top. Use your ingenuity to achieve the same effect by any other means at your disposal. Once the terrine has been weighted, put it back without its lid into the *bain-marie* in the oven and leave it to cool to room temperature – usually in about 2 hours. Then, still with its weighting system intact, set it in the refrigerator to solidify overnight. The next morning, remove the weights and put back the regular lids. These terrines will keep perfectly for at least 2 or 3 weeks. Never freeze them. You can unmold them, decorate and garnish them for the table, if you wish. You could even glaze them with a wine aspic. But I prefer to keep them in their terrine pans, where they remain moist and succulent. I do not hesitate to bring my enameled-iron, flame-red terrine pans to table and slice the meat, about ¼-inch thick, right from the terrine. Garnish the slice on the plate with *cornichons* (baby French pickles), little pickled onions, sliced tomato and sprigs of watercress. It can be an hors d'oeuvre, a main supper dish, or a snack at any time with a fine, fruity, white Alsatian Riesling or a fruity, white Riesling from the banks of the Russian River in northern California.

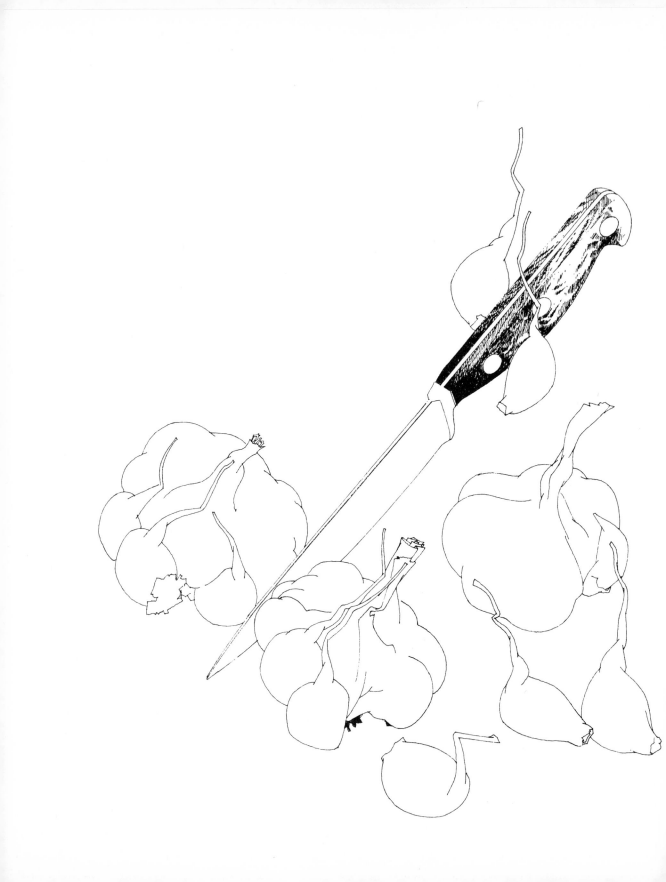

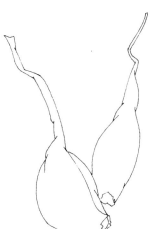

Chapter Six
Soups

in which Garlic appears, then disappears. A master
chef imparts the secret of great fish soups. A Duck
is sealed in a Dry Sack. Truffles at the Palace.
A Mushroom soup is achieved without Cream.

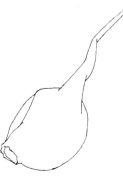

CHEF ROGER VERGÉ'S SECRETS OF MAKING GREAT FISH SOUPS

Room Five on the second floor of the Old Mill at Mougins is one of the most beautiful bedrooms in Provence. In the early morning, you step out from your bed through tall French windows onto a stone balcony where everything is at once perfumed and vivid and warm from the magical brightness of the Midi sky and sun. Behind you, the red-tiled roof slopes upwards. At your left, the old mill wheel still stands, now dry and silent. Below, on terraces at various levels, under gray- and pink-striped umbrellas, are the tables of Chef Vergé's (page 52) three-star restaurant, Le Moulin de Mougins. Surrounding the garden is a circle of giant oak trees and from the vastness of their greenery comes, morning and evening, the multitudinous orchestra of the singing birds.

A young waiter sets the breakfast tray down on the bamboo table on the balcony. There are half a dozen home-made fruit preserves to try with the *brioche*, the *croissant*, the *petits pains*, the black coffee. Chef Vergé comes up to join me for breakfast and to discuss last night's memorable dinner. "If you had carried me down here from Paris with my head in a sack," I said, "I would still have known instantly that I was in Provence by the scent of the garlic in your marvelous fish soup."

"Our Provençal garlic is something quite special," Vergé said. "When it is freshly harvested it has an almost flowery scent and a sweetness as against the bitterness that develops in the old, dried heads. With our newly harvested garlic, we can use as many as eight cloves to each cup of our fresh green Provençal olive oil. It is this combination of flavors which marries so perfectly to our fresh Mediterranean fish in the great soups of our region. The old idea in Provence was that you loaded everything with olive oil, but I have discovered that, if you control exactly the balance of flavors, you need use only about a quarter of the oil normally called for in the classic Provençal recipes. And since pure olive oil has a much stronger character than butter, less of the oil goes a longer way towards developing a memorable personality in any fish preparation."

Roger explained to me the differences between the three great fish soups of Provence. The best known, of course, is *la bouillabaisse,* which is almost a stew of chunks of a carefully balanced selection of fish and shellfish. It starts with the vegetables more or less melted into a large quantity of olive oil. The great chef, Fernand Point, once said that a true *bouillabaisse* could only be made within sight of the Mediterranean. Vergé goes even further. He never makes *bouillabaisse* in his restaurant because he believes that it is not at its absolute best unless it is boiled in the open air, on the beach where the fish have just been landed, in a huge, black, iron, open "witches' cauldron," over a bonfire of pine branches with the needles, so that the inside of the pot is licked by the flames and everything is slightly smoked by the burning of the resinous wood. "That," said Vergé, "is the marvelous, ultimate effect."

The second great Provençal soup, *la bourride,* must, according to Vergé, "be prepared with what we call *les poissons de landes,*" including the *chapon,* the white *rascasse,* the *congre* and a few *murènes.* These are boiled together with onions and the soup is then thickened with the famous *aioli,* the Provençal garlic mayonnaise. Again, with *la bourride,* oil is a primary ingredient.

"As you know, I am not from Provence," Roger continued, "but once one starts cooking here, with the magnificent products of the Provençal earth, sea and sunshine, one has to adapt one's techniques to the region. It has always seemed to me that the third great Provençal soup, *la soupe de poisson,* in which all the fish are mashed to a kind of cream, offers the best chance for cutting down on the oil and producing a dish that is digestible, healthy and light, in the tradition of the new cuisine."

Roger gave me the basic rules for his marvelous fish-garlic soup (see recipe, below). It has all the colors, the dominant character and the warmth of Provence. The fish flavors are magnified by saffron, and fennel, by bay-laurel and thyme – in their strong Provençal versions. The soup is neither very delicate nor very modest in personality. It is, historically, a peasant dish originated by the wives of the Provençal fishermen. Roger took me shopping in the fish market at Cannes and showed me the kind of fish you must buy, wherever in the world you happen to be and whatever the different names of the available specimens. He prefers fish caught with lines along rocky coasts to those dredged with nets along muddy bottoms, because the feeding habits of rock fish give their flesh a special savor. They should be small and soft-fleshed, because they are going to be puréed in the soup.

On this particular morning, Roger bought: *rascasse*, also called sea devil of the Mediterranean or hog-fish (also caught off North Carolina, around Bermuda and on the coral reefs of the West Indies); *rouquier*, the highly colored parrot-fish or sheepshead (or, off the West Indies, the "Slippery Dick"); *girelle*, the rainbow wrasse or goldfinny; *galinette* or *grondin*, also called gurnard, redfish, or sea robin; *cigale*, spider crab or water cricket; *murène*, the spotted moray (also caught off the North Sea coast of Scotland or off the West Indies where it is called the hamlet); *favouille*, tiny rock crabs (also found in the Gulf of Mexico), plus some strictly Provençal fish that simply have no English names, *capoun*, *pageot*, *sars* and *vieille*.

Roger has been so insistent on what he wants (and his local prestige is so high) that the fishmongers now have barrels of small mixed fish at their stands in the market, labeled *Poissons pour la Soupe*. I think that every fishmonger in the United States ought to do the same.

Once Roger gets the live fish back to his kitchen, he gives them only light cleaning and washing to guard their juices and then cooks them in a minimum of oil. To reduce the richness of the soup even further, Roger serves it accompanied by dry-toasted slices of French bread instead of butter- or oil-fried croutons. He rubs the bread with garlic instead of spreading it with the rich traditional *rouille* of Provence, the whipped garlic-egg-and-oil spread. (But, of course, he will make the *rouille* for you if you insist on it.) Finally, he brings the soup to table in wide, deep soup plates with the oval slices of bread floating on the surface like little boats.

THE NEAREST AMERICAN VERSION OF CHEF ROGER VERGÉ'S TRUE FISH-GARLIC SOUP OF PROVENCE

(for 4–6)

First, read Chef Vergé's advice beginning on page 132. This marvelous soup contains not an ounce of butter, not a spoonful of cream, not a wisp of thickening flour. Its creamy body comes only from the puréeing of the flesh of the fish.

Can it be reproduced in the United States? Well, naturally, not exactly. For one thing, there is a difference of mood between, say, Madison, Marietta, Minneapolis and Mougins. But I think I have proved to at least a score of my New York friends that my translation and adaptation of the Vergé recipe is an eminently satisfactory variation of the master *cuisinier's* interpretation of the traditional Provençal dish.

The balance of the fish is all-important. In New York, I buy about half a pound each from the following list: butterfish, flounder, gurnard, red mullet, fresh sardines, sea bass, sea robin, sea trout, sheepshead, whiting, plus two or three small whole blue crabs.

For maximum lightness, use only dry-toasted garlic bread as the garnish for this soup. But if you are prepared to risk the added richness of a celestial Provençal *rouille*, the recipe is below. The *rouille* is then spread on the garlic bread. A final note: you can, if you wish, sprinkle grated Parmesan over the soup and I have included some cheese in the recipe. But, personally, I am against the Parmesan. It seems to me to add a slightly clashing Italian note to a soup that belongs, completely, to the Midi of France. The cheese is offered so you can, if you wish, agree to disagree.

Mixed fish, see above, at least
6 to 8 types, all boned and
skinned, but bring home
bones and skin (about 3 to
4 lbs total flesh and bones)
Yellow onions, peeled and
chopped (1¼ lbs)
Blue crabs, small, whole in
shells (2 or 3, according to
size)
Olive oil, not too fruity (1 cup)
Tomatoes, ripe, sliced (4
medium)
Garlic (9 cloves)
Thyme, fresh in season (2 or 3
stalks with leaves)

Bay leaves, crumbled (2)
Fennel seed (2 tsp)
White wine, dry to soak the
saffron (2 Tbs)
Saffron filaments (½ tsp)
Salt, coarse crystal, to taste
Black pepper, freshly ground,
to taste
French bread, long baguette
(1 loaf)
Parmesan cheese, optional,
grated, for sprinkling on top
of the soup at table, see
above (¼ lb)

About 1 hour before serving – active preparation about 30 minutes, plus another 30 minutes of unsupervised poaching and boiling

Wash the bones and skins, then put them into a 4-quart covered saucepan with 3 quarts of cold water and ½ cup of the chopped onions. Do not add salt or pepper. Bring water to a boil and keep simmering, covered, until you need this court bouillon in the main kettle.

Wash and carefully dry all the fish and crabs, then put them, together, in a large bowl. Set a big soup kettle on top of the stove over quite low heat and pour in the one cup of olive oil. Add all the remaining chopped onions, stir them around in the oil and let them simmer for 10 minutes. They must under no circumstances fry or brown but simply become transparent and melt into the oil. Watch this carefully as you occasionally stir the onions around.

Meanwhile, add to the fish in the bowl; the 4 sliced tomatoes, 8 of the cloves of garlic, whole and unpeeled, the thyme leaves and stalks, the 2 crumbled bay leaves and the 2 teaspoons of fennel seed. Hold until the onions in the big kettle are ready. Into a very small saucepan put the 2 tablespoons of white wine, heat it to just above blood heat, then soak the ½ teaspoon of saffron in the wine, stirring it around to encourage it to exude its coloring and flavoring oils. Hold it off the heat, covered, until it is needed in the big kettle.

At the end of the 10 minutes, when the onions are perfectly done, turn up the heat to quite high and add, all at once, the contents of the large bowl with the fish, etc. Stir it all around quite vigorously, to impregnate everything thoroughly with the onion-flavored base. You should expect the fish now to begin breaking up into smallish chunks. Continue this process, with regular stirring, for exactly 10 minutes. Between stirrings, strain the bouillon from the fish bones and skins and measure it. You will need exactly 3 quarts to add to the big kettle. If it has slightly boiled down, add cold water to make up the 3 quarts.

About 30 minutes before serving – boiling the fish

The moment the 10 minutes are up, pour in the 3 quarts of fish bouillon. Stir everything around and begin tasting for seasoning. I usually find that I need, at this point, about a ½ teaspoon of salt. Do not yet add any pepper. Chef Vergé warned me that if the pepper is added too early it can cause a slightly bitter flavor. Keep the heat high under the kettle. The soup must boil hard, exactly as if it were a *bouillabaisse*, with large bubbles ensuring that all the flavors are continuously being blended together. This is the essential trick in making a perfect *soupe*. Do not cover your kettle at this point. Stir frequently. Keep everything bubbling for exactly 20 minutes.

While waiting, prepare the crusts of garlic bread and, if you have opted for the extra richness, beat up the *rouille* (see next recipe, below). Preheat your oven to 275°F. Cut ½-inch slices from the loaf of French bread – about 2 slices per person – and toast them, dry, on a cookie sheet or aluminum foil in the oven. They will usually be nicely browned in about 10 minutes. Then, either rub them with the cut side of the remaining clove of garlic, or hold them to be spread with the *rouille* when it is ready.

During this stage it is helpful to have two people working on the job. When the 20 minutes of hard boiling is up, turn off the heat under the big kettle. Strain out all the solids, set them in a bowl to be puréed and return the liquid to the kettle. Turn on the heat to low just to keep the liquid warm. Split open the crabs, take out what little flesh is left inside them, and add this to the fish, discarding the shells. Quickly purée the solids in two stages. First, pass them through an electric vegetable grinder, or a Cuisinart chopper-churner. Second, rub the ground mash through a sieve, returning the resulting purée of fish and vegetables to the big kettle. The fish fibers that do not pass through the sieve have little flavor left and should be discarded. When this job is completed, thoroughly stir the soup and bring it up to the gentlest simmering. Now add the saffron and its soaking wine. Make sure that all the coloring and flavoring oils of the saffron are gathered up from the walls of the little saucepan by rinsing it with a few tablespoons of the hot soup. Stir the soup again and watch its color change to the warm orange of Provence. Taste again and add more salt, if needed. This is the moment to grind in plenty of black pepper – in my case, usually 16 to 20 grinds. Keep it all gently simmering, covered, until ready to serve.

Serving at table

Present *la soupe de poisson* in wide soup plates, or in gumbo bowls of not less than 8 inches diameter. Bring the garlic-covered bread slices to table on a serving platter. The diner then has the choice (according to his or her love of garlic) of biting into the bread separately or soaking and working it and its garlic into the soup. If you are going to use Parmesan cheese, sprinkle it on. With this memorable dish, Chef Roger Vergé served me a dry, fruity, light white wine of the Côtes de Provence. You can serve instead a dry, light California Pinot Blanc.

AN AUTHENTIC PROVENÇAL GARLIC ROUILLE FOR LA SOUPE DE POISSON

(for 4 to 6)

Egg yolks (2)
Garlic, peeled and mashed
  (3 cloves)
Light oil, preferably Provençal
  grape (about 8 Tbs)
Salt, coarse crystal, to taste
Black pepper, freshly ground,
  to taste

Hot fish soup, from previous
  recipe, for slight thinning
  (a few tsp)
Paprika, sweet Hungarian
  (about 1 tsp)

Preparation time about 5 minutes

Arm yourself with a smallish round-bottomed beating bowl and a balloon wire whisk. Put in the 2 egg yolks and give them a few beats to break them up. Next, beat in the mashed garlic. Then start beating in the oil, teaspoon by teaspoon at first, making sure that each teaspoon is thoroughly absorbed before the next is added. As the yolks expand, the oil can go in tablespoon by tablespoon. If you beat hard and fast, with lifting strokes, getting in plenty of air, the *rouille* will soon become very fluffy and stiff. Beat in salt and pepper to taste. Then dilute the *rouille* to the thickness of a not-too-stiff mayonnaise by beating in a few teaspoons, one at a time, of the hot soup.

Serving

Spread the *rouille* on each slice of toasted bread and decorate each piece with a sprinkle of paprika (Chef Vergé thinks not more than two rounds per person, or the *rouille* will begin to dominate the soup). Serve these rounds on a separate plate.

Once you become a *rouille* aficionado, you will want to use it also in other ways: with potatoes, all kinds of green and yellow vegetables, cold meats, fish, poultry, even in picnic sandwiches. Dr. Johnson might easily have said, "Mayonnaise is for boys, *aioli* is for men, but *rouille* is for heroes!"

A BURGUNDIAN SOUP OF MIXED FISH WITHOUT GARLIC OR OIL

(for 4 to 6)

Unlike the fish soup of Provence (previous recipe), this is prepared with solid pieces of fish and poached vegetables in their natural, aromatic juices. It is a near-perfect example of a Low-High preparation, served to me by the great Chefs Jean and Pierre Troisgros (page 50), at their three-star restaurant in Roanne. This dish depends mainly on Atlantic fish and shellfish caught off the coast of Brittany and I have found it easily reproducible in New York because most of the same fish are brought in by our North Atlantic fishermen.

When Jean gave me this recipe, he advised: "Be flexible with the list of fish. Be prepared to vary the fish according to what is best in season. To make sure all the pieces are perfectly ready precisely at the moment of serving, cut the different fish into different-sized pieces according to the softness or firmness of the flesh – softer into larger pieces, firmer into smaller. Salmon should be set in the bouillon only a couple of minutes before serving. Be flexible, also, about the vegetables and herbs. If you can't get fresh thyme, use tarragon. Always better a fresh herb than a dried."

Pierre added: "We think this soup should not be brought to table in a serving tureen. That wastes time during which the fish cools and begins to lose flavor. The moment everything is cooked, set it out beautifully on large, very hot, soup plates. It must all look colorful and lovely – red crab, bright green beans, yellow carrots, pink salmon – just to look at the plate must make you instantly hungry."

Carrots, scraped (4 medium)
Celery, white, 2 or 3 stalks with leaves, plus heart
Yellow onion, peeled and chopped (1 medium)
Turbot, boned fillets (½ lb)
Red mullet, small, each about ¼ lb, boned fillets (4 fish)

Sea bass, boned and skinned (½ lb)
Blue crabs, small, whole in shells (4 to 6)
Butter (6 Tbs)
Leek white, carefully washed and desanded, thinly sliced (1 medium)

Turnip, white, peeled, coarsely
   diced (1 medium)

Green beans, small, young,
   French cut (½ lb)

Green peas, young, in season
   (½ lb)

Snow peas, young (½ lb)

Salt, coarse crystal, to taste

White wine, dry (½ cup)

Parsley (3 or 4 sprigs)

Basil, fresh leaves in season
   (8 whole leaves)

Thyme, fresh leaves in season
   (8 whole leaves)

Shallots, finely minced
   (2 cloves)

White pepper, freshly ground,
   to taste

Salmon, fairly thin slices,
   boned and skinned (½ lb)

Tarragon, fresh leaves in
   season, chopped (2 Tbs)

Chervil, fresh leaves in season,
   chopped (2 Tbs)

Lemon (½)

Black truffle, strictly optional,
   coarsely diced (1, fairly
   small)

About 45 minutes before serving – active work about 25 minutes, plus about 20 minutes of unsupervised poaching of vegetables and fish

First, make what the Troisgros call *la nage,* "the swim," the bouillon in which the fish will be poached. Into a 1-quart saucepan put 2 of the carrots, quartered, 2 or 3 chunked outer stalks of the celery with some of the leaves (hold onto the celery heart), plus the chopped onion. Pour in 1 pint of cold water and bring rapidly to a boil. Then turn down the heat and let it bubble gently, covered, until you need it in the main dish. Wash all your pieces of fish and crab, pat them dry and cut them up in the way suggested above by Jean Troisgros. Hold each fish separately until needed.

For the vegetables you will need a thick-bottomed casserole with a tightly fitting lid. The various vegetables are to be steamed in their own juices over just enough heat to produce steam, but not enough to brown or fry them. They must be undercooked to be nicely crisp. Set the casserole over gentle frying heat and melt 2 tablespoons of the butter. As soon as it is hot, put in the sliced leek, stir it around to coat it with butter, adjust the heat so that the butter is just hissing and at once clamp on the lid. Wait exactly 2 minutes, then put in the heart of the celery, chopped, stir it thoroughly, put back the lid and wait another 2 minutes. Repeat, in turn (and always 2 minutes in between each addition), for the diced turnip, the last two carrots, sliced, the green beans, the peas, and the snow peas. When all are in, add salt to taste and let them all poach, covered, for hardly more than another 3 or 4 minutes. Taste odd bits. The moment they are perfectly done, still quite crisp, turn off the heat and hold them, covered, until needed in the main dish.

About 25 minutes before serving – poaching the fish

Choose a lidded sauté pan just large enough to hold all the pieces of fish and the crabs neatly spread out without too much piling up. Put in all the fish and crabs, except the salmon. Then pour over it the ½ cup of white wine. Set the pan over gentle heat to begin sweating. Add the sprigs of parsley, then sprinkle in the basil and thyme leaves and the minced shallots, with salt and pepper to taste. Strain the bouillon from the saucepan where it is still simmering and pour enough of it over the fish so that the liquid in the sauté pan is about half an inch deep. The fish is not to be completely covered, but is to cook in the steam. Adjust the heat so that the liquid is gently bubbling, then put on the lid and leave it for 5 minutes. Begin warming up your soup plates, and a temporary platter for the fish, in an oven at keep-warm temperature, 150°F. After the 5 minutes, put the salmon into the sauté pan, re-cover and continue steaming for another 3 or 4 minutes. Now begin checking for perfect doneness. All the fish should be just flaky. Take the pieces out with a spatula, place them on the hot platter, cover with foil and return to the oven to keep warm. You must work very quickly, to avoid the fish's drying.

While the bouillon in the sauté pan is still gently bubbling, stir into it the remaining 4 tablespoons of butter, cut into slivers, until it melts. This is the professional French way of slightly enriching a bouillon sauce without allowing the butter to cook. As soon as it is melted, add to the sauté pan all the vegetables from the casserole. Gently work everything together while adding the chopped tarragon and chervil, plus a few spritzes of lemon juice, to your taste.

Serving at table

The Troisgros brothers are extremely strict about never pouring a sauce over the main ingredient on the plate, because then the flavor of the sauce tends to dominate. Instead, the sauce should first be spread across the plate and then the main ingredient laid on top. So, for this fish soup, you should first ladle the bouillon and the vegetables across the bottom of each soup plate, until you have an even layer about half-an-inch deep. Then gently place the handsomely colored pieces of fish (including one crab per person) on top of the vegetables. Finally, if you are going to splurge on that truffle, sprinkle it, diced over the top of everything. With this superb soup the Troisgros brothers served me a noble white Chassagne Montrachet from the Côte d'Or of Burgundy. The American equivalent might be a big, fruity California Sonoma Pinot Chardonnay.

A CHINESE HOT-AND-SOUR FISH SOUP FROM THE PROVINCE OF HUNAN

(for 4)

Both Chefs Troisgros and Vergé have often told me that some of their basic ideas in low-fat cooking have been drawn from the ancient recipes of China. Since dairy farming was never developed in the old China, there was virtually no butter, cheese, or cream in its cuisine. Here is a Chinese low-fat fish soup for comparison with the previous two. This soup requires the preparation, earlier in the day, or the day before, of a batch of the basic Low-High fish bouillon on page 70. (The lazy cook can substitute clam juice.)

Fish bouillon, basic Low-High, see above (7 cups)

Ginger root, fresh (1½-inch length)

Scallions (4)

Coriander, fresh, whole, leaves and stems, see page 63 (about 20 sprigs, according to size)

Sesame oil (½ tsp)

Salt, coarse crystal, to taste

White pepper, freshly ground, to taste

Vinegar, white wine (3 to 4 Tbs)

Fish, boned and skinned, non-oily – as flounder, fluke, sole, striped bass, etc. (1 lb)

Preparation in less than 30 minutes

Put the 7 cups of fish bouillon into a 3-quart saucepan, bring it gently up to simmering, and leave it uncovered. With a sharp potato peeler, skin the ginger root and drop the skins into the simmering bouillon. Grate the remaining ginger root very finely and hold it, covered. Cut the white of the scallions into 2-inch lengths, then, with a very sharp knife, cut them lengthwise into fine filaments and hold, covered. Pluck the coriander leaves from their stems. Crush the stems with a pestle or the back of a large chef's knife and add them to the simmering bouillon. Hold the leaves aside, covered.

Let the crushed stems simmer in the bouillon for another 2 or 3 minutes, then turn off the heat, strain out and discard the solids and put the bouillon back into the saucepan, but do not turn on the heat. Add to the liquid, in turn: the shredded ginger, the scallion filaments, the coriander leaves, the ½ teaspoon sesame oil, with salt and pepper to taste. Finally, stir in just enough vinegar to give you the degree of sourness that you like. Remember when tasting that the fish will absorb some of the acid, (the "Sour"), while the ginger will develop the pungency (the "Hot"). Stir the bouillon well as it continues to cool towards room temperature. When you are ready to serve, cut the fish into ½-inch cubes and add them, all at once, to the bouillon. Now quickly heat it up again just to simmering. Watch the fish carefully, lifting odd pieces with a slotted spoon. It is perfect the moment it is opaque and flaky. Warm the soup bowls. The instant the fish is ready, serve immediately. The guests must be waiting for this soup. It cannot wait for them. With it, in New York, I usually serve a noble, rich, Pinot Chardonnay from New York State.

CHICKEN HALF-MELTED IN A PROVENÇAL POTAGE PISTOU

(for 4)

Pistou is one of the most famous and universal of the one-dish-meal soups of the Midi region of southern France. Obviously, it is a subtle, French variation of Italian minestrone – a balanced blend of perfectly cooked fresh vegetables with soft chunks of chicken in an aromatic broth – which, at some time in history, traveled across the border from Genoa to Nice and into Provence. It is the ideal warming stew for a cold evening on the Mediterranean coast (or anywhere else) when the stormy mistral is howling straight down from the glaciers of the Alps and setting the palm trees clacking along the promenades of the Riviera.

This *potage pistou* is a brilliant variation by the revolutionary, young Chef Georges Blanc (page 25) at his two-star Auberge Chez La Mère Blanc in the village of Vonnas in the Beaujolais country of southern Burgundy. Since Georges has eliminated all the cheese and pasta of the original version and has cut the use of olive oil down to a minimum, this recipe comes well within the basic principles of the Low-High cuisine.

White wine, dry (2 Tbs)
Saffron filaments (½ tsp)
Chicken or capon, cut up for fricasseeing (about 3½ to 4 lbs)
Lemon, fresh (½)
Salt, coarse crystal, to taste
Black pepper, freshly ground, to taste
Olive oil, top-quality Provençal green virgin (up to 6 Tbs)
Chicken bouillon, clear, entirely fatless; or Basic Low-High Bouillon, page 000 (2 quarts)
Yellow onions, peeled and coarsely chopped (2 medium)
Leek whites, washed and desanded, sliced (2 medium)

Tomatoes, red and ripe, skinned and seeded, chopped (6 medium)
Carrots, scraped and sliced (4 medium)
Celery, green Pascal, with leaves, chopped (2 stalks)
Fennel, fresh, with green fronds, chopped (2 stalks)
Garlic, whole unpeeled cloves (6 to 8, according to taste)
Thyme, fresh leaf in season, chopped (1 Tbs)
Bay leaf (1)
Basil, fresh leaf in season, coarsely chopped (4 Tbs)
Anise liquor, Pernod or Ricard (up to ⅓ cup)
Sweet butter (4 Tbs)

About 1 hour before serving – active work about 20 minutes with about 40 minutes of largely unsupervised sautéeing and simmering

Put the 2 tablespoons of white wine into a tiny saucepan and warm it up to just above blood heat. Stir into it the ½ teaspoon of saffron and leave it to soak, covered, exuding its flavor oils and warm orange color. Clean and refresh the pieces of chicken by rubbing them all over with the cut side of the half lemon, then pat them lightly with salt and pepper. Choose a sauté pan just large enough to hold the chicken pieces snugly in a single layer – if there is too much spare room around and between them the pan will tend to overheat and burn. Before putting in the chicken, set the pan over medium-high frying heat and lubricate its bottom with 2 tablespoons of the olive oil. When it is hot but not smoking, put in the chicken pieces and lightly gild them on all sides – usually in about 5 to 7 minutes. If necessary, add a bit more oil. Then turn down the heat to simmering and carefully hiss into the sauté pan enough of the chicken bouillon just to cover the pieces. Adjust the heat to gentle simmering (as Georges would say, "the surface just smiling"), cover, and leave the chicken to poach gently until the flesh is very soft and coming away from the bones – usually in about 20 to 30 minutes.

Meanwhile, in a reasonably large saucepan, begin the cooking of the vegetables. Place the pan over gentle frying heat, lubricate its bottom with 2 more tablespoons of the olive oil and, without waiting for it to heat up, add: the chopped onions, the sliced leeks, the chopped tomatoes, the sliced carrots, the chopped celery and fennel, plus the 6 cloves of garlic, whole and unpeeled. Let them all, as Georges says, "sweat" in the oil, stirring them around fairly continuously, for about 2 or 3 minutes. Do not let them fry or brown. Then adjust the heat to simmering and pour in enough of the remaining chicken bouillon to cover the vegetables so that they are about half an inch below the surface of the liquid. Adjust the heat to gentle simmering and add: the saffron with its soaking wine, thoroughly rinsing out the small saucepan so as not to lose any of its oils; the tablespoon of chopped thyme;

the bay leaf, crumbled; plus salt and pepper to taste. Leave the vegetables to poach, covered, until they are just soft but still crisp – usually in about 7 to 10 minutes. When the vegetables are just right, turn off the heat and fish out the garlic cloves. They should still be whole, but now quite mushy inside the skins. Depending on how much garlic flavor you like, pinch a few or all of the garlic cloves and squeeze the mush into the vegetables. Discard the skins. Hold the vegetables off the fire to wait for the chicken.

About 15 minutes before serving

When the chicken is perfectly done, turn off the heat, lift the pieces out of the bouillon with a slotted spoon, remove and discard all bones and cut the flesh into bite-sized chunks. Add them to the saucepan with the vegetables. Also pour into this saucepan the remaining bouillon from the sauté pan, so as to amalgamate all the flavors. Now reheat, stirring everything, just to gentle simmering. Stir in the 4 tablespoons of chopped basil. Add, tablespoon by tablespoon the Pernod or Ricard until you have a very slight taste of licorice – I usually add about 4 tablespoons. Then carefully melt onto the surface of the liquid, curl by curl, the 4 tablespoons of sweet butter. Finally, taste and adjust seasonings.

Serving at table

Georges does not believe in serving this in a tureen, where it will begin to cool before it is all ladled out, but directly into very hot individual soup bowls, or equally hot wide soup plates. Into these, first using a slotted spoon, put a balanced blend of the various vegetables, chicken and basil leaves. Then ladle over the top enough of the aromatic bouillon to cover the solids and reasonably fill the bowls or plates. With this sustaining and warming stew, Chef Blanc served me a noble orangey-pink Tavel from the Rhône Valley. Its approximate American equivalent might be a California Grenache or Zinfandel rosé from Monterey or the Santa Clara Valley.

FINAL NOTE: If you are prepared to put up with some extra richness, Georges will serve you his *potage pistou* with that heavenly Provençal variation of garlic mayonnaise, called *"rouille."* The recipe for an authentic Provençal version is on page 139.

BASQUE PEASANT SOUP OF SALT COD AND PUMPKIN

(for 4)

This tasty and simple peasant soup – after some judicious reduction of the original amounts of the butter and cream – fits well into the Low-High pattern. The pot cheese as a thickener gives excellent body to the soup, with none of the traditional heavy cream. Don't hesitate to prepare it a day or two in advance of your dinner party, as its balance of flavors and textures improves with a few days of keeping.

Salt cod, best quality (½ lb)
Butter, lightly salted (about
  4 Tbs)
Yellow onion, peeled, chopped
  (1 medium)
Potatoes, peeled, coarsely diced
  (2 medium)
Leek whites, carefully washed
  and desanded, quartered
  lengthwise (2 medium)

Pumpkin, preferably fresh,
  chunked – or canned (¾ cup)
Chicken bouillon, clear (4 cups)
Pot cheese, low-fat (1 cup)
Yoghurt, plain, low-fat (⅓ cup)
Ricotta, Italian style, low-fat
  (3 Tbs)
Salt, coarse crystal, to taste
Black pepper, freshly ground,
  to taste

**The day before – soaking the cod – active work
about 10 minutes**

Remove all skin and bones from the pieces of cod. Wash them thoroughly under cold water, brushing or scraping off any encrusted salt, then soak the fish in cold water for about 15 hours in a covered ceramic or glass pot in the refrigerator. Change the water roughly every 5 hours.

About 2 hours before serving – active work about 35 minutes, plus about 1¼ hours of unsupervised simmering

Wash the cod pieces once more. On a wooden cutting board, cut up the cod into bite-size squares, watching carefully for any bones you may have overlooked earlier. Choose a lidded pot, for top burner use, of heatproof glass, earthenware, or enameled cast iron. Do not cook it in direct contact with any metal or the fish will darken. Put in the cod squares and just cover with cold water. Bring it gently up to boiling. The moment the first bubbles appear, turn off the heat and leave the fish soaking until it is needed for the main pot. Salt cod boiled hard becomes as tough as leather.

Set a sauté pan, large enough to hold all the vegetables, over moderate frying heat. Melt two tablespoons of the butter, then add, in turn: the chopped onion, the diced potatoes, the quartered leeks and the ¾ cup of pumpkin. With a wooden spoon, gently work everything together, then let it all lightly poach in the butter, without browning or frying, until everything is nicely soft – usually in about 15 minutes. If the bottom of the pan dries out, add a minimum amount of extra butter.

Set a 4-quart soup kettle on a top burner, but do not yet turn on the heat. This is a good moment to drain the salt cod, holding the liquid in a jug and the solid fish in a bowl. As soon as the vegetables in the sauté pan are done, turn out the entire contents into the soup kettle. Add the 4 cups of chicken bouillon, plus 2 cups of the salt cod water. Bring it all up to boiling, then adjust the heat to gentle simmering, covered, for 1 hour.

Meanwhile, prepare the pot cheese thickener. I put the cup of pot cheese, the ⅓ cup of yoghurt, and the 3 tablespoons of ricotta into the bowl of my Cuisinart chopper-churner. (Or you can use an electric blender – see page 82.) I run the machine for 7 or 8 seconds, which should give a low-fat white cream with the approximate consistency of whipped cream. Transfer the mixture to a round-bottomed bowl and beat furiously with a large balloon wire whisk using high, whipping strokes to get as much air in as possible until the mixture is fluffy and light – usually about 3 to 4 minutes.

About 10 minutes before serving

Pass the soup through a food mill several times, if necessary, until it is coarsely smooth. It should not be a mushy purée. I like to feel a few bits on the tongue. Put this purée back into the soup kettle, stir in 4 tablespoons of the pot cheese thickening cream and add the squares of salt cod. Now add salt and pepper to taste, remembering that the cod will have provided most of the required salt. Turn on the heat again under the kettle, bring everything almost but not quite to the boiling point, then serve at once in hot bowls. With this warming concoction, I used to have a noble, white, Spanish Rioja, from the vineyards of the Marqués de Murrieta. An American equivalent might be an earthy, fruity California white Riesling from Monterey.

A CURATIVE CONSOMMÉ FOR A LADY IN DISTRESS

(for 1 lady)

The last time I visited the quiet little village of Eugénie-les-Bains in the foothills of the Pyrenees mountains in southwestern France, I had a problem on my hands. We were to dine that evening with the brilliant young Chef Michel Guérard (page 35) in his two-star restaurant, Le Pot au Feu, in the luxurious, small spa-hotel which he and his wife own and run in the hot-springs village named after Napoleon's Empress Eugénie. Before reaching Eugénie, we had dined superluxuriously night after night across France, so it was no surprise when one lady in our party began feeling the pinch around her middle. In French terms, she had a small *crise de foie*. In spite of the magnetic promise of *Grande Guérard Gastronomie* in the form of a specially prepared dinner in our honor, the lady could find neither the appetite nor the strength to come down to the Pot au Feu dining room. So Michel – always a man of warm sympathy – sent up to her room a bottle of the driest and iciest Champagne, a pot of superb Chinese Keemun tea and a bowl of entirely wonderful, clear, hot, restorative, strengthening consommé, garnished with miniature doses of fresh garden vegetables shredded as finely as the feathers on angels' wings. No doctor could possibly have ordered such a supremely effective prescription. The lady analyzed each spoonful and wrote down every detail in her notebook. Together, in New York, we have translated, adapted and reconstructed this regal recipe. The lady will always be eternally grateful to Docteur Guérard.

In his professional kitchen, Michel always has an unlimited supply of perfectly made, brilliantly clear, warmly colored "white stock," which has slowly simmered through the night with beef and chicken and aromatic herbs and vegetables. When I want to serve this consommé, either to restore my stomach or someone else's or just as a light and sparkling beginning to a dinner party, I begin by preparing my own basic Low-High bouillon (page 68). Beyond preparing the basic stock the day before, there is nothing to this recipe except the delicate work of cutting the vegetables with the sharpest of knives into miniature matchsticks and transparently thin little wisps, which are the marvel of this soup. I do assure you that the result is worth the trouble. You will be praised as a professional, both in terms of gastronomic balance and technical skill.

Carrot, small, young, scraped (1)

Celery, white (1 small young stalk)

Mushroom, small, very white (1)

Tomato, cherry, peeled and seeded (1)

Bouillon, clear, best you can muster, see above (1¼ cups)

Chives, fresh, very finely minced (¼ tsp)

Dill, fresh stalks, very finely minced (¼ tsp)

(Or, if these two herbs are not available, substitute fresh parsley and/or any other fresh herb – never use dried herbs in this recipe)

Assuming the bouillon is ready – preparation time about 15 minutes

Since the bouillon will be perfectly seasoned, salt and pepper are not included in the ingredients. Using a paring knife, scrape thin slices from the carrot and celery. Then, with a small chef's knife cut the slices lengthwise with downward strokes into the thinnest possible strands. Assemble the strands in a bunch and cut them into ¾-inch lengths. Stop when you have filled 2 tablespoons. Hold them in a small covered jar to prevent drying out. Remove the stem from your mushroom and wipe the cap clean. Never wash it, since it will absorb water and lose flavor. Holding the cap down firmly on the cutting board, slice it, crosswise, into the thinnest little sheets you can manage. Then, with the sharp point of a smaller knife, cut the slices into tiny triangles each a bit smaller than a dime. Stop when you have filled 1 tablespoon. Hold these in a small covered jar. After you have skinned and de-pitted the cherry tomato, finely dice the flesh and hold, also covered. Remember to mince the green herbs finely, and pre-heat your consommé cup.

In a small saucepan, bring the 1¼-cups of bouillon up to gentle simmering. Add the carrot and celery matchsticks and simmer them, covered, until they are just done but still quite crispy – usually in 5 minutes. Then add the diced tomato and simmer, again covered, for 2 minutes more. Add the mushroom triangles, count 10 seconds, then turn off the heat and serve this curative consommé in a warm, handsome double-handled cup with a matching saucer and a silver spoon. Just before handing it to the distressed person, lightly sprinkle the top surface with the fresh chives and dill. Dry, thin toast is a good accompaniment provided the patient is not too distressed. If the patient is thirsty, the only possible accompaniment is ice-cold brut Champagne – French, Californian, or New York State.

DUCK SOUP SEALED IN A DRY SACK INSIDE A DOUBLE STEAMER

(for 4 – with some left over)

This is probably the world's most fatless soup, since it cannot successfully be prepared unless every last speck of fat is carefully and deliberately removed. It has been known to the Chinese for at least two thousand years. This noble soup, in its healthy digestibility, its lightness and its simplicity, is more *nouvelle* than even the most *nouvelle* of any *nouvelle cuisine*. It ought to be made, of course, with the very finest of Chinese rice wine, but, since none is exported by the wise Chinese, I am advised by a connoisseur friend from Peking that the closest alternative is the Spanish Dry Sack Sherry.

The "last word" on this classic Chinese dish has been written by Madame Lin Yutang in her charming and erudite book, *Chinese Gastronomy*, in which she and her daughter report that Chinese manners require that the host at a feast must deprecate his food to his guests. When duck cooked in wine is served, the host will say, "This is only a little duck, cooked with a little wine." It is, in fact, "an extraordinary combination of duck and wine, in which each spoonful of wine tastes as if it were duck and each fibre of duck tastes as if it were wine." The duck has to be "cooked in a sealed casserole, placed in boiling water," because the boiling point of the alcohol in the Sherry is lower than that of water – after a while the Sherry will begin to boil and this is why the lid of the inner casserole must fit extremely tightly, so that there can be no evaporation of the Sherry. Finally, because of the careful clarification, the soup comes out crystal clear, every trace of fat and oil having been removed, "so that the soup finally attains the clarity of brandy." The Sherry causes the duck "to separate into fibres, so that, finally, it resembles a bowl of unearthly noodle soup, consisting of very fine strands of duck meat floating in the crystal-clear broth. A small bowlful of this soup is strong enough to revive the dead!"

Duck, all visible fat removed (1 of 4–5 lbs)	**Sherry, preferably Spanish Dry Sack, of course (2 full bottles)**
Salt, coarse crystal, to taste	
Black pepper, freshly ground, to taste	**Scallions, finely minced (½ cup)**

Two days before serving – active work about 15 minutes

Thoroughly clean the duck and cut away every scrap of fat, including opening up the skin and getting out all the fat pads under the wings and all around the body. Carefully dry the duck then rub it, inside and out, with plenty of salt and black pepper. Tightly wrap the carcass in foil and leave it to absorb the salt and pepper in the refrigerator overnight.

The day before serving – active work about 15 minutes plus 4 hours of entirely unsupervised simmering and steaming

The key to success with this method is to have two tightly lidded, large casseroles, *cocottes,* or soup pots, of precisely the right sizes. One must fit easily within the other, leaving enough extra room in the larger one for a fair supply of boiling water. The French Le Creuset enameled, heavy iron *cocottes* come in appropriate sizes. Once you have chosen your casseroles take the duck out of the refrigerator. Open its aluminum covering in the sink, as a good deal of juice will have run out. Again, thoroughly dry the duck, inside and out. Now, with heavy poultry shears, cut the duck into four quarters. Place these, neatly and fairly tightly, into the smaller pot. Pour in enough from the 2 bottles of Sherry just to cover the duck, but, in any case, reserve 1 cup of the Sherry for later use. Put the lid on the pot – it absolutely must be a very tight lid – and set this pot inside the larger one. Pour boiling water into the larger pot until the level comes up to within 1½ inches below the top edge of the smaller pot. Put this entire Rube Goldberg contraption onto a large top burner and bring the water up to merry bubbling, clamp the lid on the larger pot and keep everything going for 4 hours. Every now and then add more boiling water, as needed, to keep up the level with which you started. Under no circumstances open up the lid of the inner pot. At the end of the 4 hours, turn off the heat and let everything gradually cool back to room temperature. Resist any temptation to open up the inner lid. Let everything stand as it is overnight.

The morning of the serving day – active work about 20 minutes

Now, at last, lift the inner lid, take out all the pieces of duck and lay them on a large cutting board or work surface. Pick over the duck as finely as if you were panning for gold. Remove every particle of fat, bit of bone, scrap of skin – only the lean flesh, now delicately pink and fibrous, is to be piled up in one corner of the board, eventually to go back into the soup. Minutely skim off all fat from the liquid in the smaller pot. Strain this liquid to remove any odd bits of fat that might have been left floating around in it. Pour the clear, strained liquid back into the smaller pot and then add all the pure duck flesh, the reserved cup of Dry Sack and, if taste approves, a final pinch of salt. Empty the big pot of all its cold water and, once again, place the tightly lidded smaller pot inside it.

About 2 hours before serving – final unsupervised simmering

Again, as before, fill the outer pot with boiling water to 1½ inches below the top edge of the inner pot. Bring it up to merry bubbling and keep it going, with the lid on the larger pot, for 2 hours. Add more boiling water, as necessary. Resist all temptation to open the lid of the inner pot. At the end of the time, turn off the heat, lift out the inner pot, wipe it clean and dry, say, "Open Sesame," lift the lid and serve the lovely soup with proper proportions of the duck meat. Sprinkle each bowl or plate at table with the chopped green scallions. To drink with it, have small Sherry glasses of Dry Sack.

POTAGE OF FROGS' LEGS WITH SHRIMP AND WATERCRESS ENTIRELY WITHOUT BUTTER OR CREAM

(for 4)

When this extraordinary soup was first served to me by Chef Michel Guérard (page 35), at his two-star Le Pot au Feu in Eugénie-les-Bains, it was a revelation of the success of the new cuisine. A few weeks earlier, I had been shown how to make a classic frogs' leg soup by one of the great French chefs of New York. Its marvelous richness was achieved by the inclusion of eight tablespoons of butter, half a cup of flour, a good deal of milk, eight tablespoons of heavy cream and at least two cholesterol-loaded egg yolks! All this richness is eliminated by our

basic "Crème de Fromage Maigre" (page 77). The day before, you will need to make up a batch of the Low-High basic
fish bouillon (page 70) and boil the shrimp by the basic method
(page 84).

Fish fumet or bouillon, made
  in advance, see above
  (about 4 cups)
Frogs' legs, from fancy fish
  store (1 doz pairs)
Salt, coarse crystal, to taste
Black pepper, freshly ground,
  to taste
Nutmeg, freshly ground,
  to taste
Shrimp, see above (16–20,
  according to size)

Watercress, leaves only
  (3 bunches)
Shallots, finely minced (6 Tbs)
Tarragon, fresh leaves in
  season (1 small bunch)
White wine, slightly soft,
  California Chenin Blanc or
  French Graves (2½ cups)
Pot cheese, low-fat (1 cup)
Yoghurt, plain, low-fat (⅓ cup)
Ricotta, Italian style, low-fat
  (3 Tbs)

Preparation in about 45 minutes

Assuming that you have prepared the 4 cups of fish bouillon in
advance, put it into a 3-quart saucepan and bring it up to a
boil. Add the 2 dozen frogs' legs, plus salt and pepper and a
grind or two of nutmeg to taste, and simmer them, covered,
until they are just done – usually in about 15 minutes. Then
take them out of the bouillon (saving the bouillon), and let
them cool. Pre-heat your oven to keep-warm temperature
(150°F.), and set in it the lidded tureen in which the soup will
be served. Bone the legs, keeping their flesh in bite-size
slivers. When you complete the boning, put the slivers of
frogs' legs and the shrimp into the tureen to warm.

    With kitchen scissors, snip the leaves from the three
bunches of watercress and spread them evenly across the dry
bottom of a fair-sized sauté pan. Sprinkle over the leaves the
6 tablespoons of chopped shallots and the tarragon leaves, with
salt and plenty of pepper to taste. Wet it all down with the
2½ cups of soft white wine and bring it rapidly up to a boil to
eliminate the alcohol. Pour the bouillon from the frogs' legs
into the sauté pan. Adjust heat to gentle simmering and con-

tinue, covered, for no more than 5 minutes, or the watercress will lose its bright green color.

While this simmering is in progress, prepare the thickening white cheese cream. I put the cup of pot cheese, the ⅓ cup of yoghurt, and the 3 tablespoons of ricotta into the bowl of my Cuisinart chopper-churner (or you can use an electric blender — see page 82). I run the machine for about 7 to 8 seconds until everything is smooth and blended. Turn this out into a mixing bowl and arm yourself with a balloon wire whisk and beat until you achieve first the consistency of heavy cream and finally, as you continue beating with circular lifting strokes to get in as much air as possible, the consistency of a fluffy Chantilly, or whipped cream. Hold it aside until you need it.

As soon as the timer rings for the sauté pan, purée its entire contents. I pass it first through my chopper-churner and then rub it with a wooden pestle through a fairly fine-meshed round-bottomed sieve. You can use an electric blender and/or a food mill. You should end up with a smooth green purée. Put the purée back into the sauté pan and gently reheat it to just below boiling. While it is heating, smoothly beat in with a whisk, tablespoon by tablespoon, the pot-cheese whip until you have exactly the creamy consistency you want. Finally, taste and adjust seasonings. The moment the soup is hot enough, pour it into the tureen over the frogs' legs and shrimp, and serve it at once in hot soup bowls. With this magnificent concoction, Chef Guérard served me a noble, aromatic, dry Château Laville-Haut-Brion from the Graves district of Bordeaux. At my New York table, I might serve an American wine of equivalent character, perhaps a noble California Pinot Chardonnay from the Monte Bello or Pinnacles districts of Monterey.

HERBED AND SPICED MUSHROOM SOUP WITHOUT BUTTER OR CREAM

(for 4)

Anyone who has ever prepared classic French high-cuisine mushroom soup knows that the mushrooms begin in a sauté pan slathered with butter. Then, after the bouillon has been added, it is enriched with lashings of heavy cream and often thickened with a butter-flour *roux*. All these ancient and over-rich trappings were absent from the delightfully light mushroom soup served to me by Chef Michel Guérard (page 35), at his two-star Le Pot au Feu, at Eugénie-les-Bains. For this American adaptation much depends, of course, on the excellence of the base bouillon. We are at a slight disadvantage compared with Michel who, in his French country kitchen, has wild mushrooms available to add their earthy fragrances to the bouillon. But we can find dried wild mushrooms, mainly in Chinese and Italian groceries, and these add measurably to the final quality of the soup. The day before preparing this recipe, I make a batch of the basic Low-High beef and chicken bouillon (see page 68).

Olive oil, pure green virgin (1 Tbs)	Caraway seeds, whole (½ tsp)
Yellow onion, peeled, finely chopped (1 medium)	Mace chips, freshly ground (½ tsp)
Mushrooms, fresh, wiped clean and with caps and stems thinly sliced (1 lb)	Marjoram, sweet, usually dried (½ tsp)
Dried mushrooms, see above, soaked in warm water until soft, then rinsed and chopped (2-oz package)	Tomato, peeled, deseeded, finely diced (1 medium)
	Salt, coarse crystal, to taste
Garlic, finely minced (1 clove)	Black pepper, freshly ground, to taste
White wine, dry (¼ cup)	Chives, fresh in season, minced (2 tsp)
Bouillon, basic Low-High, see above (6 cups)	

Preparation in about 30 minutes

In the bottom of a 4-quart saucepan or soup kettle heat the tablespoon of olive oil to frying temperature. Add the chopped onion and gently sauté until the onions are just transparent and beginning to melt (avoid frying or browning), usually in 2–3 minutes. Hold back about a dozen of the prettiest mushroom slices for garnishing the serving bowls and add the rest of the slices to the saucepan with the dried mushrooms and minced garlic. Stir everything around and let it poach. The mushrooms will release their water, which will bubble merrily. When this bubbling subsides, you know that the unwanted water has evaporated, usually in 3–5 minutes. The thirsty mushrooms are now ready to suck up the wine, so add the ¼ cup of white wine and adjust the heat so that it bubbles fairly hard, reducing it to concentrate and sharpen the flavors.

Meanwhile, heat up the 6 cups of bouillon in a separate saucepan just to boiling. Now pour the boiling bouillon over the mushrooms. Stir in the ½ teaspoon of caraway seeds, the ½ teaspoon of ground mace and the ½ teaspoon of marjoram. Stir again and let simmer, covered, for 15 minutes. While waiting, amuse yourself by cutting the remaining mushroom slices, with a sharp-pointed small knife, into decorative little circles and triangles. Hold, covered.

I then purée the soup by passing it, in batches, through my Cuisinart chopper-churner (or you can use an electric blender, or a hand food mill), running the machine only long enough to mix and purée everything, but not so long that it becomes a mushy paste – usually for about 5 seconds. Return the purée to the saucepan and reheat it to just below boiling. At the same time, add the diced tomato. Taste, stirring in salt and pepper to please your tongue. This final stage should not take more than 2 to 3 minutes, or the refreshing touch of the tomato will be lost. Serve at once, very hot, in warm individual soup bowls, the surface of the soup decorated and garnished with the mushroom bits and the green minced chives. With this, Chef Guérard served me a softly refreshing Alsatian Riesling which might be replaced in the United States with a white Riesling (sometimes labeled Johannisberg Riesling) from the Napa Valley of California.

THE LOW-HIGH VERSION OF THE MAGNIFICENT MUSSEL SOUP OF CHEFS JEAN AND PIERRE TROISGROS

(for 4)

This is one of the great recipes which made the fame of the brothers Troisgros (page 50) and helped to earn them their three stars at their restaurant in Roanne. Within the last few months, the brothers have been rethinking some of their most famous recipes, reducing the use of butter and cream along the principles of the new cuisine. In my translation adapted to the American way, I have replaced the Troisgros final thickening of heavy cream with the Low-High thickening of whipped, low-fat white pot cheese. This recipe requires the advance preparation of a batch of the Low-High fish bouillon from page 70. In its new American version, this remains one of the great soups of the world.

Fish bouillon, basic Low-High, see above (2 quarts)
Mussels, fresh (about 4½ lbs)
Flour, for cleaning the mussels (3 or 4 handfuls)
Salt, coarse crystal, to taste
Saffron filaments (1 tsp)
White wine, dry (½ cup plus 2 Tbs)
Carrots, finely minced (3 medium)
Yellow onions, finely minced (2 medium)
Leek whites, washed and desanded, finely minced (3)

Olive oil, pure green virgin (1 Tbs)
Garlic, peeled and finely minced (2 cloves)
Tomatoes, peeled and chopped (5 medium)
Thyme, fresh (1 small bunch)
Shallots, finely minced (2 cloves)
White pepper, freshly ground, to taste
Pot cheese, low-fat (¾ cup)
Yoghurt, plain, low-fat (¼ cup)
Ricotta, Italian style, low-fat (2 Tbs)

The day before – cleaning and fattening the mussels – soaking overnight

Prepare the basic Low-High fish bouillon. Pile the mussels in the sink under cold running water and arm yourself with a stiff wire brush and an old oyster knife. Pull off the beards, and scrape off all the clinging seaweed and barnacles until the shells "shine." Discard any half-open shells, which indicate that their owners are in a poor state of health, and any that are suspiciously heavy with internal sand. Then put them into a large bowl, cover with water, and salt to the taste of the sea. Having made the mussels feel at home, give them a Roman feast with the food that is their caviar. Throw in 3 or 4 handfuls of flour and stir around to distribute evenly. Within a few minutes there will be a gentle stirring and scraping as the mussels open up to gorge on the flour. Set the bowl in the refrigerator, where the feast continues all night, until the mussels have glutted themselves to a fat whiteness, at the same time throwing out all excrement and dirt. In the morning the water is black, and when the mussels have once more been thoroughly rinsed under cold running water they are ready for cooking.

About 1¼ hours before serving – active preparation about 35 minutes, plus about 40 minutes of unsupervised simmering

Put the teaspoon of saffron filaments into a tiny saucepan with 2 tablespoons of the wine, then warm it to just above blood heat so that the bright yellow oils and pigments of the saffron are dissolved into the wine, and leave it, covered. In the bottom of a 4-quart soup kettle sauté the minced carrots, onions, and leek whites with the tablespoon of olive oil for 2 or 3 minutes. Do not let the vegetables brown. Then add the minced garlic, the chopped tomatoes, the saffron with its wine (carefully rinsing out the tiny saucepan with a tablespoon of the fish bouillon), the thyme, and the 2 quarts of fish bouillon. Let it all gently bubble, uncovered, for about 40 minutes.

Meanwhile, take the mussels from the refrigerator. Drain and wash them thoroughly under running cold water. Put them into a lidded pot large enough to hold them all, then sprinkle over them the minced shallots, plus ½ cup of wine. Over highest heat, bring it to a rolling boil, so that the pot is filled with steam, then clamp on the lid tightly and, occasionally shaking the pot vigorously to encourage the mussels to open, leave it over highest heat for about 5 to 7 minutes. After 5 minutes begin checking and, as each mussel opens, take it out with pincers and let it cool. Continue boiling and shaking the pot until every last mussel has opened. Then, turn off the heat and carefully strain the cooking liquor (which is now marvelously flavored by the juices of the mussels) to get rid of all sand. Reserve the strained liquor. As soon as the mussels are cool enough to handle, remove the meats and drop them back into the liquor, discarding all the shells.

Now prepare the thickening pot cheese whip. I put the ¾ cup of pot cheese, the ¼ cup of yoghurt and the 2 tablespoons of ricotta into my Cuisinart chopper-churner (see page 80) (or you can use a blender). I run the machine for 7 or 8 seconds until blended and smooth and more or less the texture of sour cream, or French *crème fraîche*. Turn this out into a mixing bowl and, arming yourself with a balloon wire whisk, gradually beat until you achieve first, the consistency of heavy cream and finally, as you continue beating with circular lifting stokes to get in as much air as possible, the consistency of a fluffy Chantilly, or whipped cream. Hold it aside until you need it.

About 5 minutes before serving

Add the mussels and their cooking liquor to the main soup pot. Carefully beat in with the wire whisk, tablespoon by tablespoon, the pot cheese whip until you have the exact creamy consistency you want. Taste and adjust the seasonings, adding salt and pepper as needed, then serve at once, extremely hot. With this superb soup, the brothers Troisgros served me a noble, dry, tartly refreshing, white Sancerre from the Loire. This might be replaced by an American equivalent – perhaps a California Napa Fumé Blanc.

CHRISTMAS OR THANKSGIVING PUMPKIN INSIDE A PUMPKIN

(for 4)

Chef Paul Bocuse (see page 26) has proved to me many times in the last ten years at his three-star restaurant in Collonges-au-Mont-d'Or that pumpkin need not always be in a pie. It also comes in his *soupe de potiron*. With a dramatic Bocuse gesture, he heats and serves his soup inside the pumpkin shell.

This requires a pumpkin of about 6–8 pounds. Choose one that stands reasonably straight and cut it across the stalk end to provide a lid. I disagree with Bocuse, however, about cooking it inside the pumpkin shell. I prefer to prepare it in a thick-bottomed, tightly lidded casserole to ensure precise control of the cooking. The essential trick is to avoid overmashing the pumpkin. When you eat it, tiny bits should burst in your mouth, releasing the fruity freshness of the juice. During the heating, it does have a slight tendency to stick, so treat it gently and stir it fairly continuously. The recipe also involves the advance preparation of a batch of the basic Low-High beef-chicken bouillon (see page 68). Finally, you bring it to table in the heated pumpkin shell.

Pumpkin (6–8 lbs)
Salt butter (6 Tbs)
Yellow onions, finely chopped
  (1½ medium)
Beef bouillon, basic Low-High
  (1 pint)
Pot cheese, low-fat (1 cup)
Yoghurt, plain, low-fat (⅓ cup)
Ricotta, Italian style, low-fat
  (3 Tbs)

Meat extract, or meat glaze,
  French glace-de-viande,
  see page 78 (1 Tbs)
Milk (1 pint)
Salt, coarse crystal, to taste
Black pepper, to taste
Watercress (1 small bunch)
Parsley (1 small bunch)
Paprika, sweet Hungarian,
  to taste

The day before – active work about 30 minutes plus about 30 minutes unsupervised simmering

Using a long knife or hacksaw, cut off the top of the pumpkin to form the lid. Remove and discard the seeds and fibrous pulp. Now, with a sharp-edged spoon, begin scraping out the flesh (leave the walls at least 1 inch thick) until you have about 2 quarts of largish chunks. I then set an enameled cast iron *cocotte*, or casserole, that holds about 4 quarts, over medium frying heat. Melt 1½ tablespoons of the butter in it and sauté the chopped onions to just golden. Meanwhile, in a separate pan heat the pint of beef bouillon to boiling, then pour it over the sizzling onions. Return the mixture to a boil, add the pumpkin and simmer, covered, until soft, usually in 20 to 30 minutes. Overcooking will dilute the flavor. Then drain (reserving the beef liquid), press the pumpkin through a coarse sieve or a hand food mill. (An electric blender can be used, but only for a few seconds or it will reduce the pumpkin to an over-smooth cream.) The pumpkin purée will now be very thick and some of the beef liquid should be stirred in, but only enough to make it smooth. In this form it rests overnight, covered, in the refrigerator. The remaining bouillon and the pumpkin tureen are also refrigerated.

On the day – about 45 minutes before serving – preparing the pumpkin tureen

Preheat your oven to 350°F. Take the pumpkin tureen from the refrigerator and place it in the oven so that it is thoroughly warmed when it receives the soup.

Now prepare the pot cheese whip which gives the soup its creamy consistency. I put the cup of pot cheese, the ⅓ cup of yoghurt, and the 3 tablespoons of ricotta into my Cuisinart chopper-churner. I run the machine for 7 to 8 seconds for a paste, more or less the texture of sour cream or the French *crème fraîche*. Turn this out into a mixing bowl and, arming yourself with a balloon wire whisk, beat until you achieve the consistency of heavy cream. Hold it aside while you carefully reheat the pumpkin mixture in a thick-bottomed pan. Steadily stir with a wooden spoon, blending in the tablespoon of meat extract. Gradually thin the soup with alternating cupfuls of the milk and beef bouillon to reach the flavor balance and thickness you like. Season to taste with salt and pepper.

The moment the soup is again boiling, take the pumpkin tureen out of the oven, pour the soup in it and put it all back in the oven to stay piping hot until the moment of serving. Remember to warm the soup bowls.

Serving at table

Bring the pot cheese whip, the chopped watercress and parsley in small bowls to the table. It is best for two people to do the serving: one ladling, the other stirring in the cheese whip, sprinkling on a small circle of red paprika and a larger circle of parsley and watercress (all according to your guests' tastes, of course). With this Chef Bocuse, on his home ground, serves a white Beaujolais. On my home ground, I might substitute a white Riesling (sometimes labeled Johannisberg Riesling) from the Santa Clara Valley of California.

THE BLACK TRUFFLE SOUP OF THE ÉLYSÉE PALACE

(for 4)

When the President of the French Republic, Monsieur Valéry Giscard d'Estaing, decided to award France's highest civilian medal, the Cross of a Chevalier of the Legion of Honor, to Chef Paul Bocuse (page 26), he planned a ceremonial lunch for all the great establishment chefs at the Élysée Palace, the White House of France. The menu was Olympian. Each of the great chefs provided a dish from his native region, with the fresh ingredients brought to Paris that day. Paul contributed the first course, a fantastic, super-colossal, unbelievably luxurious soup made almost entirely of fresh black truffles – at an estimated cost of more than $200 for every four servings. In case you should ever decide to spend that kind of money on a single dish, you might find my translated and adapted version of the Bocuse spectacular quite handy. Since Paul is the originator of the new, lighter, less fattening cuisine, I am sure he will not resent the fact that I, guided by Low-High principles, have cut out his butter-layered flaky pastry crust, his cubes of foie gras and his jubilantly wild excesses of butter and cream. This version, I think, is still worthy of the Élysée Palace and would certainly interfere less with the efficiency of Monsieur le Président during the after-lunch remainder of his working day.

Sweet butter (2 Tbs)
Onions, white boiling, finely chopped (5)
Carrots, scraped and finely chopped (3 medium)
White celery, finely chopped (2 good stalks)

Mushrooms, fresh, good white color, finely sliced (½ lb)
Ham, dark-smoked, country-style, entirely lean, coarsely diced (¼ lb)
Black truffles, fresh, imported by air (1 lb)

Black truffle juice, imported
   in jars, from very fancy food
   shops (1 cup)
White vermouth, dry (½ cup)
Chicken bouillon, clear and
   strong (1½ cups)

Salt, coarse crystal, to taste
Black pepper, freshly ground,
   to taste

Active work about 30 minutes, plus 35 minutes unsupervised baking – may be prepared several hours ahead and reheated just before serving

In the bottom of a sauté pan, preferably thick copper, melt the 2 tablespoons of butter over medium frying heat. When it is melted, add the chopped onions, carrots, and celery, stirring them around until they begin to soften – usually in about 10 minutes. Then add the sliced mushrooms which very soon expel their water, causing bubbling and hissing. When this subsides – usually in 5–7 minutes – you know that the unwanted water has evaporated. Now add the diced ham, which needs only to be warmed through – usually in 3 minutes. Do not let any of the vegetables become overcooked and mushy for they must stand up to the crispness of the truffles. Now lovingly brush the truffles, cut them into coarse dice and hold them, covered.

This soup is best assembled and served in individual, lidded, heatproof pottery casseroles – of the kind that are often used for French onion soup. As soon as the mixture in the sauté pan is ready, spread it in equal parts across the bottom of each serving casserole. Divide the diced truffles into 4 equal parts and layer them into the casseroles. In a separate bowl mix together the cup of truffle juice, the ½ cup of vermouth and the 1½ cups of chicken bouillon. Taste the mixture and season it, if necessary, with extra salt and pepper, as pleases you. Spoon this liquid into each casserole to within ¾ of an inch from the top edge and cover with the lids. At this point, you may either heat up the casseroles immediately for serving, or set them in the refrigerator to wait until later in the day.

About 35 minutes before serving

Turn on your oven to 450°F. and set the four casseroles in the center. Heat them up until they are almost, but not quite, to the boiling point. Serve them at once, removing the lid as each casserole is set before the diner. The first whiff of the aroma is worth the $200. With this extraordinary soup, the President of France served a great white Burgundy, a Le Montrachet of the Domaine de la Romanée-Conti. On the American side, this great French wine could be replaced only by one of the noblest of California's Pinot Chardonnays from one of the great vineyards of the Napa Valley.

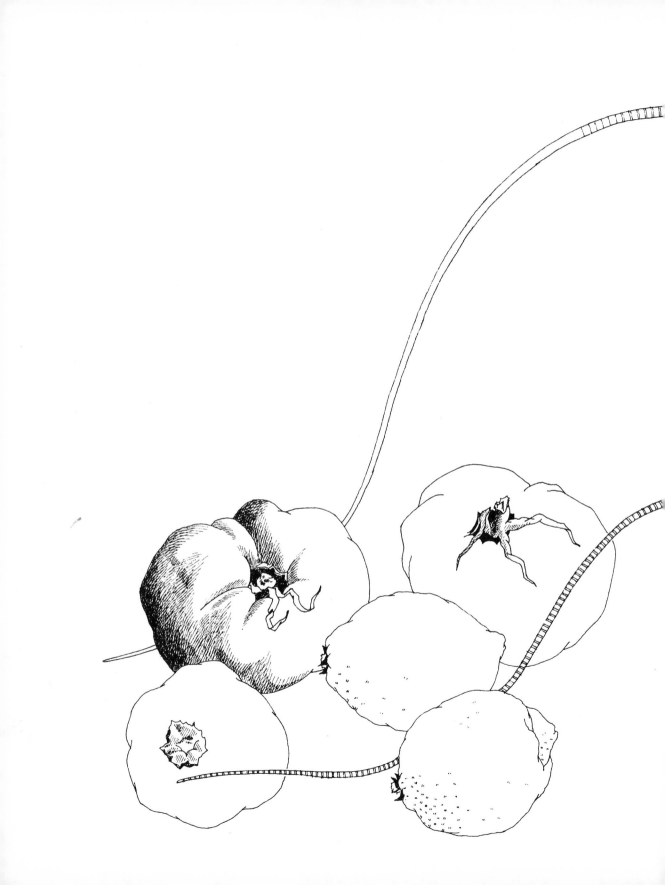

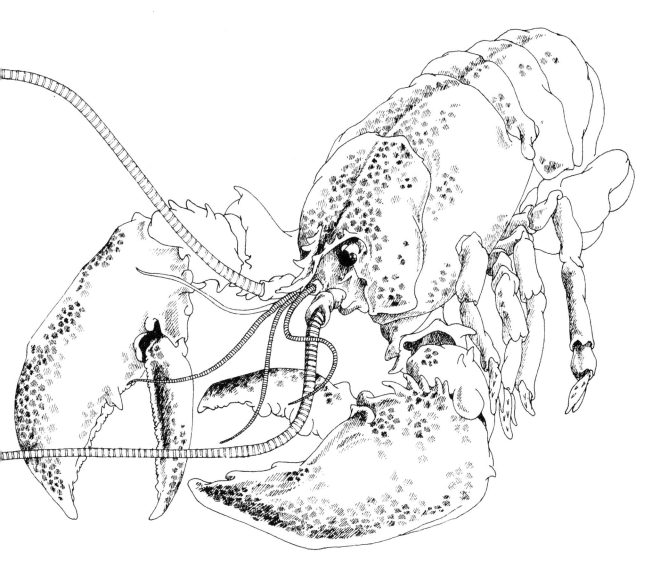

Chapter Seven
Fish and Shellfish

in which the perfect Lobster makes several
appearances, and various Fish of the sea are baked
in Salt, steamed in Parsley, poached in Bouillon,
bedded on Vegetables, wrapped in Lettuce,
interspersed with Mixed Fruit, and assembled
in a grand Pot au Feu.

CHEF MICHEL GUÉRARD'S SECRETS OF THE LOW-FAT COOKING OF FISH

After a superb dinner prepared for me by Michel at his two-star Restaurant Le Pot au Feu in Eugénie-les-Bains, we strolled in the gardens of the small resort hotel that he runs with his wife. The hotel is called Les Prés et les Sources d'Eugénie, "The Hotel of the Lawns and Springs of Eugénie." It was the beginning of October, yet we were surrounded by the extraordinary ambience of semitropical and tropical plants. Banana trees splayed out their ten-foot leaves. Orchid-like flowers were still in bloom. "You see our earth is warmed," Michel said, "by the hot spring waters rising to the surface all around us. It is good for the plants and also good for our guests who come to 'take the cure.'"

But after a few days with Michel and Christine, you have to admit that the food does slightly overshadow the waters. Each meal leads into virgin gastronomic territory. Dish after dish arrives with balances and combinations of foods beyond any previous experience. The juxtapositions of ingredients, colors, flavors and textures are impossible to compare with classic preparations. You cannot say to yourself, "This is the best version of Roast Chicken Marie Antoinette I have ever had." You must decide, entirely on your own, whether or not you like it – whether it is a lunatic mishmash, or a brilliant new idea. Michel, who plays the role of the iconoclastic *enfant terrible* of French gastronomy, takes an old, classic dish, analyzes it, questions its basic premises and then converts it into an original personal creation. Sometimes, he just dreams and invents. All this is possible, of course, only to a *cuisinier* who has mastered the classic techniques. More often than not, Michel's inventions are entirely successful.

On the autumn night when we were talking in the garden, the principal dish at dinner had been a *pot au feu* of fish. That, to a student of Escoffier, is a nonsensical title for a fish dish. The *pot au feu* – one of the national dishes of France – the dish to which King Henry IV referred when he promised the French people "a chicken in every pot" – is a stew of beef and other meats, with chicken, marrow bones, herbs and vegetables. A *pot au feu* of fish is inconceivable! "Why?" asks Michel. "Why not a mixed fish and shellfish stew, with a wide variety of flavors and textures, combined in an aromatic bouillon?" But that would simply be a *bouillabaisse*. Not in Michel's concept. The difference is that he cooks each of the fish separately, each in a completely different way, so that each develops its own strong character. Then, at the last moment, he combines all the fish, garnishes them with vegetables and lets them swim in a light, natural, clear bouillon sauce. The result is unforgettable. (Recipe, page 182).

"I steam one fish in seaweed," Michel said, "poach another in red wine, bake a third in salt, suffocate a fourth in parsley and so on. The fish is then arranged in a large soup plate, decorated with colorful vegetables. It is very important to me that everything look beautiful and that all the colors and shapes be harmonious. Above all, everything must be light, light, light. The old ways of cooking fish – frying it in a bath of oil – pouring cupfuls of melted butter over it – covering it with cream sauce – all these are as dead as the dodo. The basic trick is to find ways of cooking the fish that will prevent it from losing its flavorful juices, as it invariably does when it is boiled in water."

Bringing some of Michel's recipes back to my New York kitchen, I have tried all of the low-fat methods demonstrated and described to me by Michel Guérard and the other revolutionary young chefs of France. I will never go back to the old ways. It is not a question of giving up some of the pleasure for the sake of lightness and weight control. Once you have tasted the essence of the true flavors of fish held and concentrated within the flesh, unmasked by buttery and creamy sauces, you will feel that you have never really tasted fish before. It is as if you have suddenly found the truth after years of living with a half-truth.

When the whole fish is baked enclosed in a nest of coarse salt (page 173), the salt encrusts the fish and seals it while it is cooking. Once you have tasted the result, you will not want to turn back to buttered aluminum foil, clay pots, pastry crusts or even seaweed-covered hot stones in a pit! Another new method is that of steaming a whole fish enclosed in parsley or seaweed, which release just enough of their juices to provide steam without diluting the natural essences of the fish. (I find in the United States that parsley is better than seaweed. The parsley has an aromatic fragrance, while seaweed provides no flavor. Michel said, "It is quite anonymous." Also, there is no way of buying fresh seaweed; you have to gather it yourself on a beach. Do not be fooled by recently published recipes which propose the replacement of fresh seaweed by dried, packaged "laver" weed from China or Japan. When you are told to soak the laver before using it, you are simply injecting nicely chlorinated tap water into the cooking process.)

Other low-fat (or nonfat) methods of cooking fish used by Michel Guérard are the classic Chinese way of steaming (page 177) and a new system of steam-baking on a bed of fresh vegetables, relying on their natural juices for the lubrication of the fish (page 178).

"When I serve any of these low-fat fish," Michel added, "I often provide a slightly thickened, attractively fluffy sauce which I make without butter or cream. I take whatever juices remain from the cooking of the fish – it may be the juices from the parsley – or a part of the red wine bouillon – or some of the *nage*, the aromatic court-bouillon – and boil it down hard to reduce it, and add coarsely cracked black pepper. While this boiling is in progress, I beat two very fresh egg yolks in a copper bowl, with a small amount of water, continuing to beat very fast and hard until so much air has been injected into the yolks that they have expanded to at least four times their original volume. Then I beat in, very fast, the hot, reduced bouillon, which instantly coagulates the eggs into a form of oil-less mayonnaise. It contains so much air that a little of it goes a very long way – two yolks make entirely enough for four people. This means, in fact, that each diner consumes only half a yolk in which, after all, there is very little cholesterol!" This is the principle used by Michel Guérard for his famous "Mayonnaise Without Oil" (page 341).

WHOLE FISH ROASTED IN A NEST OF COARSE SALT

(for 4)

There is evidence that French housewives of the twelfth century used rough sea salt to enclose tightly a piece of flesh to be braised in its own juices. This recipe revives the ancient technique. In trying this method, you will find that since the salt slightly solidifies at its center, you will need some sort of rough tool such as a blunt oyster knife, a large old screwdriver, or a not-too-sharp chisel to break out the cooked fish. The salt, which is called "Louisiana Extra-Coarse White," may be bought in 10 or 20 pound sacks from one of the big companies. Or, you can often get so-called "Coarse Kosher Salt" in 3- to 5-pound packages. If the salt is from a hardware store or supermarket, be sure it is refined salt for eating, not the industrial rock salt normally used for melting ice on sidewalks, which can be strongly acid and fairly poisonous (see "Index of Sources," page 392). Although this lovely dish produces fish of an unbelievable concentration of flavor and perfection of texture by itself, two possible accompanying sauces are the *"Sauce Antibeoise,"* page 335, or the "Virgin Tomato Sauce," page 345.

Whole fish – either butterfish, flounder, gray sole, pollack, red mullet, red snapper, rock cod, sea bass, whiting or yellow pike – leave head, skin and scales on, but have fishmonger clean it, removing fins and gills (1, about 2½ lbs)
Pure rock salt to enclose the fish (about 8 lbs)
Salt, coarse crystal, to taste
Black pepper, freshly ground, to taste

About 1½ hours before serving – active work about 10 minutes at the beginning and 10 minutes at the end – in between there is not a thing you can do

The all-important point is to choose exactly the right size and type of heavy, tightly-covered, baking pot, casserole, or French-type *cocotte*. The best is one of the French Le Creuset of enameled iron. The fish must fit into the casserole without curving. Hold it inside and see that there are about 2 inches of space between the fish and walls all around and about 6 inches of space between the top of the fish and the inside of the lid. In other words, the fish must rest at the center of the casserole surrounded with at least 2 to 3 inches of salt.

Preheat the oven to 400°F. Now, before you put the fish into the pot, layer the bottom with about 2 inches of salt. This will probably use up the first 2½ pounds. Then, run the fish under cold running water and nest it, still dripping wet, in the salt on its side. Just before sealing it in, salt and pepper the inside of its open belly for flavor. Now pack the next 2½ pounds of salt tightly all around the fish, filling all the corners, but carefully avoid allowing any of the salt to fall inside the fish. Pack as much as necessary of the rest of the salt on top of the fish to make its salt shell 2 inches thick. Cover the pot, set it in the center of the oven and forget it. This is one method of roasting that requires no attention from the cook.

The problem is how long to leave it. You cannot, obviously, open it up to see how it is going. The first time, you will have to take the risk of riding with my timing, bearing in mind that your oven may be more or less efficient than mine. Then, after you have had your first experience, adjust the timing to fit in with your own equipment. For a 1½-pound fish, I allow 50 minutes; for a 2-pound fish, one hour; for a 2½-pound fish, one hour and 10 minutes. All these timings depend, of course, on the type of fish you have chosen.

At the end of the time, break the fish out of its salt shell with the blunt tool, scraping away any clinging grains of salt. Look carefully for grains which might have fallen inside the belly. Before serving, the fish must first be skinned, beheaded and boned, either at table or more formally in the kitchen. If you have decided to have an accompanying sauce, put it on the table separately so that your guests will have the pleasure of tasting the velvety flesh in its purest form. The accompanying wine served to me when I first enjoyed this dish was a fine, dry, slightly *petillant* white Alpine Crépy. The American equivalent might be a fine California Sauvignon Blanc from the Santa Clara Valley.

WHOLE FISH STEAM-BAKED IN A BED OF PARSLEY

(for 4)

Another of the great *cuisiniers* who is experimenting with the low-fat cooking of fish is Chef Jacques Manière (page 42), at his Le Pactole in Paris. When I told Jacques about my discussions with other chefs (page 171), he said: "In recent years more and more imaginative cooks have realized that to boil something in water means, almost always, to lose part of the flavor. Many of the essential juices of the fish are dissolved into the water, which helps make good soup, but detracts from the flavor of the original fish. The modern chefs are experimenting in trying to draw enough liquid from the vegetables which surround the fish to avoid the need for extra water. For example, a thick bed of parsley contains a substantial amount of liquid. The concentration of flavors resulting from this method is extraordinary."

Whole fish – butterfish, flounder, gray sole, pollack, red mullet, red snapper, rock cod, sea bass, whiting or yellow pike – leave head and skin on, but have fishman clean it, removing scales, fins and gills (1, about 2–2½ lbs)

Parsley, enough to provide a thick bed for the fish (6–8 bunches, according to size)

White wine, dry (⅓ cup)

Salt, coarse crystal, to taste

Black pepper, freshly ground, to taste

Butter, for sauce, optional (4–6 Tbs)

Basil, fresh leaf in season, chopped, optional (2 Tbs)

About 1¼ hours before serving – active work about 15 minutes with about 1 hour of unsupervised steam baking

Preheat your oven to 325°F. Choose a tightly lidded casserole or *cocotte* large enough to hold the fish without bending it. Open up all the bunches of parsley and wash thoroughly under running cold water. Do not cut off the stalks – they contain useful flavor juices. Put half the parsley – wet from the washing, without shaking it out – into the casserole and spread it, as a bed, evenly across the bottom, then pour the ⅓ cup of wine over the parsley to prevent it from burning before it has time to release its juices. Wash the fish under running cold water and, without drying it, salt and pepper its inside to your taste, then lay it, still thoroughly wet, on the bed of parsley. Cover it completely with the remaining parsley, also thoroughly wet, then clamp on the lid and let it bake in the center of the oven for about 40–45 minutes, according to the size of the fish. Do not open the lid of the casserole during this time or you will release too much steam.

After the first period of baking, take the casserole out of the oven, open it up and dig down through the parsley with two forks to check the doneness of the center of the fish. When perfectly cooked the flesh should be firm and opaque. Judge how much more cooking is needed to achieve this, re-cover with the parsley, put back the lid and continue baking for, usually, 10 to 15 minutes more. Finally, discard all the parsley and serve the fish with its natural juices from the casserole. If you feel you need a richer sauce, add a few tablespoons of melted butter into which you have incorporated the 2 tablespoons of chopped fresh basil leaves. The wine served to me by Jacques Manière was a noble, white Graves from Bordeaux, a Château Laville-Haut-Brion. At my New York dining table I might serve an equivalent American wine, perhaps a noble California Pinot Chardonnay from the Mayacamas slopes of the Napa Valley.

GOLDEN GATE ROCK COD (OR OTHER WHOLE FISH) STEAMED WITH A TOUCH OF GINGER IN THE ANCIENT CHINESE MANNER

(for 4)

Whenever I arrive in San Francisco to find the rock cod being caught in the Pacific off the Golden Gate, I hurry to prepare this dish in the traditional fatless Chinese style. If you are not close enough to the Golden Gate, it can be replaced by one of the other fish listed below. You will need a Chinese bamboo or metal steamer.

Whole fish, rock cod, butterfish, flounder, gray sole, pollack, red mullet, red snapper, sea bass, whiting or yellow pike – leave head and skin on, but have fishman clean it, removing fins, gills and scales (1, about 2 to 2½ lbs)	Sesame oil (2 Tbs) Ginger root, fresh, peeled and finely shredded (2 Tbs) Green scallions, cut into 2-inch lengths, then quartered lengthwise (4) Soy sauce, light (3 Tbs) White wine, dry (1 Tbs)

About 30 minutes before serving – active preparation about 15 minutes, plus about 15 minutes unsupervised steaming

Wash the fish and make two or three diagonal cuts on both sides, almost but not quite down to the backbone. Then set up the steamer with about ¾ of an inch of water in the bottom, placing one tier above it and the lid on top. Bring the water up to a boil and keep it bubbling fairly hard to provide plenty of steam throughout the cooking operation. Place the fish on a dinner plate, or any other kind of platter that will catch the valuable flavor juices. As soon as there is plenty of steam, set the platter with the fish in the steamer and tightly clamp on the lid. You can expect the fish to be perfectly done, firm, flaky and opaque, in about 10 to 15 minutes, according to the size of the fish.

Meanwhile, in a small saucepan (or a wok), heat up the 2 tablespoons of sesame oil, with the 2 tablespoons of shredded ginger, the quartered scallions, the 3 tablespoons of soy sauce and the tablespoon of wine. Continue heating and stirring until the scallions are very lightly cooked. When the fish is done, add the juices from its platter to the ginger sauce. Quickly behead, skin and bone the fish, pour the ginger sauce over it, and serve at once. Since rock cod is caught mainly off the coast of California, it seems proper to serve with this superb fish a fine, fruity dry Semillon from the Livermore Valley.

PIKE (OR OTHER WHOLE FISH) BAKED ON A BED OF AROMATIC VEGETABLES

(for 4)

One of the greatest cooks of France, relatively unknown because he refuses to be listed in the gastronomic guides, is Chef Lucien Sarrassat (page 48), who owns and runs his tiny restaurant in the village of Saint-Gerand-le-Puy, a few miles outside the spa city of Vichy. Sarrassat has no fixed printed menu, but relies for many of his main ingredients on the daily success of his fishing and hunting friends. If there is a freshly caught pike from the nearby Allier River, Chef Sarrassat might decide to steam-bake it, using the steam from the natural juices of a carefully balanced layer of vegetables. The minimum liquid seems to hold in the flavor of the fish, while the aromatic vapors of the vegetables are absorbed by and enhance the flesh.

Celery root, washed, peeled and diced (1 medium)

Carrots, scraped and sliced (6 medium)

Yellow onions, peeled and thinly sliced (3 medium)

Whole pike – or butterfish, flounder, gray sole, pollack, red mullet, red snapper, rock cod, sea bass or whiting – leave head and skin on, but have fishmonger clean it, removing fins, gills and scales (1, about 2–2½ lbs)

Salt, coarse crystal, to taste

Black pepper, freshly ground, to taste

White wine, dry (½ cup)

Butter, for sauce, optional (2–3 Tbs)

Basil, fresh leaf in season, chopped, optional (2 Tbs)

About 1 hour before serving – active work about 15 minutes plus about 45 minutes of unsupervised baking

Preheat your oven to 350°F. Choose a tightly lidded, oval casserole or *cocotte*, large enough to hold the fish without bending it. Cover the bottom with a bed of the diced celery root and the sliced carrots and onions. Wash the fish under running cold water, then dry it and lightly sprinkle its inside with salt and pepper. Lay the fish on its bed of vegetables and pour over it ⅓ cup of the wine. Cover the casserole and set it in the oven for the first 40 minutes. Then check the fish for doneness. When perfectly cooked, the flesh at the center should be firm, flaky and opaque. Baste the fish with the juices from the bottom of the casserole. If not quite done, set the fish back in the oven, again covered, for the necessary extra time – usually 5 to 10 minutes, according to the size of the fish.

Serving at table

Be as simple, or fussy, as you choose – according to the formality of your dinner. You can transfer the fish to a hot serving platter and bring it to table just as it comes from the oven, or you can skin, behead and bone it in advance. In either case, keep it warm for the few moments it takes to prepare the vegetable sauce. Make a smooth purée of all the vegetables from the bottom of the casserole, either with a hand food mill, an electric blender or a Cuisinart chopper-churner. Transfer the purée to a saucepan and reheat it, stirring, without letting it boil. Taste and adjust the seasonings, as needed. The sauce may be enriched, if you wish, by the working in of 2 or 3 tablespoons of butter and some chopped basil. If the sauce needs thinning, add an extra dash or two of wine. With this, Chef Lucien Sarrassat served me a fine, slightly smoky, Pouilly Fumé from the Loire. The American equivalent (also with that slight, subtle touch of smoke) would be the California Napa Fumé Blanc.

SALMON POACHED AND SERVED IN ITS AROMATIC BOUILLON

(for 4)

The cooking technique in this superb dish is a near-perfect example of the Low-High cuisine, with the court-bouillon not prepared in advance, but freshly boiled hardly more than a few minutes before the salmon begins its poaching. Note that unlike the ancient method, no fish bones are used, so there is an absolute freshness about the bouillon, which then becomes the sauce around the fish when it is served. If you prefer, however, you may eliminate the bouillon from this recipe and substitute for it a batch of the basic Low-High fish bouillon from the recipe on page 70.

For the special court-bouillon:

White wine, preferably a good dry Riesling (2 bottles)
Yellow onions, peeled and thinly sliced (3 medium)
Leek whites, desanded and chopped (2 medium)
Carrots, scraped and thinly sliced (3 medium)
Green Pascal celery, destringed and chopped, with leaves (3 medium stalks)

Thyme, fresh in season (4 sprigs)
Garlic, whole cloves, unpeeled (2)
Bay leaf (1)
Cloves, whole (4)
Black peppercorns, whole (20)
Red cayenne pepper, to taste
Salt, coarse crystal, to taste

For the sauce with the fish:

Sweet butter (6 Tbs)
Parsley, leaf only, minced (5 Tbs)
Chervil, fresh leaf in season, minced (2 Tbs)
Shallots, peeled and minced (3 cloves)

Vinegar, tarragon white wine (about 1 Tbs)
Salmon steaks, middle cut, each 1 to 1½ inches thick (4, total about 2½ lbs)

About 1½ hours before serving – active work about 30 minutes, plus about 1 hour of unsupervised simmering and resting

Choose a wide, shallow saucepan (or sauté pan, or *sauteuse*) with a lid, the pan about 3 inches deep and just wide enough to hold the salmon steaks comfortably side-by-side with not too much room to spare. If your pan is too big, it will require too much water properly to submerge the salmon. Into this pan pour the 2 bottles of wine and set it over medium heat to begin warming up. Add, at once, in this order: the sliced onions, the chopped leeks, the sliced carrots, the chopped celery with its leaves, the 4 sprigs of thyme, the 2 garlic cloves, the bay leaf, the 4 whole cloves, the 20 black peppercorns, a pinch of the cayenne pepper, with plenty of salt to taste. Bring it all up to gentle simmering, then cover it and keep it going until the vegetables are just nicely soft, so that they have released their aromatic juices – usually in about 20 minutes. Turn off the heat and let the court-bouillon cool for about half an hour, until it is time to start poaching the salmon.

About 30 minutes before serving

Fish out from the court-bouillon the 2 whole garlic cloves. They will now be quite mushy inside and will have lost most of their pungent oils. Pinch the skins to squeeze the mush into the court-bouillon. Throw away the skins. With a slotted spatula, gently rest the 4 salmon steaks on the aromatic bed in the court-bouillon. Again set the pan over medium heat to warm up. The salmon steaks will probably not be fully covered by the liquid. In a separate kettle quickly boil enough water to add, boiling, to the court-bouillon so that the salmon is just covered. When the liquid is again gently simmering, cover and keep its surface "smiling" until the salmon is just done, cleanly flaky when tested with a fork – usually in 15 to 18 minutes. Meanwhile, begin preparing the sauce. Soften the 6 tablespoons of butter in a mixing bowl and work into it 3 tablespoons of the parsley and 2 tablespoons of chervil. Work the butter hard, whipping it with a fork, until it becomes quite fluffy and increases in volume because of the air that is being incorporated into it.

When the salmon is done, turn off the heat, but leave the fish in the court-bouillon to continue absorbing its flavors as it cools slightly. Ladle out 4 cups of the court-bouillon, strain it, put it into a separate sauté pan over fairly high heat, and boil it hard to reduce it, concentrating and sharpening its flavor. Add to it the minced shallots. When it has been reduced by half – usually in 10 to 12 minutes – taste it, adjusting its seasonings, then add just enough of the vinegar, teaspoon by teaspoon, to give this sauce-bouillon a faintly acid quality. Turn off the heat and gently swirl in the whipped herb butter. As soon as it is melted onto the surface of the sauce, serve the salmon steaks on hot, wide soup plates, pouring the sauce around the fish and decorating the top of each steak with the remaining parsley. With this superb fish, I generally serve a fruity, rich Alsatian Riesling. On our American side, the equivalent might be a fine, California Riesling from grapes grown in Monterey.

FINAL NOTE: Naturally, if you insist absolutely, you can do without the herb butter. Also, if fresh chervil is hard to find, you may substitute almost any other fresh leaf herb: tarragon, basil, chives, even very finely minced scallions. Do not try to use dried herbs in the whipped butter. They will produce an unpleasant grainy effect.

THE NEAREST AMERICAN APPROACH TO CHEF MICHEL GUÉRARD'S POT AU FEU OF MIXED FISH – EACH COOKED IN A DIFFERENT WAY

(not worth preparing for fewer than 8 to 10)
If you have faithfully practiced the five low-fat ways of cooking fish in the previous recipes, you are ready to begin the Guérard magnum opus, the *grande spécialité* of his two-star restaurant,

Le Pot au Feu, at Eugénie-les-Bains (page 35). Before you try it, you should read my discussion of it with Michel on page 171. *Warning:* this recipe does involve a lot of work, and is best planned as a weekend project. It is not very difficult technically, but several separate operations have to go forward simultaneously and must all be carefully watched. It helps, on this one, to have two or three competent assistants in the kitchen.

The overall plan of the dish is simple. Michel prepares a classic boiled dinner, *pot au feu,* but with several different kinds of fish and shellfish instead of meats, plus an array of vegetables, and two very light sauces. The stroke of genius is that he first cooks each fish separately, each in a different way, each without any fat, so that his final achievement is a magnificent dish with extraordinary variety and a kind of gossamer lightness. When Michel served it to me at Eugénie, it included red mullet steamed in parsley, Mediterranean *loup de mer* steamed in seaweed, *lotte* poached in red wine, *langoustine à la nage* simmered in an aromatic bouillon and mussels steamed in wine – all finally assembled into the single dish.

The last time I prepared it in my New York kitchen (after much previous experimentation), I made up the assemblage of a whole sea bass roasted in salt (page 173), a whole red mullet steamed in parsley (page 175), a whole rock cod in a Chinese steamer (page 177), a whole pike baked on aromatic vegetables (page 178), salmon steaks poached in bouillon (page 180), a lobster poached in a basic Low-High fish bouillon (page 196), and some mussels steamed as described on page 159 up to the point where they open, but leave them in their shells. The *tour de force* is to have all these perfectly ready at roughly the same moment, so that they may be assembled with the vegetables and the sauces into what I consider to be a fine American approximation of the great Guérard fish opus.

The following are the ingredients for the final assembling of the dish. In addition you will need the ingredients for the advance preparation of the different fish in the previous recipes.

Mussels, in shells, cleaned and steamed, see above (24 to 30)

Sea bass, whole, roasted in salt, see above (about 1½ lbs)

Red mullet, whole, steamed in parsley, see above (about 1½ lbs)

Pacific rock cod, or small Atlantic cod, whole, cooked in Chinese steamer, see above (about 1½ lbs)

Pike, or pollack, whole, baked with vegetables, see above (about 1½ lbs)

Salmon steaks, poached in bouillon, see above (2, about ½ lb each)

Lobster, whole, boiled in Low-High fish bouillon, see above (about 1½ lbs)

Green beans, trimmed and chunked (½ lb)

Carrots, miniature if possible, perhaps Belgian in jars (about 1 dozen carrots)

White turnips, small, peeled and carved into olive shapes (3 or 4, according to size)

Cucumbers, peeled (2 medium)

Cornichons, small French pickles (24 to 30)

Salt, coarse crystal, to taste

Black pepper, freshly ground, to taste

Egg yolks (2)

Sweet butter (about 5 Tbs)

The day before – cleaning and soaking the mussels

The following is simply a summary schedule of the various operations. You should turn to the individual recipes (listed above) for the detailed procedures. Wash, soak, and fatten the mussels and let them clean themselves while resting in the refrigerator overnight.

On the day – about 2½ hours before serving – advance preparation of all the fish and shellfish in about 2 hours

The following operations proceed more or less simultaneously. Roast the sea bass in salt. Steam the red mullet in parsley. Cook the rock cod in its Chinese steamer. Bake the pike over vegetables. Poach the salmon in bouillon. Boil the lobster, cut it open and chunk its meat. Steam open the mussels, but leave them in their shells.

While all this is in progress, prepare the vegetables. Put the green beans, the carrots and the turnips into the Chinese steamer alongside the rock cod and cook them until just done, but still crispy – usually in about 10 to 12 minutes. Cut the cucumbers into rounds, each about ⅜ inch thick. (You will use 3 rounds for each diner.) Bore a hole in the center of each round just large enough to take the base of one of the *cornichons,* so that it sticks up vertically with the cucumber as its base. Hold aside these decorative little pylons, covered. As soon as an oven is available, set it to keep-warm temperature (165°F.) and put all the various pieces of cooked fish in it, each in a separate container, covered – also, the various vegetables as they are cooked, assembled into a single container, covered. Keep the cucumber-*cornichon* pylons at room temperature. Set your deepest and widest soup plates, plus a sauce boat, to warm.

About 30 minutes before serving – preparing the two sauces and assembling the pot au feu

Strain the fish bouillon in which the lobster was boiled and pour 2 quarts of it into a 3-quart saucepan. Boil it hard to reduce it, concentrating and sharpening its flavors. At the same time, taste it and adjust its seasoning, bearing in mind that it is to be the *nage,* the "swim," the aromatic bouillon in which the *pot au feu* will be served at table. As soon as it has reduced enough and the flavor is dead right, bring it down to just below boiling and hold it, covered. Remove all the parsley from the casserole in which the red mullet was steamed, squeezing it out to give up all its juices, discarding the greenery. Pour the parsley juice into a 2-quart saucepan and also boil it hard to reduce it. Taste it and adjust the seasoning, bearing in mind that this will be the base of the fluffy egg sauce. As soon as it has reduced sufficiently and the flavor is right, bring it down to just below boiling and hold it, covered. Now put the 2 egg yolks, with 1 tablespoon of cold water, into a copper, round-bottomed beating bowl and arm yourself with a big balloon wire whisk. Beat the eggs furiously with strokes lifted high so as to get as much air into them as possible. When the volume of the eggs has tripled or quadrupled, run into them, in a steady small stream while continuing to beat furiously, ¼ cup of the hot parsley juice, which will coagulate the eggs into a light fluff, very similar to a mayonnaise (but entirely without oil). Beat into the fluff a few good grinds of black pepper. If it becomes too stiff, work in a few more teaspoons, one at a time, of the hot parsley juice. Now transfer the fluff to the warm sauceboat and keep it at room temperature until serving time. It will hold in suspension for at least 30 minutes, if not longer.

The last job is what Michel Guérard calls the *montér au beurre*, the "mounting with butter" of the *nage*, the aromatic lobster bouillon. The new theory of the new cuisine is that butter should never be cooked into a sauce (where it breaks itself up into relatively indigestible, oily elements), but should instead be added in its natural form at the last moment. Cut ½ tablespoon of butter for each person and then slice each of these into smallish curls or slivers. Uncover the lobster bouillon (which is just below boiling) and, working fast with a light boxwood spoon, drop the slivers of butter, two or three at a time, gently onto the surface of the liquid and carefully stir them around until they melt. The objective is not to incorporate the butter into the bouillon, but to form it into a smooth layer on top. Within a couple of minutes, all the butter should be in and melted. Turn down the heat to keep-warm temperature and put on the lid.

Arranging on the soup plates and serving at table

The *pot au feu* should be served directly from the kitchen onto the individual soup plates. Each must be a work of art in arrangement, color-balance and decoration. Ladle into each plate enough of the lobster bouillon to make a base layer about ⅜ inch deep. (The new rule is that the fish should not be put in first and have the sauce ladled over them. The sauce must be under the fish, to avoid dominating their contrasting flavors.) Now put in a piece of each fish: sea bass, red mullet, rock cod, pike, salmon, lobster and about 3 mussels, in their shells, per person. Decorate the plate with three of the cucumber-*cornichon* pylons per person, plus green beans, yellow baby carrots and white turnip "olives."

Each diner can then complete the picture by dabbing on, here and there, as much or as little of the fluffy yellow egg sauce as he pleases. With his perfection of a *pot au feu,* Chef Michel Guérard served one of the greatest wines of the world, a superb, rich, white Le Montrachet from the Côte d'Or of Burgundy. On our American side, it could be approached by a noble California Pinot Chardonnay from the Napa Valley.

CHEF PIERRE TROISGROS'S SECRETS OF LOW-FAT WAYS OF PREPARING THE PERFECT LOBSTER

At the end of a supreme, three-star dinner, which had reached its peak with an *Homard à la Cancalaise,* grilled lobster just faintly touched with the flavor of Calvados apple brandy, Pierre (see page 50) joined me for coffee. I asked him at once how he had achieved, without pouring on cupfuls of melted butter, the absolute perfection of the texture of the lobster's flesh?

"Few amateur cooks seem to realize," Pierre said, "how tight is the timing for the perfect cooking of a lobster. If you remove it from the heat at exactly the right second, the flesh has the ideal elasticity and chewiness, combined with the peak of its flavor development. But if you overcook it, even for 2 or 3 minutes, it rapidly becomes almost like flavorless cotton-wool. And if you undercook it, even for just a minute or two, it will still have in your mouth a most disagreeable raw, gelatinous quality, with very little of its true flavor as yet brought out."

Pierre didn't think it mattered much how the cooking heat was applied to the body of the lobster – whether by boiling it whole in a bouillon (page 196), or by cutting it in half and baking or grilling it (page 189), or by cutting the flesh into pieces out of the shell and simmering them in a sauce (page 191) – but, if the choice is boiling, he had strong views about what kind of liquid should be used, whether you call it court-bouillon or *fumet de poisson.*

"In the old days," Pierre continued, "the professional cooks used to prepare their bouillon or *fumet* overnight by simmering the bones and heads of all the fish that had been prepared the previous day and then letting it continue to bubble at the side of the stove all the following day, ladling it out as they needed it. The theory was that it would gradually reduce and strengthen and develop a gelatinous body. I always felt – even when I was a very young apprentice cook – that this bubbling *fumet* began to smell faintly of stale fish. You know the slight odor when you go into a fishmonger where some of the fish on the slabs have been insufficiently iced and are beginning to feel the pinch of old age! This is why, in our modern new cuisine, we do not any longer use fish bones to make *fumet.*

"Nor do we do any more overnight simmering. We use fresh fish and braise them quickly in a minimum of liquid – usually with a touch of dry white wine, preferably a Sancerre from the Loire, because it has a good acidity and an aggressive flavor – plus, of course, the usual aromatic herbs and vegetables. We prepare the *fumet* just before serving the meal and it is never simmered for longer than 25 to 30 minutes. Then, at once, we remove all the solids by straining them out and rapidly reduce the remaining liquid to develop its flavor. Immediately after that, it is used in the dish. Thus our *fumet* has the quality of beautifully fresh fish and never a hint of staleness. This is, so to speak, our *nouveau fumet.* It has such a good and strong character on its own that it seldom needs to be enriched with cream or beaten egg yolks."

In the memorable dish that had just delighted us at dinner, the lobsters had not been boiled but grilled and baked in their half-shells. Pierre also had ideas on this method. He said: "When you cut a lobster in half, always do it over a large bowl so as to catch the 'blood,' the albuminous, glutinous, white liquid that oozes out of the flesh. As soon as the two halves are neatly separated, pour the white liquid back over the flesh in the shells. It helps to keep the flesh soft and makes it swell under the heat of the grill, eliminating the need for lubrication with a great deal of melted butter. Always remember, also, that you need maximum heat for the grilling. If your oven happens to have a separate control, turn it full on, as well as the grill, so that the lobster is heated from both sides at once."

When the lobster comes out of the grill (or out of the bubbling bouillon), it need not – and, in fact, should not – be served immediately. Pierre thinks that keeping it warm for 10 or 15 minutes of waiting seems to "decontract the muscles," loosening and tenderizing the flesh and, again, cutting down on the need for extra butter.

I asked about butter and cream in lobster sauces. Pierre said that, as far as he and his brother were concerned, heavy cream could almost always be eliminated. The secret of a good, low-fat lobster sauce is the use of a dominant and strong wine. "Again, we like to use the white Sancerre for its good strong body and because its aggressiveness makes our sauce *un peu nerveuse* – how do you say? – with a sort of nervy sparkle on the tongue, a kind of tiny vibration of pleasure, to complement the flesh without dominating it."

"As to butter," Pierre continued, "we do sometimes add a small amount to a sauce – seldom more than 1 tablespoonful per person – but, in these new days of the new cuisine, we never, never cook the butter. Cooked butter is indigestible and heavy. Using quantities of cooked butter was the basic principle of the old cuisine and was one of the main reasons why it was all so overrich, so unnecessarily heavy and so unhealthy. The new principle is that, when you use butter, you add it and work it in just a few moments before bringing the dish to table. This is especially necessary with a sauce for a lobster. You melt the butter into the sauce, curl by curl, just lightly blending it in and then, at once, you rush the lobster and the sauce to the table."

AN AMERICAN ADAPTATION OF THE TROISGROS'S LOBSTER FLAMED WITH CALVADOS À LA CANCALAISE

(for 4)

When Jean Troisgros (page 50) was married, it was probably inevitable that his honeymoon would be involved with a work project. He explored the rocky coast of Brittany trying each day to find a new fish or shellfish and a new way of preparing it. In the small fishing port of Cancale at a bistro called Janine he discovered this wonderful recipe for grilled flamed lobster. Bringing it back home to Roanne, to the Restaurant des Frères Troisgros, Jean and Pierre, as always, experimented together to perfect the recipe. It has become one of the *grandes spécialités* – one of the great dishes that helped to earn them their three stars. (Before trying this recipe, read my discussion of it with Pierre on the preceding pages.)

Lobsters, must be female, alive
   (2, total about 3½ to 4 lbs)
Salt, coarse crystal, to taste
White pepper, coarsely ground,
   to taste
Olive oil (about 2 Tbs)
Sweet butter, at room
   temperature (6 Tbs)

Parsley, leaf only, chopped
   (¼ cup)
Tarragon, fresh leaf in season,
   chopped (¼ cup)
Lemon juice, freshly squeezed
   (about 3 Tbs)
Calvados apple brandy
   (⅓ cup)

About 45 minutes before serving – active preparation about 20 minutes, plus about 25 minutes of unsupervised grilling and maturing

Preheat the grill to highest temperature and set the rack so that the top surface of the lobster will be about 3 inches below the heat. If you have a separate oven control, also turn it on full, so that the lobsters are heated from below as well. Humanely and instantly kill the lobsters by cutting through their main nerve cords at the central point where the tail joins the body. Thoroughly wash them under running cold water, then, preferably with a Chinese cleaver, cut them lengthwise in half, catching the white juice and pouring it back into the half shells. Clean each half by removing the gritty stomach "lady" at the lobster's "chin" and the black intestinal vein which runs down the back. Save the red "coral" eggs and the green "tomalley" liver. Sparingly salt and pepper each half. Now, lightly oil the grill pan, to prevent the shells from burning black. Lay the lobster halves, flesh upwards, on the grill pan. Slide them under the heat and leave them until the flesh is just firm and opaque – usually in 6 to 8 minutes for a 2 pound lobster.

    Meanwhile, set the four plates to get warm and heat up a

crêpe pan over a spirit lamp. Next, prepare the herb sauce. Soften the 6 tablespoons of butter in a mixing bowl and mix in the chopped parsley and tarragon, about 4 teaspoons of the lemon juice, the lobster coral and tomalley, plus salt and pepper to taste. Then add, gradually, teaspoon by teaspoon, more of the lemon juice until you have a nice tart flavor. Mix it well but loosely.

The moment the lobster is done, set the halves on the crêpe pan, lift the flesh slightly up out of the shell at the back end and spoon into the shell underneath the flesh half a tablespoon, for each half lobster, of the herb sauce. Spread the remaining sauce over the top of each half lobster.

Serving at table

Pour the ⅓ cup of Calvados onto the crêpe pan, making sure that none of it splashes onto the lobsters. Then flame and, by shaking and tilting the pan, encourage the fire to lick the lobsters. Never baste them with the Calvados or it will dominate their flavor. With this dramatic dish, the brothers Troisgros served me a noble, richly fruity, white Burgundy from Chassagne-Montrachet. Its close American equivalent is a noble California Pinot Chardonnay from the Valley of the Moon in Sonoma.

AROMATIC FRICASSEE OF LOBSTER IN SAUTERNES

(for 4)

This is one of the *grandes spécialités* of Chef Roger Vergé (page 52), at his three-star Le Moulin de Mougins, in Provence. After we had inhaled its perfumed bouquet – after we had tasted the first piece of lobster and its sauce – one of my companions said: "It is so good, it is beyond all discussion!" For me it was, perhaps, the finest preparation of lobster I had ever tasted.

The reason was clear. All of us who are lovers of wine know the extraordinary aromatic qualities of a noble, honey-sweet Sauternes. The wine in the glass seems to combine the fruity sweetness of the grapes with the essence of the smells and tastes of a sun-bathed spice garden. By slowly, slowly simmering and concentrating a whole bottle of Sauternes around the lobster, Chef Vergé imbued the flesh not so much with the sweetness as with the spiciness of the unique wine.

In working out my New York adaptation, I found that the Sauternes does not have to be a great vintage of, say, a supremely expensive Château d'Yquem. It can be of a lesser year, but it must be strongly aromatic and not too sweet. When such a wine is combined with a fresh Maine lobster, this is a dish for dreams of glory.

Lobsters, must be female,
  alive (2 or 3, total about
  4½ to 5 lbs)
Sweet butter (3 Tbs)
Armagnac (½ cup)
Shallots, finely minced
  (1½ Tbs)
Tomatoes, fine, ripe, red,
  skinned, seeded and
  chopped (3 medium)
Tarragon, fresh leaf in season,
  chopped (1 Tbs)

Sweet Sauternes, see above
  (1 bottle)
Light cream (about 2 cups)
Salt, coarse crystal, to taste
Black pepper, freshly ground,
  to taste
Carrots, celery, leek whites,
  diced and mixed in equal
  parts (1½ cups)

About 2 hours before serving – active preparation about 45 minutes, plus about 1¼ hours of relatively unsupervised simmering and reduction

First, humanely and instantly kill the lobsters by cutting the main nerve cord at the central point where the tail joins the body. Now, preferably with a sharp Chinese cleaver, cut through the shells across the tail, starting just behind the head and then making three more equidistant cuts, so as to divide each tail into 4 pieces. Then place a large, 3-quart sauté pan over medium-high heat and quickly melt in it 2 tablespoons of the butter. Before the butter turns brown, rapidly sear both sides of each piece of lobster, so that the flesh is sealed within each circle of shell. Now crack the claws and add them to the sauté pan, pour on the ½ cup of Armagnac and flame.

As soon as the fire dies down, add the minced shallots, the chopped tomatoes and the tablespoon of chopped tarragon. Lower the heat to light bubbling and stir everything around. Pour in enough of the Sauternes and the light cream (in the proportions of 3 parts wine to 2 of cream) barely to cover the solids in the pan. Set it all gently simmering, just smiling, with the lid on. Keep it going until the lobster is perfectly done, just firm and opaque – usually in no more than 20–25 minutes.

Meanwhile, deal with the lobster heads and bodies. Using poultry shears, snip off the legs, wash them and drop them into the simmering pan. They will add their flavor juices to the sauce. Cut the heads and bodies in half lengthwise and clean them by cutting away the gritty stomach "lady." Carefully remove the red "coral" eggs and the green "tomalley" liver, holding them, covered, for later use. Now add the heads and bodies to the simmering pan, topping it up, if necessary, with a little more wine and cream, in the same proportions as before.

About 1¼ hours before serving – perfecting the sauce

With a slotted spoon remove all the pieces of lobster from the sauté pan, including claws, heads and bodies, legs, and tail segments. Separate the edible flesh from the shells, cut the flesh into slices about a quarter of an inch thick and keep them warm in a covered container. Strain the contents of the sauté pan, returning the liquid to the pan, and adjust the heat to a fairly rapid bubbling, now uncovered, so that it reduces and thickens slightly. The main objective of this reduction is to bring out and sharpen the aromatic qualities of the wine.

About 15 minutes before serving – the final assembly

As soon as the sauce has an aromatic flavor and velvety texture, turn the heat down to simmering, add the 1½ cups of diced vegetables and let them cook until they are just done, but still slightly crisp – usually in about 5 to 8 minutes. While this is in progress, gently work the red coral and green tomalley into a smooth paste with the remaining tablespoon of butter. This is best done with the fingers. Then work this paste gently into the simmering sauce, smoothing it around with a wooden spoon. Add the lobster slices and let them simmer for just a couple of minutes to reheat them. Then adjust seasonings and serve at once on very hot plates. With this noble dish, Chef Roger Vergé served me a noble white Burgundy from Chassagne-Montrachet. At my own New York dining table I might replace it with a California Pinot Chardonnay from the Alexander Valley of Sonoma.

FINAL NOTE: If you are prepared to be less formal and your guests are willing to use their fingers, you can also put back into the sauce the legs and the claw and tail shells, serving them with the lobster meat. Both legs and shells are very good to suck for every last drop of juice and they add their decorative red to each serving.

LOBSTER BAKED WITH ITS CORAL WITHOUT BUTTER

(for 4)

This is another brilliant, low-fat invention by Chef Michel Guérard (page 35) at his two-star restaurant, Le Pot au Feu, at Eugénie-les-Bains. He enriches the lobster not with butter but with an aromatic whip of low-fat white cheese. In this American adaptation, our low-fat pot cheese substitutes for the French white cheese, and the result is entirely equal to what the great young *cuisinier* serves on his home ground.

Lobsters, must be female, alive
  (2, total 3 to 4 lbs)
Pot cheese, low-fat (1 cup)
Shallots, finely minced (20
  whole cloves)
White wine, dry (3–5 Tbs) '
Chervil, fresh leaves in season,
  chopped (1 Tbs)

Tarragon, fresh leaves in
  season, chopped (1 Tbs)
Lemon juice, freshly squeezed
Salt, coarse crystal, to taste
Black pepper, freshly ground,
  to taste

Preparation in about 30 minutes – active work about 20 minutes, plus about 10 minutes of unsupervised baking

In a 6-quart kettle bring about 4 quarts of well-salted water to a rapid boil. Then humanely and instantly kill the lobsters by cutting through their main nerve cords at the central point where the tail joins the body. Wash them thoroughly under running cold water. Plunge them into the boiling water and, starting the timer at the precise moment when the water returns to the boil, cook them for exactly 4 minutes. Take them out at once and lay them on a wooden cutting board. Let them cool enough so that you can handle them.

Meanwhile, prepare the cheese sauce. I put the cup of pot cheese into the bowl of my Cuisinart chopper-churner (or you can use an electric blender or a hand food mill) and hold it without turning on the machine. Instead of the usual method of sautéeing the minced shallots in butter, Chef Guérard covers and simmers them in a small saucepan with 3 tablespoons of the white wine for 3 minutes. I then add the shallots and wine to the pot cheese and run the machine until it is all thoroughly mixed and smooth, but not a mushy paste – usually for 4 or 5 seconds. Transfer the cheese mixture to a round-bottomed beating bowl and beat hard with a balloon wire whisk until it is fairly light and fluffy. At the same time beat in the chopped chervil, tarragon and just enough of the lemon juice to give a mildly tart flavor, with salt and pepper to taste. The texture, finally, should be that of a thickly creamy sauce. If it needs thinning, add a little more wine. Now preheat your oven to 450°F.

Preferably with a sharp Chinese cleaver, cut the two lobsters in half lengthwise and clean them. Remove the gritty stomach "lady" from the place where the chin would be if the lobster had a chin, and the black intestinal vein down the back. Carefully remove, preferably with your fingers, the still-uncooked, red "coral" eggs, guarding every last grain for later use. Remove the flesh from the cracked claws and press it into the main shells alongside the tail meat. Now spread each lobster half with some of the white cheese sauce. Divide the red coral eggs into four parts and carefully spread the eggs, with your fingers, across the top of each half of each lobster. Set the four halves on an open roasting pan, after lightly oiling the shells to prevent their burning, then slide them to the center of the oven and bake for exactly 10 minutes.

Meanwhile, put the rest of the white cheese sauce into a small saucepan and gently warm it up, stirring regularly. If it becomes too thick, add a little more wine. When the lobster halves are served, pour a bit more of this sauce over them. The accompanying wine chosen by Chef Guérard was a noble white Graves from Bordeaux. The American equivalent might be a dry, light California Pinot Blanc from Monterey.

HOMARD À LA NAGE – LOBSTER IN THE SWIM – IN BOUILLON AMÉRICAIN AND A CHINESE WOK

(for 4)

This is, obviously, a modernistic, low-fat version of the classic *homard à l'américaine* with the original thick, buttery-creamy tomato sauce replaced by a *nage*, an aromatically lean bouillon, with much the same qualities of taste, but with all the unnecessary richness taken out of it. This athletic and strong lobster stew is the invention of the excellent young Chef Daniel Météry (page 40), who directs the kitchen of the Restaurant Clovis of the Hôtel Windsor just around the corner from the Arc de Triomphe, in Paris. I have no idea whether Daniel has ever prepared his lobster in a wok, but I find several good reasons why it is a very suitable pan. First, the new cuisine of France owes a great deal to the ancient techniques of the Chinese. Second, Paris is now being invaded by Chinese restaurants and Oriental food shops so that pretty soon Chef Météry may be as much exposed to the wok culture as we are here. Third (and most important), the wok is a particularly efficient instrument for the Low-High cooking techniques. Its curved bottom makes the most efficient possible use of even the smallest amount of butter and oil, while its wide-open expanse encourages the quick reduction, concentration and thickening of all kinds of sauces without the addition of any starch, but simply through natural evaporation. The recipe requires the advance preparation of a batch of the basic Low-High fish bouillon from page 70, but this may be done on the morning of the day it is to be served, or even the day before.

Fish bouillon, basic Low-High, see above (3 quarts)
Lobsters, plump female, alive (2, at 2 lbs each)
Sweet butter (1 Tbs)
Sesame oil, Chinese (1 Tbs)
Carrots, scraped and minced (3 or 4 medium)
Yellow onions, peeled and minced (2 medium)
Shallots, peeled and minced (4 cloves)
Celery, green Pascal, minced (2 or 3 inner stalks)
Celeriac, skinned and minced (½ root)
Tomatoes, ripe, peeled and diced (3 medium) or Italian plum tomatoes, canned (1¾ cups)
Green bell peppers, cored and diced (2 medium)

White wine, sweet (½ cup)
Tomato paste (1 cup)
Rosemary, fresh leaf in season, chopped (1 Tbs)
Thyme, fresh in season, chopped (1 Tbs)
Tarragon, fresh in season, chopped (5 Tbs)
Bay leaf (1)
Garlic, peeled and minced (2 cloves)
Sea salt, coarse crystal, to taste
Black pepper, coarsely ground, to taste
Red cayenne pepper (pinch or two)
Parsley, leaf only, chopped (½ cup)
Lemon juice, freshly squeezed (a few spritzes)
Cognac (⅓ cup)

About 2 hours before serving – boiling the lobsters and preparing the wok in the first hour

Bring out the fish bouillon which you have made in advance and put it in a soup kettle, but do not yet heat it. Wash the two lobsters in cold water, then set them down in the bouillon. Turn on the high heat under the kettle and as soon as the liquid starts to bubble, time the boiling of the lobsters for exactly 20 minutes, then turn off the heat and let them cool in the bouillon, absorbing the aromatic flavors.

Meanwhile, I make ready my electric Chinese wok and prepare the ingredients for the sauce. Put into the still-cold wok the butter and sesame oil. In a large mixing bowl, assemble the vegetables: the minced carrots, the minced onions, the minced shallots, the minced stalks of celery, plus the minced celeriac. Also have ready, each in its separate covered bowl: the diced tomatoes (or the drained, canned plum tomatoes), the diced green peppers, and the minced garlic. Also, in a 1-pint mixing bowl, blend together the sweet white wine and the tomato paste.

About 1 hour before serving – active work about 35 minutes, plus about 25 minutes of unsupervised simmering

By this time, the lobsters should be cool enough to handle. Drain them and lay them on their backs on a wooden cutting board. With a sharp, small, pointed knife, cut away from each the "lady," the grit-filled stomach sac, from the place where the chin would be if she had a chin. Next, cut them in half lengthwise, in the standard way, using a large, broad fish knife, or, much better, a razor-sharp, laminated Chinese cleaver. Scrape out the black intestinal veins which run from the top of the back down the length of the tail. With a tea-spoon, dig out the red "coral," the caviar, plus the light green liver, and mash together these supreme delicacies in a miniature mixing bowl, holding them, covered, for the later thickening of the sauce. Now, preferably with clean fingers, pull out every scrap of the delicate flesh from tail, head and claws – cutting everything into bite-size pieces and holding, covered. Now prepare the *bouillon à l'Américaine* in which the lobster will swim to table.

I turn back to my wok and bring it up to sautéeing heat for the preparation of the classic French *brunoise*, the vegetable foundation of the sauce. As soon as the butter and oil start to sizzle, put in, all at once, the mixed minced vegetables: carrots, onions, shallots, celery, and celeriac. Keep stirring them around with a wooden spoon. They must under no circumstances brown, but rather melt and soften by the slowest of sauté poaching. As the vegetables give up their juices, they will be simmering rather than frying.

Boil away this excess liquid by, if necessary, turning up the heat to achieve a merry bubbling. When the vegetables are butter-soft, usually in 5 to 10 minutes, begin adding and stirring in, one by one, the other ingredients: the tomatoes, the green peppers, the wine and tomato paste mixture. Continuously adjust the heat so that everything keeps bubbling. Now work in the rosemary and thyme and one tablespoon of the tarragon, the bay leaf, crumbled, and the 2 minced garlic cloves. Let it all continue bubbling.

Measure 1 cup of the bouillon and work it into the sauce in the wok. Remember that you are not aiming to make a thick sauce, but a syrupy bouillon. Retaste for seasoning and, as needed, add more salt, pepper and a pinch or two of cayenne. Now cover the wok and let everything simmer, with an occasional stir, for about 25 minutes.

About 15 minutes before serving – the final assembly

Set the serving soup plates to get hot. Remove the sauce from the wok and purée it by passing it through a food mill, or rubbing it through a sieve, or, in my case, by swirling it for about 5 seconds in my Cuisinart chopper-churner. Return the sauce at once to the wok and reheat it to gentle bubbling. Check its thickness. It should be liquid, but slightly syrupy. If it is too watery, turn up the heat and boil it hard for 2 or 3 minutes to reduce and concentrate it. If it is too thick, work in, tablespoon by tablespoon, more of the lobster bouillon. When the thickness is right, finally check and adjust the seasonings. Now turn off the heat and very carefully blend in the coral-and-liver mixture, making sure that it is evenly blended throughout the sauce and does not lump. It will add slightly to the thickness. Also work in ¼ cup of the parsley, plus the remaining 4 tablespoons of tarragon and the 2 or 3 spritzes of lemon juice. Finally, recheck and adjust the seasonings. Put in the lobster meat and reheat it for 2 to 3 minutes but do not overcook. Turn off the heat. Spread carefully across the surface of the sauce the ⅓ cup Cognac and flame. (Or, if your wok is handsome enough, bring it to the table and do the flaming there.) Serve at once in hot, open soup plates, with plenty of bright green parsley sprinkled over the top as a contrast to the orangey-red bouillon. It is best eaten with silver soup spoons. The wine served to me by Chef Météry was a noble, rich Meursault, Les Genevrières from the Côte d'Or of Burgundy. A California Pinot Chardonnay from the Livermore Valley is a good equivalent.

A NAVARIN OF LOBSTER WITH AN ARRAY OF VEGETABLES

(for 4)

One of the new tricks of the new style of French cooking – a style often quite irreverent towards the historic past – is to take a classic recipe always associated with one particular kind of food and rudely to convert it into a different recipe for an entirely different food. The modern cooks, for example, have taken the classic *blanquette de veau* and made it into a *blanquette de turbot*. Now, in this recipe, Chef Paul Bocuse and Chefs Jean and Pierre Troisgros have taken a classic *navarin* of lamb – that celestial dish of pieces of young lamb surrounded by an irresistible array of spring garden vegetables – and triumphantly converted it to the service of lobster.

I am entirely unable to make up my mind whether I prefer the Bocuse version, served at Collonges-au-Mont-d'Or (page 26), or the Troisgros version prepared in Roanne (page 50). So I have simply translated and adapted the best features from each and combined them into my own favorite *navarin de homard à l'américaine*. It does require the advance preparation of a basic Low-High fish bouillon (page 70) in which to boil the lobsters.

There are two separate operations: the cooking of the lobsters with their sauce and the separate poaching of the *navarin* of mixed vegetables. The principal success of the dish depends on the crispness and freshness of the vegetables. They must be cooked precisely *à point*, just done, but still slightly crackly between the teeth. Therefore, they should be cooked last, after the operations with the lobsters, and added to the dish a moment or two before serving. This is the secret of the perfect *navarin*.

Fish bouillon, basic Low-High,
see above (3 quarts)
Lobsters, must be female, alive
(2, total 3½–4½ lbs)
Sweet butter (4 Tbs)
Carrots, scraped and finely
minced (2 medium)
Yellow onions, peeled and
finely minced (2 medium)
Shallots, peeled and finely
minced (⅓ cup, about
8 cloves)
Cognac (½ cup)
Chicken bouillon (2 cups)
White wine, dry (about ½ cup)
Tomato paste (4 Tbs)
Basil, fresh leaves in season,
chopped (1 Tbs)

Parsley, leaves only, chopped
(1 Tbs)
Tarragon, fresh leaves in
season, chopped (1 Tbs)
Thyme, fresh leaves in season,
chopped (1 Tbs)
Salt, coarse crystal, to taste
White pepper, freshly ground,
to taste
White onions (8, quite small)
Carrots, scraped and thinly
sliced (8, quite small)
Turnips, white, peeled and
coarsely diced (about 4,
according to size)
Green beans, young, trimmed
(½ lb)
Green peas, shelled (1 cup)

About 2 hours before serving – active preparation about 1¼ hours, plus about 45 minutes of unsupervised poaching

Assuming that you have prepared the fish-poaching bouillon in advance, put it into a large fish kettle and heat it up to gentle bubbling. Humanely and instantly kill your lobsters by cutting through their main nerve cords at the central point where the tail joins the body. Thoroughly wash the lobsters under running cold water and then plunge them both together into the boiling bouillon. Start your timer from the precise moment when the bubbling restarts and boil the lobsters for exactly 10 minutes. Take them out, set them on a wooden cutting board and let them cool enough so that you can handle them.

Set a large sauté pan over medium frying heat and lubricate its bottom by melting 2 tablespoons of the butter. Then add the minced carrots and onions, plus the minced shallots, stirring them around and letting them lightly poach until they begin to melt, under no circumstances allowing them to fry or brown. When everything is nicely soft and the onions are transparent, pour in the ½ cup of Cognac and scrape the bottom of the pan to de-glaze it. Now begin working in the 2 cups of chicken bouillon, ½ cup of the wine, 2 tablespoons of the tomato paste, the tablespoon each of chopped basil, parsley, tarragon and thyme, with salt and pepper to taste. Let it all gently simmer for a few minutes, covered, while you complete the work on the lobsters.

Arming yourself, preferably with a super-sharp Chinese cleaver, cut the lobsters in half lengthwise. Clean them in the standard way. Remove the gritty stomach "lady" from the place where the chin would be if the lobster had a chin, and discard. Remove the black intestinal vein that runs down the back. Using a small teaspoon, carefully remove the red "coral" eggs and the green "tomalley" liver and hold these flavorful delicacies for later use in the sauce. Now put the lobster halves, flesh side down, into the sauté pan and let them gently, gently simmer for not a moment more than 15 minutes.

About 45 minutes before serving – completing the sauce and poaching the vegetables

After the 15 minutes, at once take out the lobster halves, remove all the flesh from the shells and claws, then cut up the shells into pieces and put these back into the sauté pan to continue the simmering, uncovered, for about another 20 minutes. Preferably using your clean fingers, gently work the red coral and the green tomalley into the remaining 2 tablespoons of now-soft butter. Thoroughly blend and smooth, then hold, covered, for the sauce.

As soon as the simmering is completed, turn off the heat and remove all the lobster shells. Then taste and adjust the seasonings, adding, as you please, more tomato paste, more salt and pepper. Hold the sauce off the heat in its covered pan. Cut the lobster flesh into large dice and hold. Now begin quickly preparing the *navarin* of vegetables. It helps, here, to have several saucepans going at once.

Turn on your oven to 400°F. and, on an open baking dish, put in your 8 white onions in their skins. They should be perfectly baked in about 30 minutes. Then they can be peeled and quartered, ready for the main dish. Boil the 8 sliced carrots and the diced turnips in salted water until just done – usually in about 10 minutes. Poach the green beans in boiling salted water until done but crisp – usually in about 8 minutes. Poach the peas in boiling salted water until just done – usually in about 4 minutes.

Final assembly and serving at table

Gently reheat the sauce, at the same time carefully blending in the coral and tomalley butter. It will slightly thicken the sauce, but it remains a natural bouillon of the aromatic juices. Put in the dice of lobster and let it just reheat for a minute or two. You can keep very gentle heat under the pan, but do not let the temperature get up to anywhere near boiling. Serve this in large, deep, hot soup plates. Assemble in each a portion of white onions, carrots, white turnips, green beans, green peas, with plenty of the lobster sauce poured over them and, finally, the lobster itself spooned over the top. With this memorable conglomeration, the brothers Troisgros served me a noble, richly fruity, white Burgundy from Chassagne-Montrachet. In New York, where I might serve an American wine in its place, my choice would be a noble California Pinot Chardonnay.

AMERICAN BAY SCALLOPS DISGUISED AS FRENCH COQUILLES SAINT-JACQUES À LA MAYENNAISE

(for 4)

When Chef Henri Eudes (page 33) – after professional training in Paris and experience in some of the great restaurants of France, London and New York – opened his own small, French-style bistro, Le Café de la Gare, in Hastings-on-Hudson, the special pleasure and strength of his menu was the interpretation of some of the ancient family recipes from his mother's and grandmother's home in the country region of the Mayenne, in northwestern France. They may be old recipes, but in their tradition of lightness and simplicity they are as new as the newest of French cuisine experimentation. Since the agricultural lands of the Mayenne are roughly between Brittany and Normandy, its regional cuisine often combines the fish and shellfish of the Brittany coast with the famous Calvados apple brandy of Normandy. *Coquilles Saint-Jacques* is not, as some people think, the title of a dish, but the proper French name for scallops. All of us, of course, have eaten hundreds of mediocre and unimaginative versions of this most ubiquitous of all dishes on restaurant menus. Chef Eudes's recipe – even after the Low-High removal of a part of the butter and cream – is just about the best, most delicate, subtlest preparation of scallops I have ever tasted. (This recipe requires the advance preparation of a batch of the basic Low-High fish bouillon from page 70.)

Fish bouillon, basic Low-High,
   see above, or compromise
   with clam juice (about
   2¼ cups)
Bay scallops (1 lb)
Shrimp, very small, in their
   shells (¼ lb)
Vinegar, white wine (3 Tbs)
Shallot, finely minced (1 clove)
Sweet butter (4 Tbs)

White wine, dry (3 Tbs)
Calvados apple brandy (1 tsp)
Light cream (1 cup)
Red cayenne pepper, to taste
Salt, coarse crystal, to taste
Pepper, preferably Chinese
   Szechuan, freshly ground,
   to taste
Parsley (for garnish)

Preparation in hardly more than 15 to 20 minutes

Assuming that you have prepared the fish bouillon in advance, put 2 cups of it into a 1-quart saucepan, heat to gentle simmering and hold just below boiling, covered. Wash and dry the scallops and shrimp (the latter still in their shells), then hold them. In a 1-pint saucepan, bring the 3 tablespoons of vinegar to a rolling boil, add the minced shallot and reduce, boiling hard, until the vinegar has almost completely evaporated – usually in under 2 minutes. Quickly stir in the 4 tablespoons of butter, cut into slivers, and, as soon as it is melted, turn off the heat. Now work in 2 of the remaining tablespoons of fish bouillon, the 3 tablespoons of wine, the teaspoon of Calvados, the cup of light cream, with a pinch of the red cayenne plus salt and Chinese pepper to taste. Now gently heat it all up, stirring continuously, until it has achieved a merry bubbling. Let this continue, uncovered, to reduce the liquid and concentrate the flavors, until it tastes exactly the way you like it – usually in 3 to 5 minutes. If it becomes too thick, add a little more of the fish bouillon.

While the sauce continues boiling, bring the fish bouillon back to gentle simmering, drop in the scallops and shrimp and cook until just done – usually in about 3 minutes. Drain them at once. Now set out the scallops on warm plates and pour the sauce over them. Shell the shrimp and use them to decorate each plate. Finally, sprinkle with the parsley and serve at once. With this superb arrangement of scallops, Chef Henri Eudes served me a noble, fruity, white wine from the Loire, a Sancerre de Chavignol. As an American equivalent, try a California Napa Fumé Blanc.

COQUILLES SAINT-JACQUES À LA NAGE – BAY SCALLOPS SWIMMING IN THEIR BOUILLON

(for 4)

Here, for comparison with the previous recipe, is a more revolutionary way of preparing scallops by the young Chef Daniel Météry, who directs the new, modern Restaurant Clovis at the Hôtel Windsor in Paris (see page 46). He serves his scallops in deep, hot soup dishes, accompanied by tiny dice of vegetables, all *à la nage,* "in the swim," in their aromatic natural bouillon. It is all rather like a lovely garnished soup and is best eaten with a silver soup spoon. The recipe requires you to prepare in advance a batch of the basic Low-High fish bouillon from page 70.

Fish bouillon, basic Low-High,
  see above (1 quart)
Bay scallops, washed (about
  30, usually 1 to 1½ lbs)
Salt, coarse crystal, to taste
Black pepper, freshly ground,
  to taste
Carrots, scraped and diced to
  about the size of green peas
  (4 medium)

White onions, smallest you can
  find, peeled and thinly sliced
  (6 to 8, according to size)
Sour cream (2 tsp)
Sweet butter (4 Tbs)
Lemon (½)
Chervil, fresh leaves in season,
  chopped (1 Tbs) (or substitute fresh basil or tarragon
  or thyme)

Preparation in about 15 minutes

Assuming that you have prepared 1 quart of fish bouillon in advance, pour it into a 1½-quart lidded saucepan and gently heat it up to simmering. Then cover and keep it just below boiling, until you need it. Place your washed scallops in a 2-quart lidded saucepan, lightly salting and peppering them to your taste, then covering them without turning on the heat. Put the diced carrots into a second 1½-quart saucepan and pour over enough of the hot fish bouillon to cover them. Gently simmer, uncovered, until just cooked but still quite crisp – usually in 5 to 7 minutes.

When the carrots are done, add the slices of onion. The instant the liquid returns to the boil, turn off the heat. Working fast, pour the carrots and onions with their hot bouillon over the waiting scallops, adding more hot bouillon from the main supply, just enough to cover the scallops by about half an inch. Turn the heat up fairly high under the scallops and, timing from the precise moment when the liquid returns to the boil, cook the scallops for exactly 2 minutes – not a second more, or they will become leathery. Warm up four soup plates.

Final adjustments and serving at table

After 2 minutes, turn off the heat and, with a slotted spoon, fish out the scallops and the vegetables, dividing them equally among the four warm soup plates. Keep them all warm. Now add more bouillon from the main supply to the scallop bouillon until the volume in the saucepan is about 3 cups. Bring it up to a rolling boil and keep it bubbling hard to reduce it, magnifying and sharpening its flavors. When it is just beginning to develop a mildly glutinous body, turn off the heat and carefully work in the 2 teaspoons of sour cream. Now enrich the sauce by performing the small operation known in the French cuisine as *monter au beurre*, "mounting with butter." Turn the heat back up to merry bubbling and, arming yourself with a boxwood spoon, drop in the 4 tablespoons of butter, sliver by sliver, stirring continuously until each sliver is melted across the surface, but not incorporated into the bouillon. This follows the new cuisine principle of never cooking butter, but always adding it at the last moment. When all the butter has formed a light film on the surface of the bubbling bouillon, add a couple of spritzes of lemon juice, just enough to give the slightest sense of tartness. Taste and adjust salt and pepper, as required. Turn off the heat and stir in the tablespoon of fresh herb leaves. (Chef Météry's idea of adding them to the saucepan rather than sprinkling them directly onto the plates is to warm the leaves for a second or two, which encourages them to give off more of the flavor and scent of their aromatic oils.) Pour the bouillon sauce, in equal portions, into the four soup plates and serve instantly. Chef Météry served me with this memorable example of his creative skill, a noble, rich, white Burgundy from Puligny-Montrachet. It might be replaced on our side of the Atlantic by a noble California Pinot Chardonnay from Sonoma.

SEA BASS DRY-GRILLED AND CRUSTED WITH TARRAGON

(for 4)

When I first tasted this preparation of fish a few months ago at the three-star Restaurant des Frères Troisgros in Roanne (see page 50), it was such a dramatic improvement over the normal breaded fillets that it seemed unbelievable that there was no secret trick, that it was an entirely simple recipe. It is a new invention of the great Chefs Jean and Pierre Troisgros and the true secret of its success lies in the precision of every technical detail.

Jean told me, "This is the perfect example of our new cuisine. Our method is completely flexible. It works equally well with any fish or fresh herb in season. We add any one of a dozen possible sauces. In our new cuisine, nothing is fixed. You cook as you please. There are no more fixed and inflexible rules – no more right and wrong ways. The only inflexible demand is that the dish shall be seasoned so as to have some distinctive character, dominated by the natural taste of fresh ingredients."

All one need add is that this is one of the quickest and simplest of all fish recipes. It does require a whole fish of, say, not less than 3 pounds, otherwise the fillets may not be quite thick enough and could dry out. The final contrast between the aromatic and crackly crust and the juicy softness of the inside flesh is quite extraordinary.

Sea bass, whole, cleaned and scaled, split open – including head – but not divided, with backbone and gills removed (1, weight before boning about 3½ lbs)	Tarragon, fresh leaf in season, chopped (¼ cup) (or other fresh herb in season, see above)
Salt, coarse crystal, to taste	Sweet butter, melted (5 Tbs)
White pepper, freshly ground, to taste	Breadcrumbs or "stuffing mix," coarse (about 1 cup)

About 30 minutes before serving – active preparation about 15 minutes, plus about 10 to 15 minutes unsupervised grilling

Preheat your grill and set the rack so that the top surface of the fish will be about 5 inches below the heat. Lightly butter your grill platter and open up the fish on it, skin side down. Jean Troisgros stressed the importance of also splitting the head. Otherwise the head, which helps to transmit the heat into the flesh, if resting all on one side, tends to pull on the muscles and will tighten and harden the flesh.

Salt and pepper the surface of the fish. Sprinkle with the ¼ cup of tarragon. Moisten all over with the remaining 4 tablespoons of melted butter, to provide a kind of adhesive surface on which to stick the crust. Use your fingers to spread and press down the roughly 1 cup of breadcrumbs until the entire surface is thoroughly covered.

Slide the fish under the grill. Begin watching it carefully after the first 8 minutes. The objective is that the crust be a beautiful golden brown at the precise moment that the fish underneath is perfectly done, usually in no more than 10 to 12 minutes. If the top surface browns too fast, you can easily control it by covering it with a shallow tent of aluminum foil.

Serving at table

When the crust is the right color and the flesh is just flaky and opaque, the sea bass should be served immediately on very hot plates. If it is kept waiting, it will begin to dry out. Any of the classic fish sauces can accompany it, but my favorite is the Troisgros' own invention, their *"Sauce Antibeoise"* (page 335), or it could be the "Virgin Tomato Sauce" from page 345, or the "Green and Red Sauces" from page 336. The sauce should never be poured over the fish, but around it, so that the crust does not become soggy and lose its crackle. As the wine, the Troisgros served me a dry and fruity, icily refreshing white Viognier from the village of Condrieu, on the Rhône. I might serve in its place a California Pinot Blanc, fruity and rich, from Monterey.

BRAISED SEA BASS WRAPPED IN LETTUCE LEAF PACKAGES

(for 4)

This is another of the extraordinary specialties of Chef Roger Vergé (page 52), at his three-star Le Moulin de Mougins in Provence. He prepares it, of course, with the *loup de mer*, the "sea wolf" of the Mediterranean – a fish with an almost earthy flavor and texture. I have translated and adapted his recipe to use our sea bass and it makes an excellent conversion in the American kitchen.

Sea bass, boned fillets
   (4, about ¾ lb per person)
Salt, coarse crystal, to taste
Black pepper, freshly ground,
   to taste
Flour (about 1 Tbs)
Sweet butter (5 Tbs)
Lettuce leaves, large, nice
   green, for the packages
   (about a dozen)

Vermouth, dry white
   (about ½–¾ cup)
Shallots, finely minced (1 Tbs)
White wine, dry (2 Tbs)
Sour cream (4 Tbs)

About 1 hour before serving – preparing the packages in about 15 minutes

Wash and dry the fillets, then lightly sprinkle each fillet, on both sides, with salt, pepper and a minimum dusting of flour. Hold them.

Preheat your oven to 375°F. Fill a large, 4-quart saucepan with water, make it fairly salty, then bring it up just to boiling and dump your dozen lettuce leaves in it for hardly more than a few seconds, to soften them and make them flexible. Take them out, spread them apart and let them cool enough so you can handle them.

Choose a sauté pan large enough to put in the four fillets side by side, with enough room to spare so that they can be moved around and turned over. Turn up the heat to fairly high frying temperature and lubricate the bottom of the pan by melting in 2 tablespoons of the butter. You will not want to cook the fillets, but simply to brown them lightly and very quickly. Now put them into the sauté pan and very lightly brown them, on both sides, at maximum speed – keeping them moving in the pan almost continuously and turning them over. You just want to "seize them" (*les saisir*) as Vergé puts it, not cook them – take them out of the pan as soon as possible.

As soon as the fillets are browned, wrap each into a neat package with the lettuce leaves, tucking in the ends, so that it all holds together neatly without any need for tying. Choose an *au gratin* baking dish large enough to take the fillets side by side, with about half an inch of space between each, butter it lightly and lay the packages in it. Pour over them ½ cup of the Vermouth and sprinkle them with the tablespoon of minced shallots.

About 40 minutes before serving – braising the fish in about 30 minutes

Set the pan in the center of the oven and leave it until, pressing the packages with the tips of your fingers, you feel that the fish has lost its elasticity and is firmly set – usually in 25 to 35 minutes, depending on the thickness of the fillets. If, during the oven period, the pan shows signs of drying out, add more of the Vermouth. During the last 5 minutes of the oven time, put in the serving plates to warm up.

About 10 minutes before serving – preparing the sauce

As soon as the fish packages are done, turn down the oven to keep-warm temperature, 160°F. Lift the packages onto the serving plates with a slotted spatula and hold them warm. Pour the juices from the baking pan into a saucepan, thoroughly rinsing out the pan with the 2 tablespoons of wine. Boil the liquid in the saucepan hard to reduce it quickly until it begins to glaze and thicken. This can be used as the sauce over the fish packages, but Chef Vergé enriches it. Off the fire, he works in the 4 tablespoons of sour cream, blends it thoroughly, and heats it up almost, but not quite, to boiling. Again, off the fire, he works in the final 2 tablespoons of butter, now beating the sauce with a wire whisk. At this point, taste and adjust seasonings. Reheat to serving temperature and pour over the fish packages on the plates. Serve at once. With this superb invention of slightly earthy fish, Chef Roger Vergé served a slightly earthy wine: a fine, very fruity, Rosé de Provence from the vintners of St. Tropez. Its American equivalent might be a California rosé from the Grenache, Gamay, Zinfandel, or Cabernet grapes from any of the northern counties.

FINAL NOTE: Vergé glorified this dish by surrounding it with a dazzling array of brilliantly colored, miniature vegetables of Provence: tiny wild mushrooms, baby tomatoes, young green beans, all sprinkled with chives, all undercooked to the point of being crackly and crispy in the mouth. Roger said, "These vegetables are undercooked in the 'new cuisine' style – only I sometimes wonder whether it is truthfully *'La Nouvelle Cuisine de France,'* or whether it is not really *'L'Ancienne Cuisine Chinoise.'* "

BRAISED SMALL SMELT WITH ORANGES, LEMONS AND MIXED FRUIT

(for 4)

At five o'clock in the morning, Chef Roger Vergé and I were drinking the blackest of black coffee in the garden of his three-star Le Moulin de Mougins in Provence (see page 52). At six, we were driving furiously in his small, roaringly noisy Datsun to the farmers' market and the fisherman's wharf in Cannes. Out of the car, darting through the crowds, Roger moved from stall to stall, from barrel to barrel of fish, poking with his fingers, sniffing, tasting, handing me this or that for my appraisal and education. After two hours of shopping, we finished up with piles of things, among them a supply of a small, wrigglingly alive Mediterranean rock fish called *sars* and some of the sweetest oranges and fattest lemons I have ever experienced. From these ingredients, for my lunch, Roger prepared what is, perhaps, the most brilliantly innovative concoction of the modern gastronomic revolution.

One is shocked to discover the dish is to be a mingling of whole baked fish with warmed fresh citrus fruits. So strong was my subconscious gastronomic conservatism that I almost jumped in my chair at table when I heard the waiter say, as he set the plate before me, "M'sieur, here is your fish with mixed fruit." There is a degree of amazement in the mouth at the first bite, but, once the initial surprise is past, there follows the realization that it is a fantastic and wonderful effect. There is, after all, something new under the sun!

In New York, I substitute for Chef Vergé's tiny Mediterranean *sars* almost any small fish – fresh sardines, smelt, baby whiting, or any other local seasonal fish. For the complete success of this amazing dish, the oranges must be reasonably sweet and the lemons not too acid or bitter. This is sometimes a problem with our United States lemons compared to the luscious Provençal varieties. So I have made some slight changes from the techniques used by Roger Vergé. Although the dish can be served with oranges and lemons alone, I often add a balanced mixture of some other fruits to widen the variety of tastes and textures, including, according to the season, halved and seeded white grapes, peeled and sliced New Zealand Kiwi fruit, quartered kumquats, sliced ripe strawberries – any or all, as available. Beyond these, you can experiment, to your taste. Finally, to counterbalance the citrus acid, I add a small amount of sweet wine to the sauté pan in which the fruits are warmed. The total effect of faraway, aromatic softness almost carries the dining table on a magic carpet to Provence.

Smelt, or other small fish, whole, cleaned and scaled, heads left on (12 to 16, according to size)

Olive oil, preferably Provençal, pure green virgin (about 4 Tbs)

Sweet wine, Sauternes, or alternative (2 Tbs)

Oranges, sweet, peeled, thinly sliced and pitted (4 medium)

Lemons, peeled and pitted, thinly sliced, white inner skin and inner membranes removed (2)

Other fresh fruits, see above, according to season, also sliced (about 1 cup total)

Salt, coarse crystal, to taste

Black pepper, freshly ground, to taste

About 20 minutes before serving – preparing the fish and fruit in about 10 minutes, plus the baking time

Preheat your oven to 400°F. and set at its center a fairly large flat pan, half-filled with boiling water and with a grill rack resting across it. On this rack the fish will be laid for their brief few minutes of part roasting, part steaming. Wash and dry the smelt, leaving the skin on. Rub each very lightly with olive oil, then hold them while you prepare the fruit.

Quarter the orange slices and hold them in a bowl. Divide each lemon slice into 5 or 6 segments (according to size) and add them to the bowl. Also cut up and add the other fruits. Hold, covered.

Lightly salt and pepper the fish, place them on the grill rack above the boiling water in the oven and bake until their flesh is just firm – usually in about 8 to 12 minutes.

While the baking is in progress, cover the bottom of a medium-sized sauté pan with 2 tablespoons of the remaining olive oil, plus the 2 tablespoons of the wine and begin gently heating it up.   Add the fruits and stir them around to coat them with the oil and wine.   There is no question of cooking them or boiling them.   Just heat them enough so that they feel nice and warm on the tongue when they are eaten with the fish.

Serving at table

If you want to be formal, you can behead, skin and bone the fish before setting them on the table.   Chef Vergé expects his guests to do it themselves on their plates.   In either case, serve the fruit on and around the fish for a plate of beautiful bright colors, with a fantastic but irresistibly attractive gastronomic effect.   With it Chef Vergé served me a fine, strong, white Sancerre from the Loire.   For an American equivalent, choose a California Napa Fumé Blanc.

THE NEAREST AMERICAN APPROACH TO CHEF PAUL HAEBERLIN'S GREAT TURBOT À LA NAGE – SWIMMING IN ITS AROMATIC BOUILLON

(for 4)

I subscribe to the theory, almost universally held by the top French gastronomes, that there is no supremely great restaurant in Paris, but that there are at least four in the French provinces.   Among these, certainly the most beautiful and perhaps gastronomically the most stunning, is the three-star Auberge de l'Ill, in the tiny village of Illhaeusern in Alsace, owned and run by the brothers Jean-Pierre and Paul Haeberlin (see page 39).   Chef Paul is a true Alsatian, which means that, all his life, he has used butter and cream as if they were the lavish foundations of all that is good to eat.   But Paul is obviously great enough and sensitive enough to be influenced by the new ideas in French cooking.

The last time I dined at the Auberge, Paul presented, as a complete surprise, this extraordinary preparation of fresh turbot, lobster and vegetables "swimming around" in a clear, almost fatless, aromatic bouillon. Admittedly, it was not exactly in tune with the Haeberlin tradition or the luxurious overabundance of Alsace. But its perfect balance and variety of textures made it a deeply satisfying and memorable dish.

The huge, flat, white turbot has been, for a hundred years, the delicate, elegant, "snow fish" for great European banquets. It is not much discussed (in fact sometimes not even mentioned) in American cookbooks because it is not caught off our shores and has been comparatively rare in our markets. There is every reason, now, to change this short-sighted policy. Turbot of very fair quality (iced but not frozen) is now imported into the United States. Also, the European turbot has several close American cousins by which it can be reasonably replaced. The nearest is the smaller brill (the French *barbue*), but there is also our Atlantic sand flounder, the West Indies peacock flounder, the large Pacific sand dab and, off Southern California, the curlfin, diamond, and sharpridge turbot. All have firm, snow-white flesh.

White wine, Alsatian
  Riesling (2 bottles)
Mixed fish, with bones, heads
  and skin, but cleaned, with
  gills and scales removed
  by fishmonger (2 lbs)
Bay leaf, whole (1)
Carrots, scraped and sliced
  (3 medium)
Celery, green Pascal with some
  leaves, destringed and sliced
  (2 good stalks)
Yellow onion, peeled
  (1 medium)
Cloves, whole, to stick into
  onion (2)
Parsley, stalks only, no leaves
  (about 6)
Basil, fresh leaves in season,
  whole (about 6 leaves)

Tarragon, fresh leaves in
  season, whole (about
  6 leaves)
White peppercorns, whole (6)
Lemon, citrus flesh only, no
  skin or zest (2 slices)
Salt, coarse crystal, to taste
Lobster, must be female, alive
  (1, about 2 lbs)
Turbot, boned fillets, pieces
  about 2 by 3 inches, see
  above (about 2½ lbs)
Sweet butter (4 Tbs)
More fresh leaf herbs, in
  season, chopped, to garnish
  plates at table, say parsley,
  basil, tarragon, etc.
  (total ¼ cup)

About 1½ hours before serving – preparing the court-bouillon and poaching the lobster – active work, about 10 minutes, plus about 40 minutes of unsupervised simmering

Choose a soup kettle of about 6 quarts and pour into it 2 quarts of freshly drawn cold water and the 2 bottles of Alsatian white wine. Thoroughly wash the 2 pounds of mixed fish and add them to the kettle. Then also add, in turn: the bay leaf, the sliced carrots and celery, a few chopped celery leaves, the onion stuck with the 2 cloves, the parsley stalks without leaves (the leaves would darken the court-bouillon), the whole basil and tarragon leaves, the 6 peppercorns, the 2 slices of lemon and salt to taste. Let it all gently simmer, uncovered, skimming off scum and stirring occasionally, for about 20 minutes.

Meanwhile, in a separate soup kettle, poach the lobster, starting it in cold salted water to ensure that it dies painlessly. Turn on high heat under the kettle and as soon as the water starts to bubble, time the boiling of the lobster for exactly 20 minutes, then turn off the heat and leave the lobster in the hot water for 5 minutes longer.

About 40 minutes before serving – poaching the turbot

Take the lobster out of the water and lay it on its back on a wooden cutting board, cooling, until you can handle it. Strain out and discard all remaining solids from the court-bouillon and return the clear liquid to the kettle. Taste the liquid and readjust the seasonings. Put in the pieces of turbot and now carefully adjust the heat so that the liquid comes up to the gentlest simmering, no bubbling whatsoever, the top surface "just smiling," a lazy, slow movement of the liquid – a sort of trembling – no more than that. Let this continue, uncovered, until the turbot is perfectly done, just flaky and opaque – usually in no more than 10 minutes. Cut up the lobster, preferably with a sharp Chinese cleaver, cutting its tail into 4 segments and cracking open its claws. Remove all the edible flesh, and cut the tail pieces into slices about ¼-inch thick and the claws into large dice. Set your oven to keep-warm temperature, 150°F., and put in it the lobster meat in a covered dish and four deep, large soup plates. The moment the turbot is done, carefully lift each piece out with a slotted spatula and add it to the lobster meat.

About 15 minutes before serving – preparing the bouillon "nage"

Strain off from the kettle 3 pints of the clear bouillon. Put it into a fairly wide saucepan or deep sauté pan and reduce it at a rolling boil to concentrate and sharpen its flavors and to bring up its delicately gelatinous body. The boiling bouillon should be reduced by about half. You should end up with just about 3 cups. When its flavors and slightly gelatinous texture are perfect, turn off the heat and, as Chef Paul says, *monter au beurre,* mount it with butter. Gently stir into it, sliver after sliver, the 4 tablespoons of butter until all of it is melted onto the surface.

Serving at table

Pour enough of this bouillon into each soup plate so that you have a layer about ⅜-inch deep. Now carefully put in the pieces of turbot and lobster. Do not let the bouillon splash over the fish. The new Low-High principle is that their flavors should be kept separate until the very moment you actually take a mouthful. Lightly sprinkle each plate with the freshly chopped herbs. With this elegant fish, Jean-Pierre Haeberlin served me a noble, slightly soft, lusciously rich white Tokay d'Alsace. An American wine to accompany this dish could be one of the fruity and rich wines made from the Alsatian Gewürztraminer grape grown in the Alexander Valley of Sonoma in California.

FINAL NOTE: You can, if you wish, also garnish the turbot with a small quantity of separately poached or steamed light vegetables, say, some small green beans, or freshly picked garden peas, but obviously nothing that would dominate the fish.

Chapter Eight
Poultry and Game

in which, in high spirits, the great chefs cook
Chicken in Bouzy, Aiguillettes of Duck in Margaux,
Grape-Filled Quail with Chartreuse, and Rabbit
on Fire in Cognac. The author describes popping
the Garlic. We are induced to bury a Turkey.

CHEFS ALAIN CHAPEL AND JEAN TROISGROS ON SECRETS OF SAUTÉEING AND A NEW TRICK WITH GARLIC

I was having a July breakfast in the garden of Alain's lovely and peaceful three-star country *auberge*, Chez La Mère Charles, in Mionnay (see page 29). My rustic table and old wood lounge chair were shaded by the huge oak tree which grew out of the middle of the fountain on the green lawn behind the house. My dog was amusing herself sticking her paw into the pool of the fountain trying to catch one of the crayfish crawling across the bottom. Alain joined me for the last cup of coffee and talked about the morning's deliveries. The village postman, whose hobby was frog catching, had been out at dawn along the local stream and had brought in about one hundred of the freshest, smallest and most succulent frogs Alain had seen in years. There had also been a delivery of *poulettes de Bresse*, the finest baby chickens of France, fed entirely on corn and milk, each weighing no more than about 1¼ pounds. So, my menu for lunch was set. Alain would serve me sautéed frogs' legs and sautéed baby chicken. Our talk turned to the perfectly light sautéeing of perfectly fresh foods.

"So many amateur recipes," Alain said, "suggest that you 'throw it into the sauté pan,' as if it were a kind of easy catchall for every kitchen problem. In fact, the perfection of sautéeing is much more difficult than most people imagine. First, you must have the right kind of pan, or casserole, or *cocotte*. The best, in my experience, are tinned copper or enameled iron. But you cannot possibly use a single size of pan for every job. For lunch today, when I will sauté four of the baby *poulettes*, I will put them in a *cocotte* of a size so that they fit exactly – with no room to spare around or between them. If your pan is too big – if, for example, you try to sauté a single lamb chop in a very large pan – then, by the time you get the proper heat under your meat, all the bare parts of the pan will have thoroughly overheated and the butter will begin to smoke and burn. The pan must not be too small, either. If my *cocotte* is even a couple of centimeters too small for my *poulettes*, they will ride up, fail to touch the bottom and stew in the steam rather than sauté. That way, they will never develop the crispness and flavor of browning. Every amateur kitchen should have at least three sauté pans – one of 7 to 8 inches in diameter, another 9 to 10 inches and a third 11 to 12 inches – plus, perhaps, one even smaller and one a good deal larger. If you have the right pans, with reasonable control and experience of your heat source, it is not at all difficult to achieve the perfect sauté technique."

Hardly unexpectedly, at lunch the baby frogs' legs and the tiny chickens were sautéed to perfection and gloriously bathed in garlic!

A few days later, I was with Jean Troisgros and his brother Pierre at their three-star Restaurant des Frères Troisgros in Roanne (see page 50), where they served me almost the same dish as Alain's, but with sautéed pigeon-squab, equally rubbed and smoothed, inside and out, with garlic. I asked Jean how so much garlic could have all its bitterness and pungency so soothingly removed, while still retaining its character.

"We use our garlic in a quite special way," Jean said, "a way that involves much less work than all that old fashioned mashing and mincing and, at the same time, gives us a much tighter control of the amount of garlic that gets into the dish. In fact we control the garlic by controlling the evaporation of its flavor oils. First, we leave our garlic cloves whole and with the outer skin intact – as we say, *en chemise*, in its shirt. The skin must have no cracks or holes. Then, as it heats up, a small pressure of steam forms inside and literally poaches the flesh of the garlic, converting it to a smooth paste and, at the same time, evaporating off the bitterly pungent oils.

"Then, when the squab is cooked, if you want only a very delicate garlic flavor, you must fish out the whole cloves and throw them away. If you want a stronger garlic flavor, you pinch the cooked clove and, presto, the inside paste squeezes out like toothpaste from a tube. You throw away the slightly burned skin and incorporate the garlic paste into the sauce. Finally, if you know that your guest at table is a garlic lover, place two or three of the still-whole cooked cloves on his plate, so that he can squeeze them himself and spread his squab and its accompanying vegetables with additional garlic. You can use from one to a dozen cloves and then you can squeeze out as few or as many as your hungry little heart desires! Our method with garlic can be used in almost all forms of cooking: sautéeing, oven baking, boiling in soups and stews. . . . You must avoid it only when frying or grilling with extremely high heat. Then the garlic clove rapidly burns black and gives off a nasty, smoky-sour taste. But 90% of the time, this is the best of all ways with garlic."

Indeed, the garlic squab that Jean placed before me was the best I had ever tasted. There were two mushy and soft cloves on my plate and squeezing them was as much fun as popping balloons.

SMALL CHICKEN OR PIGEON SQUAB SAUTÉED WITH WHOLE GARLIC

(for 4)

See my discussion of this recipe with Chefs Alain Chapel and Jean Troisgros on the previous pages. For a true aficionado of garlic, there could hardly be a more memorable day of pleasure than to lunch with Alain on his baby Bresse chicken and then to drive cross country to dine with Jean on his squabs – all beautifully garlicky, yet with a surprising subtlety. Since I am entirely unable to decide which version I like better, I have simply translated and adapted my favorite details from each and combined them into my American version. *Poulettes de Bresse* are, of course, not available on our side of the ocean, so the following is for squab, but small American chickens may be substituted. You can be as flexible as you like about the garlic. You can positively bathe in it or reduce it to a tantalizing side issue.

Squabs, fresh, plump, with
   their livers (4)
Lemon (½)
Salt, coarse crystal, to taste
White pepper, coarsely ground,
   to taste
Sweet butter (2–4 Tbs)
Olive oil, pure green
   virgin (1 Tbs)

Garlic, unpeeled (24 whole
   cloves)
Chicken livers (¾ lb)
Cognac (¼ cup)
Chicken bouillon, clear
   (about ¼ cup)

About 45 minutes before serving – active work about 30 minutes, plus about 15 minutes of unsupervised baking

Preheat your oven to 375°F. Rub the squabs, inside and out, with the cut side of the half-lemon. Lightly salt and pepper the birds, then rub them all over with a minimum quantity of butter, say, about half a tablespoon per bird. They should be cooked in a tinned copper or enameled cast-iron casserole or *cocotte*, just large enough to hold them carefully so that they can be turned over individually. Set this *cocotte* onto a top burner over fairly high frying temperature and lubricate its bottom with the tablespoon of olive oil. When the *cocotte* is thoroughly hot, very quickly brown the squabs, turning them around almost continuously, until they are lightly flecked with gold on all sides – in no more than 2 or 3 minutes. Immediately take them off the heat and insert inside each bird 6 whole unpeeled cloves of garlic. Arrange the birds neatly in the *cocotte* and set it, uncovered, into the oven. After 5 minutes, baste the squabs with their juices. As they begin to brown on top, turn them over. After another 5 minutes in the oven, baste and turn them over again. Put them back into the oven and now watch them carefully. They are done when the skins have become walnut brown – usually in about 12 to 15 minutes. Meanwhile, wash the ¾ pound of chicken livers, remove the membranes and divide the livers into 4 portions. Wash and separate the 4 squab livers.

About 15 minutes before serving – preparing the sauce

When the squabs are just about done, take them out again and insert inside each a squab liver and a ¼ part of the chicken livers. Put them back in the oven just long enough to set but not cook the livers – not more than 60 seconds. Now turn off the oven and remove the livers and garlic cloves from inside each bird. Keep the squabs warm. Deglaze the bottom of the *cocotte* by pouring in the ¼ cup of Cognac and scraping off all the tasty brown bits with the edge of a wooden spoon. Quickly purée the livers (in a Cuisinart chopper-churner, or an electric blender, or by hand-rubbing through a sieve) and work this purée into the Cognac and juices in the bottom of the *cocotte*. Pick out 8 of the still-whole garlic cloves and set them to keep warm with the squabs. Squeeze the remaining 16 garlic cloves into the *cocotte,* throwing away the skins. Blend the garlic paste into the liver purée. Do not be scared by so much garlic. Most of its pungency will by now have been evaporated. Taste the purée and adjust the seasonings. If the purée remains too thick, work into it, teaspoon by teaspoon, a little of the chicken bouillon. Also, if you want to enrich it, you can work in a little of the remaining butter. Finally gently reheat the purée.

Serving at table

Place each whole squab on a very hot plate and lightly cover the bird with the purée sauce. Add to each plate two of the whole cloves of garlic which may be squeezed out by the diner. The final effect is of the subtle permeation of the flesh of the squab with the garlic. The wine the Brothers Troisgros served me was one of their finest Beaujolais poured from a *pichet,* the classic Burgundian pewter or silver pitcher. In the United States, one could substitute a fine California Gamay from Monterey.

FINAL NOTE: The squabs (or baby chickens) should, of course, be surrounded by an attractive array of fresh garden vegetables. When Alain Chapel served me, he brought a side plate of tiny wild *girolle* mushrooms, miniature carrots, baby green beans, very small onions and artichokes. Alain's chickens, quite chewy, but marvellously juicy, provided a sort of super-garlic picnic. The temptation to pick up the bones with your fingers was irresistible. It is vaguely reported that when Napoleon had his cook serve this to Josephine, she looked at him with her warmest smile and said: "This is one of the four great joys of life – I have forgotten what are the other three."

BOUZY CHICKEN FROM CHAMPAGNE

(for 4)

Do not be misled. This recipe is not a first cousin of the "Chinese Drunken Chicken." The word "Bouzy" may have a delightfully bibulous sound, but in fact it is the dead-serious name of a small village in the Champagne region of France, famous, not for any sparkling wine, but for the best red wine of the district. Bouzy wine is just now beginning to arrive in the United States in reasonable quantities.

Few people know more about cooking with Bouzy than the Mayor of the nearby hamlet of Brugny, the Countess de Voguë. Since she is young, most of her preparations are in the new, Low-High tradition. When she gave me this recipe, she said: "To make this perfectly, of course, you must use our Bouzy, but if you absolutely cannot get it in your part of America, it is possible to use, for example, a light Bordeaux or a fine Beaujolais.

This recipe, of course, is instantly recognizable as a simple variation of the classic Burgundian *coq au Chambertin.* Perhaps Bouzy is trying to steal Chambertin's thunder! Yet the fruity and light Bouzy seems to give a noticeably different flavor to the chicken. Also, in the Low-High tradition, almost all the Burgundian tricks for the enrichment of the dish have been eliminated.   Here, there is no sautéeing of the chicken in large quantities of butter – no encrusting the chicken pieces with flour – no garnishing with bits of fat pork – no thickening of the sauce with cream and flour – no serving with butter-soaked croutons.   A classic way of preparing chicken, known and admired all over the world, has been given a new and memorable delicacy and lightness.

Chicken, or young capon, cut up for fricasseeing (about 3½ to 4 lbs)
Lemon (½)
Butter (about 3 Tbs)
Cognac (⅓ cup)
Red wine, light, preferably Bouzy, see above (1 bottle)
Garlic (2 cloves)
Bay leaves (2)
Basil, fresh leaves in season, chopped (1 Tbs)
Parsley, leaf only, chopped (1 Tbs)

Thyme, fresh leaf in season, chopped (1 Tbs)
Salt, coarse crystal, to taste
Black pepper, freshly ground, to taste
Canadian bacon, entirely lean, diced or slivered (6 oz)
Mushroom caps, smallish, good color and shape (about 1 dozen)
White onions, small boilers (about 1 dozen)

About 1¾ hours before serving – active work about 30 minutes, plus about 1¼ hours of unsupervised simmering

Preheat your grill to high temperature.   Rub each piece of chicken, first with the cut side of the half lemon, then with a minimum amount of the butter.   Pack the pieces closely together, skin side up, in an open grilling pan and place under the grill at a level so that the top surface of the chicken is about 2½ to 3 inches from the heat.   Within about 2 to 3 minutes, the tops of the chicken pieces should be just beginning to be flecked with brown.   The moment this happens turn each piece over and similarly brown the other side.   Turn off the grill and pack the chicken pieces, again fairly tightly, into the bottom of a lidded casserole or *cocotte* in which the rest of the cooking will be done on top of the stove. Place the casserole over fairly high frying heat, pour in the ⅓ cup of Cognac and flame it. Pour in enough of the red Bouzy to cover the chicken by about half an inch. Bring rapidly up to simmering, at the same time adding: the 2 cloves of garlic, whole and in their skins, the 2 bay leaves, crumbled, the basil, parsley and thyme, with salt and pepper, to taste. Keep all this very gently simmering, covered, until the chicken is almost, but not quite, done – usually in an hour to an hour and a quarter. Meanwhile, place a sauté pan over medium-high frying heat, melt in it 1 tablespoon of the butter and quickly sauté the dice or slivers of Canadian bacon until they are quite crisp. Hold them, uncovered, until serving time.

About 15 minutes before serving

A few minutes before the chicken is fully done, add to the casserole the whole mushroom caps and whole white onions. Let them simmer until the onions are done, but still slightly crisp – usually in about 10 to 12 minutes. Then turn off the heat, skim off any small pools of floating chicken fat and finally adjust the seasonings.

Serving at table

The modern way is to serve the chicken directly from the kitchen onto hot, wide, deep soup plates, with the wine sauce in its natural, unthickened state – although the Bouzy does give it a certain degree of satisfactory and satisfying body. The mushrooms, onions (and any other garnishing vegetables that you may have decided to cook separately) are prettily arranged around the chicken. Sprinkle over the crisp dice of Canadian bacon. Provide each of your guests with a soup spoon for the sauce. I am sure that the Countess de Voguë would hope that you would serve with this another bottle of her beloved Bouzy, but in the United States she would doubtless approve of a California Gamay Beaujolais from the Livermore Valley.

CHICKEN WITH MADEIRA OR PORTO
AND BAKED APPLES

(for 4)

This is an example of the lightness and simplicity of many of the principal specialties of Chef Louis Outhier (page 47), at his three-star restaurant, L'Oasis, in the Mediterranean beach resort village of La Napoule a few miles west of Cannes. In the translation and adaptation of the Outhier original French recipe, I have, according to the basic Low-High principles, eliminated some of the butter and cream. Yet, in the eating, this American version has lost none of the pleasure I found in it when I first tasted it in Chef Outhier's sun-bathed courtyard, overlooking the Mediterranean. You can use either a fairly sweet Madeira, preferably a Bual (not a dry Sercial, or a very sweet Malmsey) or a good-quality Portuguese Porto. Whether you use one or the other will noticeably change the character of the dish. Try it both ways.

Chicken, roaster or capon, cut up for fricasseeing (about 3 to 3½ lbs)
Lemon (½)
Salt, coarse crystal, to taste
Black pepper, freshly ground, to taste
Sweet butter (4 Tbs)
Madeira, medium-sweet Bual or Porto, Ruby or Tawny (about ½ cup of one or the other)

Glace-de-viande, strong meat juice (3 Tbs) (see page 78)
Baking apples, preferably Rome Beauties in season, whole, cored (4 medium)
Pot cheese, low-fat (1 cup)
Yoghurt, plain, low-fat (⅓ cup)
Ricotta, Italian style (3 Tbs)

About 1 hour before serving – active preparation about 30 minutes, plus about 30 minutes of unsupervised poaching and baking

Preheat your oven to 350°F. Rub the pieces of chicken with the cut side of the half lemon, then salt and pepper. Choose a lidded sauté pan just large enough to hold the chicken pieces in a single tight layer, but do not yet put in the chicken. The pan should not be too large or it will overheat. Place it over fairly high frying heat and melt in it 2 tablespoons of the butter. When it is thoroughly hot, quickly sauté the chicken until each piece is flecked with light gold on all sides – usually in about 5 minutes. Meanwhile, mix together the ½ cup of Madeira or Porto with the 3 tablespoons of *glace-de-viande*. The moment the chicken is ready, turn down the heat to gentle simmering and pour on the wine mixture. Adjust the heat so that the liquid is now bubbling merrily, put on the lid, then let everything poach and steam until the chicken is perfectly done – usually in 25 to 30 minutes.

Meanwhile, place the 4 apples, still in their skins, on a baking platter and set them in the oven to bake until they are just done, but still quite firm – usually in about 30 to 35 minutes, according to size. Meanwhile, also, I prepare the low-fat thickening cream by putting the 1 cup of pot cheese, the ⅓ cup of yoghurt and the 3 tablespoons of ricotta into the bowl of my Cuisinart chopper-churner (or you can use an electric blender, or an electric beater). Then I run the machine until they are thoroughly blended and smoothly creamed – usually in about 7 to 8 seconds. Then transfer the mixture to a round-bottomed beating bowl and, arming yourself with a balloon wire whisk, beat hard to adjust the smoothness and texture. Thin it, if necessary, with a dash or two more wine, until you have about the consistency of whipped heavy cream. Hold this for use in the sauce.

About 15 minutes before serving – preparing the sauce

Set the dinner plates to warm. The chicken should not be brought to table on a serving platter (which involves delay, unnecessary cooling and loss of flavor), but should be handsomely garnished on the hot plates in the kitchen. As soon as the chicken is done, arrange the portions on the plates and continue to keep them warm. Turn up the heat under the sauté pan so that it boils hard to reduce the liquid, concentrating and sharpening the flavors. At the same time, scrape the bottom of the pan vigorously with the edge of a wooden spoon, to make sure that all flavorful deposits are incorporated into the sauce. When it is good and strong and shows the first signs of becoming syrupy, turn off the heat and carefully work in, tablespoon by tablespoon, the thickening pot cheese cream, until you have a consistency that will nicely coat the chicken. If the sauce tends to become too thick, thin it with an extra dash or two of the white wine. Taste, adding salt and pepper, as needed. Finally, work into the sauce the remaining 2 tablespoons of butter, sliver by sliver. While the sauce stays just warm in the pan, cut the baked apples into segments and spritz each segment with a drop or two of lemon juice. Pour the sauce over the chicken pieces on the plates and surround them with the segments of apple. Serve at once. With this memorable version of his chicken, Chef Louis Outhier served me a light, red Bandol from Provence. Its American equivalent might be a light red California Ruby Cabernet.

CHICKEN POACHED WITH FRESH LIME JUICE

(for 4)

This unusual and almost fatless preparation of chicken is an invention of the young Chef Daniel Météry (page 46), who directs the kitchens of the Restaurant Clovis of the Hôtel Windsor in Paris. It is a light, natural and simple dish, served with the sauce entirely unthickened, and fruitily refreshing with the taste of the limes. I found it quite a new experience in the serving of the ubiquitous chicken – something different, almost Caribbean. The success of the dish, of course, depends largely on the quality of the chicken. Daniel uses the finest of France, *poulets de Bresse*, which by French law are not permitted to be battery raised, but scratch, run and feed their natural way around the expansive spaces of the large farms of the region. The final result is a flesh that is firm, chewy, juicy and wonderful. On our side of the Atlantic, it is worth struggling to find a farm-raised chicken or capon, naturally fed and with a minimum of artifically induced fat.

Limes, ripe (about 5)
Chicken, roaster or capon,
   see above, cut for fricassee-
   ing (about 3 to 3½ lbs)
Salt, coarse crystal, to taste
Butter (4 Tbs)

Chicken bouillon, clear
   (2 cups)
Glace-de-viande, strong beef
   juice (1 Tbs) (see page 78)
Black pepper, freshly ground,
   to taste

About 50 minutes before serving – active work about 20 minutes, plus about 30 minutes of unsupervised poaching and reducing

Cut one of the limes in half and use the cut side to rub the pieces of chicken, then lightly salt them. Choose a lidded sauté pan large enough to hold the pieces, close together, without too much room to spare, but do not yet put in the chicken. If the pan is too large it will overheat around the edges. Set it over fairly high frying heat and melt in it 2 table-spoons of the butter. Then quickly sauté the pieces until they are flecked with gold on both sides – usually in about 5 min-utes. At once turn down the heat to gentle simmering and pour on 1 cup of the chicken bouillon. Bring it up to merry bubbling, cover, then leave the chicken to poach and steam until it is perfectly done – usually in 25 to 30 minutes.

Meanwhile, preheat your oven to keep-warm temperature, 160°F., and set in it four wide soup plates.

About 10 minutes before serving

The moment the chicken is done, take out the pieces, set out the servings on the soup plates and keep it all warm. Add to the juices in the sauté pan the remaining cup of chicken bouil-lon and boil hard to reduce, concentrating and sharpening the flavors. After about 5 minutes, when the flavor is good and strong, turn down the heat to just below simmering and work in the tablespoon of *glace-de-viande*. Then squeeze in the lime juice until you have a nice, tangy, fruity lime flavor. This usually requires the juice of 3½ to 4 limes. Gently work in the final 2 tablespoons of butter, sliver by sliver, to add, as Chef Météry puts it, "a touch of luxury to the acid leanness of the limes." Then taste, adding salt and pepper as needed. Pour this natural sauce over the chicken in the soup plates and serve at once. The best way to eat this is to cut a piece of chicken, then lift it to your mouth in a soup spoon with some of the sauce. To balance the fruity limes, Chef Météry served me a fruity, noble, rich, white Burgundy from the great vineyard of Les Genevrières in the village of Meursault, on the Côte d'Or. At my New York dining table, I might serve an American replacement – an equally noble California Pinot Chardonnay from the Livermore Valley.

NONFAT CHICKEN-IN-THE-POT WITH LOW-FAT SALAME STUFFING FOR THE EMPRESS EUGÉNIE

(for 4)

La Poule au Pot was more or less invented by King Henri IV of France, who, in a classic gesture to dramatize his hope that prosperity would be universal, promised the French people "a chicken in every pot every Sunday." The dish (if not quite the prosperity) has certainly become universal. Succeeding kings and queens of France have followed Henri IV in a devotion to boiled chicken, including the marvelously beautiful, eternally slim, Empress Eugénie, wife of Napoleon III, who gave her name to the village of Eugénie-les-Bains where Chef Michel Guérard (page 35) now runs his two-star restaurant, Le Pot au Feu. So it was inevitable – given the name of his restaurant and the name of his village – that Michel should develop his own modernistic interpretation of the peasant pot that was one of the favorites of the elegant empress.

The "*salame* stuffing" is neither an Italian *salame* nor a true stuffing. The name derives from its sausage shape (rolled in a cheesecloth), from its final function as a garnish on the plate and from the fact that the Italian word *salame* simply means "a mixture."

My translation and adaptation of this dish is best served with "*Sauce Gribette*" (page 338), which must be started the day before and marinated overnight. An ideal additional accompaniment is Michel's "Baked *Gâteau* of Mushroom,

Spinach and Tomato" (page 361), which will help to convert this basically simple pot into a magnificent Low-High feast, worthy of the fanciest dinner party.

Chicken bouillon, clear,
   entirely fatless (4 quarts)
Carrots, whole, scraped
   (10 medium)
Turnips, white, young,
   peeled (4)
Cabbage, left whole but with
   coarse outer leaves removed
   (1, not more than ¾ lbs)
Leek whites, carefully desanded and chunked (4 to 5)
Zucchini, washed and cut into
   bite-sized chunks (3 to 4)
Mushrooms, stems and caps,
   wiped and diced (1 cup)
Yellow onions, peeled and
   chopped (½ cup)
Tomatoes, peeled and
   seeded (2)

Chicken livers, quite finely
   chopped (½ lb)
Rosemary, fresh in season,
   chopped (1 Tbs)
Tarragon, fresh in season,
   chopped (1 Tbs)
Thyme, fresh in season,
   chopped (1 Tbs)
Parsley, chopped leaf (2 Tbs)
Salt, coarse crystal, to taste
Black pepper, freshly ground,
   to taste
Egg, whole (1)
Egg white (1)
Pot cheese, low-fat
   (about ½ cup)
Chicken, for stewing (3 to 4 lbs)
Lemon (½)

The day before – starting the sauce – active work about 10 minutes

Start marinating the ingredients for the *"Sauce Gribette,"* according to the recipe on page 338.

On the day – about 1¾ hours before serving – active preparation about 1 hour – unsupervised simmering about 45 minutes

Start gently heating up, in a large covered pot on top of the stove, the 4 quarts of chicken bouillon. Then take 7 of the carrots and cut them into nicely formed large olive shapes, cut 3 of the turnips into quarters, and hold them with the whole cabbage, chunked leeks and zucchini until they go into the pot.

Now start the *salame* stuffing. To produce its sausage shape, you will need a reasonably large sheet of cheesecloth. For the filling of the sausage, assemble in a mixing bowl: the 3 remaining carrots and the turnip cut into dice, the diced mushrooms, the chopped onions and the 2 tomatoes. Mix thoroughly and work into it, in turn, the ½ pound of chopped chicken livers, plus the rosemary, tarragon, thyme, and parsley, with salt and pepper to suit your taste. Finally, work in the whole egg, slightly beaten, plus the extra egg white. The mixture by now should be just stiff enough to shape into a sausage form. If not, work in a quarter cup or so of low-fat pot cheese. Now roll out the mixture into a fat sausage roughly 2½ inches in diameter and wrap it tightly in several layers of the cheesecloth, binding it fairly firmly with string and tying up both ends.

About 50 minutes before serving – stewing the chicken

Clean the chicken by rubbing it inside and out with the cut side of the half lemon. Then lower it gently into the pot of simmering bouillon. Also lower in beside it the wrapped stuffing sausage and the whole cabbage, making sure that everything is covered by the liquid. Drop into the corners the carrots, turnips, zucchini and leek whites you have been holding. Keep it all simmering gently, with the surface of the bouillon, *riant*, just smiling, as Chef Guérard says, until the chicken is done – perfectly tender, but still nicely firm and not falling away from the bones – usually in 40 to 45 minutes. Meanwhile, complete the *"Sauce Gribette"* (page 338) and the baked vegetable *gâteau* (page 361).

Serving at table

When the chicken is cooked, carefully take it out and, if you want to be very tight on fat, remove and discard its skin. Serve on very hot plates with the vegetables from the pot, the sausage stuffing cut into ½-inch thick slices, the cabbage cut into wedges, the *Sauce Gribette* and the baked vegetable *gâteau*. With this handsome assemblage, Chef Michel Guérard served me a fine, fruity, rich Riesling from Alsace. Or you could serve the American equivalent – a fruity California white Riesling (sometimes labeled Johannisberg Riesling) from the Napa Valley or from Monterey.

CHICKEN ROASTED IN A NEST OF SALT

(for 4)

This recipe is, in my experience, one of the finest (and most fatless) ways of preparing a chicken. For a discussion of the techniques of cooking in salt, see page 173. And for notes on how to get the right kind of salt, see the "Index of Sources" on page 392. Since the salt slightly solidifies during the cooking, you will need a blunt instrument (perhaps an old screwdriver) to break out the bird.

Chicken, whole, cleaned and washed (1, 3½ to 5 lbs)	**Salt, coarse crystal, to taste**
Pure rock salt to enclose the chicken (about 8 lbs)	**Black pepper, freshly ground, to taste**

About 2 hours before serving – active work about 10 minutes at the beginning and 10 minutes at the end – in between, there is nothing you can do

The all-important point is to choose exactly the right size and type of heavy, tightly-covered, baking pot, casserole, or *cocotte* (for example, the French Le Creuset of enameled iron). Hold the chicken inside the pot and see that there is about 2 inches of space between the walls all around and about 6 inches of space between the top of the chicken and the inside of the lid. In other words, the chicken must rest at the center of the pot surrounded with at least 2 to 3 inches of salt.

Preheat the oven to 400°F. Now layer the bottom of the pot with about 2 inches of salt, using up roughly the first 2½ pounds. Then, hold the chicken once more under cold running water, quickly salt and pepper it inside and lay it sideways, still dripping wet, precisely in the center of the pot.

Pack the next 2½ pounds of salt tightly all around the chicken, filling up the corners, but carefully avoiding allowing any of the salt to fall inside the chicken. Pack as much as necessary of the rest of the salt on top of the chicken, completely enclosing it. Cover the pot, set it in the center of the oven and forget it. This is one method of cooking that requires no attention.

The problem is, how long to leave it. You cannot, obviously, open it up to see how it is going. The first time, you will have to take the risk of riding with me on the timing, bearing in mind that your oven may be more or less efficient than mine. Then, after you have had your first experience, you can adjust to fit in with your own equipment. For a 3½ pound bird, I give it 1¼ hours – for 4 pounds, 1½ hours – for 5 pounds, just over 1¾ hours. At the end of the time, break out the chicken. Scrape off any clinging grains of salt, looking carefully for grains that may have fallen inside and then serve at once. If ever there was a truly no-fat way of cooking, this is it. The accompanying wine served to me was a fine, refreshing, slightly *petillant*, white Blanc de Blancs from the mountain village of Seyssel in the High Savoy. A similar American wine would be a California Pinot Blanc from Sonoma.

FRICASSEE OF CHICKEN WITH JUMBO SHRIMP À LA TOURANGELLE

(for 4)

This fine combination of chicken and shrimp is one of the memorable inventions of Chef Charles Barrier (page 23), at his three-star restaurant, Chez Barrier, just outside the city of Tours on the Loire River. This is a near-perfect example of the lightness and simplicity of the classic cuisine of Touraine and the Loire Valley. It is, basically, the cooking of the farmhouses of the region brought up to elegant perfection by a virtuoso among the great *cuisiniers*.

This recipe requires the advance preparation of a shrimp flavoring paste, which rests and ripens in the refrigerator overnight. This involves boiling the shrimp first by the basic

Low-High recipe on page 84 so you will need the ingredients
for that operation in addition to those listed below.

Jumbo shrimp, with shells
(16 to 20 according to size)
Sweet butter (about 6 Tbs)
Yellow onion, peeled and
minced (1 medium)
Carrot, scraped and finely
minced (1 medium)
Bay leaf (1)
Thyme, fresh leaf in season,
chopped (1 Tbs)
Salt, fine-grind, to taste
White pepper, freshly ground,
to taste

Chicken, fine roaster or capon,
cut up for fricasseeing
(about 4 lbs)
Lemon (½)
Salt, coarse crystal, to taste
Black pepper, freshly ground,
to taste
Pot cheese, low-fat (2 cups)
Yoghurt, plain, low-fat (⅔ cup)
Ricotta, Italian style (5 Tbs
plus 1 tsp)
Chicken bouillon (up to
½ cup)

**The day before – preparing the shrimp
paste in about 45 minutes**

Wash and boil the jumbo shrimp according to the basic Low-
High method on page 84. After they have slightly cooled
in their bouillon, shell and devein them (saving the shells)
and hold them back in their bouillon, tightly covered, in the
refrigerator overnight. I now put the shells into the bowl
of my Cuisinart chopper-churner and run the machine for just
about 1 second, simply turning it on and off, so that the shrimp
shells are chopped into small pieces. Hold them. Set a sauté
pan over fairly low frying heat, melt in it 1 tablespoon of the
butter, then add the minced onion and carrot, the bay leaf,
crumbled, plus the chopped thyme. Stir everything around
letting it just poach, without frying or browning, until it is all
fairly well softened – usually in about 5 minutes. Now work
in the shrimp shell bits and let everything simmer, covered,
for about 30 minutes. Turn off the heat and let it cool. I then
return the entire contents of the sauté pan to the bowl of my
chopper-churner (or you can use a blender), add 3 tablespoons
of butter and run the machine until it is all smoothly mixed,
but not so long that it becomes a mushy paste – usually in

about 8 seconds. Now, to get rid of the tiny remaining bits of shell, rub the paste through a very fine sieve. Finally, taste it, and add fine salt and white pepper, as needed. You should end up with about ½ cup of this superb flavoring paste to be stored in the refrigerator, tightly covered, overnight.

On the day – about 50 minutes before serving – active work about 20 minutes, plus about 30 minutes of unsupervised sautéeing and poaching

Take the shrimp and the shrimp flavoring paste out of the refrigerator and let them come to room temperature. Rub the chicken pieces with the cut side of the half-lemon, then press into them a light sprinkling of the coarse salt and the black pepper. Choose a lidded sauté pan to hold the chicken pieces just comfortably touching each other, but do not yet put them in. If the pan is too large it will overheat. Set it over medium frying heat and melt in it 2 tablespoons of the butter. Sauté the chicken pieces until they are flecked with light gold on both sides – usually in about 5 minutes. Then turn down the heat to gentle bubbling and cover the pan so that the chicken poaches in the steam of its own juices until it is perfectly cooked – usually in 25 to 30 minutes more.

Meanwhile, turn on your oven to keep-warm temperature, 175°F., and set in it the four serving plates and the still-covered dish of shrimp to warm up. The shrimp paste is to remain at room temperature. Now prepare the thickening pot cheese cream. I again turn to my chopper-churner (or use a blender) and put into its bowl the 2 cups of pot cheese, the ⅔ cup of yoghurt and the 5 tablespoons plus 1 teaspoon of ricotta, then run the machine until I have a smooth cream – usually in about 7 to 8 seconds. Transfer this to a round-bottomed beating bowl and, with a balloon wire whisk, whip it hard until it is a light, fluffy whip. Hold until needed.

About 10 minutes before serving – preparing the sauce

As soon as the chicken is done, set portions of it out on the warm plates. Now adjust the heat under the sauté pan so that the juices in it are just below simmering. Gently and gradually work into them about half of the pot cheese whip and all of the shrimp paste. Gradually add more of the whip until the sauce coats the spoon with the texture of heavy cream. Then taste and adjust the seasonings. If the sauce gets too thick, add a dash or two of the chicken bouillon. As soon as it is right, pour it around the chicken on the plates, decorating each serving with 4 or 5 of the pink jumbo shrimp and bring it all to table immediately. With this superb specialty of the Loire Valley Chef Charles Barrier served me a fine, light, dryly fruity local white from Mont-Louis. The nearest American equivalent in character and personality is perhaps a soft, rich California Chenin Blanc from Monterey.

FRICANDEAU OF CHICKEN IN RED WINE VINEGAR

(for 4)

This ancient recipe, which in recent years has spread throughout France, is a specialty of the Brothers Troisgros (page 50) at their three-star restaurant in Roanne. During the hot, steamy summers along the Loire River, every local winemaker has had the unpleasant experience of finding that some of his wine has turned to vinegar. (Incidentally, this is why the city of Orléans on the upper Loire became the "vinegar capital" of France.) However, the thrifty wives of the winemakers insist on using up some of the good red wine vinegar by putting it into the pan while sautéeing a chicken. The result is unusual and delicately refreshing. The chicken flesh becomes, so to speak, a lightly flavored salad.

Chicken, roaster, or capon, cut up for fricasseeing (4 to 5 lbs)	Chives, chopped (small bunch)
Salt, coarse crystal, to taste	Tarragon, fresh leaves in season (small bunch)
White pepper, freshly ground, to taste	Thyme, fresh leaves in season, chopped (1 Tbs)
Sweet butter (4 Tbs)	Pot cheese, low-fat (1 cup)
Garlic, unpeeled (4 cloves)	Yoghurt, plain, low-fat
Parsley, fresh (small bunch)	(⅓ cup)

Ricotta, Italian style, low-fat
(3 Tbs)
Vinegar, red wine (about
¾ cup)
Chicken bouillon, clear,
entirely fatless (2 cups)

Veal bouillon, very strong
or demi-glace – see page 78 –
brown sauce (½ cup)
Tomato paste (about 2 Tbs)
Chervil, fresh leaves in season,
chopped, optional (2 Tbs)

About 1¼ hours before serving – active preparation about 45 minutes, plus about 30 minutes of unsupervised sautéeing and simmering

This dish is entirely prepared in a sauté pan with a well-fitting lid and large enough to hold the chicken pieces and yet be able to move them around easily. If you first dry the chicken it will brown better. Rub the pieces with salt and pepper. Set the sauté pan over medium-high frying heat and quickly melt in it the 4 tablespoons of butter. Then put in the chicken and sauté to a light brown. As soon as the chicken begins to gild, put in the 4 unpeeled cloves of garlic. (See discussion on this point with Jean Troisgros on page 221.) Stir the garlic cloves around and see to it that their skins become lightly browned and crisp. Also add to the pan 3 or 4 sprigs of the parsley, about 3 or 4 tablespoons of the chopped chives, a small handful of the tarragon leaves plus the tablespoon of chopped thyme. Stir everything around, turning over the chicken pieces to absorb the flavors on all sides. When the browning is complete, turn down the heat to simmering, put on the lid and let the juices bubble gently for 25 minutes.

Meanwhile, prepare the low-fat thickening whip. I put the cup of pot cheese, the ⅓ cup of yoghurt, and the 3 tablespoons or ricotta into the bowl of my Cuisinart chopper-churner. (Or you can use a blender.) I run the machine for 7 to 8 seconds until the mixture is smoothly puréed. I then transfer it to a beating bowl and, with a balloon whisk, whip air into it until it has the spoon-coating consistency of heavy beaten cream. Hold it for later use in the sauce.

About 30 minutes before serving

Set the oven to keep-warm temperature, about 175°F., and warm up a covered storage bowl and the four dinner plates. Take the chicken out of the sauté pan and keep it warm in the bowl. Turn up the heat under the sauté pan and hiss into it the ¾ cup of vinegar, vigorously scraping and deglazing the bottom of the pan. Add the 2 cups of chicken bouillon, the ½ cup of veal bouillon or *demi-glace,* and the 2 tablespoons of tomato paste. Let it all boil hard, stirring often, to reduce and concentrate flavors. Taste the sauce as it reduces. When the nip of the vinegar has changed from mouth-puckering to agreeably zinging in the back of the mouth and throat, the sauce is ready. Strain it and put it back in the sauté pan. If it now has enough garlic flavor for your taste, discard the garlic cloves from the strainer, but for my preference I would pick them out and squeeze them so that their insides (now a soft mash) go back into the sauce. The garlic skins, of course, are discarded. Work into the sauté pan, tablespoon by tablespoon, enough of the pot cheese whip to give the sauce a smooth, velvety consistency. From this point on keep the sauce always just below boiling or it may curdle. Check and adjust the seasonings, adding more vinegar and/or more tomato paste until you have exactly the flavor that fits your taste. Put the chicken pieces back into this sauce, letting them warm up in it and absorb its flavors, covered, for about 10 minutes. Make sure that the sauce does not boil. Serve on very hot plates with the sauce and garnish with chopped fresh leaves of chervil, parsley and tarragon. With this dish the Troisgros served me a fine light red wine of the Loire. The American equivalent might be a fine red California Gamay from the Santa Clara Valley.

COLD SLICED AIGUILLETTES OF DUCK BREAST BATHED IN THE RED WINE OF MARGAUX

(for 4)

This recipe involves a fair amount of effort and time – although no serious technical difficulty. It is eminently worthwhile, both for its memorable eating and its rich red appearance. It makes a colorful centerpiece for a party buffet. It is one of the *grandes spécialités* of Chef Louis Outhier (page 47) at his three-star restaurant, L'Oasis, in the beach resort village of La Napoule, on the Mediterranean coast a few miles west of Cannes.

Since this is a cold dish, it can be assembled in separate phases several days in advance. First, find your duck. If you can get a wild mallard or a French-type Barbary or Rouennais, you will have relatively little fat to worry about and you will have perfectly rare meat by roasting the bird quickly at high heat. But if you have to use one of the ubiquitous, so-called Long Island Ducklings of the frozen food cabinets, you will have to roast it slowly at low heat and puncture the skin so that the excess fat drains out. The breast is then carved into *aiguillettes* – a French cooking term which has nothing to do with *aiguilles*, needle-shaped strips, but simply means very thin slices of breast meat.

As to the wine, Chef Outhier has a theory that the special character of the red wines of the Bordeaux village of Margaux – sometimes called the "wild-violets ambience" – has a special and near-perfect affinity for duck. This does not mean, naturally, that you have to use a super-expensive Château Margaux. There are many excellent lesser vineyards and community wines from Margaux and a bottle of one of these will provide the refreshing aspic and rich color for this most excellent of cold ducks.

If you can bear with some extra richness, you might garnish this dish with the savory pâté Chef Outhier makes from the rest of the duck. The recipe for this pâté, which he sculpts into tiny ducklings, is below.

Duck, see above (either 2 wild, 1½ to 2½ lbs each or 1 Long Islander, 4 to 5 lbs)

Chicken bouillon, clear, entirely fatless (about 1 quart)

Honey, not too strong, say clover (2 Tbs)

Vinegar, white wine (about 1 Tbs)

Yellow onion, peeled and chopped (1)

Carrot, scraped and chopped (1)

Salt, coarse crystal, to taste

Black pepper, freshly ground, to taste

Red wine, from a Margaux
vineyard (1 bottle)
Gelatin, powdered, un-
flavored (2 envelopes)
Eggshell, crushed in the
fingers (1)

Egg white, lightly beaten (1)
Vermouth, dry (¼ cup)
Plus greenery for decoration
such as sprigs of parsley and
watercress

Phase I – roasting the duck: preparation in about 1 to 1½ hours

For this dish, the duck breast meat must be rare, with the character of rare beef. To achieve this with a wild duck, set the oven at 475°F. and roast for no more than 20 to 25 minutes. For the Long Islander the oven should be at 325°F., the under-skin should be thoroughly punctured with a fork to allow the fat to drain away and the time should be just about 1 hour. (If you are going to make the pâté described in the next recipe, you will need to save the drippings that are in the roasting pan.) The bird should then cool before it is carved. Peel back the skin of the breast and, with a long sharp knife, using slow and delicate strokes, cut the breast meat into ¼-inch thick, even slices. Hold them, tightly covered, so that they do not dry out and, if they are not to be used at once, refrigerate them. Cut off the legs, thighs and wings of the duck and hold them for further cooking. Chop the carcass up into 5 or 6 pieces for the making of the essential duck bouillon. Simmer the carcass pieces in enough of the chicken bouillon to cover them. Add the 2 tablespoons of honey, then the vinegar teaspoon by teaspoon, until the taste is tangy-sweet-sour. Also add the chopped onion and carrot, with salt and pepper to taste. Let it all simmer, covered, for about half an hour, then strain out the solids and hold the duck bouillon for later use.

Phase II – preparing the aspic in about 30 to 40 minutes

Mix 1 cup of red Margaux wine with ½ cup of the duck bouillon and convert it to a clear aspic according to the basic method described on page 65. Adjust the seasoning and stir in the ¼ cup of dry vermouth.

Bring out the *aiguillettes* of duck breast from the refrigerator and arrange them handsomely on a carving platter. They should not overlap, so that each slice can be fully covered and glazed with the aspic. Bring the aspic to the syrupy stage (page 67) and start dribbling it, layer after layer, over the duck *aiguillettes*. While you are glazing the duck slices, don't worry if some of the aspic runs down onto the platter. All these extraneous bits scrape off easily after the aspic is fully set. When every duck slice is smoothly covered, put the platter in the refrigerator, protected by aluminum foil, to set overnight.

To make aspic diamonds for decorating the platter, heat the aspic remaining in the saucepan back to its liquid state, then pour it into a square, shallow baking pan to form a layer about 3/8 inch deep. Set it in the refrigerator to get very firm. Then, draw the point of a kitchen knife back and forth across this layer, cutting it into small diamonds and squares. When you are ready to decorate the platter, lift out the aspic bits with a spatula. Chef Outhier also arranges on the plates little higgledy piggledy piles of these aspic bits for the refreshment of the diner. They catch the lights and provide, as well as good taste, a decorative visual sparkle. Also decorate the serving platter with bits of greenery, sprigs of parsley and watercress and with any other colorful bits and pieces that may please you. With this simple and wonderful cold buffet dish Chef Outhier served me, hardly unexpectedly, a bottle of red Château Palmer from the village of Margaux in the Médoc region of Bordeaux. A reasonably equivalent American wine, for both the aspic and the accompaniment, might be a noble California Cabernet Sauvignon of a fine vintage from the Napa Valley.

A GARNISHING PÂTÉ FROM THE DUCK'S LEGS, THIGHS AND WINGS

(for 4)

Various chefs have different ideas on what to do with the pieces of duck remaining after the breast meat has been removed. Some grill them until the skin is crisp and serve them on separate plates so they can be lifted with the fingers and the flesh and skin eaten straight off the bone. Making a pâté from these pieces is Chef Outhier's delicious way to be conscientious. The joints of a duck which has been cooked only until the breast is just pink do, of course, need a bit more cooking.

Duck legs, thighs, wings, cooked (yielding about 3 cups of chunked meat)	**Allspice, freshly ground (¼ tsp)**
Chicken bouillon, clear (2 cups)	**Bay leaf, crumbled (1)**
Duck liver (1)	**Salt, coarse crystal, to taste**
Ham, lean, boiled, diced (1 cup)	**Black pepper, freshly ground, to taste**
Scallions, chunked (6)	**Cognac (2 oz)**
Garlic, crushed (2 cloves)	**Duck gravy, from the roasting pan, defatted (about 4 Tbs)**
Thyme, fresh leaves in season, chopped (1 Tbs)	

Preparation in about 30 minutes

Chef Outhier cuts all the meat from the legs, thighs and wings, then chunks and measures the meat. There should be about 3 cups and the amounts of the other ingredients are calculated on that basis. If you have more or less than 3 cups, adjust the other amounts accordingly. Bring the 2 cups of chicken bouillon up to simmering in a saucepan and drop in the chunks of duck meat and the duck's liver. Simmer, covered, until the raw look has disappeared – usually in 5 minutes. Meanwhile, assemble the other ingredients in a large mixing bowl: the cup of diced ham, the chunked scallions, the crushed garlic, the tablespoon of thyme, the ¼ teaspoon of allspice, the crushed bay leaf, plus salt and pepper to taste. When the duck meat and liver have finished simmering, drain them, then add to the mixing bowl. I then run all of this mixture through my Cuisinart chopper-churner until it is a fine paste – usually in about 10 seconds (or you can use a meat grinder at its fine setting). Now return the paste to the mixing bowl and, with a wooden spoon, thoroughly blend into it the 2 ounces of Cognac and only just as many tablespoons of the duck gravy from the roasting pan as are needed to make a workable thick paste. Chef Outhier sculpts this into four tiny ducklings, each standing hardly more than 2 inches high. He places one on each plate, ready for demolition by the diner, and it almost breaks your heart to slay the pretty little pet.

ROAST DUCK WITH FRESH FIGS

(for 4)

Chefs Jean and Pierre Troisgros (page 50), at their three-star Restaurant des Frères Troisgros in Roanne, serve several varieties of domestic and wild duck prepared in many different ways. This recipe, to me, is one of the greatest of their repertory – partly, perhaps, because it involves none of the standard, unimaginative, sticky-sweet dressing up of the duck. Here there are no sugar-glazed oranges, no syrup-soaked peaches; the only sweetness is the natural juice of the fresh figs – the natural savor of the duck predominates.

Long Island ducks (2, 1 about 2½ to 3 lbs and 1 about 4½ to 5 lbs)
Lemon, cut in half (1)
Yellow onion, peeled and chopped (1 medium)
Carrots, scraped and chopped (2 medium)
Celery, green Pascal, outer stalks, destringed and chopped, with leaves (2)
Parsley, fresh (3 sprigs)
Salt, coarse crystal, to taste

White pepper, freshly ground, to taste
Figs, whole, fresh in season, or canned Kadota (12)
French Orgeat, almond syrup (2 oz)
Chicken bouillon (about 2 cups)
White wine, preferably Sancerre (1 cup)
Shallots, minced (2 Tbs)
Sweet butter (2 Tbs)

About 2½ hours before serving – active work about 1½ hours, plus about 1 hour of unsupervised maturing and resting

Preheat your oven to 350°F. Rub the ducks, inside and out, with the cut sides of the lemon halves. Then thoroughly

prick the underside skin to allow the excess fat to run out.
Place them on a raised rack in an open roasting pan and roast
them until the breasts are nicely pink (but not by any means
bleeding rare) – usually in no more than 45 to 50 minutes.

Meanwhile, prepare a 2-quart saucepan in which you will
cook the duck bouillon. Put into it the chopped onion, the
chopped carrots, the chopped celery stalks and leaves and the
3 sprigs of parsley, with salt and pepper to taste. Pour in a
pint of cold water and bring it rapidly to a boil, then stir,
reduce heat to gentle simmering and let it continue, covered,
until the duck carcass is ready to go in.

Next, turn your attention to the figs. (If they are canned,
first drain all syrup.) Put them in a 1-quart saucepan. Dribble over them the 2 ounces of Orgeat, then pour over enough
of the chicken bouillon to cover the figs. Heat this up to
gentle simmering and let it continue, covered, to warm and
puff up the figs – usually in 5 minutes. By this time the bouillon should be vaguely sweet with fig juice. Lift out the figs
and keep them warm in a covered container. Now boil the
fig bouillon hard to reduce it, so that its sweetness concentrates and sharpens. When it has reduced by about half, and
it is nicely sweet, then turn off the heat and hold, covered,
until it is needed later.

About 1½ hours before serving – resting the duck while making the sauce

As soon as the ducks are pink, put the larger one into a covered
casserole or *cocotte* and let stand tightly lidded over extremely
low heat on top of the stove. It should stay there, very gently
ripening in its own juice for an hour. (This is the secret Troisgros trick with duck – to complete the cooking very slowly in
an enclosed, steamy space. Pierre said: "When the flesh rests
for an hour, its muscles decontract and the meat slowly softens
and increases in flavor.")

Now deal with the smaller duck. Carve off its breast, legs,
thighs and wings and put them in the covered casserole with
the larger duck. Using large poultry shears and a Chinese
cleaver, cut the remaining carcass of the small duck into, say,

8 pieces and put them in the 2-quart saucepan of bouillon. Press the duck carcass pieces down in the saucepan fairly tightly and then, if necessary, add more water just to cover. Continue the simmering, covered, until the bouillon is needed later.

Skim off all the fat from the oven pan in which the ducks were roasted. When only the juices remain, set the pan over a top burner and deglaze it with the cup of white wine, thoroughly scraping the bottom of the pan with the edge of a wooden spoon. Pour this deglazed mixture into the simmering duck bouillon.

About ½ hour before serving – completion and assembly

Preheat your grill. Strain out the solids from the duck bouillon, returning the bouillon to the saucepan and now boiling it hard to reduce it and concentrate its ducky flavor. Reheat the fig bouillon just to bubbling. (Pierre said: "You are now at the crucial moment for the perfection of this dish. You must taste continually both the duck bouillon and the fig stock, so that you can judge the precise moment when they should be combined. The balance you are seeking is very delicate. If you allow the sauce to become too sweet, it will dominate the duck. If you get it dead right – a very delicate and gentle sweetness – it will glorify and magnify the duck. Use your judgment. Keep it light. Avoid the slightest heaviness or thickness in the sauce. Above all remove every scrap of fat.") At the right moment, pour the fig stock into the duck bouillon and add the 2 tablespoons of minced shallots. Continue boiling hard to keep on reducing the combined sauce. Start warming your 4 serving plates. Place the figs on an open grill platter and quickly glaze them under the grill for hardly more than a minute or two.

Now carve the duck (both the whole large bird and the parts from the smaller one), set out the portions on the plates and garnish them with the glazed figs. Keep warm until the sauce is ready. As soon as the sauce has exactly the taste and texture you want, turn down the heat to below simmering and grind in a fair amount of white pepper. (Pierre said: "You must be able to taste it, but there must not be so much that it pricks your throat. There must be enough pepper to cut across the sweetness of the sauce. Also, never allow it to boil once the pepper is in, or you will get a bitter taste.")

Finally, when the sauce is dead right, keeping it just below simmering, perform the professional operation of *monter au beurre*, mounting with butter. Melt onto its surface, sliver by sliver, the 2 tablespoons of butter, to give the sauce, as Pierre put it, "A touch of luxurious velvet." Pour the sauce around, not over, the duck and figs on the plates. Then rush them, very hot, to table. Because of the slight sweetness of the sauce, red wine is not quite right with this duck, so the Troisgros brothers served me a noble, luxuriously rich, soft yet strong white Meursault from the Côte d'Or of Burgundy. At my New York table, I might serve a rich California Pinot Chardonnay from the Alexander Valley in Sonoma.

DUCK (OR CHICKEN) LIVERS SAUTÉED WITH THE NATURAL SWEETNESS OF WHITE TURNIPS

(for 4)

All over the southwest of France – where the goose is king and the duck is queen – one of the most regularly served luncheon or supper dishes is sautéed duck livers with fresh white grapes. You might call it a classic regional combination. This is exactly the kind of established dish that the revolutionary new-cuisine chefs of France like to take apart and rethink. Why must it always be grapes? Why not try other fruits? Then Chefs Jean and Pierre Troisgros (page 50) asked a more imaginative question. What about the natural sweetness of young white turnips? They experimented with their idea at their three-star restaurant in Roanne and, when they placed it before me, I was enchanted by an extraordinary marriage of flavors. It was, indeed, a revolutionary step forward.

Translating and adapting their recipe to my American kitchen, I found that duck livers are not often available in our markets, so I used chicken livers as a compromise substitute. Not bad at all! It is a light and memorable dish with which I have delighted many guests at breakfast, lunch, Sunday night supper, or even as a slightly shocking first hors d'oeuvre course at dinner. To achieve the full visual effect, you should practice beforehand the art of carving the white flesh of young turnips into neat ovals, about the size of medium olives. Large dice will do, of course, but they neither look nor taste quite as good.

Porto, ruby or tawny (1½ cups)
Demi-glace, brown sauce
   (1 Tbs)
White raisins, seedless
   (½ cup)
Black truffle, strictly optional,
   diced (1 small)
Black truffle juice, in which
   truffle was packed, optional
   with the truffle (2 tsp)

Duck or chicken livers (1½ lbs)
Salt, coarse crystal, to taste
White pepper, freshly ground,
   to taste
Sweet butter (about 6 Tbs)
White turnips, small, young,
   peeled and carved into small
   olive shapes (6 to 8,
   according to size)

Preparation in about 45 minutes

Preheat your oven to keep-warm temperature, 165°F. then start the sauce. Put the 1½ cups of Porto into a 1½-pint saucepan and boil it hard to get rid of the fattening alcohol and reduce it to concentrate its aromatic flavor. When it is about half its original volume and tastes good and strong, turn down the heat to gentle simmering and stir in the tablespoon of brown sauce, the ½ cup of seedless raisins and the optional dice and juice of truffle. Let it all simmer very gently, covered, until it is needed.

Next, deal with the livers in the normal way. Clean them, remove their membranes, salt and pepper them, then sauté them very quickly in 2 tablespoons of hot butter, until they are firm on the outside, but still nicely soft inside. Remember that they will get slightly firmer while waiting, and it is a crime to overcook them. Remove them from the sauté pan with a slotted spoon and keep them warm in the oven in a covered container. Also warm up the four plates. (Jean Troisgros told me: "Make no further use of the butter in which the livers were sautéed. It becomes too strong with liver juices. Use it some other time to fry potatoes. Under no circumstances use it for the turnips.")

Finally, the turnips. Poach them in boiling, lightly salted water until they have just lost their rawness, but are still quite crisp – usually in 4 to 6 minutes. Meanwhile, pour off the liver butter from the sauté pan, wash and dry the pan – reheat it with 2 more tablespoons of the butter over medium frying heat. The moment the turnip olives are done, drain and dry them on paper towels, then glaze them in the hot butter for just a few seconds to develop their natural sweetness. Melt the remaining 2 tablespoons of butter, sliver by sliver, into the Porto sauce and at once pour enough of it onto the serving plates so that each is covered by a thin layer. Place a portion of the livers in the center and surround them with the white turnip olives. It makes a pretty-looking plate of simple foods combined into a memorable example of the brilliant art of great chefs. With it, Jean and Pierre Troisgros served me an unusual, light red Burgundy from the normally white-wine village of Chassagne-Montrachet. The American equivalent might be a light California Pinot Noir from the Napa Valley.

ROAST QUAIL FILLED WITH FRESH SEMILLON GRAPES

(for 4)

Brilliant young Chef Claude Darroze (page 31) has now, at last, taken the advice of all his admirers and opened his own Restaurant Darroze, in the wine village of Langon in the heart of the Graves and Sauternes regions of Bordeaux. The vineyards which surround Langon are ruled by the Semillon grape, which goes into the making of both the dry whites of Graves and the luscious, sweet Sauternes. At harvest time, Claude uses the fresh grapes to add their aromatic flavor to the flesh of young quail. If you do not live in Bordeaux – or among the Semillon vineyards of California – use the most aromatic table grapes you can find.

If you are not a hunter or do not have a hunting friend, quail can still be found, in season, at game dealers, or ordered by mail from one of the famous supply houses. (See "Index of Sources," page 392.)

White grapes, nicely sweet
  (1 bunch, about 1 lb)
Quail, whole, prepared for
  roasting by your game expert,
  with livers (4)
Salt, coarse crystal, to taste
Black pepper, freshly ground,
  to taste

Juniper berries, whole (4 tsp)
Sweet butter (4 Tbs)
Green Chartreuse liqueur
  (4 tsp)
Yoghurt, plain low-fat (½ cup)

About 30 minutes before serving – active preparation about 15 minutes with about 15 minutes of unsupervised roasting

Preheat your oven to 400°F. Hold aside the 4 livers of the quail. Pick the grapes off the bunch and wash them in cold water. In the old formality and fuss of the traditional French high cuisine, each grape would then be skinned and pitted by hand, but, these days, the stress is on leaving natural foods as Nature made them. In this recipe, it saves a lot of time. Rub each bird with salt and pepper, inside and out. Divide the grapes into 4 equal parts and fill each quail with them. Place the 4 birds, breast up, in an ungreased roasting pan and put them in the dead center of the oven. Let them roast until they are lightly golden on the outside, still tenderly rare on the inside – usually in 10 to 15 minutes. It is a crime to overcook them.

Meanwhile, grind the juniper berries in a small, electric, spice mill (see page 82) and blend them in a mortar, with the 4 tablespoons of butter and the 4 livers. Blend and pound into a stiffish paste. As soon as the quails are done, flame each one with a teaspoon of the Green Chartreuse. Take them out of the roasting pan and keep them warm for a few moments. Skim as much fat as possible from the roasting pan juices, then deglaze the pan with the ½ cup of yoghurt. Blend these juices with the juniper-liver paste, divide it into 4 parts, spread the mixture over each quail and bring at once to table.

With these lovely little birds, Chef Claude Darroze served me a noble, fruity, red Graves, a Château Pape Clément. My American choice might be a fine, fruity California Cabernet Sauvignon from Sonoma.

CHEF ROGER VERGÉ'S SECRETS OF CONVERTING AN OLD, RICH DISH INTO A LIGHT, LOW-FAT INTERPRETATION

At his great three-star restaurant, Le Moulin de Mougins in Provence, Chef Vergé (page 52) offers a menu of luxurious refinement and brilliant inventiveness. Yet, as the menu changes and develops, there always remains on it one dish which stands out from all the others because of its absolute simplicity, its peasant farmhouse character, its almost-picnic-style informality. It is listed on the menu as a *gibelotte de lapin de Provence* and served sometimes as the almost shocking opening course of a magnificent dinner, or sometimes as a main luncheon course on a broiling summer day at a table under an umbrella in the garden. It is placed before you as a cold, molded aspic simply decorated with sprigs of greenery, red slices of tomato, orange curls of carrot, black and green olive rings, tiny pickles and baby sweet-sour onions. Inside the aspic are rough, savory chunks of rabbit from which you have to pick out (generally with your fingers) the large and small bits of bone in between other succulent bits of liver, lean bacon and ham, all intermingled with aromatic leaves of herbs and berries of spices. Yet, after you have taken the trouble to pick it all over, you feel deeply satisfied – you somehow know you are in the presence of a great regional dish of Provence. You believe that this might have been prepared by your Provençal grandmother. You ask Chef Vergé about it. . . .

"I agree that it is not, perhaps, entirely within the ambience of a three-star restaurant," Roger replied. "New clients may say that it is 'worth the detour,' but not completely 'worth the trip.' But you must remember that I put this into my menu years ago, before I had even one star. There are hundreds, perhaps even thousands, of my old and regular clients who would scream bloody murder if I dared to take it off my menu. And it is truly authentic Provençal."

When I asked him where he had found the recipe, he said: "It could easily have been a most ancient dish, deciphered with difficulty on the fraying and yellowing page of some old, old cookbook, *if* I had not invented it myself. It might have been a classic *civet*, a stew of rabbit, *if* I had not been determined to make it without olive oil or any other fat. So I rejected the idea of a *civet* and decided instead to shoot for a *gibelotte*, an old Provençal word for a kind of terrine of fricasseed pieces of rabbit.

"I admit, of course, that I had some old models to go on. They were extremely rustic dishes, which I have very much adapted and interpreted. They were always made with our wild rabbit from the central region of Garrigue. The cook would skin it, then cut deep slits all over the body into which she would force cubes of pork fat and fresh leaves of bay laurel, savory and thyme. Then she would *rotisse* it on a turning spit over an open, smoky wood fire. Finally, she would wrap it tightly in parchment paper to prevent its drying out and store it away in a cool cupboard to be served in the future in cold chunks. But it always did dry out and it was much too rich in fat and much too violent with its aromatic herbs. So I said to myself, this must be improved, and I took off from there, aiming to hold on to the excellence and simplicity of the old dish, while eliminating the overrichness and the heavy spicing of the meat. I solved the drying out problem by sealing the pieces of rabbit within an aspic. Instead of firing the meat over a flame, I poached it, without fat, in an aromatic bouillon in which the herbs could be strictly controlled."

I felt that Roger Vergé had given me more than the secret of his marvelous *Gibelotte de Lapin*. He had given me the key to changing almost any overrich recipe from the old, high-fat way to the new Low-High technique. Frying, grilling, sautéeing with lashings of butter, fat, or oil can always be eliminated and replaced by cooking with dry heat, in an oven, or simmering in aromatic bouillon, or steaming. In every case, unnecessary complications, overaromatic and dominant stuffings, butter and cream sauces, can be pared away without loss (generally with noticeable improvement) of the true character of the natural ingredients.

"I may have adapted and interpreted my *gibelotte*," Roger

added, "but I know that I have maintained its regional character. I would never want to 'hot it up' to some imaginary three-star standard, because it would then lose its authenticity. It would be a nothing! I suggest you eat my *gibelotte* at a small wooden table in a garden under the shadow of an olive tree on a hot and sparkling day, accompanied by a bottle of rosé and a mixed '*Salade Mesclün*' (page 355). With the first taste, in that setting, you will discover the pure, the true, essence of Provence." I would go even a step further. With Roger's *gibelotte*, you can bring Provence to your table wherever you are (see below).

THE NEAREST AMERICAN APPROACH TO CHEF ROGER VERGÉ'S GIBELOTTE DE LAPIN À LA PROVENÇALE – COLD COUNTRY ASPIC OF AROMATIC RABBIT

(not worth it for less than 6 to 8, but keeps excellently in the refrigerator sealed in its aspic)

(See my discussion with Chef Vergé on the previous pages.) I can hardly promise you that you can get wild rabbit from Garrigue in the United States markets, but if a friend can contribute a wild rabbit or if you can get the "Belgian" breed from Canada, that would be fine. The domestic rabbit, though, also does excellently in this dish.

Rabbit, beheaded, skinned
and cut up for fricasseeing,
with liver (1 or 2, for a
total of 3 to 4 lbs)
Lemon (1)
Garlic, peeled and finely
minced (2 cloves)
Shallots, peeled and finely
minced (5 cloves)
Parsley, leaf only, chopped
(¼ cup)
Rosemary, fresh leaf in season,
chopped (2 Tbs)

Thyme, fresh leaf in season,
chopped (2 Tbs)
White wine, dry (1 bottle)
Chicken bouillon, clear and
strong (4 cups)
Gelatin, powdered, unflavored
(about 7 standard envelopes)
Canadian bacon, or Italian
prosciutto ham, lean, thinly
sliced (1 lb)
Salt, coarse crystal, to taste
Black pepper, freshly ground,
to taste

For the decoration and garnishing at table, any or all of the following:

A few sprigs of parsley and/or
  watercress
Some thin slices of small
  tomato
Some carrot curls or slivers

About 1 dozen cornichons
  (baby French pickles)
About 1 dozen baby sweet-
  sour onions

**Two or 3 days in advance – about 12 hours of marination,
30 minutes of active work, plus about 2 hours of
unsupervised oven poaching – phase 1: the marination**

Clean the rabbit pieces by rubbing them with the cut sides
of the two halves of the lemon. Put the pieces into a medium-
sized mixing bowl (not too large, or you will have to use too
much wine), then sprinkle them with the minced garlic and
shallots, the chopped parsley, rosemary and thyme, then pour
on enough of the white wine just to cover. Close the bowl
with aluminum foil and leave it in a cool place but not in the
refrigerator, for 12 hours. Do not marinate the rabbit's liver.
Hold it, covered, in the refrigerator.

**The next day – phase 2: assembling the mold in
about 30 minutes**

Convert the 4 cups of chicken bouillon into an aspic by heating
it and blending in 4 envelopes of the gelatin by the standard
method described on page 65. Hold it warm enough so that
it does not set. Choose a mold, or a lidded oval casserole or
cocotte of the right size to hold the rabbit pieces fairly solidly
packed. If it is too large there will be too much aspic in relation to the volume of meat. If you use a mold without a lid,
you will have to cover it tightly with aluminum foil. Now line
the inside of the mold completely with slices of the bacon or
ham. Pack the pieces of rabbit into the mold fairly tightly
pressed together. (The reason for leaving in the bones is that
their internal marrow adds body and flavor to the aspic.) Cut
the rabbit liver into 4 parts. Wrap each part in a small slice
of the bacon or ham and bury these 4 little packages in 4 dif-

ferent places among the rabbit pieces, so that the flavors will be equally dispersed. Strain out from the marinade all its solid, aromatic ingredients and spread them around the mold. Measure the marinade and heat it up, converting it into an aspic by blending in one envelope of gelatin for every cup of liquid. As soon as the gelatin is fully dissolved, pour the hot marinade into the mold. Now add just enough of the chicken bouillon aspic to cover the solids in the mold by about ½ inch. Gently stir and taste the liquid, adding salt and pepper, as needed.

Phase 3: poaching in the oven for 2 hours

Preheat your oven to 250°F. Arrange, exactly at its center, a *bain-marie* in which the mold will stand, surrounded by steam: place an open pan, say about 2½ to 3 inches deep, on the center shelf of the oven and half fill it with boiling water. Tightly cover the *gibelotte* mold and stand it in the boiling water. Leave it to poach for 2 hours.

Phase 4: setting the gibelotte

When the *gibelotte* comes out of the oven, open it and top it up with more of the chicken bouillon aspic, so that the solids are again covered to a depth of about ⅜ inch. Let it come to room temperature, then set it, covered, in the refrigerator to solidify overnight. Pour all or part of the remaining chicken bouillon aspic into a square, open cake pan so as to make a layer about ¼ inch deep. After this has set in the refrigerator, you can cut the layer, with the point of a kitchen knife, into aspic diamonds and squares of various sizes for later decoration of the *gibelotte*. If you have plenty of chicken bouillon aspic left, you can use several pans to make a large supply of decorative shapes.

Serving at table

When you are ready to serve the *gibelotte,* unmold it onto a handsome platter and express your artistic imagination by decorating it with parsley, watercress, tomatoes, carrots, *cornichons,* baby onions and the aspic shapes. When serving, remember that you cannot slice the *gibelotte* because of the bones. Just dig into it with a large serving spoon and don't even try to be neat. It is festive picnic-style eating, so encourage the guests to pick up the bones with their fingers. With it, Chef Roger Vergé served me a mixed "*Salade Mesclün*" (page 355) and a fine, light, red wine of Provence from the district of Vidauban. An American choice might be a light California Ruby Cabernet.

SAUTÉED SQUABS FILLED WITH A RAGOÛT OF THE FOREST

(for 4)

This is a specialty of the lovely, small, two-star Auberge Chez La Mère Blanc in the village of Vonnas in the Bresse country south of Burgundy. The auberge and its kitchen are ruled by the brilliant, revolutionary young Chef Georges Blanc (see page 25), the great-grandson of the original Mère Blanc. Georges's menu is a marvelous mixture of the lightest and simplest dishes of the new-new cuisine, with a few of the richest of the ancient specialties of the surrounding regions of the Ain, Bresse and Les Dombes where they think nothing of simmering a whole Bresse chicken in a quart of heavy cream. But Georges's preparation of squab is uncomplicated, yet superbly seasoned by a filling that seems to bring to the table all the flavors and savors of the nearby forests – wild berries, various varieties of wild mushrooms, freshly harvested herbs – all difficult, of course, to reproduce exactly in an American kitchen. I believe, however, that my adaptation holds the character of the original dish – with the help of some of the dried wild mushrooms available in Chinese and Italian groceries.

Lime, fresh, whole (1)

Squabs, oven-ready, trussed, with hearts and livers (4, each about 1 to 1¼ lbs)

Wild mushrooms, dried or canned, coarsely chopped, see above (½ lb)

Shallots, peeled and finely minced (5 cloves)

Juniper berries, whole (2 Tbs)

Armagnac brandy (about ½ cup)

Madeira, slightly sweet Bual (up to ½ cup)

White wine, dry (up to ½ cup)

Chicken livers (½ lb)

Black truffles, medium-small – strictly optional (2)

Ham, boiled, entirely lean, dark-smoked, diced (½ lb)

Oregano, dried (2 tsp)

Rosemary, fresh leaf in season, chopped (2 Tbs)

Savory, fresh leaf in season, chopped (2 Tbs)

Parsley, leaf only, chopped (4 Tbs)

Mustard, French, preferably Moutarde de Meaux, to taste

Salt, coarse crystal, to taste

Black pepper, freshly ground, to taste

Sweet butter (about 6 Tbs)

Carrot, scraped and minced (1 medium)

Celery, white, minced (1 fair-sized stalk)

Bay leaf (1)

Light cream (½ cup)

Button mushrooms, whole or quartered according to size (½ lb)

The day before – active work about 10 minutes – setting the squabs to marinate overnight

Cut the lime and use the two halves to rub the squabs, inside and out, to clean and refresh them. (Never wash them under running cold water, this removes the flavor juices.) Hold their hearts and livers aside, covered and refrigerated. In a smallish bowl, mix the chopped wild mushrooms with the minced shallots and the 2 tablespoons of whole juniper berries. Divide this mixture into 4 parts and spoon 1 part into each squab. Place them in a covered storage dish, just large enough to hold them closely; if the dish is too large, the liquid will spread out and will not be deep enough for proper marination. Pour over the squabs the ½ cup each of Armagnac, Bual Madeira and dry white wine. Let the birds marinate, covered, in the refrigerator, basting and turning them over last thing at night and again first thing in the morning.

On the day – about 1¼ hours before serving – active work about 40 minutes with about 35 minutes of unsupervised oven baking

Take the squabs out of their marinade and spoon out their internal ingredients onto a wide dinner plate for sorting. Dry the birds and let them come to room temperature. If any juniper berries, etc., have fallen to the bottom of the marinade, fish them out and add them to the mixture already on the dinner plate. Hold the liquid marinade for later use. Set out a large mixing bowl in which you will assemble the ragoût for the stuffing. Pick out the juniper berries from the dinner plate, crush them lightly in a mortar and put them into the large mixing bowl. Pick out the wild mushrooms from the dinner plate and add them to the large mixing bowl. Also add: the ½ pound chicken livers, the squab hearts and livers, all coarsely chopped, the 2 diced truffles (if you are using them), all but 2 tablespoons of the diced ham, the 2 teaspoons of oregano, the 2 tablespoons each of chopped rosemary and savory, plus the 4 tablespoons of chopped parsley. Begin mixing all this lightly with a wooden spoon, at the same time working in, to your taste, teaspoon by teaspoon of the mustard, tablespoon by tablespoon of the marinade liquid, plus the requisite amounts of salt and pepper. The texture should be moist but not runny – everything should be coarsely chopped and the flavor should be strong enough to work itself into the flesh of the squabs. Let this stuffing ripen, covered, until it is needed.

Preheat your oven to 400°F. Choose a covered casserole or *cocotte*, just large enough to hold the 4 squabs snugly, with very little room to spare. It should preferably be of enameled iron so that it can be used both in the oven and on top of the stove. Again, if it is too large, the juices will be too much spread out. Lightly salt and pepper the insides of the squabs and fill each with its share of the ragoût stuffing. Tightly close each end of each bird by sewing with needle and string, or with small trussing pins. Rub each bird all over with 1 table-spoon of the butter. Hold them aside while you prepare the *mirepoix* base in the casserole.

Set it over a top burner at medium frying heat and lubricate its bottom by melting in one more tablespoon of the butter. As it is melting, add: the minced carrot and celery, the minced shallots remaining on the dinner plate, the remaining 2 table-spoons of ham and the bay leaf, crumbled. Stir them all around with a wooden spoon and let them simmer in the butter until they are just soft – usually in 3 to 4 minutes. Then add salt and pepper, to taste, plus ¼ cup of the marinade liquid. Let it all simmer, stirring occasionally, for another 5 minutes to develop and blend the flavors of this aromatic base. Then turn off the heat and put the squabs into the casserole, breasts up. Now set the casserole in the oven at a height so that the top surface of the squabs will be at about the center of the oven. Roast them, uncovered, until the skins are lightly golden – usually in about 10 to 15 minutes. Baste them occasionally with their juices, preferably using a bulb baster.

About 30 minutes before serving – the final poaching and the sauce

As soon as the gilding is complete, take the casserole out of the oven and turn the temperature down to 350°F. Pour over the squabs another ½ cup of the marinade liquid. Now cover the casserole with its lid and set it back in the oven to poach and steam the forest flavors into the flesh of the birds. After about 10 to 15 minutes, check them for doneness. They are best served slightly rare so that when pricked with a fork the juices that ooze out are pale rose in color. At the same time, the leg should wiggle easily. As soon as this happy point is reached, take the casserole out of the oven and turn the temperature down to "keep warm," 170°F. Carefully lift the squabs out of the casserole and hold them, preferably covered with foil, in the warm oven. Set the casserole back on a top burner over medium heat and deglaze its bottom, scraping it firmly with a wooden spoon, with an extra dash or two of the Armagnac. At the same time, skim off any visible excess of fat. I now transfer all the liquid and solid contents of the casserole to the bowl of my Cuisinart chopper-churner and purée them until they are just smooth and blended but not mushy or pasty – usually in about 4 to 5 seconds. Put back this purée into the casserole, again over medium heat, and work into it the ½ cup of light cream, adjusting the heat so that it bubbles merrily and begins to reduce. Now stir into this sauce the ½ pound of button mushrooms and keep the bubbling going until there has been enough reduction of the liquid, with concentration of the flavors, so that the sauce is slightly thickened. Taste and adjust for salt and pepper. While the bubbling continues, set four wide serving plates in the oven to get nice and hot.

Serving at table

Young Chef Georges Blanc belongs to the new-new school of French cuisine. He does not believe in "presenting" dishes at table on large serving platters, with the inevitable cooling off while the food is transferred to the plates. As soon as the sauce is ready, Georges spreads it across the very-hot serving plates and then carefully places one squab in the center of each. He deliberately does not spoon the sauce over the squab, since he wants to keep the flavors separate, avoiding any possibility of domination of the one by the other. Garnishing vegetables may be spread on the plate around the squab and, as each bite of squab is cut, it is lightly dipped in the aromatic sauce. With his superb invention, Chef Georges Blanc served me a bottle of what is, after all, his local wine, a fine, fresh, fruity Beaujolais from the nearby village of Morgon. The gaiety and joy of such a refreshing, young, untraveled Beaujolais is virtually unmatchable away from its home ground, but a fair American approximation, in my opinion, might be one of the magnificent California Zinfandel rosés from the Napa Valley.

TURKEY POACHED WITH VEGETABLES IN WHITE WINE À LA ROANNAISE

(for 4 to 6)

I was staying for a few days with Chefs Jean and Pierre Troisgros (page 50) at their three-star hotel and restaurant in Roanne when the talk turned to turkey. I asked whether they often served it and how they prepared it. Jean said, "Whenever I meet a turkey in a farmyard I find it unbearably stupid and with a detestable character. In a dish on the dining table, I usually find it no more acceptable. But, since they exist in large numbers and are an important source of basic protein, let us at least try to find better ways of preparing them than roasting until they are like a dried-out cardboard box. Here is our way, which makes the flesh aromatic, provides flavorful juices and gives the whole a final, rich softness. . . ."

Turkey, small, fine, fat (5 to 7 lbs)	Celery, green Pascal, trimmed, destringed and cut into 2 inch lengths (4 or 5 stalks)
Lemons (2)	Carrots, scraped and neatly chunked (6 to 8 medium)
White wine, dry, preferably Sancerre (1 bottle)	Turnips, young white, peeled and chunked (4 or 5)
Salt, coarse crystal, to taste	
White pepper, freshly ground, to taste	Green beans, washed and trimmed (1½ lbs)
Rosemary, fresh leaf in season, chopped (1 Tbs)	Broccoli, heads only, washed (1 bunch)
Leek whites, carefully de-sanded, chunked (5)	

About 1½ hours before serving – active preparation about 15 minutes – unsupervised simmering about 1¼ hours

Clean the turkey by rubbing it, inside and out, with the cut side of half a lemon. Put it into a suitably large, lidded, stewpot and cover with a 50–50 mixture of freshly drawn cold water and the white wine. Bring it up to gentlest bubbling and keep simmering, "just smiling," until the turkey is perfectly tender, yet firm on the bones – usually in about 1¼ hours.

As soon as the water comes up to simmering, add salt and pepper to taste, plus enough freshly squeezed lemon juice to give the liquid a faint citrus taste – usually 1½–2 lemons, according to juiciness and size. Meanwhile, prepare the vegetables. Make ready a separate saucepan to receive the beans with the requisite amount of freshly drawn cold water brought up to the boiling point and nicely flavored with rosemary and salt.

About 45 minutes before serving

Drop into the boiling stewpot liquid the chunked leeks and pieces of celery.

About 35 minutes before serving

Drop in the chunked carrots and turnips.

About 15 minutes before serving

Drop the beans into their separate pot of boiling water and keep them bubbling fairly hard, uncovered, for precisely 15 minutes. Now make ready another separate saucepan to receive the broccoli, with the requisite amount of bubbling water, nicely salted. At this point, you can start mixing the "Mustard Vinaigrette," below.

About 10 minutes before serving

Put the broccoli heads into their boiling water and let them bubble merrily for precisely 10 minutes.

Serving at table

The instant the turkey is done, work very quickly, to avoid overcooking the vegetables by leaving them, even for an extra minute or two, in their various boiling liquids. (Jean Troisgros believes that, if cooked vegetables have to be held, they should immediately be plunged into cold water, to stop the cooking process, and then lightly reheated at the moment of service.) Carefully remove the turkey from the pot and carve it. Serve it at once, very hot, with its dramatic array of perfectly poached vegetables from the big pot and the two separate saucepans. Add a good dollop of the "Mustard Vinaigrette" at the side of each plate. The accompanying wine served by the brothers Troisgros was a noble, rich white Burgundy from the village of Puligny-Montrachet on the Côte d'Or. The American equivalent might be a noble, rich California Pinot Chardonnay from the Napa Valley.

MUSTARD VINAIGRETTE

(for 4 to 6)

Mustard, preferably Moutarde
   de Meaux – or fine quality
   French Dijon (about 6 Tbs)
Vinegar, tarragon white
   wine (1 Tbs)

Walnut oil, French, cold-
   pressed (1 Tbs)
Salt, coarse crystal, to taste
White pepper, freshly ground,
   to taste

Preparation in about 2 minutes

Blend together in a small mixing bowl: 6 tablespoons of the mustard, 1 tablespoon of vinegar, the 1 tablespoon of walnut oil, with salt and pepper to taste. Adjust the ingredients for flavor and thickness. This mustard vinaigrette keeps excellently in the refrigerator.

TURKEY IN AN IMPOSSIBLE BAG OR IN A STEAMER-WITHIN-A-STEAMER

(for 4 to 6)

Chef Michel Guérard (page 35) at his two-star Le Pot au Feu in Eugénie-les-Bains, seems to have one big advantage over us amateur American cooks. He can, apparently, get cooking bags made of the intestinal skins of lambs or pigs that are actually watertight. So – in his extraordinary recipe for the non-fat preparation of a chicken or turkey, which he wrote out for me when I last visited him – he poaches the bird in an aromatic liquid inside the bag while it all rests in a large pot of boiling water. Michel is completely confident that none of the boiling water will get into the bag! This is a magic trick that I have been unable to duplicate with any known type of natural or plastic bag in the United States, including every "Brown-In" or "Cook-In" bag on the market. (I know, of course, that there are some packages of frozen vegetables enclosed in watertight plastic bags, which you simply dump into boiling water, but these are all mechanically pre-sealed at the factory.)

So I have translated and adapted Michel's recipe – with all the respect in the world for his brilliant skill – to an entirely different mechanical method, which I shall dare to call the "super-efficient American way"! It is the same steamer-within-a-steamer used for our "Duck Soup" on page 152 and fully described there. You need, in short, a tightly lidded casserole or *cocotte* (preferably French Le Creuset enameled cast iron) large enough to hold your small turkey with its aromatic garnishes and poaching liquid, plus a much larger lidded pot in which the smaller casserole can stand and be almost completely enclosed by boiling water, with the larger pot also covered. Armed with this double contraption, you will find my adaptation of Michel's recipe quite simple.

Incidentally, Michel uses lime flowers to add a touch of lime flavor to his turkey. Since, to my knowledge, they cannot be found in any American market, I have replaced them with a small quantity of lime juice and zest.

Lime, with good skin (1)
Turkey, small, young
  (about 5 to 6 lbs)
Salt, coarse crystal, to taste
Black pepper, freshly ground,
  to taste

Mushrooms, smallish, good
  color (16)
Apricot halves, dried (16)
Grapefruit, ripe, sweet (2)
Yellow onions, peeled
  (4 medium)

Cloves, whole (2)
Chicken bouillon, entirely
    defatted (about 5 cups)
Apple, crisp eating, cored,
    peeled and diced
    (1 large or 2 medium)

Garlic, peeled and crushed
    (1 clove)
Parsley, chopped leaf (¼ cup)

About 2¾ hours before serving – active work about 45 minutes, plus 2 hours of entirely unsupervised steaming

Scrape the zest, the thin outer skin, from the lime, preferably using a French zest scraper, then sprinkle it over the bottom of the smaller casserole (see above). Cut the skinned lime in half and use the two halves to refresh the turkey, outside and inside, by rubbing with the cut sides. Lightly salt and pepper the turkey, outside and in, then set it snugly on its side in the smaller casserole. Squeeze the remaining lime juice over it. Fit into the corners and spaces around it the 16 whole mushroom caps (with their stalks removed, trimmed, chopped and also added to the casserole), the 16 apricot halves, the strained juice from 1 of the grapefruit and the 4 whole onions (1 of them stuck with the 2 whole cloves). Then pour in enough of the chicken bouillon just to cover everything, clamp on the lid tightly and stand the casserole inside the larger pot. Now pour into this larger pot enough boiling water to come up to within half an inch of the top edge of the smaller casserole. We do not, obviously, want any of the water to get into the turkey. Turn on the heat under the big pot and set it to keep the water gently bubbling, covered, for the next 2 hours. During this time, you may not, under any circumstances, open the lid of the smaller casserole. But you may, every half an hour or so, check the water in the larger pot, to see that it is still gently bubbling and, if necessary, to top it up, so that the smaller casserole remains enclosed by as much boiling water as possible.

About 30 minutes before serving – reducing the sauce

Preheat your oven to keep-warm temperature, 165°F. Set in it to get warm a handsome serving platter for the turkey with four wide soup plates and a sauce boat. Cut open the second grapefruit, deseed it and dig out its flesh, leaving behind all the membranes, cutting the flesh into dice and holding them. Now turn off the heat under the two pots, lift out the smaller casserole and open it up. The turkey should be perfectly done. Carve it into serving pieces and lay them neatly on the serving platter, interspersed by the mushroom caps and the apricot halves. Cover with aluminum foil and keep warm. Place the smaller casserole, with its remaining liquid and solid contents, directly over high heat to bring it up to a rolling boil and continue boiling it hard to reduce its liquid, while concentrating and sharpening its flavors. Continue reducing it until it shows signs of becoming syrupy. Then rub the entire contents of the casserole through a fine sieve, throwing away the thick solids and returning the now smooth liquid to the casserole. Reheat it to gentle simmering and stir into it the diced flesh, including any juice and mash, of the grapefruit, plus the diced apple and crushed garlic. Serve this sauce at table in a warmed sauceboat with a ladle. Just before bringing in the turkey platter, sprinkle it prettily with as much as you like of the bright-green chopped parsley. With this fruity concoction, Chef Michel Guérard would serve a fruity white Gewürztraminer from Alsace. Or, I might serve an American equivalent – a California Gewürztraminer from grapes grown along the banks of the Russian River in Sonoma.

TURKEY BURIED TREASURE DOWN THE HOLE

(for 4 to 6)

When Chef Paul Bocuse (page 26) described this recipe to me at his three-star Auberge de Paul Bocuse at Collonges-au-Mont-d'Or near Lyon, his voice was at its naughtiest and his smile was at its wickedest. He has played this game with me many times. You are sure, at the moment, that the whole thing is a complete put-on. Yet when you begin investigating and trying out the recipe, you find that it is practical, deadly serious and, especially in this case, an actual ancient Burgundian tradition. Down with plain roast turkey, says

Bocuse. He promises that the flesh of his turkey will be surprisingly soft and sweet. If you haven't got a garden in which to bury your turkey, he proposed a large barrel filled with nice, damp, rich, dark loam soil. The only problem is that you may have to chain your dog.

Black truffles, absolutely
essential! (4 large)
Sausage stuffing, any recipe
you like (about 2 lbs)
Turkey, oven-ready (about
6 to 8 lbs)
Chicken bouillon, entirely
fatless (about 4 quarts)
Carrots, scraped and chunked
(8 medium)
Celery, green Pascal, de-
stringed and chunked, its
leaves chopped (1 head)
Yellow onions, peeled and
quartered (5 medium)

Leek whites, desanded and
chunked (4 medium)
Cloves, whole (4)
Knuckle of veal, with plenty of
meat, quartered by butcher
(1)
Oxtail, chunked by butcher (1)
Salt, coarse crystal, to taste
Black pepper, freshly ground,
to taste
Plus wide aluminum foil to
wrap the turkey and a burlap
feed-sack to enclose everything before burying

Three days before serving – active preparation about 20 minutes, plus 3 days of unsupervised burial

Lovingly brush the 4 truffles, skin them (carefully saving the peelings, naturally) then cut them into coarse dice. In a large mixing bowl, preferably with your clean fingers, gently work the truffle peelings and dice into the sausage stuffing. Keep everything light and fluffy. Do not press down or squeeze. Then stuff the turkey, close neck and back openings with needle and string or small trussing skewers, then tightly double-wrap the turkey in aluminum foil. Next, slip everything into the corn sack, doubling it over and sewing it up tightly.

Now – provided the weather is not too cold where you are and the ground is not frozen solid – dress warmly to avoid pneumonia, go out into your garden, and dig a hole for the turkey. Bocuse said: "The hole must not be so deep that there may be a danger of your never finding your turkey again. Nor should it be so shallow that your dog might decide to dig it up. After three days, you will find that the underground cold and dampness will ensure that the marvelous bouquet and savor of the truffles will have completely permeated all the flesh of the stuffing and the turkey. Believe me, there is no other way of achieving this complete infiltration of the essence of the truffles."

On the day – about 2 hours before serving – active work about 30 minutes, plus about 1½ hours of unsupervised simmering

Provided it is not raining, dig up your turkey, unwrap it and let it come to room temperature. In a big soup kettle large enough to hold the turkey, bring up to gentle boiling enough chicken bouillon just to cover the turkey – usually about 4 quarts – and add to it: the 8 chunked carrots, the chunked celery with its chopped leaves, the 5 quartered onions, the 4 leeks, the 4 cloves, the quartered knuckle of veal, the chunked oxtail, with salt and pepper to your taste. When it is all beautifully simmering, lower your turkey into it (not in its sack, of course, nor in its aluminum foil) and, timing it from the moment when it returns to the simmer, cover it and let it poach until it is perfectly done, almost always in about 1½ hours. Serve it with some of the vegetables from the bouillon. Bocuse finally added: "To make this quite perfect, what you should drink with it is a noble, red Burgundy from our village of Gevrey-Chambertin." There is no precise equivalent to a truly great Chambertin, but on our side of the Atlantic I feel I would also very much enjoy this dish with a noble and unique California Zinfandel in an old vintage from the Napa Valley.

Chapter Nine
Beef

in which the author introduces an Alsatian in a
hotpot, a Burgundian with Lemon and Capers,
a Japanese in a Balinese bouillon, and a Provençal
with Olives

CHEFS JEAN AND PIERRE TROISGROS'S BALINESE YAKISUKI À LA FRANÇAISE

(for 4 to 6)

This is the famous and much-publicized dish served by the Troisgros brothers (page 50) at their three-star restaurant in Roanne. On an invitation from the Japanese National School of High Imperial Gastronomy, Jean Troisgros visited Tokyo and gave a course in French cooking to its graduate students. He watched demonstrations by top Japanese professional cooks. When he returned to Roanne, he brought with him to work for a time in the Troisgros kitchen a young Japanese apprentice nicknamed Mikado (who later also worked for Roger Vergé [see page 52]).

Jean and Pierre learned how to make a Sukiyaki and then began analyzing it and rethinking it in low-fat terms. Why not eliminate the fat and the frying, cooking the meat instead by simmering in an aromatic fatless bouillon?

At that crucial moment I arrived in Roanne for a few days and the Troisgros brothers set their new dish before me. Jean said: "It is a kind of upside-down Sukiyaki – so let us call it a *'Yakisuki à la Française!'* "

It was wonderfully light. It was also a turning point in the modern history of French gastronomy. Two supreme French *cuisiniers* had thrown the traditional French chauvinism out of the window and had embraced the culinary techniques of the Far East.

My contribution to its final form was to teach Jean and Pierre how to improve their bouillon by preparing in advance an adaptation of the great Balinese clear soup, *Soto Ayam*, of beef and chicken with aromatic spices. This has since become our basic Low-High clear bouillon and its preparation is described on page 68. A batch of it must be prepared before starting this recipe.

Finally, the marvelous Troisgros trick is that each vegetable is prepared separately and in a different style, so that when they all come together almost a dozen different flavors and textures meet in dramatic coexistence, each honoring all the others while retaining its separate identity. Not a single exotic ingredient is involved in producing a spectacular Low-High party dish.

Beef, lean sirloin or top round, sliced for thin escalops (1 lb)

Veal, lean, sliced for thin escalops (1 lb)

Lamb chops, nicely lean (8)

Chicken meat, boiled and sliced (about 1 lb – see below)

Bouillon, basic Low-High (page 68), or canned beef (about 3 quarts)

White wine, dry (about ½ cup)

Saffron (¼ tsp)

White wine, sweet (1 cup)

Potatoes, peeled, sliced into rounds 3/16 inch thick (3 medium)

Mint leaves, fresh in season (4)

Parsley, chopped (about 2 Tbs)

Ginger root, fresh, grated (¼ tsp)

Salt, coarse crystal, to taste

Pepper, Chinese Szechuan, freshly ground, to taste

Yellow turnip, skinned and cut into cubes about the size of large lumps of sugar (1 medium)

Celery leaves, green Pascal, chopped (from 1 stalk)

Fennel root, carved into small, ¾ inch pyramids (1 head)

Mushrooms, fresh, cut into round about 3/16 inch thick (4 medium)

Leek whites, carefully de-sanded and chunked (2)

Carrots, scraped and cut lengthwise into ⅜-inch sticks (3 medium)

Apple, Rome Beauty, peeled and cored, cut into thin wedges about 3/16-inch thick (1)

Pot cheese, low-fat (about 2 cups)

Tomato paste (2 to 3 tsp)

Scallions, chopped (4)

The day before: advance preparation of the bouillon – active preparation about 20 minutes, plus about 3 hours of unsupervised simmering

Prepare the basic Low-High aromatic bouillon according to the recipe on page 68. The chicken from the bouillon should be saved and used in the preparation of this dish. If you use commercially prepared bouillon instead, you will need some boiled chicken meat (see ingredients).

On the day – one hour before serving – preparing the main meats and vegetables in about 40 minutes

Begin by organizing the work. Several jobs need to be done simultaneously. Bring all meats to room temperature. Skim all the fat from the bouillon you have prepared and strain out all solids. Measure 1 quart of the bouillon into a sauté pan and boil it hard for a few minutes to reduce it and concentrate its flavor. When you have reduced the quart to about 1 cup, pour it into a heatproof container and hold aside for making the sauce. In a tiny saucepan, heat a tablespoon of dry white wine until it feels slightly warm to the fingertip, then stir into it the 1/4 teaspoon of saffron, removing it from the heat and setting it aside to soak.

Carefully arrange your warming areas. I put my 12-inch (3-inch deep) copper sauté pan onto a big burner and fill it up with about 2 quarts of the now clear bouillon, heating it up and keeping it simmering during the final operations. On a second burner, I set up a *bain-marie* by filling a fair-size pan three quarters full of boiling, steaming water and placing in it a large, heatproof covered bowl in which the various meats and vegetables, after cooking, can be kept warm until serving time without toughening.

On a third burner, I organize a 12-inch Chinese bamboo steamer, heated up and ready to cook the vegetables. On a fourth burner I put a 1-pint lidded saucepan with the 1 cup of sweet wine simmering, covered.

Preheat the oven to 175°F. and warm in it a sauceboat and the large, open, shallow serving dish in which the finished *Yakisuki* will be brought to table.

Put the sliced potatoes into a small open baking dish with the chopped mint leaves and parsley, the ¼ teaspoon of ginger root, salt and pepper to taste, then steam them until just soft – usually about 30 minutes – and hold them warm in the bowl over the *bain-marie*. Put the cubed turnips into a second open baking dish with the chopped celery leaves plus salt and pepper to taste, then steam until just soft – usually in about 30 minutes – and transfer to the keep-warm bowl. Place the fennel pyramids in a third open baking dish with salt and pepper to taste, then steam until just soft, usually in about 20 to 25 minutes, then transfer to the keep-warm bowl. Drop the mushrooms into the simmering sweet wine and poach until just soft, usually in about 10 minutes, then remove and keep warm with the other vegetables. Drop the leek chunks into the large sauté pan of simmering bouillon, poach them until just soft, usually in about 10 minutes, then fish them out and keep warm. Drop the carrots into the simmering sweet wine, poach them until just soft but still crispy, usually in about 10 minutes, then remove and keep them warm. Drop the apple wedges into the simmering bouillon in the large sauté pan, poach until they are just soft but still crispy, usually in about 2 minutes, then fish them out and keep warm.

Cut the beef slices into rectangles, about 2 by 3 inches, then hold them aside at room temperature. Cut the veal slices into 2-inch triangles, then hold. Using a very sharp small knife, precisely cut out the lean "eye rounds" from the lamb chops and hold (saving the bones for some future soup pot). Skin the chicken (from the bouillon) and carve its best meat from breast and thighs into neat slices.

About 20 minutes before serving

Now each batch of the meats is dropped in turn into the simmering bouillon in the large sauté pan, poached for its precise time, then fished out and added to the vegetables in the keep-warm bowl. Precise timing keeps the meats juicy tender. The beef rectangles should be in the poaching liquid for hardly more than 1 minute – the veal triangles for 3 minutes – the thicker lamb rounds for 5 minutes – the chicken slices for 2 minutes.

Finally prepare a pot cheese whip to provide an accompanying sauce with a lovely color and a creamy consistency. I put 1½ cups of the pot cheese into the bowl of my Cuisinart chopper-churner (or you can use an electric blender, or a hand food-mill) and add 3 tablespoons from the 1 cup of concentrated bouillon which we reduced at the beginning. I then run the machine until the mixture is a smoothly blended cream – usually in no more than 4 or 5 seconds. Transfer it to a round-bottomed beating bowl and whip air into it with a balloon whisk, adjusting the flavor and thickness by working in more of the concentrated bouillon, teaspoon by teaspoon, or, if it becomes too thick, a bit more pot cheese. You should end up with the spoon-coating consistency of heavy cream. Now transfer it to a small saucepan and reheat it, stirring continuously, until almost, but not quite, boiling. At the same time, work in the saffron and its soaking wine, plus 2 teaspoons of the tomato paste. The sauce should now have a handsome orange-yellow color. Taste it and adjust the seasonings. This sauce will be brought to table in the warm sauceboat with a ladle.

Bringing the Yakisuki to table

Pour some of the still simmering bouillon from the large sauté pan into your serving bowl and decoratively arrange in it all the vegetables and meats, then sprinkle the chopped green scallions over the top and carry the *Yakisuki* to table. It makes a magnificent display of natural foods, prepared with great sophistication. Offer the sauce separately in its hot sauceboat. Serve onto wide soup plates some of the bouillon and a balanced selection of the vegetables and meats, with a creamy sauce lightly dribbled over the top. Use soup spoons for the luscious eating. When they presented it to me the brothers Troisgros served with it a fine, beautifully fruity and light, top Beaujolais from the village of Fleury. The American equivalent might be a fine and fruity California Gamay Beaujolais from the Napa Valley.

ALSATIAN BAECKAOFFA OF MIXED MEATS WITH WINE IN A HOTPOT

(for 4)

Just to prove that the Low-High cuisine is not completely all-new and all-different, here is a recipe for what is generally called the "national dish" of Alsace. It is as old as the history of the region, yet as light, as simple, as validly Low-High as anything invented last month by the three-star chefs. Considering how easy and good a *Baeckaoffa* can be, it seems strange that it is generally ignored in most cookbooks, English or French, where Alsace is always represented by a *choucroute* or a *quiche.*

In the days when most Alsatian homes still had coal-burning stoves, which dropped to a mere glimmer at night, thrifty housewives used to put together a casserole of mixed meats and vegetables, marinated with wine and herbs, then carry it down the street to the baker, whose ovens were going full tilt all night and who charged only a few centimes for baking the casserole. So the peripatetic dish was simply called, in the Alsatian dialect, *Baeckaoffa,* baker's oven, regardless of the different things that different cooks put into it.

The lid of the casserole is traditionally not lifted until it is placed before the guests in the center of the table. Then, the first puff of steam with its mingled bouquet of wine, meats, onions, bay leaves, cloves, juniper and thyme, arouses hunger pangs to the point of being unbearable. The wine is all absorbed into the vegetables, which become a kind of aromatic purée to garnish the softly winey chunks of meat. All the cook has to do is to assemble it, put it into the oven and forget it, then ladle it out at table. In my Low-High translation and adaptation, since the meats and potatoes are not first browned, they remain safely low-fat.

Beef brisket, chuck, or round, largish chunks (1 lb)

Lamb, leg or shoulder, largish chunks, with bones (1¼ lbs)

Pork, loin or shoulder, largish chunks, with bones (1¼ lbs)

Pig's foot, chunked, with bones (1)

Pigs' tails, chunked, with bones (2)

Yellow onions, medium, peeled and thinly sliced (1 lb)

Garlic, minced (3 cloves)
Shallots, peeled and minced
  (4 cloves)
Parsley, fresh, chopped
  (1 bunch)
Bay leaves, whole (2)
Coriander, whole berries (6)
Juniper berries, whole (8)
Cloves, ground (¼ tsp)
Thyme, fresh leaves (1 Tbs)
Salt, coarse crystal, to taste

Black pepper, freshly ground,
  to taste
White wine, dry Alsatian
  (about 2½ cups)
Cognac (⅓ cup)
Potatoes, starchy boiling,
  peeled and thinly sliced
  (1 lb)
Olive oil (2 Tbs)
Butter (1 Tbs)

Two days before – marinating the meats – active preparation about 15 minutes

Put the 5 meats into a large bowl, or covered dish, which will go into the refrigerator. Add sliced onions, the minced garlic and shallots, a small handful of the parsley, the 2 bay leaves crumbled, the 6 coriander berries, the 8 juniper berries, the cloves and thyme, with salt and pepper to taste, then pour over 1 pint of the wine and the ⅓ cup Cognac. Turn it all over, gently, with a large wooden spoon or spatula, so that everything is thoroughly mixed and wetted. Leave it to marinate in the refrigerator for 48 hours, turning it over first thing every morning and last thing each night.

On the day – about 3 hours before serving – about 15 minutes active work plus about 2¾ hours of unsupervised baking

Preheat the oven to 325°F. Salt and pepper the slices of potato to taste, then sprinkle them lightly with the olive oil and let them rest at room temperature. Lightly butter the inside of your large, tightly lidded, earthenware casserole and assemble the ingredients in it, in layers. First, spread across the bottom half of the sliced potatoes. Then, all the chunks of meats, including the pig's foot and tails, fished out of the marinade. Next, half of the onion slices from the marinade. Then the rest of the potato slices, with the rest of the onion slices on top. Finally, pour in the entire marinade, including all its herbs and spices.

Put the tightly lidded casserole into the oven and let it bake for about 2½ hours. It is precisely done, in the true Alsatian style, when every drop of wine has been absorbed into the meats and vegetables and when the onions and potatoes have been completely converted into a soft, winey purée, which, so to speak, becomes the sauce for the meats. You should not take off the lid for the first 2 hours, or you will lose the essential steam, but then you may check and, if the wine has been absorbed too soon, so that the meats are in danger of becoming slightly dry, add an extra ½ cup of wine. On the other hand, if there is wine left at the end, so that the potatoes are not completely puréed, continue the baking until they are. The exact timing must always depend on the efficiency of your particular oven and the tightness of the lid of your particular casserole. Serve onto very hot plates. In Alsace, extra side dishes or vegetables are never served with the *Baeckaoffa*. The wine served to me when I first had this dish was a rich and soft white Tokay d'Alsace made from the Pinot Gris grape. At my own table in New York I might choose an American alternative, perhaps a California Emerald Riesling from Santa Clara.

BRAISED BEEF WITH WILD MUSHROOMS AND ROSEMARY

(for 4)

An Italian influence is evident in this dish that is a fine example of the light and simple preservation of the aromatic, natural flavors of the ingredients. This recipe might be called an Italian variation on the French Low-High cuisine.

Butter (2 Tbs)

Olive oil, pure green virgin (2 Tbs)

Beef, fatless top round, cut by butcher into a steak 2 inches thick (about 2 lbs)

Salt, coarse crystal, to taste

Black pepper, freshly ground, to taste

Celery, green Pascal, destringed and chopped, with leaves (2 stalks)

Yellow onions, peeled and chopped (2 medium)

Carrots, scraped and chopped
(3 medium)

Italian plum tomatoes, canned,
peeled, with basil, solid
flesh only, liquid strained
off (1 cup)

Parsley, chopped leaf (¼ cup)

Oregano, fresh leaf in season,
chopped (1 Tbs)

Thyme, fresh leaf in season,
chopped (1 Tbs)

Garlic, peeled and finely
minced (1 clove)

White wine, dry, preferably
Italian Soave (about 1 cup)

Red wine, preferably Italian
Valpolicella or Barolo
(½ cup)

Wild mushrooms, dried, from
Italian or Chinese groceries
(3 oz package)

Rosemary, fresh sprigs in
season (4 sprigs)

About 2¾ hours before serving – active work about 45 minutes, plus about 2 hours of unsupervised poaching

Preheat your grill to high temperature. Cream together in a mortar the 2 tablespoons each of butter and olive oil. The fruity oil gives an extra tang to the butter. This is a Venetian trick worth remembering. Lightly salt and pepper the piece of beef, patting it strongly with your fingers. Then lightly rub it all over with some of the butter-oil mixture. Grill the meat briefly, quite close to the heat, so that it browns on each side within a couple of minutes, without cooking inside. Watch it carefully, do not overbrown or overcook. Take it from the grill and hold it.

Choose a tightly lidded casserole for use on a top burner. (The best type is French enameled iron.) It should be just large enough to hold the beef comfortably with not too much room to spare. Lubricate the bottom of this casserole with the remaining butter-oil mixture. Heat it up to gentle frying heat. Now put in: the chopped celery, the 2 chopped onions and the 3 chopped carrots. Stir them continuously with a wooden spoon, letting them melt and soften, but under no circumstances allowing them to fry or brown – usually in 5 to 7 minutes. When they are right, add the cup of tomatoes, the ¼ cup of parsley, the tablespoon each of oregano and thyme, the minced garlic and ½ cup of the white wine, stirring everything around again and reducing the heat to a very gentle simmering. On this aromatic bed lay the piece of beef, tightly clamp on the lid and let it poach for 2 hours. Check it every 30 minutes or so to make sure that the simmering is still gentle and that the casserole has not dried out. If that should happen, add another ¼ cup of white wine. After the first hour, turn the piece of beef over.

Meanwhile, put the ½ cup of red wine into a very small saucepan and warm it up to no more than blood heat. Break up by hand, or coarsely chop, the 3 ounces of dried mushrooms and soak them, off the heat, in the warm red wine. Leave them there, covered, until they are needed later.

About 30 minutes before serving – completing the sauce

Strain the mushrooms from the red wine and squeeze them out, preferably by hand. Save the wine. Turn the beef over once more and sprinkle around it the mushrooms and the sprigs of rosemary. Continue the gentle simmering until the beef is done to precisely the degree you like, usually in another 15 to 20 minutes if you are enough of a connoisseur to like it reasonably rare. During that time the beef absorbs the flavors of the mushrooms and rosemary. Then take out the beef and hold it warm while you complete the sauce. I put all the remaining contents of the casserole into the bowl of my Cuisinart chopper-churner (or you could use an electric blender, or a hand food mill) and run the machine until they are a smooth purée, but not so long that they become a mushy paste – usually in about 7 to 10 seconds. Transfer the purée to a saucepan and heat it up almost, but not quite, to boiling. Stir in and adjust seasoning. If it is too thick, add a few dashes of the red wine in which the mushrooms were soaked. Bring this sauce to table in a warmed sauceboat and serve it with the carved slices of beef on very hot plates. The accompanying wine can be a noble red Bordeaux, a Château Nénin from Pomerol. My reasonable alternative on our American side might be a fine California Petite Sirah from the Livermore Valley.

ROLLED PAUPIETTES OF BEEF À LA PROVENÇALE

(for 4)

This recipe actually comes from the Valley of La Grande Chartreuse where the flesh of the small beef achieves a remarkable quality from the lush grasses of the Alpine slopes. Here it is flavored with a basic combination of Provençal wild herbs to create a Low-High variation of the classic sliced beef, rolled and stuffed.

Ham, boiled, dark-smoked, or
Italian prosciutto, minced
(½ cup)
Parmesan cheese, grated (¼ lb)
Garlic, peeled and minced
(2 cloves)
Parsley, leaf only, minced
(4 Tbs)
Basil, fresh leaf in season,
chopped (2 Tbs)
Oregano (½ tsp)
Nutmeg, freshly grated, to taste
Salt, coarse crystal, to taste
Black pepper, freshly ground,
to taste
Egg (1)
Pot cheese, low-fat (about
½ cup)

Beef, entirely lean, top round
or rump, cut into thin slices
as for scallopini (8 slices,
total about 2 lbs)
Carrots, scraped and chopped
(2 medium)
Yellow onion, peeled and
chopped (1 medium)
Bay leaf, crumbled (1)
Thyme, fresh leaf in season,
chopped (1 Tbs)
Tomatoes, Italian plum, canned
(2 cups)
White wine, dry (1 cup)
Butter (2 tsp)
Olive oil, pure green virgin
(4 tsp)

About 45 minutes before serving – active preparation about 25 minutes, plus about 20 minutes of unsupervised simmering and grilling

First prepare the filling for the *paupiettes* by assembling, in a large mixing bowl, the ½ cup of minced ham, the ¼ pound of Parmesan, the minced garlic, 3 tablespoons of the parsley, the basil and oregano, and 2 or 3 grinds of nutmeg, with salt and pepper to taste. Then carefully and thoroughly work in the whole egg, plus as many tablespoons of the pot cheese as may be necessary to bind the filling into a spreadable paste – usually 2 to 4 tablespoons. Lay out the slices of beef on a wooden cutting board – remove any last vestiges of fat – and lightly pound them with a scallopini hammer, taking care not to tear them. Spread equal parts of the filling on each slice and roll up the *paupiettes*, jelly-roll fashion, neatly tying them with thin string.

Choose a tightly lidded, stove-top casserole, large enough to hold, eventually, all the *paupiettes* in a single layer. Spread over its bottom a layer of the chopped carrots and onion, the crumbled bay leaf, and the 1 tablespoon of thyme, with pepper to taste but no salt. Mix this layer thoroughly, then set the casserole on a top burner over medium heat and stir the vegetables around until they begin to give out their juices. Keep them moving, taking care that they do not burn. As soon as they begin to steam, neatly lay the *paupiettes* on top of them, pouring in the 2 cups of tomatoes and the cup of white wine. Clamp on the lid tightly and keep it all very gently simmering to poach the *paupiettes* until they are just cooked through, while the beef remains lightly tender – usually in about 45 minutes. While the poaching is in progress, prepare an open, shallow, *au gratin* dish, handsome enough to be carried to table, in which the *paupiettes* will be browned. Rub the inside of this dish with the 2 teaspoons of butter. About 5 minutes before the poaching is completed, set your grill to heat up.

Just before serving

When the *paupiettes* are done, lift them out of the casserole, bringing up with them as little sauce as possible, place them in the buttered *au gratin* dish, sprinkle each with ½ teaspoon of the olive oil and set them to brown, about 2 inches under the grill. Watch them. They should be nicely gilded in 3 to 5 minutes. Meanwhile, I pour the entire sauce and vegetable contents of the casserole into the bowl of my Cuisinart chopper-churner (or you can use a blender) and run it until everything is a smooth purée – usually in 10 to 15 seconds. Almost certainly, the sauce will be slightly too thin. Pour it into a sauté pan and boil it down rapidly to concentrate its flavors, while reducing and thickening it. When it is the right consistency, add body to it by whisking in an extra 2 or 3 tablespoons of the pot cheese, beating it all until it becomes slightly foamy. The moment the *paupiettes* are browned, pour the sauce over them, sprinkle them with the remaining parsley and carry to table at once. I first had with this a fine, light red Gamay de Savoie. I might substitute, in the United States, a California Gamay from the Santa Clara Valley.

SLICED SIRLOIN STEAK WITH LEMON AND CAPERS

(for 4)

This is a new invention by Chefs Jean and Pierre Troisgros (page 50) at their three-star restaurant in Roanne. The first time you taste juicy, rare, and tender sections of beefsteak, served in a soup plate with a natural sauce *au jus*, but distinctly flavored with lemon juice and the acid of capers, it comes almost as a shock – it is so completely different from any previous gastronomic experience. By the second or third bite, you begin to realize that it is an extraordinarily successful combination of flavors – the sauce bringing out and magnifying the juicy meatiness of the sirloin. And this is achieved without béarnaise, hollandaise, butter, cream or flour. With the well known soothing effect of lemon juice on the digestion, you could eat a couple of pounds of steak in this way and never feel the slightest sense of overfullness. You should prepare, to go with this, a nice mixture of light, seasonal, fresh vegetables, preferably poached or steamed, to be served around the meat as a colorful *garniture jardinière*.

Beef sirloin steak, about 1½ inches thick (about 2 to 2½ lbs)
Butter (1 Tbs)
Olive oil, pure green virgin (1 Tbs)
Shallots, peeled and chopped (2 Tbs)
Lemon juice, freshly squeezed (2 Tbs)
Vinegar, red wine (2 Tbs)
Beef bouillon (1⅓ cups)
Demi-glace brown sauce (5 Tbs) (see page 78)
Capers, drained (3 Tbs)
Salt, coarse crystal, to taste
White pepper, freshly ground, to taste
Parsley, chopped (small handful)
Tarragon, fresh leaf in season, chopped (¼ cup)

Preparation in about 25 minutes

Preheat your oven to a keep-warm 175°F. Cut every scrap of fat away from the sirloin steak and slice the remaining lean into strips, each about ⅜ to ½ inch thick and about 2 to 3 inches long. Set a heavy frypan over high frying heat and, when it is good and hot, quickly lubricate its bottom with the 1 tablespoon each of butter and olive oil. Within a few seconds, as soon as they start smoking, drop in the sirloin strips, batch by batch, moving them around and turning them over almost continuously, so that they brown and crust slightly on the outside but remain juicy, rare, and tender inside. It is all done in seconds rather than minutes. As fast as the strips are removed from the frypan, they should be kept warm on a platter, covered, in the oven. Lower the heat under the frypan to medium frying and put in the 2 tablespoons of chopped shallots, stirring them around until they are just colored, usually in not more than 20 seconds. At once hiss into the frypan the 2 tablespoons each of lemon juice and vinegar with the 1⅓ cups of beef bouillon. Stir thoroughly. Continue turning down the heat, but keep the liquid bubbling hard to reduce it, concentrating its flavors and thickening it – usually for 2 or 3 minutes. Work in, tablespoon by tablespoon, the 5 tablespoons of *demi-glace*. Keep boiling hard to continue reducing for about another 5 minutes. Add the 3 tablespoons of drained capers. Add salt and pepper, to taste. Add the small handful of chopped parsley and the ¼ cup tarragon. Now put your strips of sirloin back into the sauce and reheat them in it for not a flash more than 10 seconds, or you will commit the crime of overcooking the meat. Serve instantly in very hot soup plates with about ¼ inch of sauce in the bottom. Provide your guests with a soup spoon for the sauce. Accompany the dish with a red Burgundy – or a noble California Cabernet Sauvignon from Sonoma – and drink a toast to the Burgundian skill of the brothers Troisgros!

BOEUF EN DAUBE – LOW-FAT POT ROAST À LA PROVENÇALE

(for 4 to 6)

Here is another classic Provençal dish, but with all the preliminary frying and all the soaking of vegetables in those large quantities of olive oil eliminated without loss of the authentic character of the dish. It is all lighter and simpler than it would be in a farmhouse in Provence. But, with its garnish of black and green olives, it still keeps its Mediterranean character.

Beef pot roast, fatless, good
   rectangular shape, preferably
   top round, but could be
   bottom round or chuck
   (about 3½ lbs)
Salt, coarse crystal, to taste
Black pepper, freshly ground,
   to taste
Olive oil, Provençal green
   virgin (about 5 Tbs)
Yellow onions, peeled and
   chopped (2 medium)
Carrots, scraped and chopped
   (3 medium)
Parsley (about a dozen sprigs)
Thyme, fresh in season (3 stalks
   with plenty of leaves)
Bay leaf, whole (1)

Garlic, left whole in skin
   (2 cloves)
White wine, dry (about 1½
   cups)
Beef bouillon, clear (about
   1½ cups)
Chicken bouillon, clear (about
   3 cups)
Tomato paste, preferably Italian
   (6 oz can)
Black olives, fresh from
   the barrel in Greek or
   Italian grocery (1 dozen)
Green olives, same as above
   (1 dozen)
Cherry tomatoes (about 1½
   dozen)

About 4 hours before serving – active work about 45 minutes, plus about 3¼ hours of unsupervised oven pot-roasting

Preheat your grill to high temperature. Lightly salt and pepper the piece of beef on all sides, patting it hard by hand. Then, preferably again with your fingers, lightly rub the beef all over with a small amount of olive oil, certainly not more than 2 to 3 tablespoons. Now grill the beef quickly on each of its 6 sides, adjusting the rack so that the surface being grilled is about 2½ inches from the heat. Each side should be lightly browned in about 2 to 3 minutes – 12 to 18 minutes for the entire operation. Then hold the beef, turn off the grill and preheat the oven to 350°F.

Choose a tightly lidded casserole, or French *cocotte* or Dutch oven, of a size that will hold the beef comfortably, but with not too much room to spare, or the liquid will spread out too much and will not be deep enough. Set it first on top of the stove and melt in it the remaining 2 tablespoons of olive oil. Then add the 2 chopped onions and the 3 chopped carrots. Stir them around and let them melt and poach rather than fry and brown, until the onions are just starting to color – usually in about 5 to 7 minutes. Turn off the heat and place the beef on top of its aromatic bed. Make a small bunch of herbs by tying together the sprigs of parsley and thyme, then drop them into the casserole alongside the beef. Crumble the bay leaf and drop it in with the 2 garlic cloves. If there are any juices left behind in the grill pan rinse them out with a little of the wine and add them to the casserole. Add 1 cup of wine, the 1½ cups of beef bouillon and 2½ cups of the chicken bouillon. Over high heat on top of the stove bring this liquid mixture to the boil. Meanwhile, in a small mixing bowl, blend together half the can of tomato paste (6 tablespoons) with the remaining ½ cup of chicken bouillon. When the mixture is smooth, add it to the casserole. When everything is hot and bubbling, tightly clamp on the lid and set the casserole in the center of the oven. Leave it to poach and simmer until it is perfectly done – usually in 2½ to 3 hours. It requires virtually no attention beyond stirring it occasionally and checking the progress of the beef. Turn the beef over at roughly the half-way point.

About 30 minutes before serving – completing the sauce

When the beef is done, take it out of the casserole and keep it warm, covered. Carefully skim off any fat floating on the liquid in the casserole. Strain the liquid into a large saucepan and boil it hard, uncovered, to reduce it, concentrating and sharpening its flavors. From the solid vegetables, pick out and throw away the bunch of parsley-thyme. If the garlic cloves are still intact and have not disintegrated, squeeze between the fingers to release the now mushy inside paste and throw away the skin. I then put all the remaining vegetables into the bowl of my Cuisinart chopper-churner (or you can use an electric blender, or a hand food mill) and run the machine until the vegetables are just thoroughly mixed and smoothly puréed – usually in about 5 seconds. When the sauce has reduced by about half and is just beginning to become syrupy, turn the heat down to gentle simmering and blend in the puréed vegetables. Let it continue simmering, uncovered, while you deal with the olives.

It used to be the fashion, in the old days of high cuisine, to pit the olives and slice them into rings. But, in the new cuisine, natural foods are left in their natural state. So, if you don't want to pit the olives, drop both the black and the green into the sauce and let them heat up for a couple of minutes. You may decide, also, that it is not worthwhile to skin the cherry tomatoes, and simply drop them *au naturel* into the sauce for a couple of minutes. Taste the sauce and adjust its seasonings. You may, if you wish, also work in a bit more of the tomato paste and a dash or two of the remaining white wine. Then carve the beef onto very hot plates and pour the sauce around it, with each diner getting at least 3 tomatoes and 4 olives. A fine Beaujolais from the district of Moulin-à-Vent accompanied the dish when I first had it in France. Here, the wine could be a fine California Gamay from Monterey.

Chapter Ten
Lamb

in which we find Lamb in a fruit garden, in a
vegetable garden, in a Moussaka, and doused with
Pink Champagne.

AN AMERICAN ADAPTATION OF CHEF ROGER VERGÉ'S ALMOST-MELTED LEG OF LAMB LAYERED WITH EGGPLANT AND TOMATO À LA MOUSSAKA

(for 4 to 6)

This is pure invention – almost certainly unlike any dish that has ever been prepared before – concocted by Chef Vergé (page 52) at his three-star Le Moulin de Mougins, in Provence, out of his lifetime experience of cooking with cuisines in many parts of the world. From the culture of North Africa he brought to this dish the classic elements of the African and Middle Eastern *Moussaka,* in which, in one arrangement or another, lamb is combined with eggplant and tomato. From his experience in Central Africa, he has incorporated the technique of the slow braising of meat. He has added overtones of the historic French cuisine of Escoffier. And finally he has ruthlessly eliminated all superimposed complications, all unnecessary frills, all excessive richness, towards the perfection of a new *Moussaka.*

There is nothing particularly difficult about my translation and adaptation within the Low-High technique of the recipe which Roger wrote out for me, but since it is made up of several parts each prepared separately, it does involve a good deal of time and work. Perhaps it should be a weekend project with some help from family or friends. Each time I have brought this *Moussaka* to my table, it has "stopped the show" and the high praise of my guests has been a rich reward for the cook.   Most of the preparation is best done a day or two before the party, since the flavors amalgamate and seem to strike a perfect balance during period of resting and ripening before the final reheating in an oven casserole.

Eggplants, whole (2 large)

Olive oil, pure green virgin (1 Tbs)

Garlic, peeled and minced (1 clove)

Legs of lamb, small, with bone (2, about 3½ lbs each)

Yellow onions, peeled and chopped (1¼ cups)

Celery, green Pascal, with leaves (½ cup)

Carrots, scraped and diced (1 cup)

Turnips, white, chopped (1 cup)

Garlic, whole (1 clove)

Orange zest, the thin outer skin, chopped (1 Tbs)

Bay leaf, crumbled (1)

Black peppercorns, whole (4)

Salt, coarse crystal, to taste

Red wine, preferably old, aromatic, strong Burgundy (2 cups)

White celery, destringed and diced (¾ cup)

Mushrooms, fresh, wiped and diced (¾ cup)

Leek whites, carefully desanded and diced (½ cup)

Shallots, peeled and finely minced (4 cloves)

Butter (about 2 Tbs)

Beef bouillon (¾ cup)

Rosemary, fresh in season, chopped (1 Tbs)

Juniper berries, freshly ground (2 tsp)

Tomatoes, peeled and chunked (6 medium)

Black pepper, freshly ground, to taste

Two days before serving – active preparation of the eggplant in about 5 minutes, plus all-night unsupervised baking

Preheat your oven to 200°F.   Shortly before you plan to go to bed, wipe clean the skins of the 2 eggplants and then lightly rub them with the tablespoon of olive oil.   Place them on an open baking dish and set it at the center of the oven.   Leave the eggplants to bake all night.

The day before – preparation of the various parts in almost 4 hours

Before breakfast, check the eggplants. Both will most likely have collapsed, with the skin black and partly crisp, cracked open. The bottom of the baking dish will be covered with a black juice. With a spoon, scrape out all the perfectly cooked pulp from inside the skins and put it into a covered storage jar, adding the black juice from the pan. Also add the minced garlic. Stir thoroughly, cover, then store in the refrigerator for later use. Now you may have your breakfast.

Preheat your oven to 350°F. Next, deal with the first of the 2 legs of lamb. With a small, sharp knife, trim off every scrap of visible fat and skin. Choose an oven casserole or *cocotte* large enough to hold the whole leg snugly, but do not yet put it in. Prepare a bed for the lamb by spreading across the bottom of the casserole ½ cup of the chopped onion, the ½ cup of chopped Pascal celery, with some of the leaves, ¼ cup of the chopped carrots, ¼ cup of the chopped turnips, the whole clove of garlic, the chopped orange zest, the crumbled bay leaf, the peppercorns and salt to taste. Gently lay the lamb leg on this aromatic bed and then pour over it the 2 cups of red wine. Over high heat on top of the stove quickly bring the liquid up to the boiling point, then cover the casserole and set it in the center of the oven, leaving the lamb to braise and poach very slowly in its steam until it is extremely soft – usually in about 2 to 3 hours, according to the efficiency of your oven. Gently turn the leg over after the first hour.

Meanwhile, deal with the second lamb leg. Trim off all fat and skin, then bone it and chunk the lean meat. I then coarsely grind this in my Cuisinart chopper-churner, running the machine for hardly more than 4 seconds. (Or you can use a meat grinder.) Hold this supply of ground lamb at room temperature.

Now prepare a classic French *brunoise*, an aromatic mixture of various finely diced vegetables, by mixing in a bowl ¾ cup each of onions, diced carrots, turnips, white celery and mushrooms, the ½ cup of diced leeks, the minced shallots, plus salt to taste. Now gently sauté them in a couple of tablespoons of butter until their rawness has disappeared and they are beginning to soften, but certainly not fried or browned, usually in 3 to 4 minutes. Then pour into the sauté pan the ¾ cup of beef bouillon and simmer the *brunoise,* uncovered, for 10 minutes. Strain the diced vegetables and incorporate half of them into the eggplant purée, which should now be kept out of the refrigerator to come to room temperature. Into the second half of the vegetable *brunoise* mix the tablespoon of chopped rosemary and the 2 teaspoons of juniper. Incorporate this mixture into the ground lamb, keeping it light and fluffy by lifting and folding rather than pressing and squeezing. Then hold it at room temperature for later use.

The final job to be done while the leg of lamb is still simmering is the light poaching of the tomatoes. Put the chunked tomatoes into the sauté pan in which the *brunoise* was simmered, mixing them with the bouillon left over from that operation. Turn on moderate heat under the pan and stir the tomatoes around, mashing them down until they are a coarse, lumpy purée. If there is too much liquid, turn up the heat for a few minutes and boil it off. The tomatoes should finish up being fairly thick. Salt and pepper them to taste, then turn off the heat and hold them for later use.

As soon as the simmering leg of lamb is ready, take the casserole out of the oven still covered and let it cool for about an hour, to encourage the lamb to absorb the aromatic flavors. Then carefully and gently lift the lamb out and place it on a cutting board. Skim off all fat from the liquid in the casserole and strain the red wine sauce into a wide saucepan, bringing it to a rolling boil and letting it reduce, to concentrate and sharpen its flavors. I then put all the vegetables remaining in the casserole into the bowl of my Cuisinart chopper-churner (or you can use an electric blender, or a hand food mill) and run it until the vegetables are thoroughly mixed and smoothly puréed, but not so long that they become a mushy paste – usually in about 5 seconds. When the red wine has been reduced by about half and is showing the first signs of becoming syrupy, blend into it the puréed vegetables and adjust the seasonings. Keep it gently simmering, uncovered, until it is needed.

Now bone the leg of lamb on the cutting board and then cut the meat crosswise into slices, each about ¾ inch thick. All is now ready for the final assembly of the finished *Moussaka*. For this you will need a smaller, lidded, oven casserole perhaps 8 or 9 inches in diameter and 7 or 8 inches deep. Cover its bottom with 1 or more of the thick slices of the braised leg. Cover this with a thick layer of the puréed eggplant. On top of this a layer of the ground raw lamb stuffing. Also, if there are any odd corners of space, fill them not too tightly with some of the ground lamb stuffing. Next, a layer of the puréed tomatoes. Then repeat the sequence with more braised lamb, more eggplant purée, more ground lamb, more tomatoes, until everything is safely in the casserole. Now cover the casserole and refrigerate it overnight. Turn off the heat under the sauce, let it cool, then pour it into a covered storage jar and refrigerate it overnight.

On the day – about 3¾ hours before serving

Take the *Moussaka* and its sauce out of the refrigerator and give them 3 hours to come to room temperature.

About 45 minutes before serving

Preheat your oven to 375°F. Pour as much of the sauce into the casserole as it will accept, allowing the sauce to seep down the crevices around the edge of the casserole. There should be a good covering of plenty of sauce on top. Cover the casserole and set it in the center of the oven to warm through and cook the ground lamb – usually in 20 to 30 minutes, according to the efficiency of your oven. When serving the *Moussaka* dig the spoon straight down so that each diner gets a fair share of the various layers. Knives are not necessary for the eating – this meat is truly, as the ads say, "fork-tender." With this soothing and subtle dish, the wine served to me by Chef Roger Vergé was a soothing and delicate, fine and light red Bandol from Provence. At my New York table, I might replace it with a fine, fruity California Zinfandel rosé from the Napa Valley.

NOISETTES D'AGNEAU – TINY LAMB STEAKS IN ROSÉ CHAMPAGNE

(for 4)

I am often asked whether the new Low-High cuisine has penetrated to the top classical restaurants of Paris – those with the world-famous names that are often called "The Temples of French Gastronomy." This and the next recipe are at least two answers to that question. Here is a light and simple preparation given to me recently by Chef Georges Dumas (page 32), the second in command of the kitchen of the great three-star Lasserre. When I asked him about it, it was perfectly clear that Georges was totally aware of the new cuisine of France and was ready to launch it in Lasserre's kitchen at any time if the owners and customers demanded it.

The word *noisette* means "nut" and, in its classic gastronomic relationship to lamb, it has always meant the "nut," or "eye," the central round of lean meat of a largish lamb chop, with all fat and bone neatly cut away. Since lamb chops nowadays are so very small, many butchers cut a *noisette* of lamb from the lean fillet or leg, or rump. From whatever cut, it should end up as a delicate, miniature, perfectly tender, entirely fatless, round steak about ½ to ¾ inch thick and weighing about 5 to 6 ounces per steak. When cooked, it should be delicately pink and that lovely color is here strongly magnified by the rose of the Champagne.

Sweet butter (about 4 Tbs)	Parsley, chopped leaf (1 Tbs)
Lamb noisettes, see above (4, totaling 1¼ to 1½ lbs)	Rosemary, fresh leaf in season, chopped (1 Tbs)
Salt, coarse crystal, to taste	Thyme, fresh leaf in season, chopped (1 Tbs)
Black pepper, freshly ground, to taste	Champagne, rosé (¾ cup)
Ham, dark-smoked, country-style, boiled, diced (½ lb)	

Preparation in about 20 minutes

Start with your lamb *noisettes* at room temperature. Choose a sauté pan just large enough to hold the *noisettes* with no more than ½ inch of bare space around and between them. If the pan is too large, it will tend to overheat and burn. Set it over medium-high frying heat and lubricate its bottom by melting in 2 tablespoons of the butter. Salt and pepper the *noisettes*. When the butter is thoroughly hot, quickly sauté the lamb *noisettes* – about 3 minutes on the first side and 2 minutes on the second. It would be infanticide to overcook these baby steaks beyond the prettily pink appearance of the inside meat. Remove the *noisettes* at once with a slotted spatula and hold them, warm, covered.

Add the diced ham to the pan and stir it around, just to warm it, for hardly more than a minute. Remove the ham at once with a slotted spoon and neatly place it, divided into four portions, as a layer on top of each *noisette*. Add the 1 tablespoon each of parsley, rosemary and thyme to the pan and stir them around for about 15 seconds to warm them and encourage them to release their flavoring oils. Then pour in the ¾ cup of Champagne, letting it bubble and froth while scraping and stirring it around for one more minute to deglaze the pan. Finally, melt into the sauce, sliver by sliver, the remaining 2 tablespoons of butter. The moment it is melted and hot, pour the sauce over the *noisettes* and serve instantly. As the wine to go with this, René Lasserre would serve, obviously, a newly opened bottle of the rosé Champagne. Or the sparkle of the wine could be American – a beautifully pink California Cuvée de Gamay from the Napa Valley.

RACK OF LAMB JARDINIÈRE WITH GARDEN VEGETABLES

(for 4)

This is another recipe given to me by Chef Georges Dumas (page 32), the second in command of the great three-star kitchen of Lasserre in Paris. For a discussion of the significance of this light and simple preparation of a classic dish from a super-high-cuisine restaurant, see the previous recipe.

Cherry tomatoes, whole
(1 dozen)
Green beans, topped, tailed
and chunked (1 lb)
Artichoke bottoms (8)
Green peas, shelled (1 cup)
Salt, coarse crystal, to taste
Black pepper, freshly ground,
to taste
Yellow onions, peeled and
finely chopped (2 medium)
Carrots, scraped and thinly
sliced (3 medium)

Lamb, rack, of about 8 chops,
the main connecting
backbone split by the
butcher to make it easy to
carve the separate chops
(about 3 to 3½ lbs)
White wine, dry (1 cup)
Rosemary, fresh leaf in season,
chopped (1 Tbs)
Thyme, fresh leaf in season,
chopped (1 Tbs)
Parsley, fresh leaf, chopped
(4 Tbs)
Sweet butter (up to 6 Tbs)

**About 50 minutes before serving – active work about
30 minutes, plus about 20 minutes of unsupervised roasting**

Preheat your oven to 425°F. Begin by lightly cooking the
jardinière of vegetables in any way you prefer. I think they are
best (holding their flavors while remaining lightly crisp) if they
are steamed in a Chinese three-tier steamer. Set the water
bubbling hard in the bottom tier to provide plenty of steam
and then place the tomatoes, green beans, artichoke bottoms
and peas, each in its separate open dish, in the upper tiers.
Put on the top lid and take each vegetable out the moment it
is perfectly done – the precise time depending on the efficiency
of your steamer. In mine, I would leave the tomatoes in for
about 8 minutes, the green beans for about 15 minutes, the
artichoke bottoms for about 6 minutes and the peas for about
9 minutes. As soon as each vegetable is done, lightly salt and
pepper it, then hold it warm, separate from the others, in a
covered dish.

Meanwhile, cover the bottom of an open roasting pan with a
mixed layer of the chopped onions and the sliced carrots.
Trim all visible fat from the rack of lamb, lightly salt and pepper it and then stand it, curved side upwards, on its aromatic
vegetable bed in the roasting pan. Roast it until its inside
flesh is just nicely pink, when an inserted meat thermometer
will show 130°F. – seldom more than 20 to 25 minutes.

About 15 minutes before serving – completing the natural sauce

The moment it is perfectly done, pink inside, golden outside, take out the lamb and hold it warm. Pour off and spoon out all the fat from the roasting pan, then place the pan on a top burner and pour into it the cup of wine. Turn on fairly high heat under it and, as the wine comes up to a boil, scrape the bottom of the pan with the edge of a wooden spoon to deglaze all the succulently flavorful bits. After the wine has boiled for a couple of minutes, strain it off into a saucepan and continue boiling it hard to reduce it and concentrate its flavors. After about 5 minutes, reduce the heat to gentle simmering, carefully remove any floating fat, then taste and adjust the seasonings. Stir in the 1 tablespoon each of rosemary and thyme, with 2 tablespoons of the parsley. Finally, melt into the sauce, sliver by sliver, 2 tablespoons of the butter. Keep the sauce just under the simmering point, covered, while you set out the lamb and its garnishing *jardinière*.

Serving at table

Place the rack of lamb in the center of a handsome oval serving platter. Sprinkle it with the remaining parsley. decorate the platter with small piles of the vegetables all around the lamb, taking care to alternate and mix the colors in a logical and charming way. Bring the natural, unthickened sauce to the table in a warm sauceboat with a ladle. With a sharp carving knife, cut straight through the rack between the bones, separating each lamb chop in turn. Pour the sauce around and over the meat. Each diner who would like a little more richness may lightly dot his vegetables with tiny bits of butter. René Lasserre usually serves with this a noble, light, delicately aromatic red Bordeaux. I might serve at home a noble California Cabernet Sauvignon from Santa Clara.

PERSIAN BARREH MIVEH – LEG OF LAMB WITH MIXED FRUIT

(for 4 to 6)

I have been served this classic Iranian dish hundreds of times over the past twenty or thirty years, in the homes of Persian friends or in Persian restaurants in Teheran and everywhere else in the world where Persian food is known and admired. Yet I have never, until quite recently, thought of it as a Low-High preparation, although it conforms almost exactly to the modern principles of low-fat lightness and simplicity. So much for the newness of the new cuisine! Let's face it, the newness is simply a new application of ancient principles of good, healthy eating. The proof is here in this perpetually attractive preparation of lamb. I use dried fruits out of season, fresh fruits in season.

Lamb, whole leg, bone in, trimmed of all fat (5 to 6 lbs)
Butter (4 Tbs)
Yellow onions, peeled and thinly sliced (5 medium)
Salt, coarse crystal, to taste
Black pepper, freshly ground, to taste
Cumin seeds (2 tsp)
Beef bouillon, clear, fatless (1½ cups)
Lemon (1)

Apple slices, dried (¼ lb)
Apricot halves, dried (¼ lb)
Figs, whole, dried, preferably Smyrna (¼ lb)
Peach halves, dried (¼ lb)
Pear slices, dried (¼ lb)
Plum halves or slices, dried (¼ lb)
Prunes, dried, soft, stoned (¼ lb)
Saffron filaments (½ tsp)
Tangerine, fresh (1)

About 3½ hours before serving – active work about 30 minutes, plus about 3 hours of virtually unsupervised simmering

Choose a tightly lidded casserole, French *cocotte* or Dutch oven, large enough to hold the whole leg of lamb with enough room to spare so that it can be turned around. It should not be too wide or the ingredients on the bottom will spread out too much and there will not be the proper transfer of flavors into the meat. The casserole should preferably be of tinned copper or enameled iron, since all the cooking will be done on top of the stove. Place it over medium-high frying heat, lubricate its bottom by melting in 2 tablespoons of the butter and, when it is hot, quickly sauté the lamb leg until it is lightly browned on all sides. If the bottom of the casserole dries out, add one more tablespoon of the butter. When the lamb is properly gilded, take it out and rest it. Add one more tablespoon of the butter to the casserole, then the sliced onions and sauté, stirring them around until they are very lightly browned, but certainly not blackened or burned. Turn off the heat.

Lightly sprinkle and pat the lamb leg all around with salt and pepper. Lay it back in the casserole on its bed of onions. Sprinkle all around and over it the 2 teaspoons of cumin seeds. Pour in (at the side, so as not to wash away the seeds) the 1½ cups of beef bouillon. Heat it up to gentle simmering, just a light bubbling, then cover tightly and keep the lamb poaching in this aromatic steam for 1½ hours. Check, say, every 30 minutes to make sure that the bubbling continues at precisely the same gentle level. After 45 minutes (at the half-way point) turn the leg of lamb over.

After 1¼ hours of simmering (that is, during the last 15 minutes of this first period), make ready the dried fruits. In a 3-quart saucepan bring 2 quarts of water up to a boil and squeeze in the juice of the lemon. The moment the water boils drop in, all at once, the ¼ pound each of apples, apricots, figs, peaches, pears, plums and prunes. As soon as the water returns to the boil drain the fruits and leave them in the sieve to continue dripping until they go into the casserole. Do not squeeze them.

About 1½ hours before serving

At the end of the first period of poaching very carefully and gently turn the leg over once more (the meat is now becoming quite soft and could easily fall apart). Then place the fruits all around the lamb and sprinkle them with the saffron filaments for color and flavor. Replace the lid and continue the gentle simmering for another 1½ hours. Do not try to turn the leg over again – it will now be too soft.

Preferably using a French zest scraper, grate off the thin outer skin of the tangerine, holding the gratings in a small covered jar. Throw away the rest of the skin. Divide the flesh of the tangerine into its segments, depitting each of them and holding them.

About 45 minutes before serving

Add the tangerine segments all around the lamb and sprinkle the tangerine zest over everything. Now check to make sure there is not too much liquid in the bottom of the casserole. The fruits should be moistly soggy, but they should not be swimming in an excess of liquid. If there is too much, turn up the heat slightly so that the liquid bubbles a little bit harder and leave the lid partly askew, so that the excess of liquid is boiled and steamed away. As soon as this reduction is achieved, turn down the heat back to the gentlest simmering and re-cover completely.

About 15 minutes before serving

If there is still too much liquid, remove the lid completely and turn the heat up higher still so that there is quite strong bubbling and faster reduction of the liquid. The moment you achieve the proper moistness of the fruit garnish-sauce, again reduce the heat to the gentlest simmering and put back the lid. The trick is to achieve the perfect consistency at the precise moment when the dish is to be served. You will not need a knife to carve the lamb – it will be meltingly soft and with a memorable and most unusual flavor. Surround each serving with a balanced mixture of the fruit. Devout Persians do not serve wine, but I might accompany this with a noble, fruity, rich, white Alsatian of the spicy Gewürztraminer grape grown either in Alsace or on the foggy banks of the Russian River in the Alexander Valley of Sonoma, California.

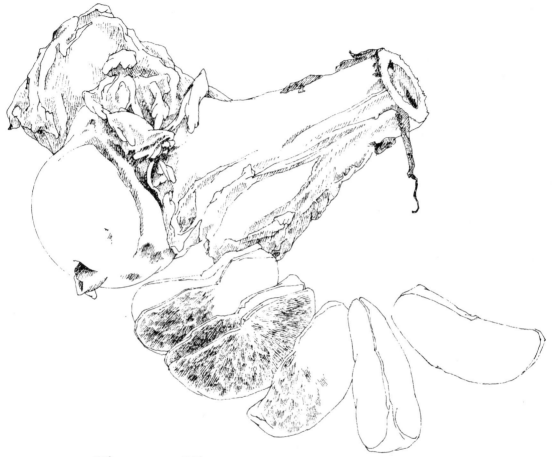

Chapter Eleven
Veal

in which Osso Buco acquires the flavor of France
and of Sweet Oranges. The riddle of a blanquette
without Cream is solved. An old family recipe
for Pot Roast with Herbs is discovered and a
chef reveals his personal recipe for Sweetbreads
with Scallions and Mushrooms.

CHEF JEAN TROISGROS'S SECRETS OF THE OLD-NEW LOW-FAT WAY OF PREPARING VEAL

Both the Troisgros brothers think that veal is one of the best and most satisfying of all meats – when it is properly prepared. It is, obviously, much lower in fat than heavily marbled beef and, since a luscious and rich quality can be developed during cooking, the diner tends to feel satisfied with smaller portions. But you have to know the secret of preparing it.

The choice of the cut, according to Jean Troisgros, is all-important. He likes, best of all, for flavor and texture, the *quasi de veau*, the whole butt, chump, or rump end of the loin (in other words, the upper part of the backside), which usually weighs from eight to ten pounds and is the perfect party piece for the Troisgros cooking method. Or, if you simply cannot use that big a piece, you can compromise with a two- to three-inch-thick steak from the same part, called, in French, *la rouelle* and, in English, a round-bone veal rump steak (see recipe on page 313).

"Never mind if your butcher screams at you," Jean said, "you must insist on getting exactly the cut you want. Also get, at the same time, some veal kidneys, each surrounded by its white fat – about one for each person – since they seem to complement the flavor of the main piece of meat. Oh, but it's difficult to explain exactly how to cook veal. It's an almost-secret way, which grandmother taught to her daughter and the daughter, in time, passed on to *her* daughter, on and on, generation to generation. . . . It's hard to put it into words on paper. The skill is in your fingers – in the judgment of your eyes."

Jean continued, "Veal cooks itself well or badly in the first ten minutes. If you don't do it right at once, you can't save it later. You go wrong if it gets ten degrees too hot – equally wrong if it stays ten degrees too cold. You must brown it dead right, but if you burn it to the slightest degree, you're lost. You can't explain, you have to do it. You have to learn by eye, by nose, by touch of the finger, by tasting with the tip of the tongue. . . . I can tell you. . . .

"The basic principle is that you start with very little butter – remember, in our new cuisine, very little – above all, not too hot, just beginning to brown. Salt and pepper your piece of veal and, then, gently roll it around in that butter. See that every square inch of it gets lightly covered with that butter, so that it then becomes gently gilded on all sides – but watch it like a hawk, that not even a corner of it gets burned. It must be golden. The moment it gets black, throw that piece of veal away and start over! Above all, your veal must look pretty. To achieve the perfect effect shouldn't take you a second longer than ten minutes.

"Then, into a medium-low oven for a few minutes of heating up the interior by dry roasting. Next, a very little bit of water around it and the lid of your casserole tightly closed for what we call 'wet cooking.' No wine. The fruity acidity of wine is no good for veal. As I said, very little water. Put it in softly, softly. Very difficult to explain. Just enough water to cover the bottom and boil and make some steam inside the tightly lidded casserole. When you sense, by eye, smell and the tips of your fingers, that the veal is beginning to soften, you can control its flavor by adding your aromatic vegetables. Choose them according to the season. In about another hour, you will have what we consider to be the perfect veal.

"This is our old family recipe. It's very difficult to pass it on. You must do it – not once, but many times. Then, at last, you will know exactly. That's it, that's all." (The precise Troisgros family recipe follows on the next page.)

CHEFS JEAN AND PIERRE TROISGROS'S OLD FAMILY RECIPE FOR A PLUPERFECT POT ROAST OF VEAL

(hardly worth doing for less than 6 to 8)

Before trying this magnificent recipe, read Jean Troisgros's general advice on cooking veal on the preceding pages. Don't be put off by his fussy stress on the difficulties. He is a worry-guts perfectionist. Even the first time I tried this recipe, I found it much easier than he had led me to expect. When you get it dead right, I am sure you will agree that this is quite the best way of preparing and presenting veal. Also it is relatively low-fat, yet has a luxurious and rich feeling on your tongue. Use whichever mixture of vegetables is best for the season. The veal seems to absorb and incorporate them all into its luscious range of flavors. For the best chance of success, even the first time, insist absolutely with your butcher on getting the precise cut you want. It should be a good, solid, squarish piece, weighing about 8 pounds, from the rump end of the animal, called variously the butt, the chump, or the rump. Leave some of the fat on it, since, after the browning, it will be melted off and discarded.

Veal, squarish piece from rump end, see above (about 8 lbs)	Tomatoes, ripe, whole (2 medium)
Salt, coarse crystal, to taste	Mixed aromatics, fresh green parsley leaves, basil, tarragon, thyme, all chopped (total ⅓ cup)
Pepper, Chinese Szechuan, freshly ground, to taste	
Butter (about 8 Tbs)	
Onions, white boiling, whole, peeled (about 2 dozen)	Garlic, whole, with skins (2 cloves)
Carrots, small, young, whole, scraped (about 1 dozen)	Bay leaves, crumbled (2)
	Veal kidneys (6)

About 2¾ hours before serving – lightly browning the veal in about 10 minutes

Choose a tightly lidded casserole or *cocotte*, preferably of enameled iron, large enough to hold the veal with a couple of inches to spare all around to accommodate the vegetables.

This is, virtually, a one-dish meal. You should start with your veal at room temperature. Salt and pepper it. (I find that Chinese pepper has a special affinity for the veal.) Set the casserole over medium frying heat on top of the stove and melt in it the minimum amount of butter starting, say, with 4 table-spoons. Stir it around and watch it carefully. The moment it is just beginning to brown – hazelnut color, as Pierre Troisgros says – begin rolling your veal around in the butter. It should be the lightest of frying, just enough to gild the meat on every side. Add more butter, tablespoon by tablespoon, if the bottom of the casserole dries out. The moment you smell any burning, or notice either butter or meat becoming darker brown, lower the flame at once. The whole job should take not more than 10 minutes. After 5 minutes, start preheating your oven to 300°F. When the veal looks pretty and golden, turn off the heat at once and move to the next phase.

About 2½ hours before serving – dry-roasting the veal for about 25 minutes

Now put the casserole, with the meat in it, still uncovered, into the center of the oven. Let it all heat up and loosen inside for about 25 minutes for an 8-pound piece. No need to watch it, but turn it over at the halfway point. Separately, in a kettle, boil up about a pint of water.

About 2 hours before serving – steaming the meat and preparing the vegetables – active work about 30 minutes

Now begin the steaming phase. Pour about ½ cup of the boiling water onto the bottom of the casserole under the meat. There should be, at all times, just enough water to keep boiling fairly hard and providing steam to continue the wet cooking. If, at any time, there is not enough water, add an extra ½ cup, always boiling. Never add more water than the minimum necessary.

As soon as the casserole is filled with steam, clamp on the lid and set the timer for 45 minutes. While waiting, prepare and assemble the vegetables. After 25 minutes check the steam and the water and adjust the heat so that the bubbling is neither too fierce nor too gentle. Re-cover and continue the steaming until the bell rings.

About 1¼ hours before serving – continued steaming, now with the vegetables for the final hour

Again, check the water, turn over the meat and neatly spread the vegetables around it: the 2 dozen onions, the dozen carrots, the 2 tomatoes, the ⅓ cup of mixed parsley, basil, tarragon and thyme, the 2 whole cloves of garlic, and the 2 crumbled bay leaves. Continue the steaming until meat and vegetables are just soft, not mushy, perfectly done. This usually takes about 1 more hour. After 30 minutes, at the halfway point, recheck the steam and water once more. By now, the juices should be flowing out from the meat and the vegetables forming the natural, aromatic sauce.

About 10 minutes before serving – sautéeing the kidneys in about 5 minutes

Peel off all fat and tough membranes from the kidneys. Melt another 2 tablespoons of the butter in a sauté pan and, over medium-high frying heat, quickly sauté the six kidneys until they are nicely crisp on the outside, but still rosy pink and soft inside – usually in 4 to 5 minutes. Then take them out of the sauté pan and hold them warm, covered.

Serving at table

Slice the veal with a very sharp knife, since the meat will now be gelatinously soft, into slices about ⅜ inch thick. Slice the kidneys about ⅛ inch thick. Divide up the casserole vegetables. Quickly pour off the sauce of the natural juices, skim off every bit of fat, reheat it and pour it over the meat and vegetables on the plates. You could be fussy and strain it. Jean Troisgros and I do not. You can also, if you wish, serve extra vegetables, prepared separately. Both the herbs and the vegetables can be varied by the seasons. The Troisgros brothers served me with this magnificent veal a wine that was the perfect frame for this perfect dish, a noble, aromatic, dominant, Burgundian red, a Corton from grapes grown on the great hill of Aloxe Corton. Such a wine is, of course, unique to the Burgundian region of France; but, for the pleasure it would bring to this superb veal, I would gladly serve a noble California Cabernet Sauvignon of a magnificent vintage from the Napa Valley.

A SMALLER VEAL CUT: THE ROUELLE STEAK BRAISED WITH BUTTON MUSHROOMS AND BABY ONIONS

(for 4)

If the large cut of veal in the preceding "perfect recipe" is just too much for your dinner, here is a very fair alternative with a rump steak which can be as small as 2 or 3 pounds. It was prepared for me by Chef René Brunet (see page 27) at his two-star Restaurant Les Escales de René Brunet in the Alpine mountain town of Varces, near Grenoble. He explained that the word *rouelle* comes from *roue,* a wheel, because this steak is always perfectly round, with the central bone where the hub of a wheel would be. An American butcher knows it as a "round bone veal rump steak" – about 2 to 3 inches thick. It is, in fact, the central horizontal cut, the heart, so to speak, of the large rump piece used in the preceding recipe.

In my translation and adaptation of Chef Brunet's new cuisine version of the classic recipe, the preliminary frying of the steak in butter is eliminated. Brunet uses wine in place of butter for the basting and low-fat yoghurt in place of cream for the sauce. Baking the onions instead of frying them is an improvement, since baking brings out and magnifies their internal natural sweetness. The slow oven-braising of the steak makes it meltingly soft while guarding its superb flavor.

Veal steak, see above (3 to
4 lbs)

Olive oil, pure green virgin
(3 to 4 Tbs)

White wine, dry (up to 2 cups)

Onions, small white, unpeeled
(2 lbs)

Mushrooms, small, good color
and shape, wiped clean
(½ lb)

Veal kidneys, entirely without
fat, diced (2)

Mustard, French Dijon (about
2 Tbs)

Yoghurt, plain, low-fat (about
1 cup)

Salt, coarse crystal, to taste

Black pepper, freshly ground,
to taste

About 2½ hours before serving – active work about 30 minutes, plus 2 hours of unsupervised oven braising

Preheat your grill to maximum temperature. Rub one side of the veal steak with the minimum amount of olive oil just to coat it, then set it under the grill, as close to the heat as possible, to brown the outside rapidly without cooking the inside. As soon as it begins to gild, usually in 3–4 minutes, turn the steak over, quickly rub the second side with olive oil and repeat the grilling on that side. Turn off the grill and set the oven at 350°F. Put the steak into a covered, fairly shallow casserole, large enough also to hold, later, the mushrooms, onions and kidneys. Pour the first ½ cup of the wine over the steak, cover and set the casserole at the center of the oven for gentle bubbling, steaming and braising for about 2 hours. The trick is to make sure that the liquid is bubbling hard enough to produce steam, but not so hard that you overcook the steak and make it stringy. After the first ½ hour or so, you may have to turn the oven down to somewhere between 350 and 300°F. Roughly every 30 minutes, turn the steak over. Do not let the casserole run dry. Add more wine, ½ cup at a time, as needed.

Meanwhile, spread the onions, in their skins, in a single layer on a baking sheet and put them in the oven, above or below the meat, to roast slowly. They are ready for incorporation into the dish as soon as they are just soft at the center, nicely juicy and delicately sweet, usually in 35 to 45 minutes. At this point, peel off their dry skins and hold.

Also have the mushrooms ready, in a covered bowl – the caps whole, the stalks coarsely chopped. Cut the 2 kidneys into large dice and also hold.

About 15 minutes before the end of the oven-braising time

Take the casserole out of the oven. Make sure that there is at least a quarter of an inch of liquid in the casserole – adding, if necessary, a dash or two more of the wine. Neatly surround the meat with the baked onions, the whole raw mushroom caps and diced mushroom stalks, plus the diced raw kidneys. Re-cover the casserole and return it to the oven for the final 15 minutes. Have ready a sauté pan for the finishing of the sauce. If the casserole is decorative enough to come to table, so much the better. If not, have ready a hot serving platter.

Just before serving

Transfer all the juices from the casserole to the sauté pan and boil them up hard, so that they reduce, concentrating their flavors. As soon as the sauce begins to get syrupy, turn off the heat and whip into it as much of the mustard as your taste prefers – between 1 and 2 tablespoons. Then, to give extra body and smoothness to the sauce, work in somewhere between ½ and 1 cup of the yoghurt. Now salt and pepper, to taste, but remember that you have deliberately not, so far, salted and peppered the steak, so the sauce should be fairly strong in character. Reheat carefully, stirring continuously, but do not let it boil. Pour over the steak and bring it to table. The wine to accompany it, chosen for me by Chef René Brunet, was a fine rich red, solid in body, Châteauneuf-du-Pape, from the Rhône. The approximate American equivalent might be a full-bodied, rich California Petite Sirah from Sonoma.

LOW-FAT BLANQUETTE OF VEAL IN A CHINESE STEAMER

(*for 4 to 6*)

This is my translation and adaptation to the American kitchen of one of the most famous, most highly publicized and most revolutionary recipes of modern times. It dramatizes, perhaps better than any other, the basic principles and techniques of the Low-High cuisine. When I visited Chef Michel Guérard (page 35) at his two-star restaurant, Le Pot au Feu in Eugénie-les-Bains, he wrote out his recipe for me by hand, saying, "I wanted to make a light version of a *blanquette de veau,* a fine old French dish, its sauce traditionally enriched with butter, flour, egg yolks, and cream. Delicious – but heavy. I decided to make it without butter, flour, egg yolks, and cream. My friends said it would be impossible. I might end up with some kind of *ragoût,* but not with a *blanquette* – a dish that evokes a strong emotional response because it has a very special meaning for many French people, who probably had it first at home made by Mother. So I conceived the idea of steaming the pieces of veal in a tightly lidded pot over a carefully balanced patchwork of the freshest of fresh vegetables, but with no other liquid whatsoever. The meat is slowly steamed over the aromatic juices of these vegetables, while the juices of the meat drip down and add to the marvelous balance of flavors. Finally, these juices are slightly thickened by being blended with a small quantity of low-fat white cheese. I once served my new *blanquette* side-by-side with a traditional version to a group of finicky experts. They agreed that my version had a finer, truer taste. No wonder, since the aromatic flavors of the meat and the vegetables are not concealed by the taste of butter, flour, egg yolks and cream."

Veal, milk fed – breast, shoulder, heel of round or shank – cut into 1 inch cubes (1½ lbs)

Leek whites, washed, desanded, sliced (usually 4 small, or 2 large)

Mushrooms, large for boiling, fresh, sliced (3 or 4, according to size)

Carrots, scraped and sliced (about 3 to 4 medium)

Yellow onions, peeled and chopped (2 medium)

Celery root, peeled and
 chopped (about ½ cup)
Watercress, leaves and small
 stalks only, finely chopped
 (½ bunch)
Cloves (2 whole)
Salt, coarse crystal, to taste
Black pepper, freshly ground,
 to taste
Onions, small, white boiling,
 peeled and left whole
 (about 16)

Mushrooms, fresh, caps whole,
 stems chopped, to be
 steamed with the meat
 (about 20)
Pot cheese, low-fat (1 cup)
Yoghurt, plain, low-fat (⅓ cup)
Ricotta, Italian style, low-fat
 (3 Tbs)
Lemon juice, fresh (a few
 spritzes)

**About 1½ hours before serving – or can be prepared ahead
and reheated – active preparation about 45 minutes
plus about 45 minutes of unsupervised simmering**

Carefully remove every last bit of fat from each cube of veal.
Wash these pieces for a second or two under running cold
water and put them, still wet, in a single layer, in the upper tier
of your steamer (see page 392). Now cover the floor of the
lowest tier of the steamer with a layer of the vegetables: the
sliced leek whites, the large sliced mushrooms, the chopped
mushroom stems, the sliced carrots, the chopped yellow
onions, celery root, and watercress, the 2 whole cloves and
salt and pepper to taste. Stir them around and mix thoroughly. Now place this lowest tier of the steamer onto a top
burner set at medium-high heat and, stirring frequently, heat
up the vegetables so that they begin to release their juices.
Keep them moving around and do not let the heat get too high,
to avoid any danger of sticking and burning. Meanwhile,
place the 16 white onions and the 20 mushroom caps in and
around the meat in the upper tier of the steamer and add salt
and pepper to taste.

As soon as the steam begins to rise from the mixed vegetable base, set the upper tier of the steamer with its meat and
vegetables above the lower tier and clamp on the tightest possible lid. Do not open the steamer more often than absolutely
necessary, or you will lose too much steam. Better to adjust

the heat by listening. There should be a merry bubbling inside. The veal is perfectly done when it is quite soft, but still nicely chewy and certainly not breaking up into strings – usually in about 45 minutes – longer if your bubbling is too low, less time if the bubbling is too high. After you have prepared the dish a couple of times, you will be able to adjust the bubbling by ear to perfection.

While the steaming is in progress, cream the white cheese for the sauce. I put the cup of pot cheese, the 1/3 cup of yoghurt, and the 3 tablespoons of ricotta into the bowl of my Cuisinart chopper-churner (or you can use an electric blender, or a hand food mill), running the machine until it is a perfectly smooth cream – usually in 7 to 8 seconds. Transfer it to a covered jar and hold for the sauce.

About 15 minutes before serving – final preparation of the sauce

When the veal is done, place the pieces decoratively on a hot serving platter, nicely garnished with the whole onions and mushroom caps, and keep warm for a few minutes, tightly covered with foil. I put the juicy contents of the lowest tier of the steamer into my Cuisinart chopper-churner and run the machine until all the vegetables and juices are a smooth purée – usually in no more than 15 to 20 seconds. (Or you can use a blender.) Transfer to a sauté pan and bring it to a boil to concentrate its flavors, while slightly reducing and thickening it. When it has achieved the consistency of heavy cream, whip into it the pot cheese cream. At the last moment, work in a few spritzes of fresh lemon juice, taste and adjust the seasonings. Reheat if necessary but do not let it boil, pour it over the veal and vegetables and serve at once. With this superb invention, Chef Michel Guérard served a noble, light, fruity red Bordeaux from St. Emilion, a Château Pavie. An American wine that approximates its character and personality might be a California Petite Sirah from Monterey.

A FRENCH VERSION OF OSSO BUCO WITH SWEET ORANGES

(for 4)

There must be very few aficionados of international eating who have not, in one Italian dining room or another, revelled in the glutinous richness of a classic *osso buco*, the neatly cut rounds of the hind shank of veal covered with butter and oil, almost buried under piles of egg pasta. All that has been sharply changed by Chef Michel Guérard (page 35) at his two-star Le Pot au Feu, in Eugénie-les-Bains. In my translation and adaptation of the recipe written out for me by Michel, the butter and oil are gone – the gentle softness of the rounds of veal is sharpened and supported by the gentle sweetness of fresh oranges. *Osso buco* has been magically transformed.

The first essential step is to do battle with your butcher to get precisely the right little cuts of veal. The shank is the middle part of the back leg which, at that point, is divided around two bones into the foreshank and the hindshank. Do not let the butcher persuade you to accept the foreshank, in which there is much less meat in relation to the size of the bone. Have him saw 4 hindshanks into 2 inch pieces, each with its neat small central bone intact, surrounded by a circle of good lean meat. During the boiling, the gelatinous marrow of the bone supplies the attractive body which gives a sense of richness without fat.

Veal, hindshanks, see above (4, total about 3 to 3½ lbs)

Lemons (2)

Oranges, nicely sweet (5)

Chicken bouillon, clear and entirely fatless (about 4 cups)

Basil, fresh leaf in season, chopped (2 Tbs)

Bay leaf, whole (1)

Cloves, whole (4)

Thyme, fresh leaf in season, chopped (1 Tbs)

Yellow onions, peeled and chopped (1½ lbs)

Salt, coarse crystal, to taste

Black pepper, freshly ground, to taste

Oil of grape pits, very light, now becoming widely available in fancy food stores (about 3 Tbs)

Brown sugar, preferably granulated natural cane (2 tsp)

Vinegar, white wine (1 Tbs)

The day before – marinating the veal overnight – active preparation about 15 minutes

Wipe the veal pieces to clean them, trim off any last traces of visible outer fat, then put them into a suitably large covered storage dish and thoroughly wet them with the freshly squeezed juice of the 2 lemons and 3 of the oranges, 2 cups of the chicken bouillon, the 2 tablespoons of basil, the bay leaf crumbled, the 4 whole cloves freshly ground just before using, and the tablespoon of thyme. Partially cover and surround everything with the 1½ pounds of chopped onions, plus salt and pepper to taste. Cover and let marinate in the refrigerator overnight, turning the veal pieces occasionally.

On the day – about 2½ hours before serving – active work about 45 minutes, plus about 1¾ hours of unsupervised oven poaching

Preheat your oven to 325°F. Choose a tightly lidded casserole or *cocotte* large enough to hold the veal pieces and the marinade. Take out the veal pieces and dry them. Pour the entire marinade, including all its solid contents, into the casserole and, on a top burner, bring the liquid up to gentle simmering. Meanwhile, place a fairly large sauté pan over medium-high frying heat, lubricate its bottom with 2 tablespoons of the oil and, when it is hot, quickly and lightly brown the veal pieces in batches, as many at a time as the pan will hold, turning them almost continuously until they are lightly gilded on all sides – usually in about 2 to 3 minutes per batch. As each piece is done, drop it into the simmering casserole. When all the veal is in the casserole, cover and set it in the center of the oven to poach, simmer and steam until the meat is meltingly soft – usually in about 1¾ hours. If the casserole shows signs of drying out add more chicken bouillon, ¼ cup at a time.

Meanwhile, prepare what Chef Guérard calls a *gastrique*, a sweet-sour flavoring essence. In a heavy frypan heat the 2 teaspoons of sugar with ½ teaspoon of water until it is all melted and darkened by slight caramelization. Turn off the heat at once, let it cool slightly and then stir in the tablespoon of vinegar. Scrape the pan to deglaze it and then hold until needed. Preferably with a French zest scraper, scrape off and grate the thin outer skin of the remaining 2 oranges and hold, covered. Then peel off the remaining white skin from the 2 oranges and divide them into their segments, removing all inner strands and depitting each segment. Hold them, covered, for later use.

About 30 minutes before serving – preparing the orange sauce

When the veal pieces are perfectly done, soft, but not coming away from the bone, take out all the pieces and keep them warm, covered. I now purée everything that is left in the casserole by putting it, batch by batch, into the bowl of my Cuisinart chopper-churner (or you can use an electric blender, or a hand food mill) and running the machine until everything is thoroughly mixed and smooth – usually in 5 to 7 seconds. As each batch is done, transfer it to a sauté pan. Now adjust the thickness of the sauce. If it is too thin, boil it hard for a few minutes to reduce and thicken it. If it is too thick, add a few more dashes of chicken bouillon. When you have it the way you want it, work in enough of the sugar-vinegar *gastrique* and the grated orange zest to give the sauce a nice sweet-sour tang. Taste and adjust the seasonings. Heat it up to just below simmering.

Serving at table

Chef Guérard, following the new cuisine tradition, serves the portions of veal directly onto deep hot plates, surrounding the meat with the orange segments and pouring around the zesty sauce. This is an *osso buco* like no *osso buco* you have ever had before. Because of its delicate sweetness, a red wine would be unsuitable, so Michel served a noble, rich, spicy, white Gewürztraminer from Alsace. Or it might be a California Gewürztraminer – a rich and spicy version from the Napa Valley.

CALF'S LIVER STEAMED À LA SOUBISE

(for 4)

Once you have mastered this Low-High technique with liver, you will never want to prepare it in any other way. In can be garnished or sauced as you choose. This version is served with a low-fat adaptation of the classic onion sauce, prepared for me by Chef Jacques Manière (page 42) at his Paris bistro-style Le Pactole.

Beef bouillon, for the steamer (about 1 pint)

Calf's liver, sliced ¼ inch thick (1½ lbs)

Black pepper, freshly ground, to taste

Yellow onions, peeled and chopped medium-fine (1 lb)

Sweet vermouth (about ½ cup)

Cognac (¼ cup)

Lemon (1)

Salt, coarse crystal, to taste

Parsley, chopped leaf (⅓ cup)

About 45 minutes before serving – active work about 20 minutes, plus about 25 minutes of unsupervised simmering and steaming

Put the pint of beef bouillon into the lowest tier of a steamer (see page 392) and heat it up to boiling, with enough merry bubbling to produce plenty of steam. Set the slices of liver in a single layer on a shallow dish or plate in the upper tier of the steamer, allowing plenty of room around the dish so that the steam can get through. If one tier of your steamer is not quite large enough, set a third tier above it and divide the liver into batches. Pepper the liver (no salt) and then learn by experience just how long your steamer takes to produce the perfect result. The time depends on the precise thickness of the slices, on the degree of bubbling and on the tightness of the lid. In my 3-tier Chinese bamboo steamer, it takes about 20 minutes.

As soon as you have started the liver going, spread the chopped onions across the bottom of a sauté pan, wet them down with ¼ cup of the vermouth and set them gently simmering, uncovered, stirring them around regularly. As they absorb the liquid and mush down, watch that the pan does not get dry. Add, as needed, tablespoon by tablespoon, first the rest of the vermouth, then the ¼ cup of Cognac, and finally the juice of the lemon. You should end up with a smooth, attractively sweet-sour, aromatic mash of onions – usually in 10 to 15 minutes.

Just before serving

At the last moment, season the onion sauce with salt and pepper as needed, work into it most of the chopped parsley, saving a small part for final decoration. Cut the liver slices into 2 inch squares and serve them on very hot plates, each square spread with the onion *soubise* and flecked with the bright-green parsley. With this velvety dish, I was served a velvety red Pomerol from Bordeaux, a Château Nenin. A fine American accompaniment could be a Pinot Noir from California's Napa Valley.

FINAL NOTE: In Roanne, Chefs Jean and Pierre Troisgros (page 50) served me this marvelous liver studded with dice of black truffles. In Vézelay, Chef Marc Meneau (page 45), at his two-star Auberge de l'Espérance, served it with a sauce based on a reduction of a white veal bouillon. However you present it, the liver comes through strongly with a delightful trueness of flavor. This is unquestionably the best of all low-fat ways of cooking liver.

VEAL SWEETBREADS WITH APPLES AND CALVADOS

(for 4)

This version of the classic French recipe was developed to eliminate the frying of the apples in butter and the super-enrichment of the sauce with lashings of heavy cream. Butter and cream are now out.

Baking apples, preferably
  Rome Beauty, whole,
  unpeeled, but cored (4,
  medium-large)
Veal sweetbreads, whole,
  small (4)
Black pepper, whole corns,
  some freshly ground, to taste
Cloves, whole (2)
Salt, coarse crystal, to taste
Raisins, seedless (16)
Calvados apple brandy (½ cup)
Pot cheese, white, low-fat
  (about ¾ cup)
White wine, dry (about 2 Tbs)
Red cayenne pepper, to taste

About 1 hour before serving – active work about 20 minutes, plus about 40 minutes of unsupervised baking and simmering

Preheat your oven to 350°F. Set the 4 apples in a shallow baking pan and place them at the center of the hot oven to bake slowly. They should be nicely soft, but certainly not mushy – usually they are ready in 35 to 40 minutes depending on their size. Save the juices from the pan.

Meanwhile, carefully wash and pick over the sweetbreads, removing any bits of membrane or hard skin. Immerse them in freshly drawn cold water in a suitably sized saucepan and bring them up to a gentle simmering. Add to this water, as it heats up, 1 tablespoon of whole peppercorns, the 2 cloves, and plenty of salt. When the water is gently simmering, keep it going, covered, until the sweetbreads are just cooked through – almost always in 10 minutes. Then take them out with a slotted spoon, reserving half a cup of their cooking water. Rinse the sweetbreads under running warm water, thoroughly dry them and put them in between two plates with a solid weight on top, to press out the remaining water and firm up. In the ½ cup of reserved cooking water, soak the 16 raisins until needed.

About 15 minutes before serving

As soon as the apples are done, peel them and cut each of them into 8 wedges, then place them in a sauté pan. Cut each of the sweetbreads into 12 wedges and add to the apples in the sauté pan. Turn on the heat to medium frying temperature. Pour the ½ cup of Calvados over the apples and sweetbreads and set it on fire, shaking the pan to encourage the flames. Now, working quickly, divide the wedges of sweetbreads equally between four hot plates, decorate each plate with 7 apple wedges and 4 drained raisins and keep the plates warm and covered.

Next, for the sauce, I put into the bowl of my Cuisinart chopper-churner the remaining liquid from the sauté pan, the apple juices from the baking pan, the remaining 4 apple wedges and ½ cup of the pot cheese. I run the machine until they are thoroughly mixed and puréed – usually in about 10 seconds. Transfer this sauce back to the sauté pan and heat it gently, adjusting its flavor and thickness. As needed, whip in a bit more pot cheese, or, to thin it, a dash or two of the white wine. Taste and adjust seasoning, also adding a pinch of red cayenne pepper. When it is thoroughly hot (but certainly not boiling), pour it over the sweetbreads and serve immediately. I drank with this a noble, light, refreshing red Bordeaux. In New York I could also enjoy it with a California Cabernet Sauvignon from Monterey.

CHEF DANIEL MÉTÉRY'S PERSONAL PARISIAN PREPARATION OF VEAL SWEETBREADS

(for 4)

In the Restaurant Clovis of the Hôtel Windsor in Paris, where he directs the kitchen, young Chef Météry (page 46) has worked out his own very personal way of preparing veal sweetbreads using a minimum of fat. He succeeds marvelously in bringing out the gentle, subtle flavors of the soft white meat. After I had tasted it and fallen in love with it at Daniel's table in Paris, I asked him for the recipe and he promised to work it out in detail and send it. When it reached me in New York, he had, like an artist sending an oil painting, signed his work at the bottom right.

Chef Météry feels very strongly that, in the standard methods of preparing sweetbreads, there is much too much presoaking and boiling. He believes that all this advance attention tends to dissolve and wash away the essential natural flavoring juices of the sweetbreads, resulting eventually in bland and dull eating at table. He has cut down the preparation to what he considers to be the irreducible minimum and his timing should be followed exactly.

I have translated the recipe from his French but have hardly dared to change a word beyond the adaptation to our American ingredients. It works out, in my kitchen, as a superb example of the Low-High technique – the preservation and magnification of the natural character of the sweetbreads, with no unnecessary covering or masking by complicated sauces. It is one of the best sweetbread recipes I have ever tried.

Veal sweetbreads, fine, white, well shaped noix, or "nuts," as Chef Météry calls them (4)

Sweet butter (about 2 Tbs)

Salt, coarse crystal, to taste

Black pepper, freshly ground, to taste

Shallots, peeled and minced (2 cloves)

Yellow onion, peeled and chopped (1 medium)

Carrots, scraped and finely chopped (2 medium)

Cognac (½ cup)

White wine, dry, preferably Sancerre (about ⅓ cup)

Chicken bouillon, clear and entirely fatless (2 cups)

Bay leaf (1)

Parsley, leaf only, chopped (1 Tbs)

Thyme, fresh leaf in season, chopped (1 Tbs)

Pot cheese, low-fat (1 cup)

Yoghurt, low fat (⅓ cup)

Ricotta, Italian style, low-fat (3 Tbs)

Scallion bulbs, trimmed away from the stalks (1 dozen)

Button mushrooms, good color and shape (16)

Egg yolks (3)

About 1½ hours before serving – active preparation about 1 hour, plus about 30 minutes of unsupervised simmering

Soak the 4 sweetbreads in cold water to swell them for precisely 20 minutes. Then put them into a saucepan large enough so that they can rest side by side on the bottom, cover them to a depth of about ½ inch with freshly drawn cold water and heat it up reasonably quickly to a boil. While it is coming up, stir in enough salt so that the water has a slightly salty taste. Watch it carefully. The moment the first bubbles appear, start the timer and let it simmer for not a second more than 4 minutes. Then, at once, turn off the heat and put the saucepan into the sink under running cold water. The objective is immediately to cool the sweetbreads right through to their centers, to stop the cooking. Place the cool sweetbreads on a wooden cutting board and, with a small sharp knife, cut and pull away all visible membranes and skin. Also, as Chef Météry puts it, "Lightly peel the sweetbreads around their edges, removing any discolored or dry bits." This careful and effective preparation of the sweetbreads is the secret of the success of this dish.

Now choose a lidded casserole just large enough for the sweetbreads to rest side by side on its bottom with, perhaps, half an inch in between them, but do not put them in yet. Chef Météry says, "The best type of casserole is of tinned copper." Set it on a top burner and lubricate its bottom by melting in it a couple of tablespoons of the butter. Lightly salt and pepper the sweetbreads. When the butter is hot, but not yet sizzling, put in the sweetbreads and let them, as Chef Météry puts it, *suer* – sweat – by just gently warming them up in the butter over quite low heat, without any question of frying or sautéeing. Turn them over after about a couple of minutes.

While the sweetbreads are sweating, sprinkle in the 2 minced shallots, the minced onion and the 2 finely chopped carrots. After 4 minutes of sweating on both sides, pour in the ½ cup of Cognac, the ⅓ cup of wine, and the 2 cups of chicken bouillon and stir in the crumbled bay leaf, plus the tablespoon each of parsley and thyme. From the moment the first bubbles reappear, time it at gentle simmering, covered, for precisely 20 minutes. Meanwhile, preheat your oven to keep-warm temperature, 165°F. and put in four deep, wide, soup plates to warm up.

Also, prepare a pot cheese whip to give body to the sauce. I put into the bowl of my Cuisinart chopper-churner the cup of pot cheese, the ⅓ cup of yoghurt and the 3 tablespoons of ricotta. I run the machine until they are churned into a smoothly creamy purée – usually in 7 to 8 seconds. Transfer the mixture to a round-bottomed beating bowl and whip air into it with a balloon whisk. Then hold it.

About 30 minutes before serving – preparing the sauce

At the end of the 20 minutes, immediately take out the sweet-breads and hold them warm, covered, in the oven. Turn up the heat under the casserole and boil the liquid hard to reduce it by about half, concentrating and sharpening its flavors. When it seems to have the right strength and is showing the first signs of becoming syrupy, strain out all the solids through a fine sieve and return the liquid to the casserole, now keeping it at a gentle simmer. Put in the dozen scallion bulbs and the 16 button mushrooms. Turn down the heat slightly so that the liquid stops simmering, and begin beating in with a wire whisk, tablespoon by tablespoon, the pot cheese whip until you have achieved a creamy, slightly spoon-coating consistency to the sauce. Turn up the heat again to gentle bubbling for exactly another 5 minutes. Turn off the heat and, with a wire whisk, quickly beat in the egg yolks, one by one, first slightly heating up each egg yolk in its cup by beating into it 1 tablespoon of the hot sauce. Then, immediately whip the heated egg yolk into the main casserole. Repeat for the 2 other eggs. Now proceed very carefully, just as if you were making an egg custard. Turn on the heat under the casserole and start bringing up the sauce, stirring all the time, remembering that you will ruin everything if you allow it to boil. Gently and gradually the sauce will (and is intended to) become a thin custard. Do not take your eyes off it for a moment. When the custard is achieved, turn off the heat and cut the sweet-breads into ⅜-inch slices, putting them into the custard to impregnate and warm them for a last couple of minutes. No more, or they will overcook. Serve the sweetbreads, mush-rooms, scallion bulbs and plenty of sauce onto the hot soup plates and bring instantly to the table. With his superb invention, Chef Daniel Météry served me a noble red Bordeaux, a Château Canon-La-Gaffelière from the district of St. Emilion. As an alternative, on our American side, I might serve a rich, red California Petite Sirah from the Napa Valley or Sonoma.

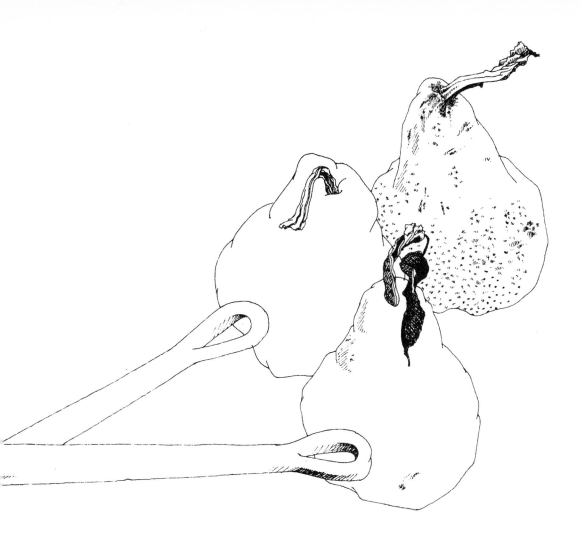

Chapter Twelve
A Few Multi-Purpose Simple Sauces

in which some of the most spectacular achievements
of the revolution are revealed, including thickening
without Flour, Béarnaise without Butter,
Mayonnaise without Oil.

CHEF ROGER VERGÉ ON THE PROVENÇAL TECHNIQUE OF THICKENING SAUCES WITH POTATO IN PLACE OF BUTTER, CREAM AND FLOUR

I had just eaten one of the most extraordinary (and super-luxurious) dishes of my life. I was dining at a small table in the garden under a huge, striped gray and pink umbrella – in the perfumed air of a Provençal July evening – at Vergé's stunningly beautiful old mill restaurant in the country a few miles outside Cannes. The waiter had set on my plate what looked exactly like a small rectangular box of hot, golden puff pastry, about three inches long and two inches wide. When I plunged my silver fork into it and opened it up, I found it entirely filled with cubes and rounds of fresh black truffles. You can imagine the bouquet that rose to dilate my nostrils! I had never in my life seen so many truffles on a single plate. I sharply put away from me any thought as to their value. Such a crass estimate might have reduced the pleasure of the eating.

Yet afterward my strongest memory was not entirely the truffles, but the brilliant sauce with which Vergé had enveloped the "black gold nuggets." The truffles were crisp in the mouth and this strongly chewy texture was dramatically balanced against the creamy smooth, velvety unctuousness of the sauce. How did he achieve it? I was bursting with that question when, with the coffee, Vergé sat down at my table.

"Is it a secret?" I asked.

"Not at all. It is an ancient Provençal trick," Roger said.

"We use a very small amount of puréed potatoes. I think there is an affinity between the potato and the truffle because both are under-the-earth tubers but, in any case, I find that the potato is a much more delicately smooth thickening agent – as well as being only about one-sixth as rich as the standard butter-flour roux. We use the potatoes raw, peeled, of course, then ground extremely fine, passed through a very fine sieve to eliminate all graininess, and worked carefully into the sauce. It is an old Provençal way, and still one of the best."

A FLUFFY SAVORY SAUCE FOR MEATS OR FISH IN THE STYLE OF A BÉARNAISE BUT ENTIRELY WITHOUT BUTTER

(about 1 quart – will keep refrigerated for at least 2 weeks) I consider this sauce to be one of the most brilliant inventions of the modern gastronomic era in France. When its inventor, Chef Roger Vergé (page 52) discussed it with me at his three-star restaurant, Le Moulin de Mougins, in Provence, he did not make any claim to his sauce's being "an imitation of or replacement for" a classic béarnaise. This is something quite different. It is a fluffy, light, savory purée of vegetables, with no butter. It does have, as does a béarnaise, the subtle tang of tarragon and vinegar. I feel no hesitation about saying that as long as I can have this, I can live without the fattening richness of béarnaise.

Roger Vergé's extraordinary "secret trick" is that he ferments the vegetables as if he were converting them into wine. Maybe that is why this sauce does have a slight winey character. Since the fermentation process involves slight supervision for three days, I always make this sauce in a minimum quantity of one quart. The recipe below is for that amount. I use it over hot or cold foods, meats, fish, poultry, vegetables, salads or sandwiches, wherever you need a touch of piquancy.

Cucumbers, peeled, cored and
 coarsely chopped (2 medium)
Yellow onions, peeled and
 coarsely chopped (2 medium)
Tomatoes, important that they
 be ripe, peeled, seeded and
 coarsely chopped (5 medium)
Red bell pepper, in season,
 or red pimiento for color,
 deveined, pitted, coarsely
 chopped (1 medium)
Green bell pepper, deveined,
 pitted, coarsely chopped
 (1 medium)
Cornichons (baby French
 pickles), coarsely chopped
 (4 oz)

Capers, whole (2 oz)
Chervil, fresh leaf in season,
 chopped (1 cup)
Parsley, leaves only, chopped
 (1 cup)
Tarragon, fresh leaf in season,
 chopped (½ cup)
Salt, coarse crystal, to taste
Black pepper, freshly ground,
 to taste
Mustard, Dijon (½ cup)
Wine vinegar, tarragon (½ cup)
Potatoes, for boiling, peeled
 (6 medium)
Olive oil, pure green virgin
 (½ cup)
Lemon juice (about 2 tsp)

Start 5 to 6 days before serving

Put the chopped cucumbers, onions, tomatoes, red and green
peppers, and *cornichons* into an enameled, glass or stoneware
storage dish (not in any metal, or they will discolor). Add the
capers, chervil, parsley and tarragon and gently but thoroughly
mix everything with a wooden spoon without crushing down.
Sprinkle on salt and black pepper to taste. Work in the ½ cup
of Dijon mustard and the ½ cup of vinegar. Again, mix lightly
but thoroughly. Cover the dish and store in a cool place, but
not in the refrigerator, for 5 to 6 days. (The secret of this sauce
is that the vegetables must ferment slightly and the average
refrigerator is too cold to allow the winey fermentation to start
and develop.) Carefully and gently stir the mixture at least
once each day.

Final preparation

Boil the potatoes and mash them, dry. Hold for the final thickening. I put 2 cups of the marinated vegetables into the bowl

of my Cuisinart chopper-churner (or you can use a blender), and add ½ cup of the mashed potatoes and 3 tablespoons of the olive oil. I then run the machine until it is all a fluffy smooth purée – usually in 15–20 seconds. Transfer into a large beating bowl, reload the chopper-churner with the next 2 cups of vegetables, again add potatoes and olive oil and purée them. Add this second batch to the beating bowl. Repeat the operation a third time with the remaining vegetables – usually less than 1 cup. Add the last of the potatoes and olive oil and add this last batch of purée to the beating bowl. Now beat the mixture thoroughly with a balloon wire whisk until it is fluffy and light.

This sauce will nicely hold its taste and texture if stored in a covered jar in the refrigerator. Use it as if it were a béarnaise sauce, remembering that it has none of the cholesterol of eggs and slightly more than half the richness of the butter that would be used for an equivalent amount of béarnaise.

CHEFS JEAN AND PIERRE TROISGROS'S SAUCE ANTIBEOISE FOR FISH

(for 4)

Pierre told me, "This sauce is our own. There is no sauce of this name in the classic repertoire. We invented it about ten years ago, and because it is dominated by the forceful character of Provençal olive oil, we named it in honor of the famous Mediterranean seaside resort village of Antibes." For true success with this superb sauce, you must get the finest quality of the purest virgin olive oil (see page 74). The aromatic herbs may be flexible according to the season, and you can experiment with different combinations. Although this sauce depends on olive oil, it is in fact about a quarter as rich as any of the classic fish sauces made with butter, cream, eggs, or flour. It goes wonderfully, I think, with the Troisgros's "Dry-Grilled and Crusted Sea Bass" (page 207).

Garlic, peeled and mashed (2 cloves)

Chervil, fresh leaves in season, chopped (1 Tbs)

Parsley, fresh leaves, chopped (1 Tbs)

Tarragon, fresh leaves in season, chopped (1 Tbs)

Coriander seeds, coarsely cracked (1 Tbs)

Olive oil, pure green virgin (4 Tbs)

Salt, coarse crystal, to taste

White pepper, freshly ground, to taste

Lemon juice, freshly squeezed (about 2 Tbs)

Tomatoes, peeled and depitted (2 medium)

Preparation time about 10 minutes – no cooking whatsoever

Put into a round-bottomed beating bowl, in this order: the mashed garlic, the tablespoon each of chervil, parsley, tarragon, and coriander seeds. Now add the 4 tablespoons of olive oil and beat furiously with a wire whisk, adding salt and pepper to taste. (For a dramatic effect, the Troisgros sometimes put in a few whole peppercorns.) Next, beat in, teaspoon by teaspoon, up to 2 tablespoons of the lemon juice. Finally, just before serving, coarsely mash the tomatoes into the sauce. They should be neither diced nor a purée, but a lumpy mash. Give the sauce a final beating before serving. The Troisgros serve it at room temperature whether the fish is hot or cold.

MIMI LENSALADE'S CONTRASTING GREEN AND RED SAUCES TO DECORATE AND GLORIFY THE SEA BASS CAUGHT ON THE BEACH AT ST-GIRONS-PLAGE

(for 4)

This is a specialty of Mademoiselle Mimi Lensalade (page 41) at her beach bistro, Au Rescapé, at St-Girons-Plage, on the Atlantic coast of the Landes, north of Biarritz.

The last time I dined with Mimi, one of her fishermen friends brought in a big sea bass which she decorated and glorified with two sauces – one a brilliant green, the other vivid red – dribbling them over the fish in a design worthy of Picasso. They lifted the taste as much as they brightened the platter. They are as simple to prepare as a cup of tea. But, in the perfection of their balance and textures, they represent true Low-High lightness and simplicity.

For the green sauce:

Sweet butter (about 6 Tbs)

White wine, slightly sweet, not too sweet (6 Tbs)

Lemon juice (about 2 Tbs)

Parsley, fresh, minced (small bunch)

Tarragon, fresh leaf in season, chopped (2 tsp)

Chives, or scallions, or shallots, finely minced (1 Tbs)

Salt, coarse crystal, to taste

Black pepper, freshly ground, to taste

For the red sauce:

Tomatoes, red and ripe, peeled and deseeded, chunked (3 medium)

Garlic, peeled and chunked (1 or 2 cloves, to taste)

Shallots, peeled and chunked (2 cloves)

Anchovy fillets (2 oz can)

Capers (about 1 Tbs)

Black olives, pitted, coarsely chopped (about ¼ cup)

Olive oil, pure green virgin (about 2 Tbs)

Black pepper, freshly ground, to taste

Lemon juice, freshly squeezed (up to 1 Tbs)

Preparation of the green parsley maitre d'hotel in about 7 minutes

In a small, 1½-pint saucepan, gently melt 5 tablespoons of the butter, then work in 5 tablespoons of the wine and 2 teaspoons of the lemon juice. Now begin adjusting the mixture by work-ing in alternately, teaspoon by teaspoon, more of the wine and the lemon juice until you achieve a nice sweet-sour effect. If you accidentally go too far, you can bring it back with a little extra butter. Stir the parsley into the sauce bit by bit until it has a bright, solid-green color. Stir in the 2 teaspoons of tar-ragon, the tablespoon of chives (or alternative), plus salt and pepper to taste. Hold the sauce, just warm – not too hot, or the greenery will wilt.

Preparation of the red modified Niçoise sauce in about 8 minutes

I put the 3 tomatoes into the bowl of my Cuisinart chopper-churner (or you can use an electric blender, or do the job in a hand mill), and add the cloves of garlic, shallots and anchovies (with their oil). Then I run the machine until it is all puréed and blended, but not so long that it becomes a mushy paste – usually in 6 to 8 seconds. Transfer the purée to a 1½-quart saucepan and gently heat it up to just below simmering. At the same time, work in as many of the capers and olives as will give the sauce a good, tangy flavor and chewy texture. If it needs to be enriched, work in a tablespoon or so of the oil, plus black pepper to taste. Finally, if your taste demands it, a small amount of lemon juice. Hold the sauce, warm – but not much above blood heat. To avoid the sauces' dominating the natural flavor of the dish, pour them around the fish.

THE NEW SAUCE GRIBETTE FOR MEAT AND FISH

(for 4)

If you need a sauce that is piquant with vinegar to provide a tang for boiled meats (for example, with "Chicken-in-the Pot," page 232), or with fish and shellfish, there are two classic and universal choices, *Sauce Grelette* or *Sauce Gribiche*, but both are a long way from Low-High requirements. *Grelette* is loaded with sour cream – *Gribiche* is heavy with egg yolk cholesterol and oily fat of mayonnaise. Three of the greatest chefs of our time – Paul Bocuse, Michel Guérard and Roger Vergé – have played around with these sauces, trying to lighten and simplify them. All three chefs have been good enough to give me their new recipes and I have translated and adapted them to the American kitchen. I like all the new ideas so much that I have decided to combine them into a brand new sauce, which I choose to call *Sauce Gribette* – a name that does not appear in any of the reference books. It is now the simplest of preparations and all the objectionable fatty elements have disappeared, but you have to start marinating the diced vegetables the day before. You can vary them according to the season.

Cucumber, peeled, seeded and
  diced (1 smallish)
Tomato, peeled, seeded, juice
  squeezed out, flesh diced
  (1 medium)
Mushrooms, caps and stalks,
  diced (2 medium)
Green pepper, seeded and
  diced (1 medium)
Cognac (½ cup)
Vinegar, Spanish Sherry (about
  1½ cups)
Pot cheese, low-fat (¾ cup)

Yoghurt, plain, low-fat (¼ cup)
Ricotta, Italian style, low-fat
  (2 Tbs)
Mustard, Dijon (1 tsp)
Tarragon, fresh leaf in season,
  chopped (1 Tbs)
Cornichons (baby French
  pickles), diced (3)
Capers, finely minced (2 tsp)
Salt, coarse crystal, to taste
Black pepper, freshly ground,
  to taste

The day before – active preparation about 10 minutes, with overnight marination

Put the diced cucumber, tomato, mushrooms, and green pepper into a covered storage bowl or jar, not too wide, so that the marinating liquids do not spread out too much. Pour over them the ½ cup of Cognac and then enough of the vinegar just to cover them. Stir gently, so as not to mash them, cover and set in the refrigerator to marinate overnight. No harm in giving them another gentle stir or two before you go to bed and again first thing in the morning.

On the day – final preparation in about 10 minutes

I put the ¾ cup of pot cheese into the bowl of my Cuisinart chopper-churner (or you can use an electric blender, or a hand food mill), adding the ¼ cup of yoghurt and the 2 tablespoons of ricotta, then running the machine until the mixture is smoothly puréed – usually in not more than 7 seconds. I transfer it to a round-bottomed beating bowl and, with a balloon wire whisk, beat air into it until it has almost the texture of whipped cream. Now drain the diced vegetables from their marinade and gently but thoroughly work them into the pot cheese, together with the teaspoon of mustard, the tablespoon of tarragon, the diced cornichons and minced capers, plus salt and pepper to taste. If you like more vinegary tang to your sauce, work in a teaspoon or two of the marinade.

LOW-FAT LEMON-YOGHURT SAUCE FOR COLD MEAT OR FISH AND SALAD

(for 4)

This recipe came from the brilliant Chef Jacques Manière (page 42) at his Le Pactole in Paris, in answer to my challenge whether he could prepare satisfactory cold savory sauces entirely without oil. I have translated and adapted it to our American ingredients.

Lemon juice, freshly squeezed (1 to 2 Tbs)
Egg yolk, hard-boiled (1 to 2)
Yoghurt, plain, low-fat (½ cup)
Shallots, peeled (3 whole cloves)

Parsley, chopped leaves (2 Tbs)
Salt, coarse crystal, to taste
Black pepper, freshly ground, to taste
White wine, dry (about 2 Tbs)

Preparation time about 5 minutes

I put 1 tablespoon of lemon juice, 1 hard-boiled egg yolk, the yoghurt, shallots and parsley, with salt and pepper to taste, into the bowl of my Cuisinart chopper-churner (or an electric blender) and run the machine until they are thoroughly mixed and smooth, but not a pasty mush – usually in no more than 4 seconds. This sauce should have body, but should be just thin enough to pour. Obviously, more hard-boiled egg yolks would thicken it – more lemon juice, or a tiny dash of dry white wine, would thin it. It keeps perfectly for several days in a tightly lidded jar in the refrigerator. Naturally, you are expected to taste it occasionally and adjust, as needed, any or all of the aromatic ingredients.

MASQUERADING MAYONNAISE ENTIRELY WITHOUT OIL

(4 to 6 portions)

This is another of the most brilliant and revolutionary, most famous and highly publicized gastronomic inventions of our time. It is the masterpiece of Chef Michel Guérard (page 35) at his two-star restaurant, Le Pot au Feu, in Eugénie-les-Bains. I have translated and adapted the recipe he gave me to our American basic ingredients, which are somewhat different from those Michel uses in his country district of southwestern France. But the version I make in my New York kitchen lives up in every way to its reputation. It is feather-light, beautifully fluffy, with the authentic egg yolk color and the savory-tangy taste (if not quite the oily unctuousness on the tongue) of the real thing. Perhaps the most amazing fact about it is that it keeps, in a tightly covered jar in the refrigerator, for about 2 weeks without separating. It is made from real egg yolks, but so much air is beaten into them that the average serving includes only about half a single yolk. The cholesterol problem is virtually nonexistent. It is the magic trick of the century. Who would ever again want to bother with real mayonnaise!

Vinegar, finest white, Sherry or tarragon (3 Tbs)
Salt, coarse crystal, to taste
Egg, whole, very fresh (1 large)
Mustard, powdered, English (½ tsp)
Lemon juice, freshly squeezed, strained (about 2 tsp)

Egg yolks, very fresh (3 large)
Gelatin, granulated, unflavored (½ tsp)
Tabasco (1 or 2 drops)
Tarragon, fresh leaves in season, chopped (from 1 sprig)

Preparation in about 15 minutes

Start cooling a 1-pint covered container in the freezer. Put into a 1-pint saucepan the tablespoon of vinegar plus about 3 tablespoons of water depending upon how sharp you like your sauce. Add salt to taste. Do not heat yet. I drop the whole egg into the bowl of my Cuisinart chopper-churner, (or you can use a rotary beater, or beat by hand), then sprinkle in the dried mustard and 1½ teaspoons of the lemon juice. I then switch on the machine and churn, beating air into the egg for exactly 2 minutes, when I stop the machine and add the 3 yolks. Continue churning and beating in air for another 4 minutes.

Meanwhile, gently heat the vinegar water in the saucepan, at the same time sprinkling onto its surface the gelatin and stirring it in, making sure that it all melts and leaves no lumps. Just as the timer nears the end of the 4 minutes, bring the vinegar mixture up to a full, bubbling boil and then, without stopping the machine (or while continuing to beat furiously by hand), throw the very hot liquid, all at once, into the churning egg mixture. The instant effect of the hot liquid is to coagulate and thicken the egg, just as does the oil in the making of a normal mayonnaise. Once the hot liquid is incorporated, continue the churning or beating for another 5 minutes.

At the end of the 5 minutes, if you are using a chopper-churner, transfer the entire contents to a round-bottomed beating bowl. The final incorporation of air must be done by hand with a large balloon wire whisk. Beat with long, high strokes to get in as much extra air as possible. This is also the point when you beat in, more or less to your taste, the last aromatic ingredients for the exact flavor of mayonnaise that you prefer. I beat in 1 or 2 drops of Tabasco, and perhaps a few more drops of lemon juice. Finally, the mayonnaise should be very light and fluffy and its volume should have increased by 3 or 4 times. Now cool it at once by spooning it lightly into the ice-cold container from the freezer. BUT DO NOT PUT IT BACK INTO THE FREEZER OR YOU WILL RUIN THE MAYONNAISE. Store in the coldest part of the refrigerator overnight. By morning, it will be completely set and will hold for several days.

Just before serving, quickly fold in the chopped tarragon.

AROMATIC COLD SAUCE ENTIRELY WITHOUT OIL FOR MEAT AND SHELLFISH

(for 4)

This is another answer from Chef Jacques Manière (page 42) in response to my challenge that he was still using, in his low-fat sauces, small amounts of olive or walnut oils for the lift they gave to the overall flavor. Could he, I asked, prepare a satisfactorily savory sauce entirely without oil? This is his answer. I have used it successfully over cold shellfish salads, as a dipping sauce for cold boiled shrimp, with cold sliced chicken, as a side garnish with cold cuts and in other, similar ways. You must judge for yourself whether the complete absence of oil does or does not represent a serious flavor and texture compromise.

Pot cheese, low-fat (½ cup)
Egg yolk (1)
Lemon juice, freshly squeezed
   (about 2 Tbs)
Red cayenne pepper, to taste

Salt, coarse crystal, to taste
Basil, fresh leaves in season,
   chopped (1 Tbs)
Green peppercorns (2 tsps)
White wine, dry (about 2 Tbs)

Preparation time about three minutes

I put into the bowl of my Cuisinart chopper-churner (or an electric blender) the ½ cup pot cheese, the egg yolk, 1 tablespoon of the lemon juice, a pinch of the red cayenne and salt to taste. Run the machine until everything is thoroughly mixed and smooth, but not until it is a pasty mush – usually in hardly more than 3 seconds. Transfer to a mixing bowl and lightly work in the basil and the green peppercorns. Taste and adjust lemon juice and salt, as you like them. This sauce should have body, but should be just thin enough to pour. More cheese will thicken it. More lemon juice, or a tiny dash or two of the white wine, will thin it. It keeps perfectly for several days in a tightly covered jar in the refrigerator.

SPICY SAUCE SAUPIQUET FOR COLD OR HOT MEATS

(for 4)

This is a light, modernized version of one of the most ancient aromatic sauces in the world, modified by Chef Paul Bocuse (page 26) at his three-star restaurant in Collonges-au-Mont-d'Or near Lyon. From the recipe which Paul gave me, I have translated and adapted the sauce for American ingredients and used it, with the enthusiastic approval of my guests, on various hot meat dishes, pot roasts, stews and terrines, as well as cold cuts and meat salads.

Shallots, peeled and finely minced (5 cloves)	**White pepper, freshly ground, to taste**
Vinegar, Spanish sherry (6 Tbs)	**Cornichons (baby French pickles), finely minced (8)**
Beef bouillon, entirely defatted (1 cup)	**Parsley, leaf only, chopped (2 Tbs)**
Demi-glace brown sauce (see page 78) (1 cup)	**Salt, coarse crystal, to taste**

About 35 minutes before serving – active preparation about 20 minutes, plus about 15 minutes of unsupervised simmering

This is the simplest of operations – all done on top of the stove in a single, 1½ pint saucepan which must be acid-resistant, preferably tinned copper, enameled iron, or nickel stainless steel. Put in the minced shallots, cover them with the 6 tablespoons of vinegar and heat up to merry bubbling. Continue boiling, uncovered, until the vinegar is reduced to less than 1 tablespoon – just a small visible layer of wetness on the bottom of the pan. At this point, add the 1 cup each of beef bouillon and brown sauce, bringing them up to gentle bubbling, uncovered, to reduce their volume and concentrate their flavors for 15 minutes.

About 15 minutes before serving

Check the consistency of the sauce and, if it is not yet showing signs of becoming slightly syrupy, turn up the heat a bit and let it bubble fairly hard to reduce more quickly. This may take 5 or 10 minutes. Finally, when the consistency is right, turn down the heat to below simmering, skim off any small pools of fat, give it a few good grinds of the peppermill and work into it the minced *cornichons* and the 2 tablespoons of the chopped parsley, plus a little salt, to taste. From this point on, it must not be allowed to boil, or it may develop a bitter taste. Keep it warm, if necessary, covered, but make quite sure that its temperature stays well below the simmering point. Serve it hot.

SAUCE VIERGE – VIRGIN TOMATO FOR FISH

(for 4)

This was served to me spooned over the magnificent Mediterranean fish, *loup de mer*, by Chef Michel Guérard (page 35) at his two-star restaurant, Le Pot au Feu, at Eugénie-les-Bains. Although the fish was placed before me hot, the sauce was at room temperature and Michel claimed that the tomato cannot be heated or it would lose its pristine freshness. Because of the noncooking, the sauce takes hardly more than a minute or two to prepare.

Tomatoes, ripe, peeled and
  deseeded (3 medium)
Garlic, peeled and chunked
  (2 cloves)
Olive oil, pure green virgin
  (about 3 Tbs)
Chervil, fresh leaves in season,
  chopped (1 Tbs)
Parsley, leaf only, chopped (2 tsp)

Tarragon, fresh leaf in season,
  chopped (2 tsp)
Coriander seed, coarsely
  cracked (1 tsp)
Salt, coarse crystal, to taste
Black pepper, freshly ground,
  to taste

Preparation in about 5 minutes

I put the three tomatoes and the two garlic cloves into the bowl of my Cuisinart chopper-churner (or you can use an electric blender) and purée them by running the machine for exactly 3 seconds. Then, without stopping the machine, I pour 2 tablespoons of the olive oil in a thin stream and let the machine run for another 3 seconds. Now, with the machine stopped, I add the tablespoon of chopped chervil, the 2 teaspoons each of chopped parsley and tarragon, plus the teaspoon of cracked coriander seed. I run the machine for 3 more seconds and then transfer the sauce to a round-bottomed beating bowl. Now, with a balloon wire whisk, beating hard with lifted strokes, fluff up and lighten the sauce by whipping as much air into it as possible, at the same time adjusting its final flavor precisely to your taste. Work in salt and pepper. Last, add, almost drop by drop, more of the olive oil until you get the perfect balance of the olive fruit with the natural acid of the tomato. This is the secret of this sauce. The stronger the olive oil, the less you would need to use of it. Naturally, you will want to use as little as possible. You can make this sauce just before serving, but it is better if given an hour or two to ripen in a covered bowl at room temperature. Give it a final whip just before serving. It is wonderful with any kind of hot or cold fish, or cold light meals.

Chapter Thirteen
Some Far-from-the-Ordinary Salads
and Vegetables

among which are included a Carrot Terrine with
Jahrlsberg, Spinach creamed with Peaches, Truffles
with Garden Vegetables, and a Wild Salad from
Provence.

AROMATIC HERB SALAD WITH WHIPPED LOW-FAT WHITE CHEESE

(for 4)

This is, in my opinion, the salad trick of the decade. Instead of being dressed with the fattening oil of a vinaigrette, the vinegar is whipped into a cream of white cheese and the result is refreshing, most attractive to look at, with a luxurious texture enclosing the aromatic qualities of fresh greenery, herbs and spices. Once you have learned the principle, you can vary this salad in a hundred ways according to the season and your taste.

The idea is now spreading all across France and it has been served to me, prepared in different ways, by such brilliant chefs as Jacques Manière, Marc Meneau, the Troisgros brothers and Roger Vergé. I have taken some of the details from all of them and combined them into my own translation and adaptation of this easiest and quickest of all simple salads. In France, they use a no-fat *fromage blanc maîgre*, which is not available here, but in the United States we have a choice of low-fat versions of white pot cheese, "imitation cream cheese," or Italian-style ricotta. (See detailed discussion on page 76.) This is the best low-fat dressing I have ever tasted.

Pot cheese, low-fat, or alterna-
tive, see above (2 cups)
Vinegar, white, Sherry or
tarragon (about 3 Tbs)
Salt, coarse crystal, to taste
Black pepper, freshly ground,
to taste
Bean sprouts, fresh, chopped
(1 Tbs)
Fennel, fresh, chopped (¼ cup)
Scallions, coarsely chopped (3)
Basil leaves, fresh in season,
chopped (1 tsp)

Mint leaves, fresh in season,
chopped (1 tsp)
Tarragon leaves, fresh in
season, chopped (1 tsp)
Parsley, fresh, chopped
(2 tsp)
Chives, fresh, coarsely
chopped (1½ Tbs)
Chinese pepper, Szechuan,
to taste

Preparation in about 15 minutes

I put the 2 cups of pot cheese into the bowl of my Cuisinart
chopper-churner (or an electric blender) with 2 tablespoons of
the vinegar and salt and black pepper to taste. I then run the
machine until the mixture is about the consistency of mayonnaise – usually about 15 second⸴. If it is too thick, churn in
more vinegar, ½ teaspoon at a time. Transfer this cheese
dressing to a salad bowl and, after whipping it for a few seconds with a balloon whisk, work in the chopped bean sprouts,
fennel and scallions plus a teaspoon each of basil, mint and
tarragon, with the 2 teaspoons of parsley. Do not overfill the
cheese dressing. You should be eating the cheese with a
garnishing array of greenery – not greenery with an almost
invisible coating of dressing. Store covered in the refrigerator
and serve quite cold. At the moment just before serving,
sprinkle on the chopped chives and grind a little Szechuan
pepper over the top.

BLACK TRUFFLE SALAD WITH GARDEN VEGETABLES

(for 4)

When Chef Michel Guérard (page 35) was running his memorable bistro in Paris, one of the dishes that helped make him
famous was his *Salade Gourmande*, in which crisply under-

cooked, superbly fresh vegetables were lavishly combined with a king's ransom of black truffles and cubes of foie gras. Now that Michel has switched his allegiance to the new low-fat cuisine, this is his defatted version of his highly publicized salad. The black truffles are still there, in a much shorter supply, but the foie gras has disappeared. It is a fine opening salad for a luxurious dinner – especially dramatic when dressed with Michel's mayonnaise made without oil (see page 341). You can expand this salad into a memorable main course for lunch or supper by adding aromatically boiled crayfish or shrimp (see page 84).

Artichoke bottoms and hearts, cooked (4 to 6)

Lettuce, Boston or romaine (enough leaves for a bed)

Black truffles (from 1 small up to largest ransom you can afford)

Asparagus, green tips, steamed (1½ cups)

Asparagus, white tips, steamed (1½ cups)

Green beans, young, cooked and chunked (½ lb)

Sweet red pepper or pimento, cooked and cut into bitesized strips (½ cup)

Salt, coarse crystal, to taste

Pepper, whole berries, Chinese Szechuan, to taste

Mayonnaise without oil, see page 341 (1 batch)

Preparation in from 15 minutes to 2 hours

This job can be either short or long depending on whether the ingredients come ready to eat from cans or, much better, fresh from the farm or the farmer's market. Trim the cooked artichoke hearts and bottoms. Wash and dry the lettuce leaves. Thinly slice the truffle into rounds of a size between a quarter and a half dollar, with a minimum of two slices for each guest.

Now cover your open serving platter with a bed of lettuce leaves and set out on it the various vegetables in a form the French call *une salade composée*, which means a non-tossed salad, with neat little single-serving piles of each of the vegetables: the artichoke bottoms and hearts, the green and white asparagus, and the green beans. Place the truffles in a circle at the center and decorate the assemblage with the strips of red pimento. Cover the platter with aluminum foil and keep the salad crisp in the refrigerator until serving time.

Just before serving

At the last moment grind over the salad some salt and Szechuan pepper. Garnish the platter with the mayonnaise without oil (from page 341), but do not completely cover the vegetables. Leave the truffles clear.

SALAD OF GREEN BEANS WITH SLICED RAW MUSHROOMS

(for 4)

When Chef Jean Troisgros was recently in New York, he paid me the charming compliment of offering to prepare dinner for a small group of my friends in my home. We agreed at once that the menu should be light and simple – an interpretation by a three-star *cuisinier* of the kind of meal that could easily be prepared by an American amateur cook. Jean started with this delightfully refreshing salad. His "secret trick" was to marinate the crisply undercooked beans in his delicate walnut dressing, while leaving the mushroom slices "undressed," so that, when they were combined a moment or two before serving, there was a sharp difference of ambience and character between the two elements of the salad. A brilliant chef had injected into a simple salad an imaginative and startling contrast.

Rosemary, fresh leaf in season, chopped (1 Tbs)
Green beans, very fresh, small and young (1 lb)
Dijon mustard (1 tsp)
Lemon juice, freshly squeezed (1½ Tbs)
Walnut oil, French, cold-pressed (4½ Tbs)

Salt, coarse crystal, to taste
White pepper, freshly ground, to taste
Mushrooms, very fresh, good shape, nice white color (about 6 to 8, according to size)

About 1¼ hours before serving – active work about 15 minutes plus 1 hour of marination

Fill a 1½-quart saucepan with freshly drawn cold water and bring it up to a rapid boil. While it is heating, salt it to a just-salty taste and stir in the tablespoon of chopped rosemary. Top and tail the green beans and chunk them into 2½-inch lengths. The moment the water boils, drop in the green beans all at once, keeping the water bubbling fairly hard, uncovered, until the beans are just tender but still nicely crisp – usually in 8 to 12 minutes, according to their age. The beans should be just covered by the boiling water at the beginning, but the water can be allowed to boil down, so that the beans are finished in the steam.

Meanwhile, prepare the dressing. In a smallish bowl, mix together: the teaspoon of mustard, the 1½ tablespoons of lemon juice and the 4½ tablespoons of walnut oil. Beat thoroughly together with a wire whisk, adding salt and pepper, to taste.

About 1 hour before serving

The moment the green beans are perfectly done, drain and dry them and lightly toss them in the salad dressing, leaving them to marinate until serving time. Set four salad plates to chill in the freezer.

About 5 minutes before serving

Trim the stalks of the mushrooms level with the caps. Do not wash them with water, since that dissolves their flavor juices. Wipe them clean with a damp cloth, then slice them very thinly across the caps. Set out the portions of green beans on the cold plates and decorate them with the mushroom slices. Serve at once, before the mushrooms have time to begin absorbing the dressing.

SALADE MESCLÜN – A NATURAL WILD SALAD OF PROVENCE

(for 4)

On shimmeringly hot Provençal days, the customers at Chef Roger Vergé's (page 52) beautiful restaurant, Le Moulin de Mougins, demand cool, crisp, refreshing salads, either to begin the meal, or in the middle, or both. So there are always two salads on the menu and, of the balance between them, Roger told me: "My menu, willy-nilly, has to have left and right pages. I find myself entirely unable to control the fact that some clients start on the left page and others on the right. Contrary to the general expectation, it seems to me that the more conservative people start on the left, while the more courageous, experimental and, shall we say, revolutionary, invariably start on the right. So, on the left page we always have an utterly conservative, classic salad, the same every day of the year. But on the right, we have the wild salads, according to the seasons and the opportunities of the market. Something different every day. This *'Salade Mesclün'* is definitely a right-hand-page salad."

One cannot, of course, find all of Roger's wild mushrooms and Provençal leafy greens in the United States, but you can, if you try hard enough, get the arugula or rocket plant in Italian markets, and the perfumed flavors of Provence come with even a minimum dose of pure, cold-pressed green, virgin, Provençal olive oil. I often make this salad for my friends and it does seem to take us back, in lovely memory, to that much-blessed land along the Mediterranean.

Incidentally, the Provençal dialect word, *mesclün,* means simply a mixed-up, shaken-up, wild assemblage of greens and vegetables. This salad is the perfect accompaniment of Chef Vergé's *"Gibelotte* of Rabbit,"* page 255.

Curly endive (1 head)
Arugula leaves, from
   Italian markets (½ lb)
Bibb limestone lettuce (2 or
   3 small heads)

Tarragon, fresh leaf in season,
   chopped (2 tsp)
Salt, coarse crystal, to taste
Black pepper, freshly ground,
   to taste

Vinegar, tarragon, white
wine (1½ Tbs)
Mustard, French Dijon (½ tsp)
Olive oil, Provençal, pure
green virgin (4½ Tbs)
Chives, fresh in season,
chopped (2 tsp)

Garlic, crushed (½ clove)
Parsley, fresh leaf, chopped
(2 Tbs)
Mushrooms, small, good color
and shape, thinly sliced (5)
Black olives, pitted and sliced
(½ cup)

Not more than an hour before serving

Wash and dry the endive, arugula, and Bibb leaves – drying
is the most important single trick of salad making. Shaking
the leaves or swinging them in a basket is not enough. The
least water held in the folds will dilute the dressing. Therefore the leaves must be pressed between absorbent towels.
The leaves are torn by hand (never cut) into the bowl, then
they are crisped and freshened by being set in the refrigerator,
covered, until serving time.

About 5 minutes before serving

Into a mixing bowl put the 2 teaspoons of chopped tarragon
with salt and pepper to taste. Add the 1½ tablespoons of
vinegar, stirring around to dissolve the salt. Then add the ½
teaspoon of mustard and the 4½ tablespoons of olive oil. Stir
and let it rest for a minute so that the flavors blend. Now add
2 teaspoons of the chopped chives, the crushed ½ clove of
garlic and the 2 tablespoons of parsley, beat slightly, then
spoon the dressing over the salad. Toss the salad at the last
moment for about 2 minutes, and decorate it with the sliced
mushrooms and black olives.

AN AMERICAN ADAPTATION OF CHEF ROGER VERGÉ'S SALADE MIKADO

(for 4)

This is the more classic salad which Chef Vergé (page 52) (as
he explains in the previous recipe) lists on the left-hand page
of his menu. He told me, "We had a Japanese apprentice in

the kitchen who also, incidentally, worked at Troisgros (page 50). Since we could not pronounce his name, we just called him 'The Mikado.' When we perfected this all-the-year-round salad we gave him the responsibility of preparing it. When we were ready to list it I thought, why look any further for a name?"

Curly endive, leaves washed and dried as in the previous recipe (1 head)

Basil, fresh leaf in season, chopped (2 tsp)

Thyme, fresh leaf in season, chopped (2 tsp)

Salt, coarse crystal, to taste

Black pepper, freshly ground, to taste

Vinegar, Spanish Sherry (1½ Tbs)

Mustard, Fresh Dijon (½ tsp)

Olive oil, Provençal, pure green virgin (4½ Tbs)

Avocado, ripe (1)

Mushrooms, fresh, good color and shape, caps thinly sliced (4 medium)

Tomatoes, skinned and seeded, coarsely diced (2 medium)

Black truffle, diced, optional (1 small)

About 45 minutes before serving – active work about 15 minutes, plus about 30 minutes unsupervised crisping

Put the torn endive leaves into a salad bowl and refrigerate them, lightly covered, to crisp and freshen them until serving time.

About 15 minutes before serving

Into a mixing bowl put the 2 teaspoons each of basil and thyme with salt and pepper to taste. Add the 1½ tablespoons of vinegar, stirring around to dissolve the salt. Then add the ½ teaspoon of mustard and the 4½ tablespoons of olive oil. Stir and let it rest for a minute so that the flavors blend. Meanwhile, peel and slice the avocado into small wedges and add them, with the sliced mushrooms and diced tomatoes, to the endive in the salad bowl. Beat the dressing slightly, adjust seasonings if necessary, and spoon it over the salad. Finally, sprinkle in the diced truffle and gently toss for about 1 minute.

TERRINE OF CARROTS WITH LOW-FAT CHEESE

(for 4)

This is translated and adapted from a recipe given me by Chef Michel Guérard (page 35), in which he uses the French no-fat white cheese. I find that cheese so bland and textureless that I much prefer to use our American low-fat white pot cheese, or imitation cream cheese, or, best of all, Norwegian Jahrlsberg, which adds a superb nuttiness while still having less than half the fat of a standard Cheddar or Gruyère. Incidentally, Michel adds flavor to his bland cheese with a tiny dose of sugar substitute. With the Jahrlsberg this is unnecessary. We are not on a slimming diet. We demand gastronomic pleasure from our Low-High dining.

Carrots, young, not too large, finely grated (1¼ lbs)
Mushrooms, caps and stems, diced (¾ lbs)
Chicken bouillon, clear, entirely defatted (about 1½ cups)
Eggs (2)
Cheese, low-fat Norwegian Jahrlsberg, grated (¼ lb)

Basil, fresh leaf in season, chopped (1 Tbs)
Tarragon, fresh leaf in season, chopped (1 Tbs)
Salt, coarse crystal, to taste
Black pepper, freshly ground, to taste

About 45 minutes before serving – active work about 15 minutes, plus about 30 minutes of unsupervised baking

Preheat your oven to 350°F. and set the racks so that the terrine will bake exactly at the center. Put the grated carrots and diced mushrooms into a 3-quart lidded saucepan and add just enough of the chicken bouillon to cover the solids. Heat it up to gentle simmering and, stirring every minute or two with a wooden spoon, cook the vegetables, uncovered, until they are quite tender – usually in 4 to 5 minutes. Add more bouillon as it is absorbed. The moment the vegetables are done, strain them from the liquid, pressing them with the back of a wooden spoon to squeeze out as much liquid as is reasonably possible. Put the carrots and mushrooms into a mixing bowl.

In a separate bowl, lightly beat the 2 eggs, working into them the grated cheese, with the chopped basil and tarragon. Then lightly fold this mixture into the carrots and mushrooms. At this point, taste it, adding a fair amount of salt and pepper. Choose an oven-proof mold or casserole of exactly the right size and spoon the terrine mixture into it. It should be well filled. Set up a *bain-marie* on the middle oven rack – using a pan about 2 or 3 inches deep, half filled with boiling water, in which the mold will stand. Set the mold, uncovered, in the *bain-marie* in the oven and let it bake until the "silver knife test" shows that it is completely set all the way through – usually in 25 to 30 minutes.

Serving at table

Unmold the terrine onto a serving platter. Serve it very hot, cut into ½ inch slices.

MOUSSE OF CELERY ROOT WITH ONION SOUBISE BUT WITHOUT CREAM

(for 4)

This is my translation and Low-High adaptation of a most excellent vegetable preparation served me by Chef Marc Meneau (page 45) at his two-star Auberge de l'Espérance, in St-Père-Vézelay. Although his basic recipe was light and simple, it did, in its original form, include some butter and heavy cream to make the mousse rich and smooth. Most of the butter and all the cream have now been eliminated.

Celery root (also sometimes called celeriac, or celery knob – in French, *celeri rave*) is one of our standard American Fall and Winter root vegetables, with a fine, subtle, celery flavor, which should make it much more popular and widely known than it is now. Chef Meneau works it into a light fluff and uplifts its perfume and personality by the addition of a modified *soubise*, the classic, delicately aromatic purée of onions.

Celery roots, whole (2 or 3,
    total about 1½ lbs)
Salt, coarse crystal, to taste
Potatoes, starchy, for mashing
    (1½ lbs small)
Veal stock, clear and strong,
    preferably homemade,
    entirely defatted (about
    2 cups)

Butter (2 Tbs)
Yellow onions, peeled and
    finely chopped (4 medium)
Black pepper, freshly ground,
    to taste
Nutmeg, freshly ground, to
    taste
Pot cheese, low-fat (¾ cup)
Lemon (1)

Preparation in about 45 minutes

Wash the earth off the celery roots under running cold water, cut away all dangling tentacles, then peel and coarsely chunk the round roots. Simmer in nicely salted water until they are just soft, but not mushy – usually in 15 to 20 minutes. Do not overcook them, or you will lose some of the celery flavor.

Meanwhile, scrub the potatoes, leaving them in their skins, then steam them until just soft enough to mash – usually in about 20 minutes.

While this is in progress, heat up, in a separate saucepan, the 2 cups of veal stock to gentle simmering and hold it warm, covered. Set a sauté pan over medium frying heat and melt in it the 2 tablespoons of butter. When it is hot, but not yet brown, add the minced onions, stirring them around and letting them gently soften until they are a pale gold – usually in about 7 minutes. Season them with salt, pepper and a couple of grinds of nutmeg. Then pour in ½ cup of the veal stock, adjust the heat to gentle simmering and let the onions mush down to a purée – usually in 12 to 14 minutes. If the purée tends to become too thick, add another tablespoon or two of the veal stock. Preheat your oven to keep-warm temperature, 175°F., and set in it a covered serving bowl.

About 15 minutes before serving – assembling and puréeing the parts

This final operation is made easy and almost instantaneous by the modern machines. You can use an electric blender, or a hand food mill, or a hand masher; I use my Cuisinart chopper-churner. I put into its bowl the ¾ cup of pot cheese. Thoroughly drain the celery root chunks and add as many of them to the bowl as it will hold without overflowing. Run the machine until cheese and celery root are thoroughly churned and puréed, but still with some tiny little lumps – usually in 5 to 7 seconds. Turn out into a large mixing bowl. Add the remaining celery root chunks to the bowl of the machine. Peel the potatoes and chunk as many of them into the bowl of the machine as it will hold, again without overflowing. Churn and purée, as before, in about 5 to 7 seconds. Add this second batch to the large mixing bowl. Put the remaining potato chunks into the bowl of the machine and add the onion purée from the sauté pan, again churning – for about another 5 seconds. Add this final batch to the large mixing bowl. Now, with a wooden spatula, or heavy beater, thoroughly work all the batches together, with a few spritzes of lemon juice, lifting rather than stirring to beat in air and fluff it up. If it is too thick, work in, tablespoon by tablespoon, more of the veal stock. Adjust the seasonings, with more salt, pepper and nutmeg, as needed. Finally, pile this aromatic mousse lightly into the serving bowl and set it back in the oven, covered, to warm everything up until the moment when it is carried to table.

BAKED GÂTEAU OF MUSHROOM, SPINACH AND TOMATO

(for 4)

Translated and adapted from the recipe given me by Chef Michel Guérard (page 35), this imaginative concoction of three vegetables looks as attractive as it tastes. It will cook almost perfectly, if you insist, with virtually no butter at all. But if you feel, as I do, that a little extra butter is worth the large extra pleasure, then you can dot the top of the *gâteau* with some extra bits of butter just before setting it in the oven. The vegetable *gâteau* goes particularly well with "Chicken-in-the-Pot" (page 232).

Spinach, fresh leaf, young, stalks removed (1 lb)

Salt, coarse crystal, to taste

Mushrooms, fresh domestic, or wild mushrooms – cèpes, girolles, mousserons, canned or dried – wiped clean and chunked into bite-sized pieces (½ lb)

Tomatoes, peeled, seeded and chunked (3 or 4 medium)

Garlic, finely minced (1 or 2 cloves)

Shallot, finely minced (2 cloves)

Parsley, fresh leaf, finely chopped (small handful)

Thyme, fresh leaf in season, chopped (1 Tbs)

Butter (1 or 2 Tbs)

About 30 minutes before serving – active preparation about 15 minutes plus about 15 minutes of unsupervised baking

Wash the spinach thoroughly under running cold water and, without shaking the water off the leaves, throw them at once into a big pot over very high heat. As they sizzle and steam, salt and mash them down with a wooden spoon. This operation takes hardly more than 2 to 3 minutes. Turn off the heat and leave them until cool enough to handle, then take handfuls of the spinach and squeeze out as much water as possible. Put the drained handfuls onto a wooden chopping board and chop, not too finely, with a sharp chef's knife. Divide the spinach into 3 equal parts.

Set your oven to 400°F. Put the chunked mushrooms into a dry sauté pan and begin heating them up, shaking them to prevent sticking. When the mushrooms start releasing their water – usually in 2 to 3 minutes – add the chunked tomatoes. Bring up the heat, stirring around, so that the water bubbles and boils off. As this process continues, add the 1 or 2 cloves of minced garlic and the 2 cloves of minced shallot. Work in the small handful of chopped parsley and the tablespoon of chopped thyme.

Choose a smallish, open baking dish or oven-proof casserole and evenly spread over its bottom ⅓ of the spinach. Next, neatly line its sides with the second third of the spinach. Now, into the center, spoon the mushrooms and tomatoes with all remaining sauce from the sauté pan. Cover the top with the third part of the spinach and dot it with 1 or 2 table-spoons of the butter according to your choice. Place the casserole in the center of the oven, uncovered, letting it bake until it is very hot, bubbly and just beginning to brown – usually in about 15 minutes. Serve wedges of this *gâteau* very hot.

SPINACH CREAMED WITH PEACHES INSTEAD OF CREAM

(for 4)

This brilliant trick was taught me by young Chef Marc Meneau (page 45), at his two-star Auberge de l'Espérance near Vézelay. The slightly gelatinous flesh of the peach is used to give the same sort of body to the puréed spinach that would come from the incorporation of heavy cream. In my translation and adaptation to American ingredients, the cream is entirely eliminated and the Low-High spinach can be made as thick as you please by simply boiling away the excess water.

Fresh spinach, stalks removed
  (2 lbs)
Salt, coarse crystal, to taste
Peaches, fresh, ripe, peeled,
  stones removed, coarsely
  chunked (3 medium)

Lemon juice, freshly squeezed
  (about 2 tsp)
Black pepper, freshly ground,
  to taste

Preparation in about 20 minutes

Thoroughly wash the spinach under running cold water and, without shaking the water off the leaves, throw them at once into a big pot over very high heat. As they sizzle and steam, salt and mash them down with a wooden spoon. This operation takes hardly more than 2 to 3 minutes. Turn off the heat and leave them until cool enough to handle, then take handfuls of the spinach and squeeze out as much water as possible. Put the drained handfuls onto a wooden chopping board and chop, not too finely, with a sharp chef's knife.

I now put both spinach and peach chunks into the bowl of my Cuisinart chopper-churner (or you could use an electric blender, or a hand food mill) and run the machine until the mixture is smoothly puréed – but do not let it become lique-fied – usually in no more than 3 seconds. At this point, it will certainly have too much water. Transfer it to a sauté pan and set it over medium heat until it begins to bubble merrily. Stir it almost continuously to avoid the danger of burning. Let it continue to bubble until you have evaporated off enough water to bring the purée to the degree of stiffness you want. Keep folding it over itself to release the water. Finally, work in lemon juice, salt and pepper to achieve the taste you like. I suspect that you will never again want to bother with spinach creamed with cream.

Chapter Fourteen
Desserts with a Minimum of Sugar

in which we are invited to revel in a Sherbet with
Smoky Tea, frozen Champagne, drunken Pears, a
Lime chaser for anger [sic]; and we come to a
rich reward.

GRANITA OF UNSWEETENED BITTER CHOCOLATE WITH ESPRESSO COFFEE

(for 4)

This is translated and adapted from a recipe given me by Chef Michel Guérard (page 35) after he had served it to me at his two-star Le Pot au Feu in Eugénie-les-Bains. I bring it to table in my best, crystal, tulip Champagne glasses. Its appearance is as attractive and unusual as its bitter-soft taste.

Champagne, good quality, French or American (1 bottle)	Egg, well beaten (1)
	Vanilla extract, pure (2 Tbs)
Evaporated skimmed milk (13 oz can)	Chocolate, unsweetened bitter (3 1-oz squares)
Brown sugar, or substitute (1 cup)	Coffee, freshly made, strong from espresso grind, say Medaglia d'Oro or imported alternative (1 pint)
Cornstarch (⅓ cup)	
Salt, to taste	Crystallized violets (4)

The day before serving – active preparation about 20 minutes, plus minimum 5 hours of unsupervised cooling and freezing

Put the bottle of Champagne into the coldest part of your refrigerator to cool. Set into your freezer to get very cold an empty, tightly lidded 1-quart storage jar. Into a small 1½ pint saucepan pour the 13 ounces of skimmed milk and gently heat it up. At the same time, work into it ¾ cup of the sugar (or substitute) with the ⅓ cup of cornstarch and ¼ teaspoon of salt. Keep smoothing and stirring almost continuously until the mixture thickens, usually in 5 to 7 minutes. Turn off the heat and let it cool for 5 minutes.

Meanwhile, set up whatever arrangements you prefer for churning and beating the mixture. I use my Cuisinart chopper-churner, but you can also use a standard, electric mixer-beater, or you can beat by hand. When the mixture in the saucepan has slightly cooled, I put it into the bowl of my chopper-churner, add the whole egg and the 1 tablespoon of the vanilla extract, switching on the machine for not more than 5 seconds. Next, with the machine still running, quickly pour in 2 cups of the Champagne and continue churning for 15 seconds more, then stop. There will be much frothing and this is the secret of the eventual lightness of the dessert. As soon as the churning or beating is completed, pour the mixture into the ice-cold storage jar from the freezer, cover it, then set it back, not in the freezer, but in the coldest part of the refrigerator until it has come down to the internal refrigerator temperature – usually in 4 or 5 hours, or overnight.

On the morning of the day – active preparatory work about 15 minutes plus unsupervised freezing for up to 1½ hours

With an electric or hand grater, coarsely grate the 3 squares of chocolate (about ⅔ cup of grated grains) and hold in a small covered jar in the refrigerator to prevent the grains from melting and sticking together. Now set up your normal ice cream freezing arrangements – electric or hand turned – in your freezer or in a tub of salted ice. Put the Champagne mix from the refrigerator into the container of the machine and freeze in the normal way. Wash out the 1-quart covered container and put it back into the freezer to get good and cold, ready for the next step. Also put into the freezer a fair-sized mixing bowl. When the Champagne sherbet has just solidified but is still workably soft, transfer it quickly to the ice-cold mixing bowl and lightly fold into it the grated chocolate. Then pile it loosely into the ice-cold storage jar, cover and put back in the freezer.

About 1¼ hours before serving – making the coffee granita – active work about 10 minutes with about 1 hour of reasonably unsupervised freezing

Brew 1 pint of strong espresso coffee using ⅔ cup ground coffee with 2 cups of water – and pour it into a standard 8-by-8-by-1-inch square tin baking pan. Sweeten the coffee with the remaining ¼ cup of sugar (or substitute) and stir in the remaining tablespoon of vanilla extract. Let it cool to room temperature, then put the pan in the freezer. Set a timer to 30 minutes, at the end of which take the pan out of the freezer and, with a strong kitchen fork or spoon, scrape off and break up all the ice that has already formed across the bottom and around the sides, thoroughly mixing the frozen part with the liquid remaining in the center. The objective is to prevent the coffee from freezing into a solid block of ice and keep it as flaky as a true Italian *granita* should be. Put the pan back in the freezer, reset the timer to 15 minutes and repeat the scraping and mixing operation. Repeat again 15 minutes later. In a normally adjusted freezer, the perfect *granita* should be ready in 1 hour. It cannot be held very long after it is ready, or it will rapidly become too hard. (After the experience of two or three makings, you will be able to judge exactly the speed of your freezer.)

Serving at table

I serve this in my best, tulip-shaped, stemmed Champagne glasses, which have been set in the freezer to become ice-cold. Fill each glass about ¼ full with a layer of the coffee granita, then ¾ full with a layer of the Champagne-chocolate sherbet, then top with another layer of the *granita*. Decorate the top, if you wish, with a sugar-crystallized violet, but not, I beg you, the cliché of a maraschino cherry. Drink the rest of the Champagne as the ideal accompaniment with the dessert.

FINAL NOTE: If some of this is left over until next day and you find that the Champagne-chocolate sherbet has become too hard, you can soften it to the right consistency by moving it from the freezer to the warmest part of the refrigerator for exactly 30 minutes. This is a good rule to remember for all sherbets. The espresso *granita* will have to be freshly made each time.

PEARS POACHED IN RED BURGUNDY SWEETENED WITH CRÈME DE CASSIS

(for 4)

For hundreds of years, it has been no very special trick in Burgundy to poach summer or winter pears in the local red wine. The new trick here is to add a goodly portion of cassis, the naturally sweet black current syrup of Dijon, made from the ripest berries that flourish on the sun-bathed slopes beyond the vineyards. The cassis contains so much fruity sweetness that the amount of sugar normally required for the pears in standard recipes can be cut virtually in half. Almost all kinds of pears can be used including the luscious Summer Bartletts and the Winter Anjou, Bosc, or Comice.

Red wine, preferably fruity young Burgundy (1½ bottles)	Pears, fine ripe, see above (4)
	Lemon juice (¼ cup)
Crème de cassis, French black currant syrup, preferably Dijon (½ cup)	Black currants, fresh in season, or canned, or whole-fruit black current jam (for garnishing)
Sugar, granulated (about 1 cup or less, to taste)	

Prepared in advance in about 45 minutes – active work about 20 minutes plus about 25 minutes of unsupervised poaching

Choose a 2-quart saucepan, which must be either enameled, or glass, or pottery, since metal tends to discolor the pears. Into it pour the 1½ bottles of red wine and add 2 cups of water, the ½ cup of cassis and as much extra sugar as your sweet tooth demands. Bring it up to the boil and let it simmer, gently, uncovered, for about 15 minutes, while you prepare the pears. Peel them, cut them in half and take out the cores. Immediately rub each cut pear thoroughly with the lemon juice, to prevent discoloration while waiting. As soon as the wine bath is ready, slip in the pear halves and let them poach, gently simmering, until they are just soft, but still nicely crisp – usually about 25 minutes, depending on the ripeness of the fruit. Do not let them, under any circumstances, become mushy. Turn off the heat and leave the pear halves to cool and soak in the wine bath for at least 3 or 4 hours.

About 2 hours before serving

Carefully lift out the pear halves and cool them, covered, in the refrigerator. Boil down the remaining wine until it is reduced by about half and is just beginning to become slightly syrupy, so that its flavors are concentrated and sharpened. Then transfer it, also, to a covered pot, and cool it in the refrigerator.

Serving at table

Serve two pear halves per person, lightly dribbled with the wine sauce and garnished, either with a couple of tablespoons of fresh black currants, or, out of season, with a teaspoon or so of top-quality, whole-fruit, black currant conserve or preserve.

MOST HANDSOME ALMOST SUGARLESS CHAMPAGNE SHERBET BUBBLING IN CHAMPAGNE

(for 4)

This is often the way dinner ends at Chef Paul Haeberlin's (page 39) magnificent three-star restaurant, l'Auberge de l'Ill, in Alsace – one of the most exalted restaurants of France. The sherbet has the texture of frozen Champagne froth. After the waiter has set down the glass of Champagne sherbet in front of you, he fills the spaces in it with fresh Champagne.

This recipe is a model of how to make perfect sherbet. It can be varied with other flavors and other wines. In my translation and adaptation I eliminate virtually all the sugar by using a slightly sweet Champagne, which adds the natural softness of grape sugar. The better the Champagne, of course, the more superb will be the sherbet. Among the sweet Champagnes I use are the new French Krug or, from California, the sparkling Muscadelle du Bordelais, or the light and fine Crémant.

Champagne, sweet, French or Californian (1 bottle)	Salt (pinch)
Sugar, natural cane, granulated (½ cup, or less, to taste)	Gelatin, unflavored, granulated (1 Tbs)
Maple syrup, pure (3 Tbs)	Lemon juice, freshly squeezed (¼ cup)

At least 1 day before serving – active work about 25 minutes, plus overnight freezing and ripening

At least 2 hours before you start the preparations, set the Champagne in the coldest part of the refrigerator. Also put a 1-quart covered jar to chill in the freezer. When the Champagne is thoroughly cold, begin by combining, in a 1-pint saucepan, the ½ cup of sugar, ½ cup of cold water, the 3 tablespoons of maple syrup and a pinch of salt. Separately, in a small mixing bowl, stir together ¼ cup of cold water and the tablespoon of gelatin until they form a thick paste. Gently heat the saucepan, stirring continuously until the solids are melted, then begin spooning in, teaspoon by teaspoon, the gelatin paste, stirring and pressing it continuously with the back of the spoon so that it completely melts without forming any lumps. There is no need to bring this mixture to the boil. As soon as it is completely smooth, turn off the heat and let it cool slightly.

For aerating and beating the sherbet mixture, I use my Cuisinart chopper-churner (or you can use an electric mixer-beater, or a hand beater). As soon as the mixture in the saucepan is finger-touch cool, I pour it into the container of the machine and add the ¼ cup of lemon juice, churning and beating for about 5 seconds. Switch off the machine. Open the Champagne, add 2 cups to the bowl of the machine, immediately corking the bottle and setting it back in the refrigerator. Switch on the machine for 20 seconds more. There will be lots of frothing and this is the secret of the extraordinary lightness of this sherbet. Pour the sherbet mix into the ice cold jar from the freezer and set it, not back in the freezer, but in the coldest part of the refrigerator and leave it to cool, overnight.

Next morning – freezing and ripening the sherbet for about 5 hours

Prepare whatever type of ice cream maker you have – electric or hand-turned – with salted ice or in the freezer. Pour the sherbet mix into the ice cream maker and let it run or turn it until you have the perfect consistency – usually in 45 minutes to 1¼ hours. Rinse the 1-quart storage jar and put it back in the freezer to rechill.

When the machine has done its work, spoon the sherbet back into the chilled storage jar and hold it in the freezer to ripen for at least 3 hours.

Serving at table

I offer this beautifully colored sherbet in my best tulip-shaped Champagne glasses. Fill each ¾ full, then top with the remaining Champagne from the left-over bottle.

SHERBET OF CHAMPAGNE-RUM PUNCH WITH SMOKY LAPSANG SOUCHONG TEA

(for 4)

Young Chef Marc Meneau (page 45) calls this sherbet a frozen punch because it is made up largely of the classic punch mixture of Champagne with a dash of rum and a good brew of fine Chinese tea. Marc told me: "There must be very little rum, just enough so that you think it is there, but are not quite sure. The best result comes when you use the fine, delicate, *Rhum de Martinique*." The Champagne, also, should be a sweet type, of good quality (not necessarily very expensive – see previous recipe), and its bubbles give a lightness to the sherbet. I always serve it in my best tulip-shaped Champagne glasses, with a final dash of ice-cold Champagne poured on top at the last moment. A lovely sight and an irresistible taste and texture.

Champagne, sweet, see
   previous recipe (1 bottle)
Tea, lapsang souchong (about
   5 tsp for brewing 8 oz of tea)
Orgeat, almond syrup,
   preferably French Combier
   (½ cup)
Maple syrup, pure (¼ cup)

Salt (a pinch)
Gelatin, unflavored granulated
   (1 Tbs)
Pineapple, crushed (1 cup)
Rum, preferably Martinique
   (½ oz)
Mint, fresh leaf in season,
   chopped (1 tsp)

The day before – active work about 30 minutes, plus overnight freezing and maturing

At least 2 hours before you start the preparations, set the bottle of Champagne in the coldest part of the refrigerator. Put into the freezer to get thoroughly chilled in advance a 1-quart, covered glass storage jar. Make an extra-strong brew of the tea. Now combine, in a 1-pint saucepan, the ½ cup of Orgeat, the ¼ cup of maple syrup, ½ cup of the brewed tea, and the pinch of salt. Separately, in a small mixing bowl, combine another ¼ cup of cold water with the 1 tablespoon of gelatin, stirring until they form a thick paste. Gently heat the Orgeat mixture in the saucepan, stirring until it is just above blood heat. Begin stirring in, teaspoon by teaspoon, the gelatin paste, pressing it with the back of the spoon against the sides of the pan, so that it completely melts without forming any lumps. Do not boil. Turn off the heat and let the translucent brown mixture cool.

For aerating and beating the sherbet mixture, I use my Cuisinart chopper-churner (or you can use an electric mixer-beater, or a hand beater bowl). As soon as the mixture in the saucepan is finger-touch cool, I pour its contents into the bowl of the machine and add ½ cup of the mashed pineapple and the ½ ounce of rum, then churn for about 5 seconds. Switch off the machine. Now open the Champagne, add 2 cups to the mixture in the bowl (immediately recorking the bottle and setting it back in the refrigerator). Add the teaspoon of mint, and run the machine for about 20 seconds more. The frothing ensures a light sherbet. Now taste the mix and play at being your own alchemist. You may add a bit more of any or all of the flavoring ingredients, until you have a mixture that exactly matches your taste. Finally, pour the mix into the ice-cold quart jar from the freezer and set it, not back in the freezer, but in the coldest part of the refrigerator, covered, leaving it to cool and ripen overnight.

Next morning – active work about 15 minutes, plus about 4 hours of unsupervised freezing and maturing

Proceed exactly as for the Champagne Sherbet of the previous recipe.

Serving at table

I offer this to my guests in my best tulip Champagne glasses. Fill each about ¾ full with the sherbet. Top each serving with about a tablespoon more of the crushed pineapple. Just before eating, fill up each glass with the remaining Champagne.

SHERBET OF GREEN LIME AND RED CHASSE SPLEEN

(for 4)

Chef René Brunet (page 27), at his brilliant two-star Alpine *auberge* at Varces, near Grenoble, claims to have made a remarkable gastronomic discovery. He finds that the relatively little known Bordeaux red wine of the small château with the joyous name, Château Chasse Spleen (literally, "chase anger"), in the Medoc village of Moulis, has an extraordinary affinity for lime juice and that they can be combined and frozen into a superb sherbet.

Limes, with unblemished skins (3)

Sugar, natural cane, granulated (¾ cup, or less, to taste)

Red wine, preferably Chasse Spleen, see above (1 bottle)

At least 1 day in advance – active preparation about 15 minutes plus overnight freezing and maturing

Set a 2-quart covered storage jar in the freezer to chill. Peel the thin green outer skin from the 3 limes, preferably with a French zest-scraper, then hold this grated or minced skin in a covered jar.

Put the sugar into a 2½-quart saucepan of tinned copper, enameled iron, or heatproof glass (bare metal interacts with the acid of the fruit). Add 3 cups of freshly drawn cold water and the lime skin, then bring up to boiling, stirring, to dissolve the sugar. Now turn down the heat to gentle bubbling and keep it going, uncovered, for as long as it takes to get a good limey-zesty flavor into the mix – usually in about 10 minutes.

When the flavor is right, turn off the heat and pour in the bottle of red wine. Cut the 3 peeled limes in half and squeeze out every drop of their juice, straining out pits and pouring the juice into the wine mixture. Let it cool to room temperature before pouring it into the storage jar from the freezer. Then set it, not back in the freezer, but in the coldest part of the refrigerator, covered, to cool and ripen overnight.

Next morning – freezing and maturing the sherbet in about 5 hours

Proceed exactly as for the Champagne Sherbet on page 372.

Serving at table

If the sherbet has become too hard in the freezer, defrost it by transferring it for half an hour to the warmest part of your refrigerator. It should then become workably soft.

HOT SOUFFLÉ OF BUTTERLESS SUGARLESS CRUSHED PEARS

(4 individual soufflés)

When Chef Michel Guérard (page 35) served me this at his two-star Le Pot au Feu in Eugénie-les-Bains, I was almost sure that it was the lightest and fruitiest soufflé I had ever tasted. The natural sugar of the pears provided all the sweetness that was necessary and, since there was only half an egg yolk in each individual soufflé, there was hardly a cholesterol problem.

In my translation and adaptation of the recipe which Michel wrote out for me, I have eliminated his use of sugar substitute and replaced it by the added natural grape sugar of sweet wine – either a Sauternes from Bordeux, a Quarts de Chaume from the Loire or a Sweet Semillon from California. Provided you can find perfectly ripe pears, there is no reason why it should not be just as good whether made in Eugénie-les-Bains or Eugene, Oregon.

Pears, very ripe, best in season (2 large)	Vanilla bean (1, whole)
	Egg whites (5)
Sweet wine, see above (about 2 cups)	Egg yolks (2)

About 40 minutes before serving – active preparation about 20 minutes, plus up to 20 minutes of reasonably unsupervised baking

Peel, core and chunk the two pears and put them into a 1-quart, enameled or heat-proof glass saucepan (to avoid darkening the fruit). Pour in just anough of the sweet wine to cover them and heat to gentle simmering. At the same time, add the vanilla bean, split in half lengthwise and quartered. Continue simmering, stirring regularly until the pear flesh is thoroughly soft, nicely sweetened and well flavored with vanilla – usually in 8 to 12 minutes.

Remove the pieces of vanilla, wash, dry and store them for

reuse. Drain the pears and purée them in any way you prefer. I swirl them for a few seconds in my electric chopper-churner. At this point, they will usually be much too liquid. Return them to the dry saucepan and boil them down to evaporate their water and concentrate their flavor, usually in 3 to 5 minutes. Then let the thickish purée cool.

Meanwhile, preheat your oven to 375°F., placing the lower rack about 2 inches from the bottom and the upper rack high enough so that it will not impede the rising of the soufflés. On the upper shelf, place a shiny cookie sheet to reflect the heat downwards onto the tops of the soufflés.

Now beat, with a balloon wire whisk, the 5 egg whites in the normal way, to the stiff peak stage. As soon as the pear purée is fingertip cool, quickly work into it the 2 egg yolks. Now gently heat the pear-egg mixture, stirring continuously, until the yolks have just thickened, usually in 3 to 5 minutes.

Quickly fold the pear purée and the egg whites together, lightly pile into individual soufflé dishes (each about 4½ inches across and 2 inches deep) filling each dish to within about half an inch of its top, then sliding them at once onto the lower rack in the oven. When the soufflés have risen about half to three-quarters of an inch above the edge of the dishes and the tops are lightly browned, usually in 18 to 20 minutes, zip the soufflés instantly from the oven to the waiting diners at table.

ALSATIAN SOUFFLÉ OF LOW-FAT WHITE CHEESE WITH LEMON

(for 4)

In Alsace, this is traditionally made with a superrich, buttery-flaky crust as a *Tarte au Fromage Blanc*. This Low-High adaptation eliminates the crust. The lovely, light filling is baked and served in a low soufflé dish of white china or ceramic pottery decorative enough to be brought to table.

Pot cheese, low-fat (1 lb)

Sugar, natural cane, granulated (about ½ cup, or less, to taste)

Lemon rind, grated (2 tsp)

Salt, to taste

Egg yolks (4)

Flour, all-purpose, sifted (¼ cup)

Light cream (1 cup)

Vanilla, pure extract (1½ tsp)

Egg whites (4)

Cream of tartar (¼ tsp)

Sweet butter (2 tsps)

The day before serving – active work about 20 minutes, plus about 2 hours of unsupervised baking and ripening

Gently and lightly mix together the 1 pound of pot cheese, as much of the sugar as your sweet tooth demands, the 2 teaspoons of lemon rind, about ¼ teaspoon of the salt and the 4 egg yolks. Now beat this mixture to a smooth fluff in any way you prefer. I put it through my Cuisinart chopperchurner for about 5 seconds, but you can use an electric rotary beater. Preheat your oven to 300°F. Transfer the cheese mixture to a beating bowl and whip air into it with a balloon whisk, at the same time incorporating the ¼ cup of flour, the 1 cup light cream and the 1½ teaspoons of vanilla extract.

In a separate bowl, beat the 4 egg whites until frothy and just beginning to stiffen, then beat in the ¼ teaspoon of cream of tartar. Continue beating until fairly stiff, then beat in a tablespoon or two of the remaining sugar. Continue beating until the whites hold stiff meringue peaks. Then, gently and lightly fold the whites into the cheese mixture, using lifting strokes to hold in as much air as possible for maximum fluffiness.

Using minimum butter, rub the inside of the soufflé dish and lightly pile in the soufflé mixture. Bake in the center of the oven until the cheese mix has risen slightly and is completely set all the way through – usually in 45 minutes to 1 hour. Then turn off the heat, but leave the soufflé in the oven, with the door closed, for one more hour. Refrigerate overnight, covered with foil, to complete the ripening.

Next day – about 2 hours before serving

Let the soufflé come back to room temperature and serve in its baking dish. It goes wonderfully with a sweet Alsatian wine.

A MODIFIED PARISIAN VERSION OF THE CLASSIC MIRLITON OF NORMANDY

(for 4)

Because *mirliton* is a well-known regional dish of Normandy, it is surprising that it is missing from every major American-French cookbook, even from those claiming to teach you how to master the art of the French cuisine. In the few French reference books where it can be found, the recipes are so much garbled that they offer nothing of the finesse, balance, or delicacy of this wonderfully inventive interpretation by Chef Daniel Météry (page 46) at the Restaurant Clovis in the Hôtel Windsor in Paris. He has lightened and simplified it into a memorable new balance of flavors and textures. It is so near to perfection that it demands to be included in this survey of the current work of the great chefs of France.

But – it is not entirely Low-High! It does contain a reasonable amount of butter, honey and nuts. However, this version is certainly not nearly so rich – not even half so rich – as if it were prepared with layers of whipped cream and icing sugar by a classic Norman cook in, say, Rouen. So I cannot resist including it as one of the last recipes of this book. Shall we say that, if you have meticulously prepared every previous recipe on these pages, you will be in such perfect condition that you can afford this final slight blow-out as your rich reward.

In my translation and adaptation I have made one substantial change. I have eliminated the buttery-flaky crust with which Daniel surrounds his *mirliton*. I bake mine in a low copper pan, about the size of a standard 9-inch layer cake pan, from which it is spooned out and served.

Apricot halves, dried, chopped (7 oz, about 1 cup)

Honey, not too strong, say, clover (½ cup)

Hazelnuts, shelled and toasted, then chopped (⅓ cup)

Orange liqueur, Grand Marnier (5 oz)

Almonds, powdered (1¼ cups)

Sugar, natural cane, granulated (1¼ cups)

Eggs (4)

Sweet butter, melted and browned to light walnut (1¼ cups)

Sweet butter, for greasing pan (1 Tbs)

Egg yolks (2)

Preparation in about 1 hour, including about 30 to 40 minutes of unsupervised baking

This is best served at room temperature, so you can prepare it at any time ahead of your meal. Set out two mixing bowls and, in the first, assemble the ingredients for the bottom layer: the cup of chopped apricots, the ½ cup of honey, and the ⅓ cup of chopped hazelnuts. Work them together thoroughly and wet them with ½ cup of the Grand Marnier. Leave them to marinate while you assemble the second layer in the second mixing bowl: the 1¼ cups of powdered almonds and the 1¼ cups of sugar. Then begin thoroughly to work in the 4 whole eggs, first lightly beaten, then gradually mix in as much of the browned butter as is needed to make it all into a workable paste.

Preheat your oven to 325°F. Lightly grease the 9-inch layer cake pan with a minimum of the remaining butter, then spread evenly across its bottom the apricot mixture and make a second layer above it of the almond paste. Bake in the center of the oven until it is all softly firm, usually in 30 to 40 minutes.

About 10 minutes before the end of the baking time

In a small bowl, make a glazing mixture by beating the 2 egg yolks with the remaining 2 tablespoons of Grand Marnier. When the *mirliton* is almost done, take it out of the oven and, using a pastry brush, paint its top completely with the yellow egg-liqueur mixture. Set it back in the oven for about 5 minutes more to produce a shiny, smooth, yellow glaze. Finally, let the *mirliton* cool almost to room temperature.

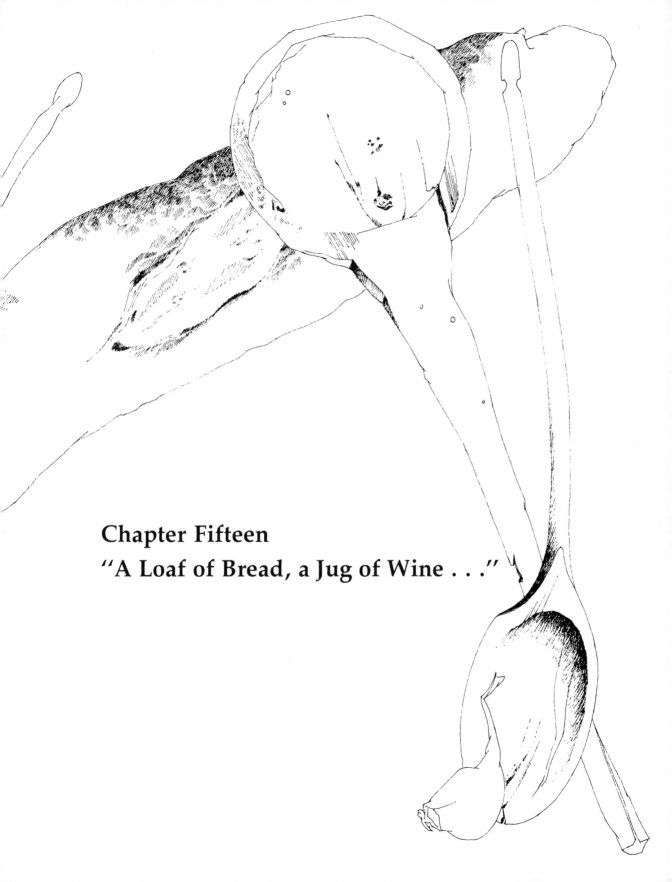

Chapter Fifteen
"A Loaf of Bread, a Jug of Wine . . ."

LOW-FAT POT CHEESE NATURAL BREAD THAT NEEDS NO KNEADING

(makes three loaves)

I am devoted to the pleasures of home-baked bread. I am not devoted to the hard work of making it. So here is my bread-without-the-work – made with low-fat ingredients and natural stone-ground, unbleached, wholewheat flour. It stays fresh longer than the average and can be frozen for several weeks. Above all, it has an excellent, slightly nutty flavor, delicately savory with a subtle touch of cheese and onions.

I learned most of what I know about baking natural bread from my friend Beatrice Trum Hunter, who is not only an effective and literate teacher but has written more good books about natural foods than anyone else in or out of town. The dough for this loaf involves no more work than stirring with a wooden spoon and waiting for it to rise. I bake my loaves in three enameled-iron terrine pans, each with an inside length of 11½ inches, thus producing a long loaf with even 3-inch by 3-inch slices. This has become, over the years, my standard, all-purpose home bread.

Yeast, dry granulated, fresh
(2 standard 1-tablespoon-
each envelopes)
Sugar, natural cane, granulated (¼ tsp)
Honey, preferably Swedish
wild flower, unprocessed or
similar type (¼ cup)
Grape pit oil, imported from
Provence (2 Tbs)
Pot cheese, low-fat (2 cups)

Yellow onion, peeled and
grated (1 medium)
Dill seed, freshly ground
(1 Tbs)
Salty sea kelp, granulated
(2 tsps)
Eggs, lightly beaten (2)
Wholewheat flour, coarse,
stone-ground (up to 5 cups)
Salt butter (about 2 Tbs)

Mixing the dough in about 20 minutes, plus about 2½ hours of unsupervised rising and baking

Start by activating the yeast. Empty the 2 envelopes into a smallish bowl, sprinkle with the ¼ teaspoon sugar and cover with ½ cup of warm water at precisely the right temperature. This is the key to success. If the water is only lukewarm, it will not start the yeast going. If it is too hot, it will kill the yeast stone dead. The right temperature is between 105° and 115°F. The proof that you are right comes in about 5 to 10 minutes when the yeast water must start bubbling. If this does not happen, the yeast may be too old. Throw it all away and start over.

When the bubbling is going well, pour the yeasty liquid into a larger bowl and work into it with a wooden spoon: the ¼ cup of honey, the 2 tablespoons of oil, the 2 cups of pot cheese, the grated onion, the 1 tablespoon of ground dill, the 2 teaspoons of salty kelp and the 2 lightly beaten eggs. Mix thoroughly. Now begin sprinkling the flour over the top, cup by cup, working each cupful in before adding the next. You are aiming at a thick batter and it usually requires between 4 and 5 cups of flour. Do not let it get too thick. When it seems right, beat it thoroughly, then cover the bowl with a cloth and set it in a warm place to rise until it has doubled its bulk. This usually takes about an hour, according to the temperature and weather.

My own trick for assuring a consistent temperature in my

"warm place" is to turn on my oven to 500°F., leave it on for exactly 60 seconds, then immediately turn it off, place the covered bowl of bread dough in the oven, close the door and wait for the dough to double its bulk.

When the dough has risen properly, punch it and stir it down to expel its air bubbles. I then take my three terrine pans, lightly grease them with the butter and spread enough dough into each one so that it is exactly half-full. Then cover each with a cloth and set them, again, to rise in that essential "warm place" (I repeat my oven trick) until the dough has again doubled in volume. That point is reached when the dough has risen sufficiently so that each terrine is now almost full to the brim. This may take 40 to 50 minutes.

When the dough has risen and is obviously very light, remove the terrines from the oven and heat it up to 350°F. Then set the three loaves on a center shelf to bake. They should rise at least another inch or so to a rounded top, with a deep toasty-brown color – usually in 30 to 45 minutes.

Brush the tops with a minimum quantity of melted butter and set the unmolded loaves on a wire rack to cool to room temperature.

THE GREAT THREE-STAR CHAMPAGNE CUP OF THE VILLA LORRAINE

(hardly practical for less than 8 to 10 thirsty people) This is the most luxurious and superb Champagne Cup I have ever tasted. It is served as an apéritif before dinner at the greatest French restaurant of Brussels, The Villa Lorraine – the only restaurant outside France to be honored with three stars. At the center of the main Garden Dining Room, with picture windows looking out onto the illuminated trees in a wooded park outside the city, there is a table with a magnificently colored display of the piled-up fruits of the season. At the center is a huge bowl of crushed ice in which stands a cut-glass carafe half-filled with fruits, topped up with this entirely sugarless Champagne Cup which is poured for the diners.

This recipe consumes two bottles of Champagne and you

must use the best that your pocketbook will allow. Also, you must gather a balanced mixture of the very best fresh fruits of whatever season of the year.

Fresh fruits, a balanced mixture, certainly, whenever possible – apples, apricots, nectarines, peaches, pears, raspberries, strawberries, etc. (about 4 lbs, total mixture)

Lemon peel, grated outer rind, and juice (1)

Orange peel, outer rind only (from 1 orange)

Dry white wine, preferably first-class Alsatian Riesling (½ bottle)

Cognac (3 oz)

Maraschino Cherry liqueur (2 to 3 oz)

Champagne, French or American (2 bottles)

Orgeat, almond syrup, preferably French Combier (1 oz)

Mint, fresh leaf in season (about 1 dozen whole leaves)

Two days before – marinating the fruits – active preparation about 15 minutes, plus 48 hours of entirely unsupervised soaking

Choose a tightly lidded, 2-quart, refrigerator storage jar, preferably of glass so as to avoid discoloration of the fruits. Divide all your fruits exactly in half and set aside one half to keep fresh and to ripen for the next 2 days. Prepare the second half by washing the fruit and trimming off the stalks, bruises, etc., but do not peel any of them. Put small fruit whole into the refrigerator jar – put in the larger fruits coarsely chunked. Add the lemon and orange rind, the ½ bottle of white wine, the 3 ounces of Cognac and about 2 ounces of the Cherry liqueur – or a bit more if your sweet tooth demands it. It is the only outside sweetening that will go in – for the rest, we depend on the natural sweetness of the fruit, which is the secret of the marvelous refreshment of this *coupe*. Stir gently with a wooden spoon, so as not to break up the fruit, then store, tightly covered, in the refrigerator for at least 48 hours.

On the day – about 1 hour before serving – active preparation about 15 minutes, plus about 45 minutes of unsupervised ripening

Separate the now-fruity liquid from the solid fruits (which have given their all) by straining through a fairly fine sieve, pressing the fruits gently to give up their last drops of juice, but certainly not hard enough so that fruit pulp gets through into the liquid. Rinse out the storage jar, put back the strained liquid and return to the refrigerator. Choose your handsomest, large, wide-mouthed fruit-cup jug and put it in the freezer to get thoroughly cold. Prepare the second half of your fresh fruits in exactly the same way as you did the first half – small fruit left whole, the larger coarsely chunked. When your serving jug is thoroughly cold, put into it the fruity liquid, plus all the new fruits, then, again, stir gently and, finally, pour in 1 bottle of the Champagne, plus the 1 ounce of Orgeat syrup and, if it is to your taste, a spritz or two of lemon juice. Then let it fizz, froth, rest and ripen for 30 to 40 minutes in the refrigerator, while you set up the serving arrangements. The jug should stand in a large bowl of ice. You should thoroughly chill your best Champagne glasses (flute or tulip) by setting them in the freezer.

Serving to the guests

Fill each ice-cold glass ¾ full with the Champagne Cup (which, by this time, will have lost a good deal of its bubbling), then fill up and refresh each glass with new, ice-cold Champagne from the just-opened second bottle. You may, or you may not, as you wish, stand a long glass spoon in the serving jug and spoon a piece of fresh fruit into each glass. Finally, garnish each drink with a fresh leaf of mint.

When I said to the owner of The Villa Lorraine, Marcel Kreusch, that this seemed a pretty complicated recipe for a simple fruit cup, he replied: "My father taught me that nothing which is too easy can possibly be outstandingly good."

Index of Sources

The ingredients used in this book are now so widely distributed in specialty food stores throughout the country that it would be quite impossible to compile a complete national catalog. However, in case readers find certain items difficult to obtain, the author lists here his sources for the ingredients that were used in testing recipes in this book.

Anchovies: see Fish

Aromatic Herbs and Spices: Fresh herbs, of course, are always the best, but they present the problem of tracking down local suppliers or growing them yourself. We get our rooted plants from the Nicholas Garden Nursery at 1190 North Pacific Highway in Albany Oregon, which will ship to all parts of the country. Otherwise, good dried herbs are worth searching for, as nationally distributed brands have often sat on supermarket shelves long enough to lose much of their flavor oils. We order hard-to-find dried herbs and spices from the Kobos Company at The Water Tower, 5331 Southwest Macadam in Portland, Oregon.

Arugula: A leafy salad plant, also known as rocket plant, generally available at Italian groceries.

Bacon, Canadian: see Hams and Bacons

Bonito Tuna, Dried: see Japanese Specialties

Bouzy: Bouzy, the red wine of the Champagne region of France, is quite unevenly distributed across the United States and may be hard to find. It can be replaced by a first-quality light red wine—say, a Beaujolais Villages, a Gamay from the Savoy, or a Bourgeuil or Chinon from the Loire.

Cheeses: From Ideal Cheese at 1205 Second Avenue in New York City, we get a *New York State pot cheese* at 4% butterfat, a *farmer's cheese* at 12%, and a whole milk *ricotta* at 16%. Skim-milk ricotta with 5% butterfat, as well as the regular whole-milk variety, is generally available in supermarkets throughout the country. For an extra-low-fat natural pot cheese (less than 1%), a soft farmer's cheese with 5% butterfat, and a hard farmer's cheese with only 0.5% butterfat, we go to Miller's Cheese shop at 13 Essex Street, New York City.

Chilis: Mexican Serrano chili peppers can be ordered from Casa Moneo, 210 West Fourteenth Street, New York City.

Chinese Steamer: We bought our three-tiered Chinese bamboo steamer at Cathay Hardware on 49 Mott Street in New York City.

Cod, Salt: The best quality in the U.S. comes from Canada and can be found in Greek stores (where it is called *bakaliaro*), in Italian (where it is *bacalà*) and in Spanish (*bacalao*). In New York, we order from the Kassos Brothers at 570 Ninth Avenue.

Coriander, Fresh: We find it at Wing Fat at 35 Mott Street, and United Supermarket at 84 Mulberry Street, New York City.

Cornichons, French: Baby sour pickles bottled by Dessaux Fils of Orléans; available from fancy food stores.

Cuisinart Chopper-Churner: see Kitchen Equipment

Farmer Cheese: see Cheeses

Fish:
Anchovies. The best anchovies are the salted whole fish in barrels, available by the pound from Kassos Brothers, 570 Ninth Avenue, New York City. Among the canned varieties, our favorites are those packed by the Masso family in Vigo, Spain and those sold under the Bonavita label (Portuguese) and under the Jean-Gui label (French). The latter two come in 2-ounce or 1⅔-ounce

cans, either as flat fillets or rolled with capers, and are available in fancy food stores. All of these canned anchovies are imported and distributed by Lankor International in Carlstadt, New Jersey. *Eel, Haddock, Herring,* and *Kippers* are available from a firm that specializes in smoked and salted fish, The Meyer and Thompson Company at 146 Beekman Street in New York City. *Katsuobushi* (dried tuna): see Japanese Specialties

Game: Czimer Foods, R.R. #1, P.O. Box 285, Lockport, Illinois will send a printed list of their game birds and other animals. They are experienced in shipping to all parts of the country.

Glace de Viand or Demi-Glace: If you don't have time to make *demi-glace,* one of the good canned sauces is Howard Johnson's Brown Beef Gravy. A small quantity of Valentine's concentrated beef extract, which is sold in drugstores, can replace *glace de viand.*

Greek Specialties: We shop at Kassos Brothers, 570 Ninth Avenue, New York City.

Hams and Bacons, Dark Smoked and Aged: Some reliable mail-order sources for sound country hams and fine pieces of dark smoked slab bacon are Jim Kite's Hams in Wolftown, Virginia; the Rose Packing Company, R.R. 3, South Barrington Road, Barrington, Illinois; and Winston's, 338 Waughtown Street, Winston-Salem, North Carolina. We get authentic Smithfield hams from Gwaltney, the V.W. Joyner Company, or the Smithfield Packing Company, all in Smithfield, Virginia.

Ice Cream Machine: see Kitchen Equipment

Japanese Specialties: For the *kombu* (leaf kelp) and the *katsuobushi* (dried bonito tuna) we go to Katagiri & Company at 224 East Fifty-ninth Street, New York City.

Kala Marsala: This is an authentic form of Indian curry powder obtainable across the country from Indian groceries.

Kelp: Powdered kelp is generally available from health food stores. For leaf kelp, see Japanese Specialties.

Kitchen Equipment: Readers may request from these companies the names of retail outlets in their areas that carry the machines. *French Chopper-Churner:* Cuisinart, P.O. Box 352, Greenwich, Connecticut. *Ice Cream Machine:* The Salton Company, 1260 Zerega Avenue, Bronx, New York, which will also answer queries about their Quick Mill for Spices.

Meat Extract: see *Glace de Viand*

Mushrooms: One of the prime sources for packaged, dried wild mushrooms is Custom Cultures at Broken Bridge in Gibbon, Oregon. They will send a printed list and will also ship fresh wild mushrooms by air to all parts of the country.

Oils: One of the keys to the success of the recipes in this book is the use of absolutely first-quality oils. They add a marvelous character and flavor to the dishes that the ordinary supermarket oils simply do not have. The best *olive oil* comes from the first pressing of the olives with no heat applied and is thus termed cold-pressed virgin olive oil. After the first pressing, the olives are pressed again a second and perhaps a third time. Finally heat is applied to extract the last oil, which is of much lesser quality. Our favorite brands of cold-pressed virgin olive oil are Bénédictin (35-ounce size) and Puget (8½-ounce size) from France, and Madre Sicilia (½-gallon size) from Sicily. For lighter oils, we use Bénédictin's *grape stone oil* (35-ounce size) and G. Vivier's *walnut oil* (17-ounce size). *Sesame oil* is available at health food stores and Chinese specialty shops. We get all the above oils at Bloomingdale's Gourmet Shop at 1000 Third Avenue in New York City.

Olives: The best olives come out of barrels from Greek, Italian, or Spanish groceries. Canned olives of strong character are imported from the same countries. Much gentler olives are the canned types from California.

Pepper: We think the best of the *black peppercorns* is Indian Tellicherry Black Pepper available from White Flower Farms in Litchfield, Connecticut. *Chinese Szechuan peppercorns* can be obtained from Chinese groceries. *Green peppercorns* are difficult to find. Write to Cuisinarts at P.O. Box 352 in Greenwich, Connecticut, or Lankor International in Carlstadt, New Jersey, and ask for the names of local dealers.

Pot Cheese, Low Fat: see Cheeses

Paprika, Hungarian: We get fresh paprika from H. Roth & Son, 1577 First Avenue, and from Paprikás-Weiss, 1546 Second Avenue, both in New York City. Both stores will also send printed catalogs and ship by mail.

Ricotta, Low-Fat: see Cheeses

Rocket Plant: see Arugula

Spice Mill: see Kitchen Equipment

Salt, Rock (to enclose poultry or fish for roasting): We have used "Louisiana Extra-Coarse White Rock Salt" that comes in 10- or 20-pound bags from the Diamond Crystal Salt Company, 1010 Clifton Avenue, Clifton, New Jersey. The Morton Salt Company, at 939 North Delaware Avenue in Philadelphia, Pennsylvania, will no doubt also direct readers to outlets carrying their brand of the product. An acceptable substitute to the coarse rock salt is kosher salt, available in 3-pound boxes and carried by most supermarkets.

Syrups: *Almond.* French Combier Orgeat can be found in fancy food stores. *Black Currant.* We use the kind produced by Frederick Munier in Dijon, France, distributed by André Prost in Little Neck, New York.

Turmeric: This spice can be found in Indian groceries. See also Aromatics.

Tea, Lapsang Souchong: We order from the Grace Tea Company, 799 Broadway, New York City.

Tarama: see Greek Specialties

Truffles: Truffles are an ingredient difficult to find in the United States. The finest, of course, are fresh and available only in France. Occasionally fresh truffles are shipped in by air at enormous expense. Canned truffles have generally lost much of their flavor and savor from having been pasteurized at high temperatures. However, a new type of canned truffle that has been processed at much lower temperatures is available by mail order from The French Caterer, P.O. Box 352, Greenwich Connecticut.

Vinegars: The French *red wine vinegar* and *tarragon white wine vinegar* bottled by Dessaux Fils of Orléans are among the best in the world. Our most luxurious *sherry vinegar* is the Spanish "Juan Santa Maria," bottled in Jerez de la Frontera. We order French and Spanish vinegars from Susan Wagner Imports at 505 East Eighty-second Street, Casa Moneo at 210 West Fourteenth Street, and Bloomingdale's Gourmet Shop at 1000 Third Avenue, all in New York City.

Index

The items in this Index that are recipes are in **boldface type;** all other entries refer to discussions of techniques, principles, history, chefs, and restaurants.